GANNA
DIVA OF
LOTUSLAND

Brian Adams

"Lotusland: the lotus-eaters' dreamy
forgetfulness of the outside world."
Charles Glass (after Homer "The Odyssey")

"Money talks - but you can't make it sing."
Chicago press comment

"She was one of those all-or-nothing girls."
Effie Alley

"Paris without Ganna is not Paris."
Alma Mahler

Also by Brian Adams

La Stupenda: *biography of Dame Joan Sutherland*

Australian Cinema: *the first eighty years*
(with Graham Shirley)

Portrait of an Artist: *biography of Sir William Dobell*

The Flowering of the Pacific: *Sir Joseph Banks, botanist
on Captain Cook's first voyage of discovery*

Such is Life: *biography of Sir Sidney Nolan*

Sidney Nolan's Odyssey: *a life*

A Pain in the Arts! *Culture without Cringe
in Australia*

To Loraine and Daniel

Contents

Preface

I had never heard of Ganna Walska. When her name was mentioned during a visit to friends in California, it suggested to me some long-forgotten vamp of the silent screen like Pola Negri or Theda Bara. I was half-right because she *was* a femme fatale, but in other walks of life, and somebody mentioned that she was perhaps the inspiration for one of Orson Welles's most memorable characters in *Citizen Kane*. I discovered that Madame Walska's legacy in America was based solely on the series of themed gardens of her Montecito estate which, since her death in 1984, became one of Santa Barbara's must-see visitor attractions. My hostess, Anne Jones, happened to be a trustee of the Ganna Walska Lotusland Foundation and wanted me to see it. I'd written a book ("The Flowering of the Pacific") about Sir Joseph Banks, the precocious young botanist on Captain Cook's first global voyage of discovery, and was lukewarm about spending time looking at flora when there was much else to see around town, like its splendid Hispanic origins.

Visiting Lotusland out of politeness, I was immediately captivated by what I saw. There, in thirty-seven verdant acres, was Southern California's version of a sixteenth-century European folly: a horticultural extravaganza serving no practical purpose except to satisfy the soul of its creator and delight the senses of visitors. Artfully stage-managed settings of rare, shiny cycads vied for attention with dense stands of dragon trees; an elegant allée of gnarled olives - a vivid reminder of my home in the south of France - contrasted with a formal English rose garden; the broad green lawnscape was framed by soaring Euphorbias; and a pink stucco mansion in the middle of all this beauty suggested 1920s Hollywood. And of course, there was a profusion of lotus flowers. I saw much much more, too contradictory, too rich - even too bizarre - to be appreciated during a single visit.

"Who was the woman who created this?" I wanted to know. "What was she like, and what motivated her to produce such a gripping spectacle?"

I absorbed random snippets of information about Polish origins, alluring beauty, a lifelong love of cats, Imperial Russian connections, the award of France's prestigious Légion d'honneur, multiple marriages, wealth derived from several beneficial divorce settlements; and, above all, the lady's dashed aspirations to be a great opera singer. She sounded like a latter-day hunter-gatherer whose burning ambition had been foiled by a missing melody gene. Having written the biography of the great Australian diva, Joan Sutherland ("La Stupenda"), I *was* interested in singers.

The staff at Lotusland referred reverentially to "Madame" Walska, though she had no formal title and Ganna Walska was not her real name.

"Why don't you write her story?" my hostess suggested. "There's a huge collection of personal papers and memorabilia stored in the house."

Back in France, overwhelmed by the impact of an all-too-brief visit to Madame's extraordinary domain, I knew I must return to learn more about this intriguing woman and her long, galvanic life, which included escaping the horrors of the Russian Revolution, charming Paris as the owner of one its most famous theaters, and finally embracing the American Dream.

This biography, thanks to Anne, is the result.

Lotusland trustee Anne W. Jones

Prelude

In 1984, Dr. Warren Austin, just back from an overseas trip, rushed to Santa Barbara's Cottage Hospital when he heard that that a former patient and friend had been admitted. He opened the door of her private room and was immediately transfixed by a pair of eyes recognizing him, as if saying "Why did you let them bring me here?"

Madame Ganna Walska was unable to speak, and it was impossible for anyone seeing her in this state, connected to drips and tubes, the face badly blotched by pigmentation from working countless hours under the relentless Californian sun, to realize that she had been a great beauty with a peerless complexion.

The owner of the Lotusland estate had outlived six husbands, long ago turned her back on her dizzy social life on two continents, and nobody remained to recall the heady days around the turn of the 20th century when, as a young Polish beauty, she captivated the Imperial Russian court at St. Petersburg, eloping while still in her teens to become a baroness through marriage. Details of her early life were lost in the mists of time, and even her exact age was unknown. Austin could be in the presence of a woman in her mid-eighties, or approaching a hundred.

Years before, she had made him promise never to send her to hospital, and finding dear Ganna smoldering with silent rage mortified him for failing a friend and neighbor. He found himself unable to respond to her parlous state, suddenly realizing that he knew so little about her life, now nearing its end.

Some of Dr. Austin's former patients lived in Hollywood, where his love of show business combined with matinée idol looks and a voice uncannily like Cary Grant's, forged friendships with several movie stars, especially when they learned that this former army doctor became the Duke and Duchess of Windsor's de facto physician (and fourth hand at bridge) when the exiled former King of England sat out the war in the safety of the Bahamas. Arriving in Santa Barbara in 1947, he was the first physician to practice in the exclusive Montecito area, marrying into money to become

7

seigneur of one of the great estates, Val Verde, while continuing his medical practice for nearly forty years.

Breast cancer and a mastectomy preceded Ganna's current plight, followed more recently by a succession of falls that confined her to a wheelchair. The music-loving, art-collecting Austin had heard that in her younger years, she strove with brains, beauty and boundless ambition to beguile the world with her singing during a golden era when Caruso, Farrar, Chaliapin, and Melba were superstars of the lyric art. It never happened, however, and her default career as a femme fatale - famous for being famous – had waned to playing the minor role of a recluse cloistered within the pink-washed walls of her estate, like one of their friends, Gloria Swanson, in *Sunset Boulevard.*

Ganna Walska was now unrecognizable, and most people hearing the name would relegate it to another era - the Roaring Twenties perhaps - making it impossible to understand how this diminutive, desiccated figure Dr. Austin was visiting, a former mistress of excess and self-proclaimed enemy of the average, had once known - in varying degrees of intimacy - some iconic figures from the first half of the 20th.century. They included, from what she'd told him during conversations, Toscanini, Mussolini, Chaplin, Roosevelt, Caruso, Goering, Stokowski and Pavlova.

He knew that Ganna, assisted by her dedicated English secretary, and propped up awkwardly in a wheelchair pushed by one of Lotusland's dwindling staff, had gone out to view her lush domain through fast-fading eyesight until recently. Few other private gardens could boast such an eclectic feast of flora from the four corners of the globe, creating a vista of color and beauty that was almost theatrical, reflecting perfectly Ganna's complex personality. She had certainly triumphed in that part of her long life, which, being an estate owner himself, Austin understood better than most.

Over the years of their friendship, he had managed to piece together some of Madame's extraordinary story, though the mosaic of her many ventures and adventures contained so many gaps that it produced only a fragmented picture of people, places and events. It was fascinating to see her at home in the preternatural ambiance of the Lotusland mansion crammed with Buddhist art, which she regarded as her passport to nirvana, and he had heard that Ganna married for the last time a handsome young American scholar

8

named Theos Bernard, who conned her into acquiring the property as a future center for Oriental studies.

For a life nearing its end on a high note, with growing acclaim for her outstanding display garden, Warren Austin found it disturbing to imagine how many times this resourceful woman, who developed a surprisingly strong feminist streak, must have faced failure. During their many lunches at Lotusland, he'd heard about her attempts in 1920s Paris to market perfumes and cosmetics to challenge the great French labels, together with her management of a leading Paris theater, making him wonder if she would have been more successful if married to fewer, less-wealthy, men - or not married at all. She once confided to him about having wanted children, but there were none, although a fellow physician who was her New York doctor during the 1940s, had told him there was no obvious gynecological reason for her not being a mother.

Austin also knew that before residing permanently in the United States, Madame Walska's efforts in nurturing French culture were rewarded with the Légion d'honneur, an honor she cherished. He remembered her proudly displaying its ribbon on whatever she wore: sometimes pinned to a grubby apron in the kitchen at Lotusland.

Those who knew Madame Walska only during her Lotusland years were unaware of the time when she tried everything money could buy - and there was plenty of that - to fulfill her ambition of becoming a latter-day Jenny Lind, or thoroughly-modern Malibran. For years, the international press dubbed her "the Polish opera singer" and repetition had the effect of certifying a mythical talent, which obscured the fact that she was no Slavic nightingale: more a female phantom of the opera. Marriage, too, was always a lottery for Ganna Walska, from a ravishing young beauty eloping with her handsome Russian nobleman, to when she had become rather matronly on divorcing her sixth husband: the duplicitous American guru. She wrote about all six of her spouses in an autobiography, so dense and non-linear that Dr. Austin found it impossible to form any coherent impression of Ganna's life, after she insisted he read it. One quality, however, shone through her disjointed memoirs like a beacon: an intense pride in being Polish, which never deserted her.

As she lay mute and immobile in the Santa Barbara hospital bed, Madame Ganna Walska's long waltz through life, with its moments of mad mazurka and impassioned polonaise, was quickly fading, and Warren Austin knew there would be no recovery. She should be returned to Lotusland and spend her last hours on this earth among the sweet sounds of birdsong and heady fragrances of her beloved estate.

Birth of a Legend
1887-1910

A much harsher environment, half a world away, provided the setting for the birth of Hanna Puacz: the baby girl who would become the talk - if not always the toast - of two continents as Madame Ganna Walska. Her parents lived in the border town of Brescz nad Bugiem, better known as Brest-Litovsk, and simply Brest in today's western Belarus. This unremarkable place that little Hanna would come to know as her first home, situated on the main rail and road link between Warsaw and Moscow, had been controlled from the east for the past eighty years. Its language and customs reflected the vast region known as White Russia, though the Polish-speaking minority population remained true to their heritage by looking west to Warsaw as their rightful capital.

The baby's birth certificate from the Roman Catholic parish church of the Holy Cross in the Pinsk diocese records the child born on June 24, 1887 as the daughter of Napoleon and Karolina Puacz (née Genneberg).

The unambiguous document, penned in Polish, was a straightforward record of birth and subsequent baptism, revealing none of the maverick traits that would lead this infant, born under a wandering star, to become a far-from-average addition to the population. Hanna's religion was registered as Roman Catholic in a predominantly Russian Orthodox and Jewish society, and her family remained resolutely Polish in spite of the overwhelming social and financial pressures to conform to Russian ways. The date of birth entered in the Pinsk parish register, however, would assume an elasticity that allowed pretty little Hanna to vary her age as it suited. In later life, this would lead to passports, marriage certificates, pre-nuptial agreements, contracts and divorce papers displaying a range of ages, either through ignorance, indifference, carelessness, or intent. In the 1950s, responding to a lawyer's request for information about her father and mother to support an application for United States citizenship, Ganna Walska responded, "His name was Napoleon Puacz and my mother's maiden name was Karolina Heneberg . . . both parents were born in Poland - where I do not know. I never knew. But anyone of our family was always born in Poland. That's all I can say."

Parents' portrait

Her birthplace straddled the banks of the often turgid Bug, a tributary of the mighty Vistula, the region's longest and most important river, as a rather melancholy staging post between East and West. Its community remained divided in this age of political turbulence leading to regularly shifting borders, with Poles never forgetting the violent riots of 1830-31 and 1863-64, when the Russians tried unsuccessfully to suppress their culture. Memories of those dark times remained etched on the collective conscience, affecting their texture of life, and Brest-Litovsk was a place to pass through on the way to somewhere more important. Those who stayed needed to accept its divided loyalties.

Swampy surroundings, with endless reed and grass marshes, peat bogs, and lakes reflecting broad skyscapes, offered little to lift the spirits, whichever ethnic or language grouping the citizens belonged to. Only a distant backdrop of hills offered any visual relief from a brooding landscape where the rare European bison still roamed the primal forests and peasants scraped a basic living from growing flax, hemp, potatoes and sugar beet, as well as fishing the river. It was a demanding existence in a notoriously harsh continental climate vacillating between the extremes of long, freezing winters, and brief, stifling, mosquito-ridden summers.

The bourgeois family Puacz lived comfortably enough, with the parents doting on their bright and beautiful daughter, raising her according to the strict tenets of the Roman Catholic church, while making sure she absorb Polish ways by shielding young Hanna from what they regarded as corrosive Russian influence. Napoleon Wladyslaw Puacz was an educated man, handsome, with a striking dark beard and moustache, taken to wearing neat suits to demonstrate his standing in the community, where he worked at a variety of jobs including real estate and for the railways. Many years later, his granddaughter, Hania Tallmadge, would recall hearing that there were only two social classes in the town: peasants and landed gentry, and the Puacz family was emphatically not from the former. "They had a coat of arms," she explained, "they were not poor. My grandfather traveled, and his wife always wore beautiful clothes."

The child baptized as Hanna would acquire several identities during her life, and from an early age was known affectionately within the family circle as Andzia. Ganna Walska would look back with mixed emotions on her earliest memories; attention was lavished on her, but the household was suffocatingly conventional, forcing Andzia to conform, except where books were concerned. Lighting a candle after bedtime prayers to read something from Napoleon's bookshelves would have been regarded as a mortal sin - not to mention hazardous by setting fire to the bedding - but she learned to read in this fashion, sometimes reciting poetry in the softest whisper for fear of being overheard. Soon, rebellious little Andzia knew about many things she would have been forbidden to experience, had her parents or their priest known about them.

Theater remained out of bounds because, as she explained later, plays and operas were about love, and a Polish girl was supposed to know nothing about that until married. The circus, however, did not violate any moral or social codes, and it was there that the Puacz daughter first heard lusty folk melodies and popular marches

13

performed by a circus band. Those roughly-played tunes nurtured an early taste for music that would flourish illicitly, and had the effect of increasing her self-determination. "I knew so little about music when I was a girl," she recalled. "Yes, I sang songs I heard the peasants sing while at their work, but not the music from church. I didn't want to sing that."

There was a piano at home and Andzia was encouraged to practice for the purpose of accompanying her father's violin playing after dinner. But she never really took to the instrument and loathed being forced to play, preferring to sing. "As a rule, poor piano-playing was a necessary attribute of a well-educated girl!" she reminisced. An aunt complimented Napoleon on his daughter's voice which showed promise, suggesting he hire a teacher to train it.

"Why?" he questioned her with genuine surprise. "You say she sings all right now."

In later years, Ganna Walska had no recollection of playing with dolls because she claimed to have too much curiosity about what was happening around her in the real world. On leaving church one Sunday morning, the congregation came upon the disturbing sight of a woman in distress, shamefully displaying a naked breast, with blood staining a once-white blouse. Her lank blond hair hung down, Ophelia-like, as she staggered along the middle of the street staring ahead with unblinking eyes and mumbling incoherently, while a mocking crowd of youths followed mimicking her sounds and movements. Andzia watched fascinated, wanting to know why this woman was acting in such a peculiar manner. Karolina turned her little head away from the ugly scene, explaining she was mad, but the child's reaction was to think it would be wonderful to be crazy like that.

The normal playthings of childhood may not have featured much in Ganna Walska's growing up, but cats did; it was an affection that lasted throughout her life. Hanna amused herself with them for hours, and when a particularly appealing kitten was taken away from her, she became distraught, running down to the bank of the Bug River and threatened to drown herself. In summer, the water level was down: so low, in fact, that it only reached up to her knees on wading in. Something in the mud on the bottom took hold of her big toe in a painful pincer grip, making Hanna scream so loudly that somebody came running to rescue her from an aggressive freshwater crayfish. Suicidal thoughts quickly evaporated, but the girl was becoming a handful for her conventional parents, who were increasingly mystified by their daughter's aberrant attitudes.

Hanna Puacz received her first communion at the age of ten, in 1897, and the priest, perhaps suspecting heretical tendencies, asked if she had heard of somebody called Charles Darwin, whose theory of evolution without the Almighty's guidance was anathema to Roman Catholic teaching. The name was unfamiliar, and not knowing the reason for the question - unsure if she should recognize this person or not - she answered truthfully in the negative. During the week, Hanna happened to come across a Polish translation of "On the Origin of Species by Natural Selection" on her father's bookshelf and secretly tried to read it by candlelight. She failed to understand anything at all about evolutionary biology while holding the weighty tome in one small hand and a candle in the other, trying to avoid the tallow dripping onto the sheets. Persisting, however, and skipping pages to the end, she experienced a heady sense of achievement, going to church the next Sunday and cheerfully informing the priest that she now understood what this Mr. Darwin was all about.

On the threshold of her daughter becoming a teenager in 1900, Karolina died suddenly at the age of thirty-eight of an unspecified illness. The life of the Puacz household was thrown into turmoil, and following a respectable period of mourning, the overwhelmed Napoleon decided he must take a new wife to help raise the family. His granddaughter, Hania Puacz Tallmadge, speculated: "Ganna probably didn't get along with her stepmother, and never forgave her father for remarrying." This could have been the reason for the few reminiscences about the family which, according to Mrs. Tallmadge, may have comprised the three children from Napoleon's first marriage: her own father, Leon - almost four years younger than Hanna - and possibly an older boy, because, "I remember hearing a story that there was one more brother from that first marriage who, at the age of sixteen, decided to seek his fortune in the United States but was never heard of again."

A faded photo from this troubled time shows Hanna and her father posed in a rustic setting, probably set-up in a studio. The girl is perched uncomfortably on a fake rock wearing high-button boots, a black mourning dress and clutching a cane. "To see my face," Ganna Walska recalled, "the photographer made me take off and put by my side the hat veiled with a long, practically non-transparent crepe that hung over my eyes."

Napoleon Puacz stands beside his daughter, his left hand thrust stiffly into a coat pocket, with a walking cane dangling from the other arm. Black-hatted and stern, the two stare into the camera showing no bond of intimacy. It was the only picture, apart from a portrait of her biological parents that Walska retained from her childhood, and it symbolized sorrow.

Her cousin came on a visit to Brest-Litovsk, the son of Napoleon's brother, Josef, who had studied art in Warsaw and Paris, and subsequently attracted some attention in the French capital for his cautiously modern portraits. Hanna went out walking along the river with the young man who sang a melody so unlike the familiar peasant songs that she found it impossible to get out of her head.

"It's from a brand-new opera by an Italian named Puccini," he explained. Everyone sings it in Paris. It's all the rage."

"What's opera?" Hanna asked innocently.

Her response provoked a look of disbelief at such provincial naiveté. "So you see how little I knew about music," Walska would tell an American reporter some twenty-five years later. "That aria from *Tosca* – 'E lucevan le stelle' - I heard my cousin sing entranced me and I would sing it to myself repeatedly, going off across the fields where my father couldn't hear."

Her sheltered life continued through the early teenage years under Napoleon's watchful eye and she would recall growing up knowing little of the world, and less about love: "I hated those lonely days and the regular bridge games. I kept singing that one piece from *Tosca*, though being warned that stage people were to be despised and performing in public was sinful." She had also heard her cousin sing 'Vesti la giubba' from *Pagliacci*, and the haunting sadness of Leoncavallo's music found its echo in the stirrings of her adolescence.

Napoleon's weekly bridge evenings often needed a fourth hand to make up the numbers, which invariably went to Hanna and required such intense concentration not to disgrace her father that it led to migraine headaches that often took days to disappear. By the age of fifteen, increasingly unhappy with her stepmother, and worried about a future offering little more than early marriage into the town's Polish-speaking bourgeoisie and producing several children in quick succession, she became restless. Hanna was blossoming into a real beauty, proud of her origins, aware of her charms - if not yet how to use them - and at the same time was thoroughly familiar with the Russian language through her schooling. Keeping his daughter under control until she was safely married loomed as a big problem for Napoleon, and he must have welcomed a neat solution offered by his brother Josef. He and his wife had moved to St. Petersburg to work, and they offered to have Hanna come and stay.

In 1905, the excited seventeen-year-old, left home in a spirit of high adventure - and not a little trepidation - eager to cast aside White Russian provincialism for the refined sights and sounds of the capital of the Tsars. The marshy lowlands she saw from the train window on approaching the great city may have reminded her of home, but everything else would be different in this, the first Russian metropolis built in the style of the great European cities, with magnificent palaces, wide boulevards, spacious squares and broad canals, reminiscent of Paris, Vienna and Venice. The facades of the neoclassical cultural institutions were overwhelming - even threatening - to the impressionable newcomer, and her nervous entrée to an elegant lifestyle on the fringes of the Imperial court, made Hanna feel quite provincial at first.

Uncle Josef moved in these circles as a society portraitist, and was in a good position to introduce his charge to St. Petersburg's many attractions and the upper crust people supporting them. Not all was beauty and harmony, however, because of chronic unrest among the proletariat. But well-shielded from the grimy shipyards, factories and fish processing plants of the city, pampered citizens and their followers led lives of privilege, assuming that the Romanov dynasty would rule for a millennium. By that calculation there were still 708 years to run.

St. Petersburg's effect on Hanna was dramatic, transforming a rather gauche teenager into a confident young lady after she began mingling with Josef's Puacz's clientele, who came to his studio to sit for flattering portraits. She began to absorb the manners and foibles of the court as if by osmosis, and many a dashing young cavalry officer was dazzled by Hanna's delicate beauty and intrigued by her spirited, almost revolutionary, independence. She gained the reputation of being quite a flirt, though her father was kept in the dark about that when Josef sent off his regular letters to Brescz nad Bugiem, reporting on his niece's sojourn.

Mingling with "the chosen of the world," as she would call them later, Josef's ward had opportunities to sit close to the Tsar and Tsarina at Sunday ballet performances, and observe the royal couple during charity functions or passing on the street in their carriages. The Sovereign of All the Russias, however, seemed to act so diffidently that she thought it kinder not to glance in his direction, "and thus save him the embarrassment he obviously suffered at the stares of the curious."

A distant war in the Pacific combined with the festering social unrest at home Nicholas II seemed powerless to control, may have been one reason for his public scowling, which gave the impression of being totally aloof from his subjects. The conflict had started the year before Hanna arrived, when the Japanese fleet made an unprovoked attack on a Russian squadron at Port Arthur, a treaty base in northeastern China. As a consequence, many young officers, whose previous duties were mostly decorative in gracing St. Petersburg parties, were sent away to defend the national honor. The hostilities dragged on until diplomatic pressure from Europe and the United States led to the signing of a peace treaty in September, 1905, recognizing Korea as part of Japan's sphere of influence and shelving the problem of what to do about Manchuria.

The Russian capital regained its former gaiety sooner than anyone had dared to hope, with its boulevards colorful again with the uniforms of officers just back from the Far East. One who returned from duty as a veterinarian was a handsome young man in his mid-twenties from a wealthy landowning family, whose father was one of the Tsar's many doctors.

Hanna met Baron Arcadie d'Eingorn (above) at a party and immediately fell in love with him; she thought he looked attractively foreign because of being clean shaven, which was contrary to the current fashion for luxuriant beards and waxed mustaches. For the best part of a year they met and flirted at balls and social gatherings, to Josef Puacz's mounting apprehension and Napoleon's disapproval of a Russian liaison for his daughter.

Arcadie's own family was equally hostile about the couple's attraction, anticipating a member of St. Petersburg's aristocracy as their son's future bride, rather than a bourgeois Polish girl, however vivacious and beautiful.

Approaching the age of twenty, Hanna, no longer a child, ignored what her family thought and threw caution to the wind by eloping with Arcadie in June, 1907. They journeyed to Russia's far south to be married in a brief ceremony at Essentuky, a resort town in the northern Caucasus, a remote and romantic mountainous region lying between the Black and Caspian Seas. There, Hanna acquired the title of baroness, experienced physical sex for the first time, and during the couple's subsequent honeymoon in Moscow, delighted in attending lyric theater. The latter was apparently more appealing to the young bride.

"So this is what opera is all about: a love story in song," she commented to her loved one after a performance of Rimsky-Korsakov's fairy tale work, *Sadko*.

The baroness's romance would tell a different story, with the d'Eingorns' vastly different backgrounds soon leading to some serious schisms. She loathed his self-destructive nature, which seemed to her a typically Russian characteristic, often brooding about the world's troubles and drowning his sorrows in vodka and champagne. Being married to a hard-drinking, chain-smoking, wild-living aristocrat shocked this young woman from a sheltered upbringing, who never touched alcohol or smoked a cigarette. But, as she was to recall later when trying to accommodate Arcadie's failings, "We got along very nicely, in spite of clashes over his assumed household responsibilities and my overt self-reliance."

During social gatherings at their St. Petersburg house, Hanna would entertain guests with a song or two, many of whom remarked on her beautiful voice, though she could never contemplate turning a promising amateur talent into a professional career because it was inappropriate for a society lady. She was unquestionably that now: a baroness with plenty of roubles to spend on extravagant dresses, and the freedom to live lavishly in a city where the gap between the haves and have-nots was all too obvious. But she needed to occupy her days with some sort of activity while Arcadie was out carousing, and learned that it was perfectly acceptable for a lady to pursue interests on her own, as long as they were artistic.

The ballet ruled at the center of St. Petersburg's cultural life, with numerous Russian works premièred in the nation's preeminent theater, many becoming international favorites like Petipa and Ivanov's version of *Swan Lake* with music by Tchaikovsky. During her frequent visits to the Imperial Mariinsky Theater, Ganna Walska would almost certainly have seen a performance of the Petipa/Ivanov/Drigo revival of the work, and been moved by its dark message of fatal love in the story of a princess turned into a swan by an evil sorcerer's curse.

During this first decade of the twentieth century, a new spirit permeated St. Petersburg's great theater, fostered among others by its most innovative choreographer and teacher, Mikhail Fokin (who would later adopt the French version of his name: Michel Fokine.) A former graduate of the Maryiinsky's ballet school who became a brilliant soloist, he had just created *The Dying Swan* for the peerless Anna Pavlova when Hanna met him, and was working on a new romantic piece called *Chopiniana*, which revised would become famous as *Les Sylphides* - the world's first non-narrative, or plotless, ballet. For a brief time, the Baroness d'Eingorn became one of Fokin's pupils, though having no formal dance training, and nearly twenty-one, she could not expect much more than enhanced deportment from the lessons to augment her other charms.

The young couple's life revolved around the court, and their busy rounds of engagements were often in aid of worthy causes. That was how Hanna met the Grand Duchess Marie Pavlovna, the Tsar's aunt, who arranged annual bazaars for her combined charities where handiwork made by the Empress and her daughters was offered for sale. The Baroness d'Eingorn was put in charge of one of the stalls to be visited by the Tsar's mother, Empress Marie. She was nervous at the prospect because helpers like her were instructed on the strict etiquette demanded for such an encounter. "No matter how low Her Majesty might hold her hand," she remembered, "we must bend down to it but never - oh never! - lift it to our lips."

The d'Eingorn's wealth gave them freedom to travel extensively, and they journeyed extensively in Russia as well as going to Paris, where Hanna was able to put some of Fokin's tuition to good use at a Montmartre cabaret-restaurant. There, to her surprise, Arcadie introduced his wife to a handsome young man who proceeded to monopolize her on the dance floor for the whole evening, while her husband - who disliked dancing - sat at their table drinking and smoking. "I was extremely flattered," she recalled, "that a smart Parisian was so attracted to a young provincial girl such as myself." The evening ended in farce, however, when her partner asked for something to remember him by. Hanna thought it inappropriate to offer a handkerchief or a token flower from her corsage, and pointed to where her husband was waiting. "My heart stopped," she remembered. "Certainly a duel was imminent, for my frightened eyes saw with horror that Arcadie's right hand was reaching in a pocket for his revolver." She almost swooned from the tension of the moment. "But no! Arcadie took out some gold louis and paid off the [professional] dancer for his services."

Another small incident early in their marriage reflects the brittle nature of their relationship. They went north in winter to the university town of Dorpat (called Yuryev in Soviet times, and now Tartu in independent Estonia) and while she was skating at the local rink a little girl of three or four caught her eye and Hanna smiled back. The child approached as if intending to say something, stumbled and almost tumbled to the ice. She extended her arms to steady the infant, and at that instant a woman of about her own age rushed forward to snatch the tiny hand away.

"What do you want of my daughter?" Leave her alone! If you care for children so much why don't you have your own?"
The confrontation lodged in her memory, and whenever facing tragic moments, she would recall the jealous mother. "At each sorrow," she noted in her diary, "I have wanted to disappear, to die, or the earth to swallow me up, just as I felt after that painful scene."

Further misery clouded the couple's relationship when Arcadie's health declined and the doctors he consulted diagnosed that he was suffering from "galloping consumption." Shattered by the news, Hanna was prepared to consider any solution, wondering if her husband's life would be spared by going to Switzerland, which she heard, was the best place for the treatment of tuberculosis - as well as having the reputation for being one of the most romantic countries in Europe. The spirit of romance still suffused her vision, with imagined vistas of towering, snow-clad mountains particularly appealing to someone who came from the marshy lowlands of Central Europe.

Girls like her were raised without the need to develop personal initiatives or to make important decisions, but Hanna proved she'd learned a thing or two since coming to live in St. Petersburg by consulting the professors at the Medical Institute: gray-faced old men with the longest beards she ever saw. They dismissed her idea of Arcadie going to Switzerland for treatment.

"My dear child," she was told patronizingly, "he certainly could not stand the journey. He is too far gone."

"How long does my husband have to live?" she asked in desperation and the chilling consensus was that it might be only a matter of weeks.

Hanna refused to believe them.

From Russia with Love
1911-1914

The thought of separation filled Arcadie with dread. "My bridegroom," Hanna noted, "consented to stay for three years in that health resort, only if I agreed to stay beside him, selfishly announcing that otherwise he preferred to die immediately at home rather than be buried alive for three long years alone." She became, in effect, Arcadie's prisoner by consenting to stay with her husband at a sanitarium in Davos, and agreeing to follow the same rigorous routines as the other gaunt-faced patients to avoid creating a demoralizing impression.

In fact, Hanna appeared to be the only fit person in this gloomy Swiss establishment where even the medical staff had a sickly air about them. There were few pleasures for her during this bleak period of sleeping in separate rooms, with constant intimations of mortality. The daily dialogue with the doctors was equally depressing.

"How's my husband's temperature this morning?"

"Not very good!"

"Perhaps it will improve by noon?"

"Let's hope it will be down by evening so he can have a peaceful night."

"What about tomorrow?"

"If his temperature holds steady for five days, he may be allowed to sit outside in the sunshine for a few hours."

The patients were weighed each Friday, raising her anxiety while waiting on tenterhooks for Arcadie's results. Hanna was not allowed to accompany her husband to consultations and shuffled around her room aimlessly, wringing her hands and clenching her teeth, willing the time to pass. She tried to stop herself straining to hear his footsteps outside her room, knowing it was pointless because everyone wore rubber slippers which made little noise. Arcadie would appear after what seemed an eternity; she searched his face for signs of a favorable result from the scales, and hoped against hope that he had not lost weight. If he had gained only fifty grams, they could start making plans for the future.

The strict house rules were observed: going outside only during the permitted hours, and dining in an era when treatment for tubercular patients included eating a lot, and often. The institutional meals reminded her of the way piglets were gorged before slaughter at Easter in Poland, or how turkeys were said to be force-fed prior to Thanksgiving in America. The medical advice was to eat very slowly, and, as she wrote her diary: "No one was ever in a hurry to go back to his prison cell anyhow, as the dining room was the only diversion for those lucky enough to be allowed to leave their beds."

A meal might meander through eighteen small courses, and to pass the time Hanna folded the day's written menu after each dish. "Sometimes," she recorded, "oh, rarely, it was a wonderful surprise to have the potatoes served together with the meat!" That made two lines out of my menu at the same time! Hurrah!" Mindless mealtime games served to ease the abject boredom of life in the sanitarium.

With the devastating *charme slave* that allowed Arcadie to get his own way - spoilt by his family, by money and by women - her restless, reckless husband made the situation worse by refusing to accept any form of austerity. Smoking and drinking were taboo on the premises, and his former excesses, including a bottle of champagne with lunch every day, became a tantalizing memory when suffering the indignity of lying in bed without even a light after the doctor's night rounds. His wife's room was next door, but she was allowed to visit him only during the hours of daylight. In complying with the rules, Hanna, too, had to observe lights-out and sleep with the door wide-open. "In that breath-paralyzing cold," she recollected, "I was covered with feather quilts three storeys high."

One night, in the mental hinterland between consciousness and dreams, she sensed that something was happening around her bed, as if it were raining inside the room.

"Yes, it must be rain . . . No, it's too big for that, it's hail . . . Large hailstones . . . Ouch! One has fallen on my neck. It hurts!" She turned over and tried to sleep, but after a lull the mysterious bombardment continued.

"Hailstones are falling again. One just hit my forehead."

Hanna discovered a small pebble on the pillow beside her.

"A stone? . . . A nightmare?"

She slipped out of bed, stepping onto the freezing floor with bare feet, to feel her way in the dark to Arcadie's door, listening for his irregular breathing. There was only silence.

"Good, he's sleeping peacefully for once."

Scurrying back to a bed that had already given up most of its warmth and needing body heat to make it bearable again, she rolled herself into a ball like a cat.

"A few minutes longer and I'll be warm again. Just a few minutes more . . ."

Before drifting off, something fell again and she gingerly extended a hand from under the covers to discover what was happening, and found another small stone, then another. Then one hit the floor with a loud thwack and rolled across the parquet, making a deafening din in the still of the night. Hanna willed her eyes to pierce the darkness, squinting hard to make them focus and managing to make out a faint outline of the open porch door where the missiles must be coming from.

Now wide awake, she jumped up, shuffled to the balustrade and looked out, but there was nothing to see. She thought she heard murmuring, and strained to hear what it was. Wraithlike forms appeared below, just visible against the blanket of snow, and, though it was impossible to make out who or what they were, this was certainly no hallucination. Suddenly her name was whispered by a voice that was unmistakably Arcadie's.

"Andzia, Andzia, come down and open the front door. It's locked. Andzia are you there?"

Three shapes materialized and she recognized her husband, who was performing a kind of choreographic pantomime that Fokin would have been proud of, gesturing in the direction of the front door with one hand, and miming the action of turning a key in the lock by the other.

Hanna stood rooted to the spot, still barefoot, so shocked by these events that she hardly felt the glacial chill creeping up her legs under the nightgown. The realization that her beloved's delicate condition was threatened forced her to react by dashing back into the room, running along the corridor and down the

26

staircase to reach the main entrance. Struggling to unlock the outer door with her hands sticking to its icy ironwork, the shadowy figures of the night pushed and pushed until it opened, entering through a cloud of fresh, powdery snow blown in by a cutting wind. Arcadie and his two companions dashed up to their rooms without exchanging a word, leaving Hanna to return to bed.

Next morning, her husband revealed that after the nurse's last visit, when everybody slept, he was in the habit of dressing and going to the *kurhaus* (spa rooms) in the village with a couple of like-minded patients, to play poker, drink, and smoke. "And breathe stale casino air!" she scolded him.

He told her they would return to the sanitarium around five in the morning and enter through the front doors, which were usually left unlocked. Knowing he would be expelled if the medical director learned of their escapades, and unwilling to implicate his friends, he'd relied on his wife to resolve the dilemma when they found unexpectedly barred last night.

Hanna noted in her diary: "My husband's generosity would not permit him to bring such punishment on his companions for his audacity, so he chose that ingenious solution to crush my heart. He swore on his love for me he would die that instant if I did not forgive him." She wanted to leave Davos immediately; he sensed it, and in a melodramatic scene of Russian roulette pulled a gun from a pocket pointing it at his head, suggesting he would carry out the threat if she were to go. Hanna stayed.

An all-pervading atmosphere of physical decay in the institution was stifling for a healthy, socially-ambitious young woman just reaching the age of twenty-one, and when Arcadie continued his nocturnal gambling and drinking sprees, the outcome was a repeat of the previous incident. When challenged, he swore on his oath that he would never do such a thing again, wept copious tears, and was forgiven for the moment. But eventually, Hanna had to threaten him with the ultimatum that if there was one more recurrence of his behavior, she would be off. Like the plot of one of Anton Chekhov's plays that were all the rage in St. Petersburg, he inevitably weakened, and, after spending yet another riotous night with his cronies at the casino, Hanna, true to her word, refused to stay for a moment longer.

The Baroness d'Eingorn had the wherewithal to go anywhere she chose, although the thought of deserting her husband, however cruel his behavior, left her sad and broken as she hurriedly packed before leaving to take stock of her misery in one of Europe's most fashionable winter resorts, forty-five miles away. She wrote in her diary: "When I arrived at the Palace Hotel in St. Moritz that afternoon, entirely overwhelmed by excessive emotion and in the gloomiest of spirits, I could not even find the necessary energy to open my suitcase. Still in my traveling coat I threw myself on the bed and lay there for hours dry-eyed. I suffered rather from not being able to suffer anymore, not being able to feel any more."

A loud knocking on the door of her suite jolted Hanna out of her self-pity, and before she could ask who it was, Arcadie burst in. The first thought that flashed through her mind was that the intense cold of St. Moritz would kill him, then, like the offender, she heard herself begging forgiveness for deserting her husband. He proposed staying overnight; suggesting they dine together in the hotel, watch the dancing, and promised not to drink anything. They would take a table beside the dance floor to avoid breathing in too much cigarette smoke, and agreed to be in bed by ten o'clock. This precious moment of togetherness, he said, would make him so happy. "Naturally I consented," she recalled. "How could I refuse him anything? The quarrel was forgotten. Love has such a healing power." But Arcadie was strangely reluctant to depart the next morning, finally confessing to his wife that he'd been banished from further treatment because of his bad influence on the other patients. He could not return to Russia in such a delicate condition, and arrangements were made to enter another establishment whose regulations for patients were less draconian.

Hanna found it difficult to cope with their new agreement, which allowed an occasional trip to St. Moritz, and her next visit there was during the height of summer, with the social élite of several continents gathered at the Palace Hotel, reveling in the luxury that wealth and status accorded them. She enjoyed being in the company of magnificently gowned women and distinguished-looking, immaculately dressed, men again, meeting English visitors who impressed her by their exquisite manners. Hanna was embarrassed, however, when women her own age curtsied in deference to her married state. Continental society was easy to understand because it conformed to what she experienced in St.

Petersburg, though she had trouble placing one tall guest dressed in vivid colors that she assumed only *cocottes* (prostitutes) would be brazen enough to wear. This young woman played tennis with the men and was apparently unmarried, yet never accompanied by her mother or a chaperone. In fact, if she hadn't been in the company of women known to be *comme il faut*, Hanna would have placed her without hesitation among those called politely *femmes légères* (courtesans).

This red-hatted, purple-gowned person intrigued her so much that Hanna had to ask someone who she was.

"Celle-là? Oh! C'est une americaine!" was the response.

She noted later: "Obviously in America a woman could dress individually and eccentrically even if she belonged to society without necessarily being thought an actress, which was then considered to be the criterion of frivolity. I also came to understand that in America it was possible for young girls to go out with men who were not of their family unescorted by a *dame de compagnie*. I felt that her unconsciously natural behavior, which would have irrevocably ruined the reputation of a Polish girl, presented only an irresistible attraction."

This aimless life in Switzerland could not last, and Arcadie encouraged his wife's return to Russia, while he stayed to complete a full course of treatment, and Hanna found herself back among the Russian aristocracy during the winter of 1909. She tried to forget about sanitarium life by participating in one of the social rituals taking place most afternoons along St. Petersburg's fashionable thoroughfares beside the River Neva. Her ornate sled pulled by two fine horses was controlled by a coachman dressed in bulky clothing that made him look excessively fat, with Hanna enveloped in an ermine coat with matching hat, passing to and fro, waving to friends and acquaintances until the horses began to foam at the mouth from their slippery exertions and needed a rest. She then stepped down to mingle with the smartly-dressed crowd, strolling and chatting beside the frozen waterway.

On one occasion, while accompanied by two officers who'd been Arcadie's colleagues during the Russo-Japanese war, a distinguished-looking hussar approached them and her companions suddenly stood rigidly to attention and saluted him. He introduced himself as the Grand Duke Boris, cousin of the Tsar, and Hanna recalled having seen him in the company of King Constantine of Greece during the d'Eingorns' visit to Paris. This meeting in the snow began what Hanna called a "flirtation" with the Grand Duke, who revealed that he had noticed her at the Café de Paris, where he made a bet with Constantine that she was Polish. Hanna coquettishly confirmed her nationality and Boris smiled in mock relief, saying he could now collect his dues next time he met the Greek monarch. "My wonderful flirt with Grand Duke Boris," she confided to her diary, "consisted of hearing music together, going to the theater, or dining with the songs of the Tziganes, hidden by heavy *portières* [drapes], lending much charm to the atmosphere." These Hungarian Gipsy musicians with their evocative, soul-stirring melodies were best heard screened-off, it seems, because they were neither good-looking nor clean.

Another man who flirted with Hanna during Arcadie's absence was the means of firing her passion for singing, describing him only as "the second-richest man in Russia." A clue to his identity is her diary entry "our eyes had met in St. Moritz," suggests that he was not a total stranger. When her Mr. X. left St. Petersburg on a three-day trip, Hanna locked herself away at home to suffer the agonies of separation in a typically Slavic way, and, as dawn broke after a long sleepless night, she sat down to write him a long letter. "In my girlish romantic head I had only one thought," she noted. "He had insinuated that he could not be loved except for his money. Very well! Not for the world would I let him know that I was in love with him. Proud and overcome with the fear that he might guess my feelings, I wrote a thousand lies to confuse him." Without mincing words, she said he had every right to suspect that he would not be loved for his own sake . . . without his fortune no one would ever look at him . . . it was enough to know his *parvenu* background to realize that fundamentally he was a peasant in spite of his education . . . his father would be allowed in her parents' home only by way of the service entrance . . . his sister married a count thanks only to her dowry.

The object of her affection failed to appear after three days and Hanna sent a telegram imploring him to return her over-emotional correspondence unopened. She was helpless to judge between fantasy and reality in the romantic fiction she wove around the relationship, finding it unbearable to live normally after sending him such an impulsive letter. Accepting that he wouldn't be rushing back to her, Hanna left on a visit to the Crimea where the Tsar and Tsarina, together with their children Olga, Maria, Nicholas, Anastasia, Alexei and Tatiana, spent summers beside the sea at the royal palace in the resort city of Yalta. It was rumored that her hero was with the royal party holidaying beside the Black Sea, and she arrived there desperate to reconcile their differences, but after a week of fruitless searching, Hanna had to leave the balmy southern climes to return to the chilly, changeable north.

She seemed to have made the right move when learning that her quarry had accepted an honorary post at the Mariinsky Imperial Opera House, and her next step was obvious: "I went to the opera every night expecting to meet him there." Hanna sat through interminable performances of nationalistic works by Borodin, Glinka, Mussorgsky, Rubinstein, Arensky and Tchaikovsky from Russian opera's golden age, but for three weeks there was no sign of her man as she watched hours of incomprehensible stage action and listened to unfamiliar music. "I experienced genuine torture sitting there for hours night after night, unable to appreciate, let alone understand, the operas . . . I could not even find distraction in watching the audience, for in those glorious days of St. Petersburg it was not the thing to go to the opera. It was fashionable only to attend the ballet on Sunday nights when the Tsar came with his magnificent court and all the military men were in gala uniform."

Her blind faith was finally rewarded on encountering her phantom lover at the entrance to the theater one night. He bowed politely, but coldly, and that was all. Already an accomplished little actress, she returned the gesture in such a way as to suggest she hardly remembered who he was: "But my heart - oh my heart! How fast it beat, and how my legs trembled as they carried me to my seat. I really do not know how I managed it." On the way home that night in a wretched mental state Hanna had a brilliant idea: she would sing on the stage of her idol's theater. "Surely such proximity would conquer him - he would no longer be able to resist me!"

Achieving this, however, proved both daunting and not a little humiliating. "There was very little distinction made between a cabaret singer and an Imperial Opera prima donna - it was just as wicked to be on any stage," she wrote. Just as she had paid Mikhail

Fokin for dance lessons, she proceeded to engage a coach for her voice, the leading baritone, Joachim Tartakov, who was also stage director at the Mariinsky. If he would accept her for singing lessons, it would present the perfect excuse to be nearer to Mr. X.

The experience was brief and chaotic. "It seemed that I always arrived so late it was almost time for Tartakov's next pupil," she revealed. "Like all those who are extremely busy doing nothing, I could not get there on time. Nobody ever was. And to tell the truth I really did not feel that I needed to take those singing lessons but I could not say to my teacher: 'Here are ten roubles, do not trouble yourself to bother me about the singing, just tell me if you saw Him today . . . What did he say? . . . What prima donna did he talk to?'" Hanna did receive sketchy news of her man, but it was no help because Tartakov did little to hide his distaste for Mr. X.

To further scramble the Baroness d'Eingorn's overheated emotions, Arcadie arrived home from Switzerland a changed man, with his health in a dangerously delicate state, sad and soulful from being unable to indulge in his former freewheeling pleasures. Their marriage was all but over, with his ambitious wife of twenty-five no longer the impressionable innocent of a few years before and the relationship drifted into leading separate lives.

The Empress Dowager, Maria Feodorovna, was a former Danish princess with family ties to many of the royal courts of Europe, with her sister Alexandra queen consort of Britain's Edward VII. The mother of the Russian monarch loved family parties, dancing, delicate embroidery and fine pearls; she was also a good watercolorist and was the inspiration behind some of the court jeweler Fabergé's most famous creations: the Imperial Easter eggs. This artistic background led her to issue an order for painting the portrait of a lady at one of the city's society balls who most typified the beauty of Slav womanhood; the chosen subject sitting for a canvas which, after public exhibition, would be hung in the Imperial collection. Hanna was understandably dizzy with surprise when she was selected for this honor. The painter, Alfred Eberling, claimed to be overpowered by his sitter's beauty, with a string of complimentary comments about her flawless face: "What a mouth! What a nose! What exquisite nostrils!"

She sat for a second portrait during 1912, and what emerged could be regarded as a summation of an extraordinary age: a languorous, sexy image of the Baroness d'Eingorn in expensive finery about to grace a glittering St. Petersburg social occasion. She was posed by the artist Victor Stemberg on an ornate chair, leaning forward slightly, and lightly supporting her head on one hand as if being asked to pause for a photograph. His full-length portrait became a sumptuous evocation of privilege that Russia's revolutionaries living in exile might have cited as a reason to overthrow the Tsar and his circle. Hanna is dressed in the brocaded finery of an off-the-shoulder evening gown, revealing in its enticing *décolletage* a generous expanse of creamy skin extending from tilted chin to generous bosom. A long rope of lustrous pearls caresses her neck, and a white ermine coat with a glistening silk lining sis draped nonchalantly over one shoulder. In fact, Stemberg captures the face better than any photograph, with an enigmatic Mona Lisa half-smile playing around cherry-red lips and a dreamy, distant look in his subject's dark eyes.

Portrait 1912

Hanna's unrequited romance with Mr. X steered her in the direction of a singing career and also to acquire a new identity, because it would have been a serious breach of etiquette for a married society woman to have her name in print, who didn't even dare to show an address on her visiting cards. The same restriction forbade the use of her husband's name when she was invited by friends to sing at a charity cabaret in Kiev, where the lyrics of one of her numbers went: "Isn't it a shame to sleep - why don't you waltz?" She would recall: "At the eleventh hour I had to think up a substitute [name] and, like all Poles, I loved to dance: especially the waltz. So suddenly I said: 'Waltz. . . Valse. . . Walska!' The Russian version of Hanna was Ganna, and little Anna Puacz from Brest-Litovsk, who became the Baroness d'Eingorn by marriage, would henceforth call herself Ganna Walska when performing.

A subsequent trip to Paris for voice study with a celebrated compatriot, the internationally renowned tenor Jean de Reszke, coincided with the heyday of the city's reputation for wild permissiveness. Every excess, whether artistic, sensual or flagrantly sexual, was openly practiced, and its darker fringe embraced a drug culture based on morphine and hashish, often accompanied by absinthe, resulting in oblivion for many a Left Bank bohemian. But all that was a world away from Walska's experiences in the French capital because financial independence allowed her to live in a fashionable *arrondissement,* from where she initiated divorce proceedings by serving a writ on Arcadie through a Russian Orthodox priest living in Paris.

As with Tartakov in St. Petersburg, she approached her two lessons a week far too casually, trusting in determination to see her through. De Reszke, a tenor of almost legendary reputation now retired from the international opera stage, regarded her as just another of his affluent students with a pleasant voice whose ambitions were social rather than artistic and, in reality the two of them were literally Poles apart. As a result of the tuition, however, newly-named Ganna Walska was offered a few cabaret engagements which were successful, but not what might have been expected for someone with such a distinguished teacher.

Time flew for Walska during the first half of 1914, with more occasional cabaret appearances, continuing her singing lessons, and regular visits to the opera. It was all too easy to ignore the consequences of what happened at the end of June in the Balkans for someone with a minimal interest in politics. Archduke Ferdinand, the heir presumptive of the Austro-Hungarian Empire, and his wife were killed by a Bosnian Serb assassin on their visit to Sarajevo and a month later the Austrians declared war on Serbia. Then Russia ordered the mobilization of its armies in response to these events, and Germany issued an ultimatum to Russia, giving twelve hours' notice to disband its forces. When that failed, war was declared, and four days later Germany repeated its action against France. In Britain, the Liberal politician, Edward Grey, summed-up the situation with his gloomy epitaph for an era: "The lamps are going out all over Europe; we shall not see them lit again in our lifetime."

Ganna Walska found herself stranded in Paris with borders closing across much of the continent. She was alone with no family, no obligations and nowhere to go, feeling the urge to contribute in some way to the Allied cause. "I could not have gone to the front," she noted in her diary, "because the merest drop of blood almost made me faint, and so I knew I would only be a nuisance to the doctors and a hindrance to the sick." Instead, she played her modest part in the French war effort by sewing sheets for soldiers, though she shouldn't have bothered because her needlework was a disaster, coming from a woman who'd never needed to learn how to boil an egg, or any other domestic skills.

At first, Ganna felt safe enough, speculating that it was impossible for the City of Light to be invaded because a German advance would surely be repulsed by brave French, British and Belgian troops. But the war news became increasingly grim when the Germans threatened to encircle Paris, with friends advising her to leave and visit America for a few months to be safe. "It was not an uncommon belief at the beginning of the European conflict;" Ganna noted, "that three months at the maximum would mark the end."

France slid into chaos as many Parisians made frantic preparations to flee the capital for the provinces, along with the government heading west to the relative safety of Bordeaux. Sea crossings were disrupted, and for a while it looked as if the only escape routes were south through the Alps to Italy, or across the Pyrenees into Spain. A shipping agent mentioned that transatlantic services still operated, and if Madame Walska managed to get to Britain, she might find an onward passage to New York.

There had been talk of her performing the title role of *Tosca* in Puccini's opera at the Opéra Comique during the forthcoming winter season, but all entertainments were suspended during the invasion scare. Baroness Hanna d'Eingorn, however, was a beautiful woman who had now acquired an almost mythic feeling about opera singing in general, and divas in particular. They were somehow above the rest of humanity: their gift of art so potent that they were allowed everything - and forgiven all. She was determined to become one, war or no war.

Packing up some belongings - a few clothes and a wealth of jewelry - she headed for London with a woman companion named Renée Davennes, and then on to the port of Liverpool, to wait anxiously for a steamer passage to America. The demand for tickets in any class far outstripped availability, with every day's delay increasing the threat of America-bound liners being torpedoed by predatory German U-boats known to be operating off the coast of Ireland.

Eventually, Ganna Walska managed to secure a berth on the "Arabic" at the end of December, to face 1915 and an uncertain future.

The Promised Land
1915-1918

The White Star liner survived the wintry, storm-tossed North Atlantic, avoiding the German submarine blockade of Britain, which came into force a few weeks later. The New York *Star* reported on February 10, 1915 the arrival of Madame Walska "the Russian-Polish singer" who would shortly make her appearance, either in the new Winter Garden show or on a vaudeville bill, presenting a sketch she had staged in Paris called "Taken by Surprise," which was said to have been a great success at both the Théâtre Fémina and the Théâtre Boulevard des Capucines.

According to the story, - with "Madame" now prefixing her stage name in the fashion of operatic divas and leading actresses of the day – Walska played the role of a Russian prima donna about to make her American début. She dresses and rehearses in full view of the audience, and leaves for the theater. Burglars break into the apartment, but are interrupted by her sudden return for some sheet music. While searching for it, she is startled to see the reflection of the thieves in a mirror, and, with quick thinking, acts as if unaware of their presence, frightening them off with what looks like a revolver, to retain her precious jewels and other valuables. It was rather remote from Ganna's ambition to conquer the loftier realms of opera, and failed to happen according to the newspaper report because of terminating her engagement after receiving cabled news of Arcadie's death on the Prussian battlefield just hours before she was due to make her first New York stage appearance.

Walska's entry into New York's vibrant theater scene was assisted by an unidentified American producer who befriended her on the voyage from Liverpool, though she remained secretive about him, mentioning only that she sang at the Century Theater through the "generosity" of Otto H. Kahn, a wealthy financier who supported the Metropolitan Opera Company, and was widely applauded as a leading patron of the arts in general.

Ganna was soon installed in an apartment somewhere on Manhattan's West Side - she couldn't remember exactly where when asked about it years later - and within three months was performing in French operetta at the Century. *"Mlle Nitouche"* by Henri Meilhac and Albert Millaud with music by Hervé had a featherweight plot about a convent girl who becomes a popular singer. The celebrated Russian couturier Romain de Tirtoff - known professionally as Erté - claims in his gossipy memoirs that the famous Broadway producer, Lee Shubert, a key figure in American show business whose family's theatrical holdings were worth millions, met Walska soon after she reached New York and was so dazzled by her beauty and sex appeal that he cast her in the operetta. According to Erté, by the time the show was in rehearsal, Ganna was his mistress and on one occasion when the conductor complained of Madame's inability to follow the score, Shubert ordered him: "Never mind the music. You follow her!"

Femme fatale

In her autobiography, Walska would confirm that Mr. Lee Shubert, "who was most kind to me and wanted to be of service," acted as her agent, though even a man with his show business clout

38

found it hard to place the newcomer. Claiming that Metro offered her a three-year contract in motion pictures, Walska said she was only interested in occasional film appearances until accepted as an opera singer, and was told by the studio that it would not be worth it for them "because they would first have to spend a fortune to build-up my name." There was the chance of a single screen engagement, however, when a producer urgently needed to find a substitute player, and Shubert provided his car and driver to take her to the studios in New Jersey. Determined to make a good impression, she wore a Russian sable coat over her best Paris dress, with a string of expensive pearls around her slender neck, and recorded the experience in her diary.

"At Fort Lee I was shown to an almost empty ugly office with ordinary wooden chairs, one of which I disdainfully took. Five minutes later a heavy man with an eternal cigar glued to his mouth burst into the room, looked around as though he did not even see me and shouted loudly: 'Where is that girl? Where *is* that girl?' A boy ran in and simply pointed to me as I sat there in all my finery. 'What? That!' said the man with as much disgust and contempt as the mouthful of cigar would allow. 'Get me Shubert on the phone,' he screamed in a thunderous voice. 'Hello! Lee? For God's sake, what do you mean? Making fun of me? I ask you for a Broadway girl and you send me Queen Mary of England!' he shouted."

That brief brush with the burgeoning new entertainment medium ended Ganna Walska's flirtation with movies for the moment and with Lee Shubert forever.

Although inconsequential - and flattered by being described as vaudeville operetta instead of musical comedy - *Mlle Nitouche* was staged in a serious venue, even if its acoustics were poor and the venue was fast gaining a reputation for being the wrong house, in the wrong place, at the wrong time. When Walska performed at the Century Theater during 1915, hopes for its brilliant future had waned, and the original name of the New Theater changed, only six years after it opened. The backers were some of the nation's richest and most influential men: John Jacob Astor, Alexander Smith Cochran, Henry Clay Frick, Otto H. Kahn, J. Pierpont Morgan, Cornelius Vanderbilt and Harry Paine Whitney, who intended their fine new playhouse to become America's answer to Richard Wagner's Festspielhaus at Bayreuth. With a revolutionary design, its location, adjoining Columbus Circle and fronting Central Park West, was unappealing and inconvenient for patrons, and the distinguished founders soon discovered they had thrown away their money in creating, not a temple of high culture, but a costly white elephant fit only for the occasional French cabaret and movie shows.

The former Hanna Puacz - whatever the nature of her relationships with Kahn and Shubert - was sure she had overcome many of her previous inhibitions about performing on stage, and now billed as Madame Ganna Walska could use her continental charm to get most of what she wanted. If it had meant sleeping with Lee Shubert for a few weeks, she probably accepted it as the means to an end, in spite of her avowed fustian principles. Ganna was well aware that most actresses at the time faced a casting-couch dilemma if they wished to succeed, although a few years later, when being interviewed, she was adamant that sexual pressures played no part in her experience of American show business:

"This is so wonderful a country. So much opportunity here, she gushed to a reporter. "For women, especially when they are pretty, it is so different from Europe."

She explained that where she came from, a woman seeking success in opera always had to compromise herself:

"First the director makes love to you, then the stage manager then the orchestra leader. If the girl did not accept this, there was no chance of a career on the European stage."

Madame insisted that things were different in America:

"Here a girl is treated as an artist. It is a business and the conductors, directors and stage managers are business people. They are interested in your work and not in your love."

One of her endearing traits was wishful thinking, which often obscured - or dignified - a humble past. Regular reports began appearing in the press about her, all mentioning the lyric stage as her goal. "To me art is everything," she informed reporters confidently. "I like the stage better than any other thing."

After leaving Lee Shubert she became romantically involved with Lowell M. Palmer Jr., the son of a wealthy Brooklyn businessman, philanthropist and art connoisseur. Their romance introduced her to his circle of friends, who must have been bowled over by this glamorous eastern European creature with her fractured English and alluring ways, possessing every attribute a woman could possibly desire: exceptional beauty, sharp wit, and limitless talents. Approaching the age of twenty-eight, however, Ganna was leaving her bid for stardom rather late.

During the first year in the United States when not performing - which was most of the time - she tried to keep busy meeting producers, having publicity photographs taken, and hearing as much music as possible. "I go every day to the opera, to musicales and the symphony," she wrote. It was not unusual to attend a morning song recital in the Biltmore Hotel at eleven, listen to a concert at Carnegie Hall during the afternoon, and dress up for the Metropolitan Opera in the evening. "It was with music that I sought to bury my troubles," she stated in her diary, referring to a nagging problem with voice production which no amount of coaching seemed able to overcome. In private, Madame Walska could trill like a canary, but when fronting an audience an iron band threatened to throttle her. One evening, she was in her regular seat at the Met to hear Geraldine Farrar sing *Madama Butterfly,* regarding the performance as one of the most memorable days of her life. "After the second act," Walska noted, "I broke down and cried. It was so wonderful."

She went home in a daze, wondering how to achieve the acclaim received by Farrar that night: "All the feeling of shame for professional life left me. From that day I worked without resting to overcome all obstacles that I might become a success in opera." With her personal life now secondary to a career, Ganna proceeded to hire a succession of teachers, each trying to wrest the best from unresponsive vocal cords and tight neck muscles, leaving her admirer in a quandary. Lowell Palmer managed to convince his fiancée that she needed his total support during this testing time, and announced in October, 1915 they were engaged to be married.

The papers were full of stories about disastrous losses for the Allies with the German military machine riding roughshod across Europe, leaving Ganna relieved that she had responded to friendly advice in Paris and escaped the madness. She worried about what might be happening to her family and friends, but unable to receive any news of them, continued to lead her life in the way most peace-loving Americans were doing. She accompanied Lowell to a New Year's Eve party to welcome in 1916 given by someone whose name meant nothing to her, whose invitation she had been reluctant to accept at first. Her fiancé insisted on her going with his assurance of the host's high social standing, but warning that she should on no account make mention of footwear in his company.

They arrived at a lavishly decorated Fifth Avenue mansion and after introductions Walska was waltzing with the host when the high heel detached itself from one of her shoes. He expertly put it back into place with a minimum of fuss and they continued to dance, allowing Lowell and his buddies to have a good laugh at Ganna's expense, and reveal the mystery about needing to keep quiet about the host's occupation. He owned the flourishing firm of Herman Shoes, and knowing his fiancé's rather snobbish attitudes, Lowell had refrained from saying whose party they were attending for fear of her refusing to accompany him to the house of a mere cobbler.

With Ganna Walska's rather snobbish attitudes absorbed during her years in St. Petersburg society, the romance was probably doomed. It was soon announced that there was to be no marriage, with her insisting that the arrangement had never been formalized, explaining later to a newspaper reporter why she terminated the so-called engagement:

"He propose to me, yes. But I refuse him. Then the papers print this story that we are engage. He call me up on the telephone. 'Is it true?' he ask me. He was a nice man, Mr. Palmer, and so when they ask me I just tell them that I care more for career than marriage. It was the only thing I can say. How can I tell them he has ask to marry but I do not care for him? So I just say husband is a hindrance to art and let it go that way.'

In the meantime, Madame was preparing for the leading role of Helen of Troy in Offenbach's *La Belle Hélène* and was chosen by the well-known artist and illustrator of beautiful American womanhood, Coles Phillips, as "a type that seemed to him more individual than eight other beauties of various nationalities." His "Blue Portrait" of Ganna, which she acquired, depicts the sitter as an ambitious, thoroughly modern woman, whose looks fully justify the praise heaped upon her.

Rehearsals went ahead for Offenbach's masterly *opéra-bouffe,* with her finding it difficult to sustain a role that should have been perfect for a beautiful woman with a light soprano voice. But her throat became constricted again, leading to a hoarseness that alarmed everyone. Otto H. Kahn, after watching one stressful rehearsal, suggested that he might be able to help by referring her to a doctor friend, and it was announced in the press that Madame, having temporarily lost her singing voice, would appear in motion pictures "while she is undergoing treatment with a specialist."

Blue Portrait

In July, 1916, she presented herself at the Metro-Rolfe studios where director William Nigh was engaging players for his latest movie. He liked what he saw and immediately offered Walska a supporting role in *The Child of Destiny,* starring Irene Fenwick and Robert Elliott, which would mark Walska's screen début. Being a silent movie, it required minimal vocal effort on her part, but having continuing hoarseness, she remembered Kahn's glowing words about his friend: "Dr. Joseph Fraenkel is not an ordinary practitioner; he is an artist, a poet, a great man, a genius!"

She phoned his consulting rooms only to discover that he was away on summer vacation. A few weeks later, someone suggested that her problem might be psychological and recommended visiting a leading New York psychoanalyst. Walska searched up and down West 56th Street looking for his office, failed to find it and wondered if Dr. Fraenkel was back in town yet. After trudging across ten city blocks to East 66th Street, she discovered that "the great man" had indeed returned and could see her immediately.

The secretary led the way up a spiral staircase to a dark, wood-paneled library and after her eyes adjusted to the gloom, Ganna became aware of standing in front of a small, long-haired man with the air of a philosopher about him, his enormous desk littered with papers and medical tomes. Joseph Fraenkel took off his dominating tortoiseshell eyeglasses, studied the patient intently for an embarrassingly long time, and then motioned her to sit on a chair facing him.

"What can I do for you, my child?"

She began explaining the problem, but was interrupted in mid-sentence by Fraenkel's German-accented voice.

"You need help, my child, but I am not interested in the entire *curriculum vitae* of your throat!"

"How can you help me if you don't know all the circumstances?" she responded.

"Do you think I am a fool?" he barked back, starting to write out a prescription. "Do you think I have studied all these years to be laughed at by an ignorant young lady like yourself?"

"What! Don't you even want to examine my throat?" Walska countered his arrogance.

"Listen to me young lady," he lectured her with a little more restraint after her feisty response, "I am afraid that you will go to some other doctor who might ruin your health forever with an operation. If you would feel better about it, I will look at your throat, but I already know what the matter is. It was obvious the moment you stepped into this room."

She was on the point of running away from this bizarre situation, but hesitated on remembering Otto Kahn's glowing description of this man. Fraenkel opened a drawer in his desk and took out the picture of an attractive dark-haired woman, waved it in her direction, and then returned it, proceeding to write down the patient's name, repeating it several times over as if trying to remember some association. This surprised Walska because the doctor hardly looked the type to waste his time reading show business gossip in the populist press.

He opened another drawer and rifled through a pile of loose papers, bringing out a single sheet, read it silently, and then asked if she knew anyone named Jim McVicker. She shook her head. "Oh, yes you do," he insisted, thrusting the page at Ganna. She noticed some spidery writing and made out the phrase "Don't have anything to do with that Walska woman," and she panicked, about to run when Doctor Fraenkel recovered the paper and put it away without further comment.

The volatile little man causing such confusion for his patient was an 1889 graduate of the Vienna University Medical School who arrived in the United States before the turn of the century to specialize in diseases of the nervous system. Despite his untidy appearance, he possessed compelling social qualities which had established him as a darling of New York society, renowned for dinner-table conversations full of wisdom, eloquence and humor. Joseph Fraenkel was passionate about music, literature and art, with his conviviality and medical expertise respected by professional colleagues. He'd been a teacher at Cornell and was one of a small group of specialists who organized the New York Neurological Hospital, as well as serving on the board of the Montefiore Home and Hospital for Chronic Diseases. Nearing fifty - but looking and acting much older - he was currently pursuing another facet of his career as a neuro-endocrinologist. He published monographs in the *Medical Record,* and one of the more obvious rewards of success was ownership of a fashionable town house at 94th Street on the corner of Park Avenue.

With Dr. Fraenkel

The photograph Fraenkel flashed in front of Walska's eyes was

45

of Alma Mahler, the beautiful young widow of the famous Viennese composer Gustav Mahler, who conducted at the Metropolitan Opera from 1908 and became musical director of the New York Philharmonic a couple of years later. Dr. Fraenkel had been Mahler's medical advisor during his final illness, and would urge the beautiful Alma to marry him after her husband died. Ganna had obviously rekindled warm memories of Alma for the doctor, which explained why, during the second consultation in his rooms, Madame was greeted with a trembling handshake and a proposal of marriage.

Walska knew nothing about Joseph Fraenkel's obsession with the multi-talented Alma Mahler: how after a respectful interval following her husband's death from a rare heart disease in 1911, he had gone to Vienna to woo the widow, taking her on a romantic trip to Corfu in Greece. But whatever transpired, he evidently failed to meet the expectations of the lusty Alma who, after a conflict between her intellectual, and his sexual proclivities, described Joseph in her memoirs: "He was one man for whom even I was too earthy." Mission impossible, Dr. Fraenkel, an unlikely lothario at the age of forty-four, and ruthlessly dismissed by his hoped-for wife as "an elderly, sick little man quite unheroically nursing a fatal intestinal ailment," returned to New York. There, he received a final crushing blow from her in the form of a letter:

"When it comes to living you are a miserable failure. At best men like you are put between book covers, closed, pressed, and devoured in unrecognizable form by future generations. But such men never <u>live</u>."

Madame Ganna Walska accepted Joseph Fraenkel's proposal of marriage, and whatever reservations she had about the man soon to become her second husband, instead of Lowell Palmer, were probably discounted by the comforts she had come to expect in life, together with his contacts in the world of music. She had now received a document from the Russian Orthodox Church granting an ecclesiastical divorce from Arcadie d'Eingorn before his demise on the Prussian battlefield, which provided sufficient evidence for the New York authorities, in lieu of a death certificate, for them to be married on September 7, 1916. Walska moved into the doctor's spacious home, with servants to look after her every whim, and money enough to salve any financial stress. She would not know about her husband's Alma Mahler connection for several years, but did find out about the mysterious Jim McVicker.

Apparently, Olive Whiting, social secretary to Mrs. W. K. Vanderbilt's niece, whose life had been saved by Dr. Fraenkel, dabbled in the occult and wrote the strange message with McVicker guiding her hand during an after-dinner séance. "It seemed that Mr. McVicker was very much surprised at seeing my name," Ganna recalled, "and explained that it was uncanny because 'Walska' was the name of a Russian girl (as he then erroneously thought I was) whom he had seen in Paris and with whom he had unsuccessfully tried to dance."

One result of becoming Mrs. Joseph Fraenkel was pursuing an interest in psychic matters to resolve her singing problems. Several false predictions would damage Walska's trust in mediums, though she persisted in her quest, and her new husband made little effort to dissuade her. He was far too busy attending to his medical practice, as well as worrying about the conflict in Europe when America declared war on Germany in April, 1917.

Dr. Fraenkel contended that the Great War would leave its mark on subsequent generations through the physical defects received by the military, being balanced by moral and mental benefits for the United States. According to him, the Napoleonic Wars reduced the physical stature of the French people and decreased their chest measurements. On the other hand, he cited the population of northern Italy, which historically suffered from goiters, but when war came, "there were children born of the hardy men of another section. The result was, of course, beneficial."

These questionable notions also addressed the problems of wounded troops returning home from the front, theorizing that it was more natural for women to marry disabled men, than the reverse. "I have enough confidence in the American woman," Fraenkel wrote, "to believe she will prefer a man to a slacker, and will pick her husband for his character and manhood rather than for a beautiful exterior." The doctor concluded that whatever the imbalances and disadvantages wrought by warfare, nature would always restore the balance.

The *New York Times* published a long and rambling article on this subject, under the bold headline "Effect Of The World War On The Babies Of America," with the author revealing that many of his opinions were based on "Divine Providence." Ganna's response to her husband's bizarre theories is not recorded, but many *Times* readers must have regarded Fraenkel as a Hippocratic oaf rather than a highly-acclaimed neurologist. Walska, in searching for her own identity, received little relief for her throat problems from her husband, but might have learned from this newspaper article that he considered all medical operations criminal, having lost faith in surgery because, "If nature gave us certain organs it was not for the purpose of having them taken away."

Companionship, combined with readily-available affluence, seem to have Madame's principal reasons for entering into this aberrant relationship, and the relative calm that marriage brought to her life led to indulgence in the occult and to continue singing lessons for what she regarded as her destiny. Ganna was astute enough to know that the key to a career was publicity, and worked hard to ensure that influential journals helped to promote an image of Madame Ganna Walska as a contender for greatness by feeding them a heady mélange of stories to attract opera company managers and concert promoters.

A prominent article appeared in *Musical America* informing readers of her pedigree descended from "the great Stanislaus Laszczynsky," a former Polish ruler whose daughter, Marie, became the Queen of France by marrying Louis XV. There was a passing reference to cabaret singing in Kiev, but no mention at all of performing in operetta, or screen acting. The piece concentrated instead on her preparation for the great operatic roles, while her present activities were largely those of a concert artist. A few weeks later, the same magazine printed two pictures captioned "Ganna Walska Enjoying Life;" one of them taken at the beach wearing a daring neck-to-knee bathing costume and accompanied by Thamara Swirskaja, prima ballerina of the Chicago Opera Company. The other - modern woman that she'd become - showed Ganna driving her own Cadillac, though she freely admitted to friends that engaging the vehicle's reverse gear remained a total mystery to her.

At the end of 1917 billed as "the Polish soprano" she began performing in New York at charity events, including the Emergency Relief Fund at the Waldorf-Astoria, and the Christmas Fund of the *American* newspaper held at the Hotel Astor. It was also announced she would be one of the artists in a forthcoming celebrity recital, and perform with the Minneapolis Symphony Orchestra and the New York Mozart Society.

In February, 1918, the *Herald* ran a prominent advertisement for the final Biltmore Musicale of the season in the grand ballroom of the luxurious new hotel, which had become a focus of New York's social life following its opening five years earlier. Enrico Caruso was the featured artist and seat prices peaked at five dollars, when tickets for an all-Beethoven concert by the Russian Symphony Orchestra under the direction of the distinguished Henri Verbrugghen, ranged from seventy-five cents to a top of two dollars, with a percentage of gross receipts donated to American Friends of Musicians in France. Caruso's associates at the Biltmore were to be an American cellist, the tenor's regular piano accompanist, and the soprano Madame Ganna Walska.

This billing to sing with the world's most famous tenor came through Caruso's accompanist and close friend, Richard Barthélemy, who happened to be one of the singing teachers Walska engaged after arriving in New York. She claimed to have "flirted with the great tenor by correspondence," sending five dollars for his caricature, which he drew for her, and kept the money. At the time, Ganna was lodging at the smart Knickerbocker Hotel on Times Square and had the thrilling experience of lunching with Caruso - also a resident - and another leading opera singer, the baritone Antonio Scotti. That occasion, together with Barthélemy's professional connection, some strategic magazine articles, and newfound social influence as Dr. Fraenkel's wife, apparently landed the prized engagement.

The recital began at eleven o'clock on the Monday morning of February 18, attracting such a huge crowd that many music lovers were turned away disappointed, in spite of extra seats brought in to fill every inch of space in the Biltmore's huge ballroom. The city's savvy concert goers knew that the darling of the Met's golden voice was always sweeter on Mondays, after a Sunday rest. Caruso was billed to appear three times during the program, singing a group of Italian songs, then an aria from *Pagliacci*, and finally a duet from Bizet's *Les pêcheurs de perles* with Madame Walska.

With all attention on the celebrity tenor, her contribution was largely ignored, being little more than a vanity appearance, but it did attract some of the attention she craved by singing a group of Russian songs competently, and partnering Caruso adequately in the Bizet - with a little help from her stellar partner. During the big moment in their duet when a high C is required from both singers, she produced her full voice and was horrified to realize that, although he appeared to be singing, nothing could be heard of his silky tenor voice. "I became afraid that I had done something wrong," she recalled, "and toned down to *pianissimo*."

"Why you not sing *forte*?" he whispered in her ear while acknowledging the generous applause.

"I started to but I couldn't hear you."

"But I am Caruso and everybody know Caruso can sing high C. It's your début and I wanted to give you chance to show what you can do."

Ganna knew that had he produced his famous *forte*, her light soprano would have been swamped.

Next day, the *Times* headlined "Enrico Caruso Responds Eagerly to Many Encores. Sings Tirelessly and Beautifully at Musicale - Mme. Walska Among Other Artists." The paper's music critic praised the lavish manner of the tenor's singing: "He sang and sang, tirelessly, beautifully, sentimentally, heroically . . . and so eager to sing that he gave encore after encore and sang so much that it was a joy to his admirers to be there." The critique mentioned nothing about Walska's efforts, however, only that the musicale ended with the famous *Pearl Fishers* duet before the crowd dispersed without the singers performing "The Star-Spangled Banner," as was customary during the war. It would not become the official national anthem of the United States until 1931.

Dr. Fraenkel adored his beautiful young wife and agreed to her every demand, although she sensed that being the decorative partner of a senior medical man, however distinguished, meant giving up some of her own identity. It became increasingly obvious in their social life and made Ganna restless when the greatest New York and Newport homes were open to her and she could count Mrs. George Henry Warren and Mrs. Vincent Astor among her new friends. Fraenkel's religion also saw them mixing with prominent Jewish families spurned by the social register, such as the Schiffs, Warburgs and Nathans, and regarded by his wife as "the only representatives of a bourgeoisie in America." They knew her as "the young wife of Dr. Fraenkel," but to most of the people they met, Ganna was just a Polish beauty with a cute foreign accent, called "Baby" by the great man in his avuncular manner.

She was far too smart, however, to spurn the advantages offered by the marriage, admitting to wishing "by all means to participate with the full enthusiasm of my juvenile heart in the wonderfully instructive talks of that exceptionally illuminated man." Ganna was no longer a juvenile, in spite of retaining the bloom of youth, and, over thirty, needed to prove her own intellectual worth. Consequently, her adoring husband began boasting to friends that having studied Goethe for thirty years - it was his favorite bedside reading - he was unable to grasp certain concepts of the great German *romancier* until he discussed them with his "Baby wife." Joseph believed that a woman's intuition was stronger than any acquired knowledge, because it was infallible. And who was she to disagree? As time passed, however, Ganna came to realize that her "great Aesculapius," as she called him in a fit of ostentation, lacked "goodness," which she ascribed to hardships during a difficult childhood in Austria, and the fact that he suffered from increasing gastric problems – disadvantages that Alma Mahler had discovered when he wooed her years before.

Dr. Fraenkel's pains were bad during the day, but frightening after dark. "Every night," his wife recorded, "even if he closed his door tightly in his desire not to waken me I would hear those groans that so cruelly tore my heart to pieces." When disturbed from her sleep, she would jump out of bed, plug-in an electric boiler made ready for the purpose, and give him hot water to sip. She had to hold the glass in a towel, but he would swallow its contents straight away, his pain being greater than the searing effects of the liquid. Sometimes Joseph would crawl on his knees and cling to her nightgown, screaming to have mercy on him and demanding she put an end to his suffering. But Ganna could never condone mercy killing - even if she had the means to carry it out - and his misery continued: a physician powerless to treat himself.

To counter their domestic stress, Walska immersed herself in music, taking ever more singing lessons. "I trained my voice as a dramatic soprano," she said, "but always met with disappointment when success was near." Among her teachers was a famous prima donna, Mme. Frances Alda, the New Zealand-born wife of the formidable director of the Metropolitan Opera, Giulio Gatti-Casazza. Famous for her recordings with the Victor company she, too, had adopted a stage name - understandably perhaps having been born Fanny Jane Davis - and insisted that her rich student should become a lighter soprano.

"The day will come," Alda warned, "when you will regret the years you have spent training your voice wrongly."
Walska was at a double disadvantage because the resourceful and down-to-earth Kiwi not only sang supremely, but was also an accomplished homemaker, prompting Mrs. Fraenkel to note in her diary: "Unfortunately I can neither cook nor sew, and when Madame Alda, whose excellent cooking I have enjoyed, presumed to advise me to take up cooking instead of singing, she flattered me by judging me by herself."

Singing lessons and soirées, music and musicians became the cornerstone of Ganna Walska's life, and financial security from her marriage, offered the freedom to indulge in whatever took her fancy. On a hot summer's day at Islip, Long Island, there was a fashionable wedding in the Knapp family (of Union Carbide fame) and Ganna was walking in the garden with dozens of other guests to attend the wedding breakfast when her attention was drawn to a man in the crowd who returned her look rather provocatively. She noticed that he had one arm in a sling and looked somehow foreign, perhaps even Polish. Dr. Fraenkel didn't know his identity when she pointed him out, but thought his face familiar. During the meal the stranger was seated at a nearby table, and, while the other guests around her chatted away, he became the center of Ganna's attention. She overheard that he had broken the arm while playing polo, but no name was mentioned. Dr. Fraenkel then remembered that they had met years before, and went in search of him, but in vain: he had probably left. "So did I," Walska noted, "taking the vision of that sickly and pathetic-looking figure." Inexplicably, she kept thinking about him long afterward, and her husband would make pointed remarks about her obvious interest, commenting as she left the house dressed in extravagant finery on regular visits to the Metropolitan Opera, "If so-and-so sees you he certainly will be lost!" On returning home, Dr. Fraenkel would emerge from his study to ask: "How was it? Did you see Him?"

After making discreet inquiries, one of her friends, hearing from Joseph Fraenkel that it would give his wife pleasure to meet this mystery man, invited him to a dinner party "I was very excited as I entered Anna McCullough's parlor that night," Ganna admitted in a diary note. Her hostess's guilty expression, however, told her that Mr. Alexander Smith Cochran would not be present: he had telephoned his regrets a short time before. Cochran, as Walska had already found out, was a wealthy bachelor, an avid polo player, hunter, international yachtsman and philanthropist; a remote, rather eccentric man who was difficult to get to know. She said later that her thoughts were vitalized every few months by asking questions about him and wondering about the inexplicable spell he cast on her. "He existed for me in the same way as does some book already written but not yet possible to obtain and read," she told her diary.

– 4 –
Unlucky in Love
1918 -1920

Approaching the fall of 1918, newspaper headlines were dominated by news of successful military campaigns in Europe. Following a series of crushing defeats, the German forces retreated to the relative security of their Hindenburg Line; in early September thousands of American troops took part in the bloody Battle of the Meuse-Argonne in northeastern France and there was, at long last, a whiff of Allied victory in the acrid air. It increased in October when the new German chancellor was sent to the United States to broker a peace treaty. Soon after, the northern French city of Lille became liberated by the British; Germany and Austria-Hungary agreed to President Wilson's peace terms; and at the beginning of November an armistice was signed with the Ottoman Empire. The German armistice commission met an Allied delegation in a railroad car in France and agreed to a general armistice, effective November 11. In Times Square on Armistice Day, Enrico Caruso stood at the window of his suite in the Knickerbocker Hotel and led a huge crowd below in singing "The Star-Spangled Banner." Two days later, the Russian government, amid the chaos of the Bolshevik revolution, annulled the oppressive Treaty of Brest-Litovsk signed with the Central Powers eight months previously, liberating the long-oppressed Baltic provinces and Russian-occupied Poland.

Such momentous events - particularly those concerning her birthplace - brought home to Ganna Walska the full impact of a conflict that would have ravaged her own life, like Arcadie's, had she not escaped from Europe four years before. The future now looked brighter for her beloved Poland, as well as the American boys returning home to heroes' welcomes, not to mention Madame's career. She received an invitation to perform in Havana, a city not usually noted for the lyric art, but there was some urgency for her to make an opera début. Ganna had striven to perfect her technique; singing in public with Caruso boosted her confidence, and now there was an opportunity to prove herself worthy of her husband's esteem by following a dictum of Dr. Fraenkel's bedtime companion, Goethe: "If you desire that a person possess certain qualities, attribute to him publicly those qualities." She was determined to make Joseph proud of her, even if it meant the inconvenience of having to travel all the way to the Caribbean.

By now, Mrs. Fraenkel was thoroughly familiar with the Metropolitan Opera's repertoire, occupying her front-row seat - number fourteen - five times a week, enjoying most of what she heard, except for Wagner. Her husband preferred orchestral concerts, and when querying his wife's almost total obsession with singing, she responded by attending the important symphony concerts with him as well, and inviting some of the leading musical personalities of the day to their home. They included the virtuoso violinists Fritz Kreisler and Eugène Ysaye, and there were also opera singers and conductors at the Fraenkels' soirées, among them the celebrated Russian bass Feodor Chaliapin, Frances Alda, Pierre Monteux and Leopold Stokowski. In this stimulating company, Walska became, she said: "music-mad and sound-intoxicated."

It was a dancer, however, originally from St. Petersburg, who confirmed for her that perfection in art could exist. She was about to perform on the same stage as the world's most famous ballerina, Anna Pavlova, who was a huge attraction for the rich Americans who flocked south like migrating birds to Cuba's capital city during the northern winter. The grand hotels, casinos, night clubs and balmy air of Havana made it the western hemisphere's equivalent of France's Côte d'Azur, and if the divine Pavlova was on the bill to present dance interludes during opera performances, patrons would flock to Havana's Grand National Theater, whatever else was offered. Madame Walska's engagement by an American-based Italian impresario was to sing the title role of the Russian princess, Fedora Romanova, in Umberto Giordano's popular work, *Fedora,* which had premièred in Milan twenty years before with the scarcely-known tenor named Enrico Caruso in the cast. This seemed a perfect vehicle in the most auspicious of circumstances to launch an operatic career over the Christmas-New Year holidays during the world's blessed return to peace.

Her absence from New York during this period resulted in a flood of tender letters from Joseph: handwritten notes suffused with love, loneliness, longing and pain. Ganna was greeted on arrival in Cuba:

"May all good fairies greet, lead and protect you there," and when he heard that his wife had arrived... **"My Dear Baby, I am glad that you reached Havana safely. I pray that your stay will be happy and successful . . . I am as usual up and down - more ups."**

But her first rehearsal with the opera company was an unqualified downer.

"Walska, now for you!" the stage director called.

Madame Walska, please!" she responded, affronted by such *lèse-majesté*, and giving him a withering look that would have frozen Niagara Falls. She recalled later: "The Queen of England might have envied my attitude of dignity at that moment," though her hauteur was returned in full measure.

"Oh no! In the opera house one calls for 'Caruso,' not '*Mr.* Caruso.'"

Another letter arrived from New York just before opening night to make her feel wanted again:

"My Dearest Baby, I am all there with you tomorrow: I feel very strongly that you are capable and deserving of great success and happiness and I am grateful to God that He brought me into your path . . . Baby dear, write oftener and more. It gives me courage all during the day to work after I heard from you."

Joseph Fraenkel wrote almost daily, as absence made his words grow ever fonder:

"I have been around you all day today! I am so full of some joy - I am sure that you knew it - and I have so little to say. I know you knew it - feel it better than words could tell it. Love, love, love and be kind and more kind. Put it into your music and your art and by giving it, Santa Claus will give you always more."

But no amount of encouragement from a loving husband could save the opening night of the poorly-prepared *Fedora* from being a fiasco. By Ganna's own admission it was a disaster because she suffered the worst stage fright ever experienced, almost paralyzing her body, with many notes emerging as embarrassing croaks. Sections of an increasingly restive audience jeered as she took her curtain calls, some pelting the stage with fruit demanding their money back - which they got from the management. Had it not been for Pavlova's sublime artistry during intermissions, the evening might have turned into a riot. Subsequent performances went little better, with Ganna needing her husband's medical advice, together with more cash. On January 7, 1919 he wrote

"My dearest Baby, I have this morning your two letters and telegram - It gave me a wonderful feeling. I send you love and all the best there is in my heart. . . and a medicine for sleeps . . . I am also sending you the money - and most of all send you all the best of me!'

A dejected Mrs. Fraenkel returned home to New York a nervous wreck, frantic about where her career could go from here. The only blessing was that no American critics had been present, and news of her failure never reached mainstream musical circles.

Looking back on her marriage to Dr. Fraenkel, she would complain of losing her personality during this difficult time. Their relationship, with an age gap of almost twenty years, continued with his increasing dependence on her companionship, understanding and care, while she experienced the frustration of failing to be accepted as a serious artist in New York's burgeoning music scene. In a diary entry, Ganna speculated that she had been brought into Joseph Fraenkel's life "to soften his soul" which had been hardened by struggles to prove himself in autocratic Austria, "where traditionally there was no room for a poor Jew eager for learning."

She continued to attend the opera, and during 1919, the Chicago Opera Company - second only in status to the Metropolitan in the United States - played a long season at New York's Lexington Theater, with Ganna a regular at their performances. One night, she became aware of someone in a proscenium box watching her intently each time the lights went up between acts, but she was at a disadvantage because poor eyesight prevented her from seeing if the attention was worth reciprocating - and opera glasses were never to be used for this purpose. Next day, continuing her headlong pursuit of musical immersion, she attended a recital given by the famous Italian soprano Luisa Terrazzini, overhearing a socialite from Chicago talking about the previous night's opera audience, and mentioning that Harold McCormick had been seen there. His generosity, Ganna heard, made the existence of opera in Chicago possible as well as financing this season in New York. Her keen hearing also picked up that McCormick had been sitting in one of the boxes last night, and she thought he might have been the person ogling her. It was her wish to sing with that company ever since she auditioned for its musical director, Cleofonte Campanini, when he judged she would make a good Fedora, which had led to her engagement for the debacle in Havana.

A short time later, Ganna read in a newspaper that Mr. Harold McCormick, president of the International Harvester Company, and son of the man who revolutionized world agriculture by inventing the mechanical reaper, was in New York staying at the Plaza. On impulse, she decided to telephone him and, to her surprise, the call was put straight through to his suite.

Harold McCormick

"This is Madame Walska, Mr. McCormick. You don't know me. My name means nothing to you, but I would like to meet and speak with you."

"I'm very sorry, Madame, a meeting is out of the question because I am returning to Chicago today. I already have an appointment at noon and after a quick lunch with my son must catch the train."

"Please Mr. McCormick," Walska pleaded in her most seductive middle-European voice, "just say you don't wish to see me, for I simply refuse to believe that one can't find five minutes when one really wants to."

This novel approach must have intrigued the busy captain of industry, coming from a voice of mysterious promise as well as "glorious timbre and beauty" - as he would describe it later.

"Oh no," he hastened to assure his caller, trying not to show offence, "I really mean I have no time - it's not an excuse. Perhaps you could write me?"

"I could, but I won't. What's the use? If you cannot allow me five minutes, it would be useless to bother you. From a man who cannot find five minutes I expect nothing!"

"Wait a minute," came the response that Walska was fishing for. "If you were to be here at noon - exactly at twelve o'clock - and only for five minutes?"

"Certainly, I will be there as you request. Thank you, Mr. McCormick - and *à bientôt*."

It was only a short, chauffeured drive from the Fraenkels' Park Avenue residence, and Madame had time to change into a charming new day dress and have the maid fix her hair before arriving at the Plaza on the stroke of midday to face a little unexpected confusion at the reception desk.

"Which Mr. McCormick do you wish to see, Madame," the desk clerk wanted to know. "Junior or senior?"

After a moment's hesitation, remembering that McCormick had mentioned his son earlier, she opted for the latter.

When the top industrialist arrived in the sitting room and introduced himself, it was immediately obvious to Ganna that he was not the person who had stared at her throughout the evening at the Lexington Theater. But she was struck by this man's kindly disposition, as they shook hands and sat down.

Turning on the maximum charm, and making sure to be brief, she stated her desire to sing with the Chicago Opera, and mentioned her previous meeting with Campanini - making sure to say nothing about Havana - explaining that she had been preparing Leoncavallo's *Zaza*. It was the composer's most successful work after *Pagliacci* and in the company's forthcoming repertoire. McCormick knew that its title role of a French cabaret performer demanded a singer with considerable dramatic and vocal gifts.

"Do you think you can do it?" he asked, fixing her with his blue

59

eyes. "Yes, I think so," she responded. He promised to speak to the company's musical director, and Walska reminded him of his lunch engagement.

After hearing nothing for a week, she sent a letter to McCormick and received a prompt reply in the form of a handwritten note, explaining that singers for the forthcoming winter season were already under contract, though he held out the hope that the company's new maestro, Marinuzzi - who had succeeded Campanini after his recent death - might want to audition her at some stage. He added: "As to the impression you made at our meeting, I must say it was a very favorable one," suggesting that he might try to see her on one of his regular New York visits "if you have me care to do so - and you say you do, so I accept." Several weeks passed until he phoned to ask permission to visit Madame Walska.

This was an era when beautiful European women like Ganna were often assumed to be French: endlessly mysterious creatures skilled in the art of seduction. But those with theatrical aspirations were most likely to be adventuresses like Elizabeth Rosanna Gilbert, the now-legendary Lola Montez, stage name of the Irish-born Spanish dancer and courtesan who had numbered Franz Liszt, Alexandre Dumas père, and King Ludwig I of Bavaria among her conquests. Harold McCormick, one of the most prominent men in America, married, but long separated from his wife, J. D. Rockefeller's daughter Edith, was not at all sure what he would find when, accompanied by his son Fowler for the sake of propriety, he arrived at the Fraenkels' East 94th Street address. Instead of the proverbial purple boudoir perfumed with intoxicating incense, they found themselves in a very respectable town house, its well-stocked library prominently displaying the works of Goethe and Dante. McCormick's astonishment must have multiplied when Madame, dressed demurely, entered on the arm of her husband, whose reputation extended at least as far as the Midwest, because Dr. Fraenkel was recognized as Harold's cousin's physician. The surprise was complete when it was revealed that Madame Ganna Walska, diva-in-waiting, was in fact *Mrs.* Joseph Fraenkel.

Returning to Chicago on the Twentieth Century Limited after their sophisticated encounter, Harold penned his thoughts as the

New York Central Railroad's prestige express train sped alongside the Hudson:

"The name of the car I am in is 'Cold Springs,' first, I feel, the 'cold' is by contrast, because somehow, there arises in me a little warm stirring of feelings - very gentle and very delicate but none the less remarked by me." He told Madame that such a response was a novelty because his emotions had been repressed by circumstances **"which I should be glad to tell you of if the appropriate situation arises and if you care to hear."** This veiled pass failed to get Ganna any closer to performing in Chicago, but she had made a hit with one of the richest men in America, and seized the opportunity to keep him interested.

As part of her strategy, she made sure to learn more about the person who could hold the key to a singing future. By asking around, Walska discovered that McCormick's wife, Edith, was the youngest of the four Rockefeller children and had a reputation for being the most rebellious of the clan, constantly querying her role as a member of one of America's most powerful families, and being drawn to psychological and metaphysical matters which distanced her from the others. When she had married Harold twenty-five years before, it was not only a fairytale union, but also the conjunction of two powerful dynasties. The fact that the outspoken Edith was mentally unstable, and the sporty Harold tended to drink too much, were minor blemishes on an otherwise perfectly-matched, modern marriage. By uniting two powerful families whose patriarchs - John D. Rockefeller and Cyrus McCormick - were the ultimate expressions of the American Dream, had prompted the press of the day to hail the nuptials of Edith and Harold as "the Princess of Standard Oil" becoming the wife of "the Prince of International Harvester."

In spite of their massively affluent backgrounds, both the Rockefeller and McCormick children were raised in surprisingly austere circumstances, though when freed from parental restraints, Edith and Harold threw off the Spartan pasts with gay abandon and splashed money in every direction from their stone mansion at 1000 Lakeshore Drive, Chicago.

With an extravagance reminiscent of the French Second Empire, including dinners for two hundred guests under glittering chandeliers with liveried footmen in attendance, the couple also pursued a wide range of cultural interests. They staged musicales at home featuring the greatest performers, collected fine art, and became principal patrons of the city's opera, with Edith sponsoring several translations of Italian libretti into English. In their palace overlooking the lake, they flaunted their version of American royalty in which she adopted an *hauteur* that tended to place her somewhere in the stratosphere, insisting on being called Edith Rockefeller McCormick as a gesture of independence, while the more down-to-earth Harold managed to keep his feet on the ground - except when indulging in his passion for flying light aircraft.

It became obvious to their circle that Harold and Edith were seriously mismatched, with his gregarious nature finding difficulty in accommodating her haughty manner. She believed herself descended from La Rochefoucauld nobility of France, though the Rockefellers were of mixed English, German, Scottish and Irish origins. Two of their children died young, which drove Edith into a cloistered world of her own making, and in 1912 she met the Swiss experimental psychiatrist Carl Jung in New York who diagnosed her condition as latent schizophrenia. She began treatment with him, responding so well to the sessions that Jung was asked to stay in America, where Edith promised to fund him work. When he declined the offer, she left with him for Europe in 1913 and remained there in spite of the combined efforts of her father and husband to persuade her to return to the United States. By 1914, Harold also became interested in the work of Jung's Zurich group, which embraced a philosophy of striving for personal integration and wholeness, resigning as treasurer of International Harvester to spend time in Switzerland, though remaining on the company's board and returning from time to time for meetings in Chicago.

Inevitably, their lengthy separations led to the McCormicks drifting apart, with Edith becoming one of Jung's most fervent disciples, as well as supporting musicians and writers - and having affairs with several of them. Harold, alone in Chicago, sought the company of captivating women, and, being the principal backer of the opera company, had access to many an attractive company member. In 1918 he was named president of International Harvester, which committed him to spend most of his time in the Windy City.

Dr. Fraenkel's health deteriorated rapidly during the winter of 1920, and Ganna's spirits were kept buoyant by regular letters and cables from Harold, who counted on seeing her on his next visit to New York, when he hoped they could get better acquainted. He wrote from Lakeside Drive in reply to one of her cables:

"It did me good to hear from you that you had strong music stirring within you on Sunday. I too felt music in the air, and stirring about the strings for softness - but it was real music . . ."

McCormick was able to separate Madame Ganna Walska, aspiring prima donna, from her real-life role as Mrs. Joseph Fraenkel caring for a sick husband. "How strangely near you I feel tonight," he declared with little attempt to hide his feelings. "It almost makes me shudder in a way because there seems so much 'business' I know not of going on within me at one time." He revealed plans to sail for Europe, where he would discuss the future of his marriage with his estranged wife.

Next time, there was a letter of sympathy over Dr. Fraenkel's illness, its concern barely disguising what was a passionate love letter, addressed without the formality of "Madame Walska:" **"Ganna, I am wondering what goes on in your mind. Do you know that your face comes to me clearly now at any time - your countenance and your figure."** Instead of "Harold F. McCormick" of the previous correspondence, he began sign himself simply "Harold." She telephoned him regularly in Chicago, sent publicity pictures, and he eagerly responded by mail before visiting her in New York: **"Ganna, the more I see of you the lovelier and more capable you become. Kindliness and firmness, beauty and simplicity reign with you."**

Harold obviously regarded Ganna as a potential conquest, commenting, **"I presume, as you hinted once, you have sometimes a fight with yourself, not to allow your charm play the devil with you and with others!"** And as his ardor increased: **"My beautiful Ganna, my thoughts go to you these days, and the spirit of my life springs from the beauty of your soul . . ."**

Joseph Fraenkel's chronic illness worsened and his wife had to forego singing lessons and opera visits to spend more time at home caring for her husband, while further letters and telegrams of support arrived from Chicago, making Walska feel totally vulnerable again - as during the darkest moments of Arcadie's tuberculosis. Joseph was finally relieved of his excruciating pains when he died in the Post Graduate Hospital on April 24, 1920, aged sixty, plunging his wife into mourning. In a diary note she described her Joseph's passing as "a terrific calamity [that] crushed

63

my mind, broke my heart and blackened my soul." Regular telephone conversations with Harold were halted by the stark telegram Ganna sent him: **"Doctor Fraenkel Died At 11am"**

There was some consolation for her in receiving eloquent condolences from Chicago, as well as the practical suggestion: **"I don't know what you would like me to do about coming to the funeral, or whether you would rather I come on some time later - just when you want me - that is the time I prefer."**

Harold had been working hard behind the scenes to secure an engagement with the Chicago Opera, finally persuading the new musical director to have Madame Walska sing the title role in *Zaza* during the coming winter season. With that to sustain her, she tried to carry on as normal by planning to take a house in the Catskills for the summer to work with her singing teacher there on the opera's score, and to invite Doctor and Mrs. Mills, friends of her dead husband, to stay with her in the mountains of New York State.

Ganna expressed her fears to Harold that Dr. Fraenkel's family had the power to "cut short all meanings of my living and may even force me to leave the house in 24 hours." If that happened, she would be unable to spend time in the country, and "if I do not study, if I have no costumes, I cannot expect to go to Chicago and fulfill my contract." She claimed, without apparent foundation, that the Metropolitan Opera had asked her to join their company, but "with such conditions that I cannot accept - Farrar is singing all my parts - so I have to pray to God that she should get sick at the last moment and I will take the part."

The Mills changed their plans and decided to visit Europe in July, persuading the increasingly distraught Ganna to go with them on the pretext that Paris was the best place to have her opera costumes made, hoping that by distancing her from familiar surroundings - and perhaps the attentions of the still-married McCormick - her life might return to normal. When Harold learned about the trip, he immediately made arrangements to travel on the same ship for a planned visit to Edith in Switzerland.

It was sensible for Walska to be absent from New York during that summer because several claims were pending on her late husband's will, which had left her an estate valued at $338,575. One challenge came from Dr. Fraenkel's brother, Emil, a New

York lawyer, contesting the contents on behalf of the family. There was the additional question of two thousand dollars said to be due to Mrs. Bustead, Dr. Fraenkel's maid. Walska's own attorney, Phelan Beale, partner with John Vernou Bouvier Jr. (the future Jacqueline Bouvier Kennedy Onassis's grandfather) in the law firm of Bouvier Beale at 165 Broadway, advised Ganna to be cautious about spending money until the objections were heard. The court case was set for October, though he expected no conclusion for at least a year.

Dressed in black, the widow Fraenkel boarded RMS "Aquitania" bound for Cherbourg and Southampton on Saturday, July 31. On her way to her first class accommodation, she passed a notice board displaying the passenger list, and standing beside it was someone who reminded her of the man from the Long Island wedding party: the subject of past fantasies. Ganna could not be sure if it was the elusive Alexander Smith Cochran because she'd seen him only once, four years ago with his arm in a sling at Islip. He moved away and she immediately searched for his name on the alphabetical lists, checking both the Cs. and the Ss., but it was not there. "It couldn't be him," she told herself. "It must be a mistake. Still, I'm not on the list either, since I only booked my passage at the last minute." Their names may have been absent from the notice board, but the Cunard Line's shipboard booklet listed a "Mr. Alex Smith Cochrane [sic] and valet" as passengers, together with "Mrs. Gana [sic] W. Fraenkel" and "Mr. Harold F. McCormick."

The first act of what would become a burlesque on the high seas, which could have provided the book for Cole Porter's future smash-hit musical *Anything Goes* - is the familiar bustle of a transatlantic embarkation, with a band playing on the quay, late arrivals scurrying to board the great liner, and white-clad stewards carrying bags and guiding passengers to their accommodation. A sense of adventure fills the air, as friends wish Walska and the Mills bon voyage. While all this is happening, she notices the man she thought might be Cochran standing and watching her, a cigarette dangling from the corner of his mouth. Walska would write in her memoirs that he was "looking apathetically at me, at us, at the space in front of him, for not a muscle of his face showed he saw us, was looking at me, or even that his eyes were voluntarily fixed on anything."

The next act takes place at sea during a calm crossing of the Atlantic, with the hot weather of high summer, making the ship uncomfortably stuffy, prompting Madame to keep the door of her stateroom open to allow cooling sea breezes to circulate. Cochran's own quarters are on the same deck and she glimpses him occasionally passing by in the corridor, but he never seems curious enough to glance inside. Going on deck, she finds him asleep in a deck chair and for the first time is able to study his face. She recalled: "He appeared very plain to me . . . that is to say his face had no soul, no life, and its lines were the kind one gets from the wind and not from the experiences of life when every wrinkle means suffering - tangible records of deep feeling." Ganna thought he looked dry skinned and bitten by the elements; in other words, a

Smith Cochran

typical Joseph Conrad sailor.

The enigmatic Alexander Smith Cochran sometimes referred to in the press as "the most eligible bachelor in the world" because of his great wealth, led a life of ease as the sole heir to the most successful businesses of its type in the United States. He was the principal owner of Alexander Smith and Sons Carpet Company of Yonkers, New York State, with about seven thousand employees -

more than half the town's industrial workforce. The business had revolutionized carpet manufacture with the development of new weaving techniques, and their high-quality products were sold around the world. In 1892, for instance, they consigned a large shipment to Moscow for the coronation of the Tsar, and Smith carpeting was selected by the Russian Empress for the Winter Palace in St. Petersburg. The Baroness d'Eingorn herself may well have stepped daintily upon it.

Though the press characterized Cochran as a free-spending playboy, a 'sealebrity' through mixing with the international ocean-racing set, and a society sportsman playing polo with maharajas in India, the substance behind the celebrity image was usually ignored. The man was passionate about literature and had donated generous gifts to his university, as well giving large sums of money to worthy causes in and around Yonkers. As a result of collecting first editions of Shakespeare, Spenser, Milton and Bacon during fox-hunting trips to Britain, he offered to underwrite the cost of establishing a literary and social club at his alma mater, Yale, where students could relax and converse with the noble aim of "the promotion among the members and in the community of a larger appreciation of literature and the arts of social intercourse." He was also one of the Metropolitan Museum of Art's benefactors, with important gifts of Islamic art.

Whether any of Cochran's sporting, literary or artistic credentials impressed Ganna at this moment is questionable because Harold McCormick was also aboard the "Aquitania," keeping a discreet distance to avoid her embarrassment. In Walska's memoirs she mentions coyly that he "happened to be on board - and perhaps not by chance." But Harold remained a married man, and social propriety demanded that they observe the utmost discretion in the confined and very public surroundings of a great ocean liner, where the faintest whiff of scandal would spread through the ship like wildfire and be reported in the American press.

Act three of this comedy, finds Madame sitting on deck enjoying refreshing breezes in Harold's company when Cochran appears, strolling back and forth. He has a lady with him who stares at Walska each time they pass, and finally stops, hesitates, and then whispers to her that she wants to meet because she had been a friend of Dr. Fraenkel.

"All friends of my late husband are welcome indeed," Walska responds, but the woman scarcely listens, turning away to signal her companion to come over.

"May I present Mr. Alexander Smith Cochran?" she asks, whispering with embarrassment, "Please forgive me. He begged so much to be introduced. I couldn't help it."

Cochran coolly takes the seat next to Walska just vacated by Harold, who had stood up to greet Mrs. Frank Henderson - the lady persuaded to make the introduction - and engages Walska in earnest conversation, totally ignoring the others. The awkward encounter is saved by the first call for dinner and Cochran leaves to go to his suite and dress, vowing to himself, as he revealed later, "I will marry that woman if she will have me or I will never marry at all!"

The finale of this farce sees the two of them meeting in the pool room of the ship after dinner. With the excuse that the atmosphere is too smoky for a lady, he leads Ganna to the top deck, and in the full moonlight and gentle airs of a warm night, abruptly asks her to marry him. She is shocked into silence, unable to find words, but he becomes insistent, imploring her to see him in Paris.

Harold McCormick was furious at Cochran's interest, having planned to comfort the mourning widow during the voyage, but there were few opportunities and he admitted later: "I was even then in love with Madame Walska but I throttled my feelings. Cochran, however, was free. He never pursued anyone as he did Madame Walska." Early the next morning, Alexander Smith Cochran, whose destination was London, disembarked by tender off Plymouth without communicating further with Ganna, or explaining his precipitate offer of marriage.

The liner proceeded to Cherbourg, and she soon found herself back in the French capital after an absence of five fast-moving years during which her life changed radically. Walska was barely settled into the hotel, however, when there was a telephone call from London; it was Cochran, who knew where she was from the Mills, asking over a crackly line if she would dine with him that evening if he flew to Paris immediately. Flattered by the extravagance of the approach, she accepted; he arrived in good time and proceeded to propose marriage again during their meal. For a second time, without any discussion, she rejected him with a shake of the head, and her persistent suitor, irritated at not getting his way, abruptly rose from the table and departed. He left Paris to go hunting in the south-west of France near Pau, close to the Pyrenees, but came back to the capital within a week, thrusting an exquisite oriental pearl ring from Cartier on Ganna's finger as soon as they met.

"If by January you still do not want to marry me," he told her, "I will understand that Harold McCormick is too much on your mind."

A third marriage by the age of thirty-three was the last thing Walska wanted, only four months after Joseph Fraenkel's death. And if the thought of choosing to be the second Mrs. Harold McCormick or the first Mrs. Alexander Smith Cochran arose at all, it was no contest because Cochran had the advantage by being a bachelor and, therefore, a free man. McCormick was in the throes of battling Jungian psychology to persuade his wife to give him a divorce, and that might take an eternity. The renegade Rockefeller daughter had by now resolutely rejected her family and America itself, supported by a monthly allowance of $2,500 from an alienated father, which would soon be doubled in his desperate efforts to entice her back home. Whatever the outcome of this tortuous triangle, Ganna was in Paris being wooed by two of America's richest men: one, a self-centered, world-weary forty-six-year-old Yale alumnus, and the other a Princeton man, gentle, balding, and a flabby forty-eight.

Femme Fatale
1920

Ganna Walska made arrangements to return to America following her eventful sojourn in Paris, while Harold McCormick went off to Switzerland attempting to negotiate a divorce from Edith, and Cochran played polo at the exclusive Hurlingham Club in Britain. A couple of days before she boarded the liner, Alec - as Ganna insisted on calling him - phoned and pleaded with her to meet him the next morning, saying he was anxious to see her the moment he arrived in the French capital. He followed up the call with two cables to the Ritz, where she was staying: "Am Coming Back Immediately" and "Crossing Tonight. Meet You At Ten In Morning. Staying Crillon."

Soon after greeting each other in that most fashionable of Parisian hotels, Walska received a further proposal of marriage, with Cochran insisting in an emotional - but hardly chivalrous - outburst that it was the only solution for his miserable life. Even if she did not care for him, he said, she must consent to their wedding as an act of charity. In a scene of low melodrama following the high farce on the voyage over, he appealed to Ganna's humanitarian sympathies, begging her to become his wife, crying, "Save me! Save me!"

She was nonplussed by the approach, but he did strike a chord in making her aware that she might be able to bring some happiness into his life, as she had for poor departed Joseph Fraenkel, and the hapless Arcadie before him. Walska's decision to accept Cochran's proposal of marriage was influenced by the fact that she had heard nothing positive from Harold, except for brief telegrams announcing his movements, like going to the mountains for the weekend "to think." She could only assume that after ten days in Switzerland his mission to wrest a divorce from his recalcitrant wife had failed.

Mourning for Joseph Fraenkel came to an end much sooner than she expected when Ganna accepted the offer to become Alexander

Smith Cochran's wife, but only under certain conditions: the most important being to allow continuation of a career in opera, explaining to her husband-to-be that she was not the type of woman who could ever be happy living as decoration for a wealthy man. Making plans for their future, it was agreed that after the wedding he would return to England to hunt, and she would sail back to America to prepare for the *Zaza* engagement in Chicago.

The question of when, where and how the ceremony might take place was answered by a brusque reply from the groom: "This afternoon, of course!" Ganna assumed it was one of his little jokes, knowing that French law did not encourage haste in these matters. But Alex was used to getting his way in everything, and would brook no obstacles. He contacted his Franco-American lawyer at noon, briefing him to prepare the necessary papers before three-thirty because the American Consulate closed at four o'clock and the couple would need to present themselves a little before then to have their documents certified. Attorney Charles Loeb responded to the request by saying that even if his client were President of the Republic, the French bureaucracy would never allow a marriage ceremony at such short notice.

"Never mind," Cochran responded dismissively, "you go away and prepare the papers, I will bring the authorization."

By 15.40 that afternoon, the bride had the necessary papers in her hand, rushing them to the astonished Loeb, while the groom took a taxi ride to the consulate to ensure it remained open. Ganna never knew - and was afraid to ask - how the notoriously intractable laws were sidestepped, but when Loeb saw the license, complete with its array of *timbres fiscales* and showy signatures, she thought the eyes would pop out of his head.

"He must have bribed everyone from the prime minister down to the last bailiff!" was all the lawyer could mutter.

Alexander Smith Cochran and Ganna Fraenkel were united in matrimony during the late afternoon of Wednesday, September 15, 1920 at the American Cathedral of the Holy Trinity on Avenue George V by the rector, Frederick H. Beckman, with the Loebs as witnesses. The marriage certificate describes the groom as a bachelor aged forty-six, his bride a widow of twenty-nine, though she was four years older. An accompanying Book of Matrimony contains the order of ceremony, together with quotations from two

71

poets - Cowper and Longfellow, which must have pleased Alex as a literary man and Ganna for their optimistic view of togetherness after two stressful previous marriages:

> **What is there in the vale of life**
> **Half so delightful as a wife**
> **When friendship, love and peace combine**
> **To stamp the marriage-bond divine?**
> **The stream of pure and genuine Love**
> **Derives its current from above;**
> **And Earth a second Eden shows**
> **Where'er the healing water flows."**

William Cowper (1666-1709)
Love Abused.

and

> **"As unto the bow the cord is,**
> **So unto the man is woman;**
> **Though she bends him, she obeys him,**
> **Though she draws him, yet she follows;**
> **Useless each without the other."**

Henry Wadsworth Longfellow
(1807-1882)
The Song of Hiawatha.

After a wedding dinner in the company of lawyer Loeb and his wife, the groom was in such a hurry to be alone with his bride that when the head waiter offered liqueurs and coffee he was rudely sent packing. The couple went to the Crillon, Cochran's hotel of choice, never suggesting that she might prefer to remain at the Ritz instead. While Walska was at the church, the maid had transferred her possessions from Place Vendôme to Place de la Concorde, worried that Madame would not find everything in order because of the unseemly haste. Alex suggested she check her wardrobe while he took his customary stroll before bedtime.

An hour later, Ganna heard him return, entering the sitting room of their royal suite, and as soon as the door was closed there came the sound of unrestrained laughter. "He laughed and laughed quite joyfully," she recalled in her memoirs. "At every step he took toward my room his laughter became more hilarious. When he finally stopped on the threshold of my room, I asked the reason for his extraordinary gaiety." Cochran tried to explain, making several spluttering attempts but on each occasion collapsing into hysterics.

Finally pulling himself together, he managed to describe walking along the Champs-Elysées where the *filles de joie* called out offering him their services. As he neared the end of his nocturnal promenade, almost back at the Crillon, one prostitute became over-insistent and Alex said he responded by telling her: "No, not tonight, my dear. Tonight I am married! Ha-ha-ha-ha." His bride wondered if that irritating bray - let alone his sense of humor - would be their downfall, and retired alone to her bedroom.

While the marriage ceremony was taking place that afternoon, Harold McCormick finally succeeded in persuading Edith to grant him a divorce after discovering she was having an affair with a young Austrian named Edwin Krenn. He had undergone analysis with her, and with no apparent means of support, Edith gave him money and assisted in obtaining Swiss nationality, convinced that he was going to be a brilliant architect, ignoring Carl Jung's warning that their affair would end in scandal. Harold also learned that his wife's accumulated debts were nearing a million dollars, and she needed to be bailed-out with the proceeds from the sale of some Standard Oil of New Jersey stock.

He was now in a good position to press for legal separation, and prepared to leave Zurich's Bauer-au-lac hotel in high spirits, hopelessly happy and whistling an opera melody, on the way to inform his beloved Ganna the good news. About to set off for the telegraph office, he came across the hotel's messenger boy in the lobby.

"Hello my little friend," Harold called out jovially, "I have a wire for you."

"So have I, Mr. McCormick," the lad responded, handing over a telegram just received from Paris. It was from Ganna and read: "Just Married Alexander Smith Cochran. Hope You Will Understand And That We Will Always Be Good Friends."

The smile disappeared from Harold's face, to be replaced by a look of stunned incredulity. Instead of news about his divorce, he cabled the intention of coming to Paris almost immediately, convinced that her action - as he told his attorney later - was the result of being "lonely and spiritually adrift, and, without my counsel, she finally accepted the advice of a European friend and married Cochran. I was never so shocked and crushed in my life as when I heard of the marriage."

After sending the telegram, McCormick sat down in the hotel's writing room to compose a letter explaining his state of mind, desperately disappointed about the terrible timing:

"I was going to leave Saturday to join you. I was happy and contented, yet tired, worn and torn. My object with the children was so to leave the situation that they would be prepared to see you as I saw you and to love you as a companion. I meditated some and looked at my souvenirs of you and at your photographs, I read 50 pages of the book you gave me and then today came your telegram. You say 'hope you will understand.' Understand what, Ganna Dear - that you love me still as you said at our parting, that I was your 'last love?' I take it that way. I love you dearly in my poor broken way . . ."

With money no object for one of America's leading industrialists, he hired a private plane to fly him from Zurich to Paris at dawn the next morning, phoning Ganna from the airport at Le Bourget and insisting on seeing her immediately he arrived in the capital. "Afraid that something would happen to him," she recalled, "I accepted his proposal to breakfast with me." Their meeting might have come from Georges Feydeau's classic 1907 French farce *La Puce à l'oreille* (*A Flea in Her Ear*) with its improbable situations and exaggerated characters. While Alexander Cochran slept soundly in the adjoining room on his first full day of married life, his wife, wearing a white chiffon *peignoir*, poured coffee for her defeated suitor in the sitting-room, who sat slumped in a chair wearing a hangdog expression.

"No sugar please," he requested politely, and then revealed: "Edith has finally consented to give me a divorce. Now *you* must divorce Mr. Cochran and we will be married as soon as possible. I am sailing with you!" Ganna was flabbergasted, able only to mumble incoherently about an impossible situation. Yes, she was sailing for America soon, but accompanied by her new husband who'd just canceled his plans for England. That was upsetting enough for her because the winter season in America was no place for a restless sportsman whose life, as she understood it, revolved around racing yachts, polo ponies and fox hunting. "I feared he would find it more than dull without his sole distractions of ponies in the daytime and women-less clubs at night," she noted acidly.

"It's impossible for you to sail with me, Harold," Ganna protested. "Think about the scandal when the press discover that the chairman of International Harvester was seen in the company of the woman who has just married the richest bachelor in the United States, embarking on her honeymoon with a man married to Rockefeller's daughter: a man with grown children!"

Knowing that he shunned publicity - except when promoting the opera company - she succeeded in calming McCormick, by convincing him to take a different ship home. The next couple of days in Paris, spent were "sadly comical," according to her, with the threesome spending time together in brittle harmony, lunching, dining and going to the theater. They even visited Ganna's dressmaker, and, when she went to a hairdresser on her own, Cochran - gentleman that he was - stayed behind at the Crillon to keep company with the gloomy Harold.

McCormick prepared to make a melancholy return to Switzerland, and once he'd left, Alex tried to secure his wife's loyalty by plying her with extravagant gifts. She was unimpressed, however, showing little delight when he announced the purchase of a town house on the fashionable rue de Lubeck for their future visits to the French capital, and presented her, after lunch at the Café de Paris, with a gleaming monogrammed Rolls-Royce, complete with its uniformed chauffeur - or *mecanicien* as Parisian owners of the cherished British *marque* tended to call their drivers at the time. Previously, there had been a million francs worth of sable coat waiting in her room as a wedding present, together with a note giving *carte blanche* to choose any jewelry she desired from Cartier, where Cochran kept an account. Her new husband also arranged a Paris bank account for Ganna to receive a hundred thousand dollars a year "pin money." All that passed her by, she claimed in her autobiography, "without actually touching my inner being." Madame, however, if not a devotee of conspicuous consumption, could ill afford to show contempt for the very handy pin money.

She continued to maintain contact with Harold through regular correspondence, making no attempt to hide it from her husband, who assumed it was for professional singing reasons. The other man in her life wrote her from Zurich four days after the wedding:
"Darling Ganna - My Baby - I am suffering, I am tortured - hardly have I slept – I abandoned you in Paris - I left you to yourself and to him – your sweetness and gentleness are for me - 'Tis I who understand your beauty of character and all - it seems he valued them more because he came there and

got you – I can't think now of you being his and not mine."

Cochran's accommodation on the ship back to America was confined and uncomfortable, being one of the last cabins available because of his last-minute change of plans. The newly-weds found themselves on different decks, and, unlike the eastward crossing, the Atlantic weather was appalling with the honeymoon trip turning into a nightmare that all the money and possessions recently heaped upon Ganna could not mitigate. She was confined to bed suffering badly from *mal de mer* throughout the voyage, leaving her Alec to take his meals alone. To make things worse, he reveled in the stormy conditions being a longtime ocean racer. In 1910 he had sailed his schooner "Westward" from America to Britain in fourteen days to compete in European waters, and during 1914 built the sloop "Vanitie" as a trial yacht for the America's Cup races, which were canceled because of the hostilities in Europe. In January, 1917, after America entered the Great War, Cochran turned over his steam yacht "Warrior" for service with the British Navy and accepted a commission of Commander in the Royal Naval Reserve, for which he was awarded an honorary CBE by King George V.

Returning to New York, the couple stayed for a month at Dr. Fraenkel's house, which was haunted by too many ghosts from the past for Ganna, and remained the subject of a legal challenge over his will. Life there with her Joseph may have been challenging, but their social circle embraced many people from the world of music and the arts as compensation. With Cochran's society buddies, however, she found the company frequently vacuous and the atmosphere claustrophobic. They clamored to meet Alex's bride and the Cochrans dined out frequently; on the occasions when they remained at home, it was only to offer reciprocal hospitality, with Mrs. Cochran looking stunning in a slinky new evening gown from Paris. She had been too preoccupied with the turmoil surrounding the two men vying for her to acquire *Zaza* costumes for her Chicago début, and ordered just this one black garment from the almost legendary fashion house of Callot Soeurs. It made such an impression on its repeated New York outings that her husband joked to friends about having married an economical little wife; as misconceived a remark he ever made.

Such warning signs about his behavior did not auger well for the stability of their marriage, and the first lunch party they gave at home only served to highlight her new husband's mutability. After eating, the guests moved from the dining room to Madame's singing studio for coffee, when Alex formally kissed her hand, offered thanks for a charming time, and departed. Ganna needed to resort to acting to conceal her dismay at this eccentric behavior. After everyone left, the phone rang; it was her husband calling from his club and laughing like a whinnying hunter.

"Guess what happened to me?" he asked with arch naiveté. 'When I thanked you for lunch today and left, I entirely forgot that I was married and was, in fact, the host. I have only just realized my mistake. Isn't that funny? Ha-ha-ha-ha. . . ."

The gossip columns continued to show interest in their marriage, though Cochran's austere personality had rarely offered much for them in the past, except occasionally on the sports pages for his hunting, shooting and yachting activities. Ganna, however, was becoming a celebrity and provided the sort of chatty copy journalists sought. One New York newspaper ran a small piece accompanied by a flattering photograph of "Mme. Ganna Walska" under the heading "To Continue Stage Career as Wife of Millionaire," in which she was quoted saying that marriage would make no difference whatsoever to her career.

A longer feature appeared almost simultaneously in the Boston *Post* revealing their relationship in sharper focus by a young man named Olin Downes, already one of America's leading music critics. His interview was accompanied by an embarrassing picture of Ganna captioned "A new member of the Chicago Opera Company" taken during the war when she sang "La Marseillaise" at a charity concert dressed as a gawky *sans-culotte* clutching a limp tricolor in one hand and brandishing a sword in the other, looking like a parody of the famous Delacroix painting known as "Liberty Leading the People".

Downes' article was significant because he found it impossible to extract any substantial information from his subject. Instead, he watched her every movement closely, noting that Madame Walska's eyes were the bluest he ever saw; she was a charming talker; and her slender hands made eloquent gestures to emphasize points. He glimpsed a milky white leg beneath the long blue morning gown, with a pretty Polish ribbon over an exposed ankle.

1920

"The whole impression," he wrote with the precision of a vivisector, "is of small bones, taut muscles, general firmness, compactness, strength and youth and animation and charm of personality." These last qualities were complemented by Madame's provocative - almost feminist - statement that, having married a rich, former confirmed bachelor, she refused to live with him: she made him live with her in a substantial and admirably appointed home in New York's fashionable Nineties. "If Mahomet won't go to the mountain," Downes quipped, "we all know what the mountain must do."

Harold McCormick remained in Europe during October 1920 and continued to pour out his feelings in self-pitying letters about lost love, and concern about Ganna fulfilling her opera engagement in Chicago. He described how he motored from Paris through countryside desolated by terrible battles, impressed by the courage of the local people forced to start their lives over again, living in "small shanties" being built to house them. He visited the International Harvester plant in Lille and then traveled on to Belgium and occupied Germany to assess the condition of his company's factories after four years of war. Returning to the

French capital, he found that everything reminded him of Ganna: "the shops, Place Vendôme, the King George restaurant . . . How I long to reach America and you," he wrote. "The time seems endless. How good it will be to see you again and to have you once more near me."

Alexander Cochran's annoying quirks continued, including a loathing of smoking in an era when most men indulged in the habit. It happened to be one of the few things he had in common with his wife, forbidding anyone to light up a cigarette until coffee was served in their drawing room, and even refusing his brother's dinner invitations. But he seemed to be apathetic about almost everything else, exercising his demons regularly and prompting Ganna to recall Joseph Fraenkel's love of Goethe and the poet's comment about a selfish heart being unable to escape the torment of boredom. She would write in her autobiography:

"He was extremely cruel, with the cruelty of those who do not have sensibility, who cannot feel. He also had that lack of tact which characterizes the insensible. . . For instance, when I went to dine for the first time at the house of his sister, Elinor Stewart, suddenly Alec stopped eating and pointed to a Gainsborough portrait of a lady hanging in the dining room and said, 'Elinor, I gave you that picture as a present but now that I'm married, I think I'll take it back and give it to my wife.'"

Ganna hoped these problems would be left behind after leaving for Chicago, having suggested it would be better if she went there alone for the rehearsals. Alex reluctantly agreed, making arrangements to go to Aiken in South Carolina on a polo playing trip. He sent his wife a hastily-penned note en route to this wintering spot for wealthy people:

"Dear Ganna, Just made a hurried dash off the train to send you a telegram and when I tried to think of something to say which meant anything, of course it had nothing but 'love' and I had not the courage to write just that with a stupid telegraph operator standing there waiting. Anyway that's what I meant to send."

In late November, he cabled "Thanksgiving Remembrances" to Chicago, where Walska and her entourage, including her maid and a doctor, were comfortably installed in a suite of rooms at the Blackstone Hotel, arranged and paid for by Harold McCormick in the luxury twenty-one-story establishment, famous for its celebrity guests, including several U.S. presidents. Over the next few days, Cochran sent cables signifying an intention to join his wife earlier than she expected - or wished.

November 23: "Hope You Are Well And Comfortable."
November 26: "Please Send Word All Goes Well. Love To You."
December 1: "Telegram And Letter Received. Will Be In Chicago Early Next Week Via New York Sunday."

His return letter from South Carolina revealed his restlessness:

"Dear Ganna, Another day I had hoped for a letter. But the Chicago mails I imagine don't come very rapidly. I want to hear that all is going well as you had expected etc. (a big etc.) It's very dull here getting thro' the evenings. One gets worked out at riding green ponies by four o'clock and the sun begins to go down and one stares ahead at bed time as tho' it was ages away. Last evening we had a Thanksgiving turkey and nothing but polo gossip. Tonight I'm going to bed at 8.30. My love, Alex."

It would be stressful having him around, but there was nothing Walska could do about her husband's arrival in Chicago.

Bonjour Paree!
1920-1921

Harold McCormick had to remain discreetly distant in public from the woman he had pursued like a hunter and now yearned to have for himself though it failed to deter speculation in his home town about the effect she would have on the talented group of temperamental and well-paid *artistes* who made up the celebrated Chicago Opera company. Ganna accompanied him to a lunch party in honor of a guest singer, the French soprano Yvonne Gall, given by one of the leading families, whose son watched Madame Walska's launch into Chicago society. "She was one of those rare types of classical beauty," Arthur Meeker remembered, "so fine, so regular, so overwhelmingly bewitching that none could resist it. Her eyes were large, dark and flashing; her features pure Greek; her skin of a dazzling pallor."

Madame Gall was also a beauty, and a genuine prima donna with a fine international reputation on stage and for her recordings. But none of those present knew anything about Madame Ganna Walska, although the impression she made led many to assume similar triumphs in the great European opera houses as well. Otherwise, they reasoned, Mr. McCormick, as president of the company's opera's board, would not be promoting her as a new star. Somebody overheard Ganna joking that every man proposed the second time he met her, and one of the guests remarked: "Yes, but she doesn't say what they propose!"

Cochran reached Chicago on December 14, having arranged with his wife to lunch at the Blackstone before she went off to rehearsal. He entered the dining room and asked to be directed to Mrs. Cochran's table; the head waiter checked his lists and could find no reservation in that name and Alex insisted imperiously that there must be a table because his wife had confirmed it with him on the telephone. Looking around the beautifully appointed room, he could not see her and stormed out in anger, gathered up his bags and headed for the railroad station to take the next train back to

New York. During a brief stop at Syracuse, he wired his wife: "Feel Like A Deserter But May Get Back Sunday." This blunt message was followed by a letter explaining his precipitate action:

"Dearest Ganna, My feelings are so confused about my leaving. It seemed like desertion ... As a matter of fact my sympathy is more with you when I am not seeing my wife mixed and torn by what I feel are ugly (the very word) conditions and situations ... "

He should have been aware that his wife was registered at the Blackstone under her professional singing name, explaining that personal prejudices got the better of him on these occasions, asking Ganna to be strong, believing that his love had nothing to do with success or failure:

"It's just there, I think, when you want it; buried under all sorts of personal egotisms and mistrusts and doubts, habits etc. My Dear goodbye, Alex."

Arriving in New York, he made arrangements to leave for Europe, staying at the Park Avenue house, but using it only to sleep, taking meals in his club and writing to her confirming his departure within a few days.

"I'm just sitting here and wondering and musing - it's a rotten lazy habit that seems to grow on me...It seems I have nothing I can write except the details of coming and going. It doesn't seem satisfactory and must bore you to read them. But at least they are short."

Ganna Walska found it impossible to concentrate on her stage role while the tensions generated by the hotheaded Cochran swirled around her like a Chicago winter fog, and they had a profound effect on the other singers who expected a prima donna performance from her. She tried to reason what was best for herself, for Alec, for colleagues, deciding there were only two choices: husband or career. Alec, for all his foibles, provided her with every material comfort she had ever dreamed of, while dear Harold was stymied without a date for the start of his divorce proceedings. "Alec?" she asked herself out loud to a dressing room mirror. "Yes, certainly Alec! But with him - and no resources of my own on which to fall back - it would be such an empty life."

Ganna was in a deep quandary and sought advice from the opera company's leading baritone, Tito Ruffo. His response was far from encouraging, admitting that he had been thinking of giving up the singing business for some time now, but having lost money on a bad investment, was resigned to continuing for a few years longer to pay off his debts. In fact, Ruffo revealed candidly that it was impossible to speak about his art without asking himself how to escape its servitude. She questioned another cast member, the American tenor Edward Johnson, and he responded in a similar vein.

"Madame, I look at you and wonder why, having money, you would want to pursue the most ungrateful and hardest of all careers!"

Their harsh opinions made Ganna consider quitting Chicago there and then, but she hesitated, engulfed in doubt, wiring a close friend of her late husband asking what to do. The next day Mrs. Paul (Nina) Warburg, a member of the prominent financial and philanthropic dynasty, and wife of an early advocate of the U.S. Federal Reserve System - replied with a four-line telegram in the form of a poem:

> **"Why expose yourself to the critics' slander?**
> **Why with the restless stage wander?**
> **Why to the fickle public pander?**
> **Go home and belong to your nice Alexander!"**

With Christmas fast approaching, and *Zaza* about to begin stage rehearsals, with opening night scheduled for December 21, Madame Walska decided to follow the advice in Nina Warburg's doggerel, by quitting the production "because coming in such frivolous form, it paralyzed the best in me. I felt lonesome, small, useless . . ."

Nothing had been mentioned publicly about problems with *Zaza*'s leading lady, but Ganna left for New York with rumors rife in Chicago about difficulties. Some said her voice constantly cracked at rehearsal, that musical director Marinuzzi had thrown down his baton in disgust at her singing, and Tito Ruffo stuffed fingers in his ears before storming off the stage. Perhaps the most reliable account came from the tenor Edward Johnson, who kept his friends, the Meekers, *au fait* with all the opera gossip. He told them that until the orchestra rehearsal nobody had actually heard Madame Walska sing, and the others assumed she was "marking" - resting her voice for the performance. Gino Marinuzzi insisted on hearing it at full strength, however, to balance the singers with his players. "But Maestro," she had called out across the footlights, "didn't you know? It's what I've been doing ever since we started to rehearse." Johnson said it was all the voice Madame possessed, and not nearly enough for such a demanding role.

The only certainty in a flurry of speculation was that Ganna's trunks were packed by her staff, taken from the Blackstone Hotel, and Madame left Chicago without explanation, muttering darkly at the railroad station that others would soon be doing the same when her friend "Mistair Mac-Cor-meek" avenged the terrible insult she had suffered. Harold must have been shattered by these events because *Zaza* was left stranded with no other soprano available to take over the role at such short notice, and the company's sellout Christmas attraction was canceled.

When the press finally got hold of the story, varied explanations were printed in a torrent of innuendo. *Town Topics*, however, took a singular approach, intimating that Mary Garden, the company's star soprano for the past decade, known as "the Sarah Berhardt of opera" and about to become its director - or *directa* as she insisted in a rash of cultural correctness - did not relish the prospect of being usurped by a Polish pipsqueak hiding behind a stage name. The designer and couturier Erté, recalled many years later that Ganna's voice, which he described as never better than mediocre, was so frozen with stage fright at the first *Zaza* rehearsal that Tito Ruffo had indeed stalked off the stage, and conductor Marinuzzi was forced to dismiss the singers and musicians for the day, reporting to the management that Madame's future with the company was, in his opinion, nonexistent.

The lady at the center of this vortex remained tight-lipped at the time, but would complain later that the papers had printed "terrible lies," insisting that she did not rehearse with Marinuzzi: "He has never heard my voice." As for the conspiracy theory about Mary Garden, "She was not even in Chicago at the time." Walska did admit, however, that the stories produced some sensational headlines, and, if she had performed the role successfully, the various journals would have had little to print about her. "I tell you why I leave Chicago," she told a reporter, "Mr. Cochran had become determined I was to have my opera or him - but not both. He became more insistent. Every day his telegrams come to me and I keep thinking: 'Shall I go to Mr. Cochran or shall I stay in opera? Shall I go or shall I stay?'" Her decision, apparently, was to be with her Alec (which she continued to call him to his eternal annoyance) for better or for worse.

The Park Avenue residence retained many memories of Joseph Fraenkel as Ganna prepared to mark the festive season in traditional Polish fashion. With no family of her own to entertain, she dedicated the event to the young daughter of a friend, Rosemarie Baruch, niece of the Wall Street financier and presidential adviser, Bernard Baruch, inviting a few other acquaintances and their children to share an elaborate ritual in which Ganna played Santa Claus, when she should have been singing *Zaza* in Chicago.

That frosty Christmas Eve, she stood ready to go downstairs wearing her crimson costume and disguised by a snow-white beard, hauling a large sack loaded with presents onto her slim shoulders, when the maid handed her a small package. Having just positioned the costume's enveloping hood, Ganna was unable to see properly and asked for the parcel to be put down somewhere for later.

"But Madame, it's from Mr. Cochran - his Christmas present."
She saw embarrassment on the maid's face, who knew that this impersonal way of gift-giving would infuriate her mistress. Santa's sack was put on the floor while Walska opened an elegant jewel case to reveal inside a Cartier gold ring inset with a huge heart-shaped diamond. She recalled later: "I also saw - and how much more important - through tear-filled eyes my beautiful Christmas spoiled because my husband did not sense the difference between putting his present directly on my finger, hanging it on the Christmas tree for me to discover, or hiding it under my pillow rather than sending it through a servant."

Regaining composure, the tears were brushed away and Ganna proceeded downstairs to stand hidden on a window sill in the drawing room behind heavy curtains, and with everyone assembled, broke one of the small glass panes behind her with a hammer to give the impression of Santa Claus crashing through. She wanted her charade to be perfect to counter any skepticism from the children, remembering the first Christmas she did this with Dr. Fraenkel, who completely ruined the effect by immediately calling a glazier to come and fix the icy blast.

Cochran's jealousy over his wife's career disappeared once she returned to New York, and he became more relaxed than she had ever known. After abandoning her opera commitment, Ganna was free to sail for Europe, which delighted him, suggesting another extravagant present to celebrate their going away.

"Wouldn't you like some pearls?" he asked. "Cartier has shown me some of exceptional beauty."

She detested his detachment, remembering the scene a few weeks previously at the Cartier showroom on Fifth Avenue when looking at bracelets, because it was the height of fashion to wear as many as possible on one arm. Ganna had recalled the story of an uninhibited American woman in Paris during the war who asked each of her lovers to give her a bracelet, until she had enough to display them from wrist to elbow, and some wit had commented: "Service stripes!" She was wondering if the fad really suited her when her husband's reflection appeared in the mirror. Alex asked what she was buying and Ganna explained, having already decided that it would be too vulgar to hide her alabaster-like arms beneath the artificiality of diamonds, emeralds and rubies set in platinum bands. A couple of days later, he knocked on the door of her room and then threw a package on her desk.

"Here's the proof of my unselfishness!"

Ganna refrained from comment for fear of upsetting his fragile sensibilities, and on opening the parcel, several of the expensive bracelets she'd examined at Cartier came tumbling out. Her immediate reaction had been disgust, but she controlled her emotions enough to ask what he meant by proving his unselfishness.

"Well, you see, when I saw you trying on bracelets the other day," he responded in his matter-of-fact way, "it never occurred to me that by chance it might give you pleasure to have some. Today I was bored, with almost an hour to waste before luncheon and I didn't know what to do with myself. I was passing Cartier's when an ingenious idea came into my head. I said to myself that Ganna had looked at bracelets the other day; if I got them for her today it would kill a few moments of my time. So I did, you see! Ha, ha, ha, ha. . . ."

Before they left for Europe, she wrote a flattering letter to the fashion designer Erté, who lived on the French Riviera at Beausoleil, near Monaco, wishing to make the acquaintance of "the most imaginative man in the world," and asking him to design costumes for *Fedora* and *Thais*, which she claimed to be singing in

Chicago next season, in spite of the recent *Zaza* fiasco. Walska enclosed a photograph of herself, and the young couturier impressed by her looks, accepted the commission. His partner, Nicolas, also of Russian origin, remembered seeing Madame Walska singing in a Kiev *café-chantant* some years before, recalling the unexceptional quality of her voice, and expressing surprise that she had graduated to leading roles with one of the leading opera companies.

Early 1921 saw the Cochrans in Paris again, though their house in the fashionable *seizeième arrondissement,* bought in a few minutes before their rushed departure four months before, was not yet livable. Instructions had been left for its speedy refurbishment, but almost nothing was finished. Ever footloose, Alex decided to leave immediately to hunt with friends southwest France, and his wife offered to accompany him.

"Oh no!" he responded, laughing in his annoying bray, "women are always a nuisance when men go hunting."

He returned to the Pau area, where the snow-clad Pyrenees provided a picturesque backdrop for his sport, having first made arrangements for Ganna to spend her time in the more equable climate of Cannes, where a suite of rooms at the Carlton Hotel was reserved for her and her staff. The intention was for her to travel there by train with half-a-dozen servants and enjoy the sunny winter days at leisure on the most fashionable part of the Côte d'Azur.

The scenery may have been exceptional for Cochran in the French southwest, but the hunting was disappointing and he decided to relocate to Melton Mowbray in England, hoping for something more productive. On January 28 he set a telegram from Pau to Walska at the Ritz: "Arriving Paris Saturday Morning And Going Melton Sunday. Much Rather Hunt There While You Are Away Than Staying Here . . . Lunch Saturday And Send Love." After receiving mail from his wife, Alex immediately sent off a second wire: "So Happy To Get Your Letters This Morning. Meet You Ritz On Arriving." His plans allowed them to lunch together at the appointed time and place; he stayed overnight at the Crillon, she remained at the Ritz, and next day the couple went their separate ways: he north to foggy, freezing England, and she south by the overnight sleeper to the French Riviera.

Walska had grown to dislike hotel life because of being a non-smoker, a teetotaler, and hating the idea of casinos. At the Carlton, overlooking the Mediterranean in Cannes, these seemed to be the principal pastimes of the mainly British clientele. "I had been sent like a beautiful doll to obey my master's orders to enjoy myself," she would remember. "Naturally he wanted me to be happy so that his hunting season would not be the least bit spoiled by the thought that I preferred to be with him or that it was not by my own choice that I was in the South of France during the smartest month of the year!"

After five aimless days, she rejected her husband's idea of Eden and returned to the capital on the pretext of supervising the decoration of their house, living at the Ritz until it was ready for occupation. Erté came to see her there, impressed that his new client was even more striking than her photograph, although the observant thirty-year-old of exquisite taste and manners noticed that she was putting on some weight around the hips. Soon after, Walska traveled south again to visit him at Beausoleil, turning up without notice.

"I know you are not expecting me today," she remarked at the front door, "so how is it that your house is so tidy and you are dressed as if going to a party?" Erté was mystified by the question, being impeccably dressed and fastidiously presented, explaining that his villa was always in this state. It was not until much later, on getting to know her better that he discovered if she was not expecting visitors, Madame Walska would spend all day in what he described as a grubby old bath robe - but making sure to wear her priceless Cartier pearls.

He accepted Ganna's commission to design costumes for the leading roles she expected - or more likely hoped - to sing in the near future. The list had lengthened to include Zaza, Fedora, Gilda in *Rigoletto,* Aphrodite, Nedda in *Pagliacci*, Tosca, Butterfly, Marguerite in *Faust*, Monna Vanna, Louise and *La bohème's* tragic Mimi. It would have been an extraordinarily eclectic repertoire for the greatest prima donnas of the era, with Erté himself using the term "staggering" to describe it. But he proceeded, as instructed and was paid handsomely for his beautiful designs.

The Cochrans were reunited in Paris after their travels; with springtime finding them busy making the rounds of the capital's *antiquaires* to complete the furnishing of their comfortable town house in one of the most fashionable parts of the French capital. A nice decorative touch amid the brownness of everything else came from Erté's framed costume designs, adding a bright, contemporary look to rather somber, club-like interiors. There was much heavily-patterned wallpaper above dark wood paneling, together with heavy furniture from various periods, bought without the couple referring individual pieces to each other first.

But having their own home in Paris soon became a disaster instead of a delight. "Fortunately we rarely dined alone," Walska recalled, "because Alec insisted on entertaining various friends night after night. If however we chanced to lunch by ourselves, he actually did not open his mouth unless it was to be rude to the excellent cook or to abuse the perfect butler we had, while with each morsel of food, I swallowed my tears to conceal them from Alec and the servants - as if we can hide anything from these silent witnesses of our daily life!"

One of his acquaintances in the French capital was Marie-Emile Walter Marrast, a talented forty-five-year-old musician of mixed English and Armenian background Cochran first met in America. Like Walska and Erté, Marrast had changed his identity; by using an anagram of the family name, together with adopting the style of Walther from the hero of Wagner's *Die Meistersinger von Nurnberg* and was known professionally as Walther Straram. With a passion to promote French culture, he sensed an opportunity of furthering this with Cochran money channeled through his ambitious wife. Straram's greatest ambition centered on the exciting new Théâtre des Champs-Elysées, situated, not as the name suggests on one of the world's most beautiful thoroughfares, but around the corner in fashionable Avenue Montaigne, as the ideal venue for his ambition.

When the building opened in March 1913, with its combination of styles suggesting late Art Nouveau and early Art Déco, it was described by Marcel Proust as a fine temple of music, architecture and painting. With a richly decorated *grande salle* and incorporating a smaller playhouse, the performing complex was widely regarded as a model of contemporary public architecture, with construction cognoscenti hailing the daring use of reinforced concrete by its principal architect, Auguste Perret. In spite of that largely hidden feature, the building employed a relatively traditional layout, but it was the breathtaking modernity of its lavish interior that caught the imagination of the opening night audience on March 31, 1913, who thrilled to a monumental performance of the Berlioz opera *Benvenuto Cellini*. A season of Diaghilev's Ballets Russes followed, including the world première of Nijinsky's highly controversial *Le sacre du printemps* (*The Rite of Spring*) to Stravinsky's earth-shattering score.

That marked an historic date in the development of dance and music, making the Théâtre des Champs-Elysées world-renowned. The Great War affected its reputation, however, and when peace returned, Proust's former temple of high art had fallen on hard times, resorting to vaudeville and cinema shows after the former glories of Berlioz, Stravinsky and Diaghilev.

Walther Straram's dreams of restoring the theater to its former prominence as a showcase for the capital's culture were frustrated by a lack of funds, and because the performing lease was held by Jacques Hébertot until 1928, who demanded an extortionate sum to relinquish it. Madame Walska, still fired with a burning desire for operatic fame, toyed with a scheme to overcome the obstacle. She was not short of her husband's cash, including his lavish pin money; perhaps now, instead of ever more Cartier baubles, bangles and beads he would agree to buy her an interest in this wonderful theater. Alex agreed, and Ganna acquired a controlling interest in the building itself, and, by augmenting the company's capital, the principal shareholder. She became, in effect, the owner - naming Cochran's friend, Walther Straram, as her future administrator. The fact that Madame Walska would need to rent performing space like any other impresario for as long as Hébertot remained the lessee, failed to worry her as she started taking regular singing lessons with Straram from May 1921.

She should have been ecstatic about this turn of events, but partnering an erratic husband continued to be unsettling. Ganna had experienced a three-year trial of subservience to Dr. Fraenkel's intellectual brain, and then endured an agonizing period of having to nurse his disability. She had agreed to marry her Alec in order to grasp the spirit of freedom. "Instead," Walska now admitted, "I met egotism in its most infinite degree and limitless extent," complaining that her husband constantly sought distractions, which probably explained why he had never married before. It was too late for him to want children, though Ganna - having previously shown little interest in motherhood - felt deprived without having a family of her own on which she could lavish love and affection.

Alexander Cochran suffered from tuberculosis - which his wife knew nothing about - and he never admitted to thinking of a divorce. Walska claimed later that she would have willingly consented, in spite of its social stigma, because their life together was as if they had been divorced from the moment they married, making any subsequent legal action a formality. Cochran left her alone in Paris saying he needed to spend a couple of days in London, from where he wrote: "I am going to stay over here for a while." The rest of an impersonal communication concerned itself with paying the domestic staff at the Paris town house and settling domestic bills, together with the arrangement for a business associate to drop-in "to find out what you wished to do as regards staying in Paris; for we never can talk (you and I) to any purpose or success."

Walska was sick with worry, feeling trapped in France and

wanting to return to New York, but nothing was clarified until the first week of July 1921, when her husband, still lodging at Claridge's in London, wrote again:

"Dear Ganna, Your letters are received. I am glad you are feeling better. About leaving Paris in July. The concierge is there to look after the house. So about your servants it's only a question of your own circumstances as to whether you keep them or not. I sent word to Duveen to send the four pictures, brought in under bond, back to America. I will find out about Elsie's bill and who paid it. Yours ASC."

He never returned to rue de Lubeck, or to his wife.

The Reaper Prince
1921-1923

Alexander Smith Cochran went home to New York following his extended London sojourn visibly shaken from the brief experience of marriage, apparently glad to resume the life of a confirmed bachelor. Divorce was accepted now as inevitable by both parties with Ganna wishing it could be in "a less ugly way" as she faced the melancholy task of packing up her possessions at the Paris town house and discharging the staff. She was desperately worried about what the future might hold, "not knowing if or when I would be back in France," in spite of the Tribunal de Commerce's formal approval of her controlling the Théâtre des Champs-Elysées on July 29, 1921.

Harold was still in the throes of trying to free himself from Edith, his infatuation for Walska remaining undiminished. He decided to throw caution to the wind by suggesting a rendezvous in the far-from-romantic setting of the northern French fishing and ferry port of Dieppe, where, among the trawler men, mariners and an all-pervading smell of fish and engine oil, he thought they would be safe from prying eyes. But the wily Cochran had engaged a detective to follow McCormick's every move during his European trip, to gather evidence against his wife, hoping to avoid paying her huge amounts of alimony. The "secret" assignation proved to be a disaster for the couple, with Ganna worrying about Alec's divorce strategy, and Harold constantly on guard nervously looking over his shoulder, and admitting a lack of understanding in the circumstances. The only positive outcome was the detective's failure to gather any incriminating evidence.

Walska was furious when she learned from her housekeeper that Cochran had removed furniture from the former Fraenkel house after obtaining a writ to enter the premises and repossess what he regarded as his property. Some of the pieces had belonged to Joseph, and her anger mounted when she suspected that her husband's attorney, Samuel Untermayer, was trying to get evidence against her by using further spy tactics. The lawyer was one of the most prominent in the United States - a Yonkers man like Cochran - notorious for charging fees of a thousand dollars a day and widely admired for supporting worthy causes as a financier, reformer, civic leader, traveler, philanthropist and art lover. Untermeyer's eloquence was reputed to transform trial cases into dramatic spectacles, and, in spite of suffering from ill-health at the age of sixty-two, he remained a formidable force in the courtroom.

Arriving back at rue de Lubeck following her fallow tryst in Dieppe, Ganna was shocked to find a realtor's *à vendre* (for sale) notice on number 14, unable to enter the property because of being locked out. After spending the night at the Ritz, she managed to gain admittance next day through a ruse perpetrated by her lawyer, Dudley Field Malone, who engaged the concierge in conversation while an associate broke the chain securing the front door and took down the sale notice. Once inside, Ganna discovered that her estranged husband's business associate, referred to in his letter, or perhaps Alec's valet, had taken away his clothes and possessions during her absence. Now she would have to fight for what was hers, and remained virtually barricaded inside, like defending a castle under siege, only relaxing a little when Malone informed her that by attempting to bar his wife from the conjugal home, Mr. Cochran gave her grounds for a French divorce.

Ganna returned to the United States for a brief visit after she decided, on reflection, to make her home in the French capital. While in New York, she checked the state of the Park Avenue house inherited from Dr. Fraenkel – but now denuded of much of its furniture and art work after Cochran's grab - and discussed with her attorneys tactics to be employed in the divorce action. Newspapers headlined the forthcoming litigation after a war of words broke out between the rival camps, with Samuel Untermayer accusing the opposition of trying the case in the press, and stating that his client was being overgenerous in offering $10,000 per annum to get rid of the "much-married lady."

Yet another transatlantic voyage took Ganna back to Europe in her accustomed first-class style, while Harold remained in Chicago waiting for his own freedom, resigned once more to keeping in touch with his beloved across the ocean by letter and telegram. He also arranged to send his own trusted informants to Paris charged with reporting back to him. Dr. R.E. Moore and his wife were based at the Grand Hotel right next to the Opéra, and Samuel J. Cawse took up residence in the elegant Plaza Athenée. They would provide information about the woman who was expected to become the second Mrs. McCormick and he her fourth husband

Moore also gave regular "daily treatment" for Ganna's throat problems over a period of several months, and in a letter to McCormick about her health, wrote: "I should say [it] is in excellent condition - she sleeps better - has no nervousness or excitement of any kind which I can see." Moore and Cawes, working in cahoots, were sure that Ganna was being closely watched by Cochran's detective, who posed as an artist while trying to gather evidence. He sent flowers to the house, and even painted a portrait of Madame which she bought and hung on her wall. Moore reported unequivocally, "We all know he is a spy."

Samuel Cawse worked as a household manager - a major-domo - to assist in carrying out proposed opera appearances and a concert tour, though Walska seemed reluctant to give him any dates or other details. He informed McCormick: "I bought her a large mirror, so she can see how her dresses look, and attitude while singing." Cawes meticulously logged the daily routines: "Mrs. C. [Cochran] goes to the theater quite frequently, usually two or three times a week, and above all to the Opera-Comique! . . . Mr. Straram comes daily, and usually stops for lunch, and again in the afternoon stopping sometimes for tea."

According to the detailed information, Madame spent most of her time indoors, only going out during the day to buy sheet music - scores of it from Durand & Cie on Place de la Madeleine. An antique dealer was a frequent visitor, and she apparently spent money with him like water, to the annoyance of Cawes, who controlled the purse-strings of Harold's budget. "Do I understand Sir that I buy everything?" he queried his employer, "as at times I am afraid to spend so much." Cochran's "spy" in the best tradition of cheap thrillers, continued to pretend he was an artist, resulting in Moore advising Cawes "to let him be around as much as he wants and keep tabs on him to see what is going on," informing Madame that he had seen her painter in the lobby of the Grand Hotel. She admitted to being well-aware that the man was no artist: "He is a detective for Mr. Cochran and cost him a lot of money at Dieppe this summer, and he does not know anything."

Two days before Christmas 1921, Dr. Moore sent an end-of-year report to Chicago stating that their charge had yet to give a concert; Straram was going away for a month and she could not face an audience without him. Madame's personal maid, Mary Placek, had told him that Walska and Straram were often engaged in violent quarrels, resulting in her mistress having "this choking of the throat," and had not improved in her singing, stating bluntly that Mr. Straram was just like the rest: waiting to get his hands on Walska's money. That was to be the final reportage after months of bizarre, unproductive but highly expensive sleuthing, because Moore and his wife were forced to make a hasty exit from France when the authorities started hounding them when their visas expired.

In order to establish the rightful ownership of Mr. and Mrs. Cochran's disputed possessions, Samuel Untermayer took a deposition from Nicolas E. Landau describing in detail what had been removed from the Park Avenue house to Cochran's apartment at 820 Fifth Avenue. Landau had been contacted by Madame during October, 1920 - a year before - to assist with the move, and according to his sworn statement approximately one-third of the furniture was moved out to be replaced by items from Cochran's apartment. In response, Walska's attorney, Malone, then initiated an action in the New York Supreme Court on behalf of his client to regain the disputed goods, estimated to be worth $50,000. She would also seek an extra $10,000 in damages because her estranged husband took vases, paintings and antique furniture from the residence without permission.

Dudley Field Malone, an American specializing in French divorce law, discussed the situation with Ganna in Paris and on return to the United States confirmed a previous report that Cochran had offered his wife $10,000 a year if she would "call it quits." When prepared to double the offer, Ganna reacted, "If he wants to get rid of me he must pay until it hurts, for his own good. He must be made to realize that a woman is not a toy to gratify a whim and then be cast aside like a house, a yacht, or a racehorse."

Meanwhile Edith Rockefeller McCormick, accompanied by her lover Edwin Krenn and his friend, Edward Dato, ended eight years of exile by returning to the United States where Harold's lawyers promptly filed for divorce on the grounds of his wife's adultery. McCormick was far from blameless because of his multiple infidelities, but the Rockefeller family pressured an early settlement to minimize the scandal, after resigning themselves to the impossibility of reconciliation. Edith had to accept harsh terms, including payment to Harold of nearly three million dollars for their houses, receiving nothing in return by way of alimony as she faced a new life by establishing a center for Jungian psychology in Chicago, assisted by Krenn and Dato. Following this final split, Harold remained on friendly terms with the Rockefeller patriarch, the now-legendary J.D., while Edith shied away from ever seeing her father again, suffering from a phobia that none of her psychological knowledge acquired from close association with Carl Jung could overcome.

Malone and Untermayer conferred on several occasions during the winter of 1921-22, attempting to settle terms for the Cochran divorce, and confirming that complaint in a suit to be instituted against Madame Walska had been drawn up and verified. This revelation, at the end of March, 1922, was prompted by a newspaper story that Malone was about to file for divorce against her former husband, naming a prominent society woman, to which Untermayer responded: "This eleventh-hour yarn is the first time anybody has suggested that Mme. Walska has any complaint against Cochran or that she contemplates bringing any suit against him." He said that his client had been holding off filing papers for more than two months in response to urgent and repeated requests from Walska's lawyers, adding: "Mr. Cochran came from Europe to sign the complaint in his suit for divorce against the lady on the grounds of her various acts of misconduct." He dismissed this latest skirmish as so much dust kicked up to create the impression that Madame Walska held a grievance against her husband.

During this frustrating time of legal cut and counter-thrust, Ganna and Harold carried on a long-distance relationship: he eager to maintain her interest in marrying him, and she worried sick about money, having lost any hope of access to the Cochran millions. Now, with an expensive Paris theater for her to administer, McCormick sent reassuring sentiments, acknowledging that performing was her prime interest: "I only wish that my love could help the singing in place of the chance that it might be in the way." But Walska could see only dollar signs, and Harold, madly in love, was confronted by the full force of her desperation: "When we were in Paris last fall you said in response to my plea that we 'commune.' We cannot 'commune' until you fix me more secure financially, because I am very nervous about it now, and until you learn to trust me absolutely - to feel that when Ganna says so-and-so it is true because she said it." He answered by assuring the love of his life that he would attend to the matter of her financial security immediately.

Final terms of the Cochran settlement were never made public, though figures mentioned seem far from generous, considering his wealth. Apart from household items like furniture and paintings, the principal benefit was a $300,000 trust fund for Ganna; under its conditions Alex was obliged to pay annually the equivalent of the difference (in case of a shortfall) between what the fund earned and a guaranteed $20,000. That meant an income which, by Madame's freewheeling spending habits, would give her only a fifth of the "pin money" her husband had provided when they married. It was certainly not enough to pay for running her theater and forming a fine symphony orchestra to play there, as she had promised Walther Straram.

Fortunately for her peace of mind, Harold established his own fund for Ganna before her divorce was heard, transferring 20,000 shares of common stock and 1,286 of preferred stock in International Harvester, whose quarterly income of $25,000 would be paid into her Paris bank. A second trust held 6,693 shares of common stock. She could expect to receive a guaranteed minimum of around $120,000 a year, when Cochran's contribution was included.

Speculation about a Walska-McCormick marriage increased in Harold's home town through tittle tattle surrounding a surgical operation to boost his libido. The urologist, Victor Lespinasse, was a pioneer in the treatment of sexual disorders - particularly impotence - and McCormick sought his help. The doctor specialized in the current medical novelty of gland transplants, with a widely-quoted mantra "A man is as old as his glands." The treatment was probably based on techniques developed by a famous French surgeon of Russian extraction, Serge Voronoff, in which testicle tissue from baboons and chimpanzees was grafted onto human testicles in the hope of "regenerating old men." The precise nature of Harold's surgery was not disclosed, but before marrying the glamorous and sexually-desirable Ganna, he prepared himself for nights of ecstasy by being admitted to Chicago's Wesley Hospital.

The procedure, much in vogue during the 1920s, was openly discussed at Chicago's more sophisticated dinner parties, and ribald songs were chanted about "monkey gland operations," as they were known. Harold's hospitalization was intended to be a secret, but wire tappers got to work, and stories about his sexuality - or lack of it - were splashed across the populist press, with much speculation about the type of gland tissue he would receive. If not from a monkey, it surely had to be human, and, what better source than a lusty individual like a young blacksmith?

Harold only succeeded in attracting greater attention to his condition by threatening to sue the first newspaper that mentioned his operation, and by then all classes of society, from those aloof in their spacious lakeside mansions to the habitués of smoky downtown saloons, chuckled at a parody of Longfellow's "The Village Blacksmith" doing the rounds:

> "Under the spreading chestnut tree,
> The village smithy stands;
> The smith, a gloomy man is he,
> McCormick has his glands."

Walska would refer to Dr. Lespinasse's surgery in her autobiography. "In those days all members of the McCormick family were great favorites with the press. It started with the scandalous news about Harold's secret operation (As if anything can be secret or sacred to the press!!) Then his children disputed the doubtful privilege of being in the limelight. The same news about Mr. Jones or Mrs. Smith would have been worthless to a newspaperman but the name of the rich McCormicks was like honeysuckle to a bee."

The couple finally tied the knot at the Mairie of the Passy district in Paris on August 11, 1922 - four days after Ganna's divorce from Alexander Smith Cochran became final. The wedding party for the six-minute ceremony comprised five people in the mayor's office at 10.30 a.m., with the bride and bridegroom accompanied by

Dudley Field Malone and his wife as witnesses. When news reached the United States, it was reported that Harold's seventeen-year-old daughter, Mathilde - characterized as "a good pal of Madame Walska" - warmly approved of her father's remarriage. Her mother would not be drawn, however, as she attempted to establish a new practice intended to make Chicago the psychology center of the world. "Mrs. [Edith] McCormick has no comment to make," was the tight-lipped response from her secretary. Harold's eldest daughter, Muriel, had been kept in the dark about her father's intentions and when a reporter telephoned her the news, she reacted, "So he has gone and done it!"

The newlyweds honeymooned at Salzburg during the city's annual Mozart Festival, where the press hounded them, cabling reports to the United States describing Ganna following the music from miniature scores, apparently an unfamiliar sight for journalists, though it was not unusual for ardent music lovers to score-read during performances. The couple rubbed shoulders with some of the world's cultural élite, sharing a notable meal at the Grand Hotel de L'Europe with composer Richard Strauss, his librettist for *Der Rosenkavalier*, Hugo von Hofmannsthal, producer Max Reinhardt, Walther Straram, and the lessee of the Champs-Elysées theater, Jacques Hébertot.

The publicity surrounding the wedding and honeymoon resulted in offers from agents in the United States and France eager to capitalize on Walska's growing notoriety, though it was getting late for her to establish an international singing career at the age of thirty-five. Typical of the approaches was one from R. E. Johnston of Musical Celebrities with an address on New York's Broadway. He had written to her just before the nuptials, on July 24, 1922: "You certainly have the entire country interested. For newspaper mention and articles you have taken the lead, and Mary Garden as a news getter is relegated to the background in comparison." Johnston offered musical fame and fortune for Madame Walska by appearing with singers of the caliber of Tito Ruffo, Beniamino Gigli, Giuseppe de Luca and John Charles Thomas - on the condition that she pay for the exploitation. A figure of not less than $25,000 was suggested, and in return she could expect to receive a minimum of $500 a concert.

Her cabled response did not dismiss the outrageous terms out of hand, but said she could not commit herself exclusively to Musical Celebrities, failing to mention she was currently in discussion with the New York impresario Jules Daiber for a concert tour of the United States during the early part of 1923. The opportunistic Johnston replied a few weeks later offering concerts with Gigli and Ruffo in Chicago and New York: "I would be very happy to put you on each one of them, if you will pay $1,000 toward the expenses for the appearances. It is worth it. It is great advertising."

Another approach came from Louis P. Verande, the artistic director of American & Continental Co. on the Avenue des Champs-Elysées in Paris. He wondered if Madame would be interested in going to Australia with a company chosen by herself for the impresario Thomas Quinlan, former manager of the Beecham Opera in England. Her answer was no because her friend Chaliapin once told her that Australia, apart from being impossibly distant, was an uncivilized place, full of kangaroos, and a desert for lovers of fine singing.

Ganna felt happier with herself when, as a tryout for the American tour, she took to the road and gave recitals in ten provincial cities of France during October, 1922, apparently in control of her nerves and charming the audiences. As always, she looked magnificent, beginning at the Salle des Conférences at Tours wearing a light blue gown, *décolleté* with a deep V at the back, ornamented with pearl and diamanté embroidery. Her jewelry included her trademark triple string of lustrous Cartier pearls. The New York *Herald* reported that she was particularly appealing in songs by Léo Delibes and Claude Debussy, while the Chicago *Tribune* enjoyed hearing her Enesco and Gounod's "Ave Maria" which won enthusiastic applause. There was praise from both correspondents for the sweetness and tone of the singing and, after the concert a beaming Walska told the *Tribune* that she was happy to be known in the provinces by her work, rather than for the shallow notoriety she attracted in the United States.

With newfound confidence she was now ready to face a Parisian audience, after being engaged to sing the solo soprano part in the final movement of Beethoven's Ninth ("Choral") Symphony at a concert given by L'Orchestre Pasdeloup under the direction of André Caplet in December, 1922. Erté designed a special Empire-style costume in white crepe with *appliqués* of shaded mauve, long tight sleeves and a flowing skirt intended, he told his client, to symbolize the spirit of the composer's great work. He came from Beausoleil for the performance and admitted to being unashamedly dazzled by Madame's beauty - if not the voice. Harold McCormick, entertaining a party of friends, was said to be delighted with his wife's success and waxed lyrical about her future career.

American reporters sent to cover Walska's appearance were obviously unfamiliar with classical music, some cabling their editors that she had done well in the chorus, noting Madame's new fashion of wearing a handkerchief attached to the wrist while singing - a stage gimmick much favored by Luciano Pavarotti half-a-century later. The New York *Times* correspondent wrote: "The audience which had hoped to judge the singer had no occasion to do so as the singing was confined to quartet singing and a few passages in the upper register." Ganna complained, with reason, that the press "cabled stories that I have but little to sing, never more than two or three minutes at a time. They hold me up to ridicule again."

She spent the rest of December preparing for the all-important American concert tour and was scheduled to leave France at the end of the month, which had to be changed when Harold needed an emergency appendectomy, and Jules Daiber was cabled on January 4, 1923 saying that her itinerary must be rearranged. He wired back urging Walska not to cancel Carnegie Hall "because it will shake the confidence of the general public that will not believe you are coming and jeopardize the whole tour. I had such a wonderful tour booked and can save it if you arrive in time for New York." Daiber's star attraction at this time was the temperamental Italian soprano, Luisa Tetrazzini (Melba's bitter rival) and the agent waited on tenterhooks for the unreliable Ganna Walska to make up her mind where and when she was prepared to sing. Pittsburgh, Philadelphia, Montclair, New York and Chicago were all struck from the list, and the American concert tour cost her $1,831.47 in penalty charges before singing a note.

The community of Elmira in New York State never aspired to be a great center of high culture, but the town turned out in force to see the much-heralded Polish beauty on the first appearance of her rearranged schedule in historic Park Church, wearing a trailing gown of lavender velvet and a long rope of pearls. They were a present from Harold, who could not be there because of the pressure of International Harvester business in Chicago. One woman telephoned the box office to ask if Mr. McCormick would be present, saying she would not attend otherwise, but everybody else came to see Ganna and were won over by her charm, grace and friendly manner. She commented afterward: "They had not expected that I could sing, having been led to believe the contrary from so many newspaper reports, and went only to see the girl who married two great millionaires, one after the other."

GW concert

Jules Daiber told her to expect some flattering notices after the next recital, in Detroit's Symphony Hall, because a Chicago critic had shown him a favorable write-up of her Elmira appearance which stated that Madame Walska not only had a voice, but knew how to use it. Walska noted in her memoirs, "I was awakened the next morning [after the Detroit performance] by persistent telephone calls from the press asking if they might announce that I was through with singing, that I was going to my hubby and would never sing again." She couldn't understand what the fuss was all about until the newspapers were delivered to her suite. The music critic of the Detroit *Free Press* was scathing: "That Mme. Walska is in earnest, valiantly striving to reach her ambitious dreams is clearly evident, but nature at the start has endowed her neither with the vocal gifts nor the keen intelligence to ease her path." She protested at this and other critical mauling during a hurriedly-assembled press conference, asserting that the city's papers were biased, leaving Detroit vowing to prove them wrong.

The McCormicks spent a brief time together for a second wedding ceremony, required under Illinois state law to legalize their union, solemnized in the presence of a few friends at the family's Lake Forest estate. Truckloads of flowers filled the rambling house, a twenty-piece orchestra played the wedding march, and catering from a downtown Chicago hotel provided the elaborate wedding breakfast. Later, Harold chatted to the press gathered around a roaring log fire and sent them food from the feast as his wife made ready for her travels.

What followed, after she canceled half the original engagements, was no triumphant whistle-stop tour of America's musical heartland; Niagara Falls, Nashville, Greenville and Boston - apart from the latter – would not appeal to discriminating music lovers because most would be attracted by Walska's notoriety, not to hear delicate renditions of Mozart arias or Hugo Wolf art songs. When she innocently asked Daiber why there seemed to be more interest in the concert gowns than her voice, he replied pointedly that if the press were to decide Walska could sing, she would be of no interest to them at all.

Feeling elated after the Boston matinée, however, she described her feelings to journalist Robert Murray preparing a feature article for national syndication by the Hearst press. He carefully noted Ganna's speech patterns, with overtones of Polish, Russian and French accents, as disjointed and often grammatically incorrect, but always colorful:

"Did you hear that applause?' she asked me, 'and they all called me Ganna. In Boston! Ganna! I have never been called by that name before. One old lady with white hair rushed up to me and said 'Oh! Ganna, now I know the secret of your success.' Well, it is over. The critics, they will probably say terrible things but I sing for the people and not the critics. 'Have you wired Mr. McCormick,' I was asked. "No. I cannot do that - It seems so silly, yes, to wire him 'I was a great success Harold' - it is so stupid."

Mary Placek placed her mistress's copious baggage in the sleeping compartment, and then Madame was ready to be interviewed further in the sitting room of the train, leaning back on a chair, intoning a "Whew!" and instructing Murray, "Now you may begin." He was won over, describing her as one of the most beautiful European women to come to America: refined, aristocratic, and with a peculiar reserve that fascinated him:

"Walska was dressed in a filmy affair of georgette so transparent below the knees that a shapely pair of bare legs peeped out. It was very effective to say the least. On the left hand sparkled a heart-shaped solitaire diamond five-eighths of an inch in diameter. On her right hand blazed a sapphire twice the size of the diamond. As she talked she fingered a rope of pearls for which Mr. McCormick paid $600,000 as though they were glass beads."

The smitten journalist eased his subject into the more delicate question of married life.

"After I married Dr. Fraenkel he helped me so much. He was a wonderful man. Such a thinker and at the same time so sweet.' Walska's eyes shone and her bosom heaved. 'He was a Mozart, a poet, a Christ, all in one.' Walska sighed and then looked startled. 'But I forget I talk for the paper. We must not get so personal, please.'"

Her truncated tour ended with Madame receiving some welcome crumbs of comfort from Herman Devries, the highly-respected music critic of Chicago's *Evening American*. He claimed Harold as a genial friend, and telephoning him for an appointment to discuss a personal matter, was invited with his wife to Rush Street one afternoon where they were received by both Mr. and Mrs. McCormick. "Tea was poured," he reported, "and simplicity, harmony and hospitality were the characteristic elements of the reunion." Devries was astonished to find the new Mrs. McCormick completely unostentatious, "displaying neither pose nor pompous dignity, affectation nor self-sufficiency." He asked when he would have the opportunity of hearing her sing again, and, encouraged by her husband, Ganna agreed to give him a miniature recital, assisted by Jeanne Krieger, her accompanist, who happened to be in the house at the time.

The resulting music-making convinced Devries that it was only stage fright that had created unfavorable impressions during Ganna's recent concert tour. The *American* reported this as a scoop, running his account under the headline "Walska Can Sing, Says Critic of American" alongside a flattering picture of the lady in question. Perhaps he was right about the stage fright, because Ganna seemed to find it impossible to transfer the vocal gems Devries heard during a relaxed family afternoon in the McCormicks' drawing room to the opera and concert stages.

A disillusioned Jules Daiber sent his bill for expenses incurred by the tour cancellations, and then went through the motions of planning another concert tour for Madame Walska at the end of the year, though nothing could compensate for the damage to his reputation as an artists' agent.

A Musical Mentor
1923

Before making arrangements to return to Europe, Ganna met Harold's aging mother for the first time at House-in-the-Woods, Lake Forest, Illinois during February, 1923, finding Nettie Fowler McCormick sympathetic and charming, and full of concern that her new daughter-in-law should take care of her "dear boy." In March, the couple visited the McCormick matriarch again in the warmer climes of San Diego, California with Walska staying at the family's Lacey House while Harold took an important trip to visit his brother Stanley, who lived near Santa Barbara in strange circumstances.

The pair had been very close as young men until their lives diverged, with Stanley attracted to artistic pursuits and going off to study at the bohemian Académie Julian in Paris, instead of devoting his life to the family business. He did work for a while as International Harvester's comptroller, however, and seemed set for a long and distinguished career with the company, like Harold, his elder brother. Stanley married a beautiful and talented Bostonian, Katharine Dexter - only the second woman to graduate from Massachusetts Institute of Technology - and with the McCormick fortune at their disposal, they seemed to have everything a young couple could desire, and then some. But by the age of thirty-three, schizophrenic Stanley became possessed by demons: developing a sexual mania that left no woman safe from attack and he had to be removed from society.

The solution was to sequester him in a rambling and barred Southern Californian mansion set in ninety acres of well-maintained gardens located between the ocean and the foothills of the Santa Ynez Mountains at Montecito, then an unincorporated community on the eastern fringe of Santa Barbara. Named Riven Rock, the estate became Stanley's world without women: a solitary prison of extreme privilege. He languished there guarded by exclusively male attendants, while a large domestic staff arranged entertainments for him with private symphony concerts and films. Riven Rock also housed a huge library of books and a large art collection to stimulate its prisoner while he was being treated by a succession of specialists.

Ganna was told there seemed to be little prospect of Stanley's McCormick's release, in spite of his wife spending her life and a considerable tranche of their wealth on his rehabilitation. Harold was on a committee supervising his brother's welfare and received regular medical and psychological reports which were forwarded for Walska's perusal. They might have given her misgivings about being married into the McCormicks, a family that one of their close Chicago friends, the novelist and journalist Arthur Meeker Jr., described as being noted for "a certain not undistinguished goofiness."

Just before returning to Paris, Ganna was approached by the manager of the Chicago Summer Opera at Ravinia Park with the offer of an engagement for next season and urged to sign a contract for a thousand dollars per performance. Strangely, Mr. Epstein showed no interest in hearing her sing, there was no discussion of repertoire, and she could only assume that he wanted her simply because of the publicity power of the McCormick name. She agreed to the offer, realizing that it would be very convenient to combine her work with a vacation at the family's summer residence. The contract was to be signed the day before she left for Europe, but Epstein had disappeared by then, and it was not until later Ganna discovered that Edith Rockefeller McCormick had promised to underwrite the forthcoming opera season, on the condition that the manager would never have "that woman" in his company.

Far away in Poland, the Puacz family knew only the sketchiest details of their celebrity member's whirlwind existence on both sides of the Atlantic: that she had become rather rich through marrying Mr. McCormick, whose International Harvester machinery was well-known in their country, and he was rumored to have bought her a theater in Paris for her own use. She, on the other hand, managed to hear about them through friends like Feliksa Krygier of Philadelphia, who wrote telling her of a recent party she attended in Warsaw at the home of the Radkiewiczs (the maiden name of Ganna's stepmother). Mrs. Krygier had met the aging Napoleon Puacz there, who was said to be moved to tears on hearing that she knew his daughter.

On March 28, 1923, Walska prepared to sail from New York on the CGT Line's "Paris" - the largest and most luxurious ship sailing under the French flag - telling a reporter that she had signed a contract for a season of opera in the French capital, and expected to make a concert tour of Poland soon and was looking forward to being reunited with her family after such a long absence. Harold accompanied his wife to the berth where they were greeted quayside by about a hundred flag-waving Polish fans waited to see Madame off. Looking chic in a grey suit with a squirrel collar, and wearing a brown-veiled toque to match, she chatted with them before receiving a goodbye kiss from Harold. Then there was time to talk to journalists in her deluxe suite filled with orchids, assuring them that she was treated fairly in the news columns of the papers.

"As for those music critics - pouf!" Walska exclaimed with a dismissive gesture. "My tour here was a success. My audiences liked me, and that's all I care about." She denied there was anything hasty about her leaving, ridiculing suggestions that unfavorable comments caused her to abandon the concert tour.

"It is sensational to say Ganna cannot sing," she insisted, borrowing her agent's previous comment. "It is not to declare Ganna *can* sing. Of course, they had to have me on the front pages, and that was the one way of doing it."

Home in Paris at the beginning of April, Ganna accepted an engagement to sing at one of the capital's most beautiful concert halls, the Salle Gaveau, with the orchestra conducted by André Caplet. It was a taxing program of modern French music under the baton of the popular French maestro: Debussy's *Images*, Ravel's *Pavane pour une infante défunte* and *La Valse*, together with one of Mozart's fiendishly difficult arias from *Die Entfuhrung aus dem Serail*. Music critic Louis Schneider was impressed:

"This ability in the *vocalises* is the principal quality of Mme. Ganna Walska; adding her personal grace and courage to pit herself against any hazards. The great Lili Lehmann, who at the height of her career, offered this aria at a concert given at the Conservatoire before the war, told us 'I have spent sixteen years, and now I understand a little about it. Mme. Ganna Walska has time in hand; she also has this magnificent and rare energy to triumph over all difficulties, even vocal ones' she said."

Nobody from the American press was there, which was a pity because, even with its sting in the tail, this critique produced one of Ganna's most satisfying notices.

Living apart from his new bride meant a self-proclaimed life of agony for Harold, and he bridged the gulf of separation by sending tender love letters across the Atlantic addressed, according to a variable scale of longing, to "Dearest Deevah," "My Sweetheart Wife," "My Beautiful Lamb-Wife" and "My Boss." Some of them recall intimate moments spent together:

"You sat on the sofa and beckoned me to sit by you and you listened to what I had to say - Ah if you only knew (I think you did) what joy and love that gave me. It was so confiding, so loving, so patient, so understanding. You saw how quickly I appreciated it - In five minutes it was over. "

Harold yearned for his beloved, hinting that his libido-enhancing operation may not have been a total failure:

"These nearly three months will soon be over - they must end and then for the time I will be with you I will see you, hear you, feel your dear presence, touch you Dear - hold you fast as though we were never to part again."

But litigation rather than the joys of togetherness was uppermost in his wife's thoughts at this time with the settlement of Dr. Fraenkel's estate still unresolved. Ganna's New York attorney, Phelan Beale, had suggested it might take a long time, and, true to form, Joseph's family continued to be obstructive three years after her second husband's death. Objections were filed in the Surrogates' Court by the brother, Louis, contending that a payment of $15,000 to Beale for counsel fees in acting as the estate's executor were excessive, asserting that an agreement to disregard the will had been reached in December, 1920 to divide the residue equally between the widowed wife and other members of the family. But an enormous claim of $108,000 was still outstanding against the late Dr. Fraenkel from a New York stockbroking firm that happened to be associated with executor Beale. The court was expected to appoint a referee to hear the objections, though Beale reassured Walska that the Park Avenue house was safely hers. As a wealthy society attorney, he and his wife, Edith Ewing Bouvier, were in the process of acquiring a splendid 28-room ocean-front mansion in East Hampton named Grey Gardens which, many years later, would achieve show business notoriety on both stage and screen.

As well as the legal demands on her time, Walska continued taking daily singing lessons with Walther Straram, helping him establish a symphony orchestra to conduct – it had to be the best in Paris - and seeking mystical experiences to give meaning to a rather bleak existence. After being disappointed with spiritualism when married to Dr. Fraenkel, she had turned to the Ouija board and received encouraging results when the *planchette* pointed to letters at the rim in answer to her questions, though the Havana fiasco (which she claimed it had predicted) and false information about a stolen pearl necklace eventually turned her off séances. Ganna embraced yoga when a gentle Hindu taught her how to develop voice control by holding her breath for as long as possible, and this led to her accepting that good singing was learning how to exhale slowly and smoothly. Later, a Western yogi, Dr. de Kerlor, who was the Polish ex-husband of the famous Italian fashion designer, Elsa Schiaparelli - a fierce rival to Coco Chanel in the bitchy world of French *haut couture* - also promised help with her development, insisting that correct voice production resulted from always having the fingers of both hands in contact so as not to lose body magnetism. "I shall never forget how in my simple-hearted way," she recalled sarcastically after this technique failed her, "I desired to warn Caruso always to keep his hands together while on the stage."

Ganna Walska's search for enlightenment was not always treated so flippantly, and she gave most methods a fair trial, becoming interested in astrology, guided by a Polish woman theosophist who wrote a hypothetical horoscope containing details of what should happen to her almost hourly. "On Wednesday morning for instance," Ganna noted cynically, "I was to feel badly depressed and I did feel badly depressed! Humiliated, I decided to counteract the indications of the horoscope - just to test it - and I succeeded in blasting all the predictions and proved to myself that will power is stronger than environment or fate." This lady theosoph admitted that she could not make Walska happy and advised her to see a Dr. Mills, in her opinion the only person able to help. He called himself a metaphysician - a title Ganna found difficult to comprehend, let alone pronounce, and was already eighty when they met. But Mills would be added to a long list of disappointing experiences, after boasting that he could bring the dead back to life, but was uncertain about curing Madame's migraines.

When living with Alexander Smith Cochran had become unbearable, Ganna turned to other beliefs, on learning from a New York friend - a former member of Dr. Mills' meditation class - that she was helped by Christian Science. She soon realized that this had everything to do with Biblical beliefs and owed little to pure science, after seeking the cult's assistance and was assured that her husband could be cured of his intense introversion, but only if he asked personally because it was a rule never to help people who did not seek it themselves. Ever skeptical, Walska wrote in her diary: "Indignantly I replied: 'If a man is dying, knocked down on the street, is it then your Christian idea that a doctor should not help him because he has personally not made a previous appointment?'"

Now, with a fourth husband, and notorious on both sides of the Atlantic for her multiple marriages, she attempted to rationalize her feelings by self-analysis, wondering why she had such an extraordinary effect on men. Ganna's sheltered Roman Catholic upbringing in Poland, the jealous guarding by Napoleon Puacz after her mother died, and being chaperoned by an uncle in St. Petersburg, had produced a woman for whom the ideal of romantic love was paramount, and, in the reverse of brother-in-law Stanley McCormick's hapless condition, Walska developed an almost manic indifference to the physical side of relationships. Much of the time spent with Arcadie had been against the background of his debilitating tuberculosis, which probably blunted his sex drive, and both Dr. Fraenkel and Alexander Cochran suffered from chronic illnesses that made them less sexually active - if at all - than normally healthy men.

But she faced a bigger challenge with Harold McCormick, whose "monkey gland" transplant had led him to believe that he could indulge in sexual pyrotechnics with his new bride like a Titan of the boudoir. His past reputation as a drinker and womanizer was well-known, and long separation from Edith had allowed free rein with a range of beautiful women. He now intended to take full advantage of his conjugal rights with his Ganna, though "the delicately perfumed soul of Harold McCormick," as she expressed it - trying not to sound too vulgar in her memoirs - clashed with his "wrongly applied goods."

112

The McCormicks

She had been dismayed to discover that her latest husband idolized "the physical expression of love," becoming insatiable in his demands. But Harold's desire was "unattainable by him anymore," and, therefore, all the more unpleasant to experience. Apparently, Dr. Lespinasse's surgical expertise had achieved little more than to raise Harold's hopes - and little else - because Ganna would write in her memoirs: "Nature, in her wisdom, having fulfilled him by giving him four children, had chosen for his second wife an idealist who was able to put so much richness on the value of his soul that she could not even imagine the possibility of his preferring to seek further for a gross and limited pleasure."

Socially, Madame now gained a reputation for being an unfeeling woman, which she claimed as her own invention for self-defense. As the major shareholder in a famous Paris theater, owner of the fashionable rue de Lubeck house (after Harold bought it from Cochran) and with a green monogrammed Rolls-Royce with chauffeur on call, she could flaunt all the materialistic trappings of a pampered wife. Rather than exhibiting frivolity like most Parisiennes, however, Madame Walska preferred to maintain the levelheadedness of a shrewd business woman with executive ability and judgment, which prompted some close friends to call her "a leader in skirts." Those who knew her less well, regarded the grinding schedule of singing lessons, managing the affairs of her theater, and being separated from an adoring husband for long periods, as a conversion to feminism.

Celebrity circles gossiped that Ganna Walska had become as frigid as the North Pole - in spite of her outward appearance - leading the life of another age when, as she expressed it, "women only smoked exceptionally, when they cut their hair only after typhoid fever, considered black coffee as a drug, when they preferred early retiring to a smoky restaurant, night club or dance hall." She referred to Wolf-Ferrari's popular comic opera, *Il segreto di Susanna* (*Susanna's Secret*), about a wife suspected of having a lover when her husband detects tobacco smoke in her room, not imagining for one moment that Susanna might be a closet cigarette smoker. Walska's inhibitions stretched all the way from smoking and drinking alcohol to sex, priding herself on being a teetotaler and now abhorring the intimacy of social dancing.

As a leading industrialist, as well as member of the Rockefeller Foundation and a trustee of the University of Chicago, Harold McCormick was committed to remain in the city for long periods where, as president of International Harvester, he guided the worldwide business of the enterprise founded by his father Cyrus, which produced; with associated companies, much of the world's agricultural machinery. But Erté, continuing to design ever more sumptuous costumes for Ganna's planned or phantom performances saw her becoming a different woman once Walther Straram started guiding her career. When Harold heard about this, he was far from amused, but could do little about it, separated as he was for long periods by time and distance. What was more, her Svengali - as some were describing him - now conducted the fine symphony orchestra financed by Cochran and McCormick money, receiving rave reviews for playing what the Chicago *Tribune* called "ultramodern music." Their concert at Ganna's Champs-Elysées theater on April 22, 1923 was a triumph before a capacity audience, with hundreds turned away, and reading about its success in his hometown press, must have left Harold with very mixed feelings. At least he could have the satisfaction that his wife

114

was doing something right for once, even if with the wrong person.

Walska's opera début in Paris, in spite of previous discussions with Erté about costumes for works by Debussy and Mozart, would be Verdi's *Rigoletto*, and not in her own theater, but the National Opera as a one-night charity gala in aid of the staff pension fund. Erté promised to come from Beausoleil for the occasion and was invited to join Madame for supper after the performance, assuming it would be a success; if not, she would be too upset to see anyone. He created four different costumes, each with an individual name, to complement the drama, informing his client: "I am convinced that all these costumes worn by you, will have a great impact; don't think about the costume traditions of this opera, consider my designs as an illustration of the drama."

The brilliant young designer, still only thirty-two and now noted for his *Harper's Bazaar* magazine covers, was given full freedom to express his considerable talents. The other members of the cast, however, would wear different designs, which made many assume that Madame Walska had paid to land the principal role because every aspiring diva wanted to perform with the prestigious national company. She wrote in her diary, however: "Those singers whose careers were behind them, and had no hope of an engagement in the future, would not forgive me for getting a chance, wrongly imagining that the chance was bought." But it was not surprising that she found herself ostracized, a predicament not helped by a newspaper article claiming that Madame paid a million-and-a-half francs (around $60,000 at the going rate of exchange) to appear. Under threat of litigation, the journal quickly retracted their story, but the damage was done.

On the morning of the performance, Walska was contacted by "some Russians" who insisted on meeting "for my own sake," telling her she would be very sorry that night if she failed to listen to them. Later, just before the curtain rose, she learned that the baritone, Joseph Schwartz, billed to sing the role of her father - the deformed jester of the opera's title - had withdrawn because of a sudden illness. The management found a replacement Rigoletto in Jean Mauran, who could sing in Italian, but Walska had no idea who he was, and then it was announced from the stage that he would not be appearing, either. "And so for my Paris grand opera début," she noted, "I saw my partner for the first time when we were actually in action, without knowing anything about his acting." She failed to admit that he, too, faced the same situation.

The Salle Garnier was packed, with many Americans paying three times the normal seat prices to watch this latest bid by Harold McCormick's wife for operatic glory. According to Erté, she looked splendid, and the Russian tenor, Dmitri Smirnov, was in excellent voice as the licentious Duke of Mantua. Walska herself thought the act went well enough, with a concluding high note that she and most of the audience appreciated, though there was an eruption of hissing in the house. She recalled, darkly, "I knew then that the Russian visitors of that morning were keeping their word."

During the second act, Erté watched Ganna's performance disintegrate when, while wearing a costume he had named "Innocence" to express Gilda's pure soul, the moment arrived in the garden scene for the famous soprano aria "Caro nome," with Walska standing at the top of a flight of steps carrying a lighted candle. She recalled singing it correctly: "Or if you prefer just as badly as others who had sung there the week before or might be singing the week after." Her designer watched with alarm as she opened her mouth, and no sound emerged. The correspondent of the *New* York *Times* was seen to wince when it did - as a squeak - and Gabriel Groviez directed the orchestra play more slowly, while Walska, completely disoriented, hitched up her skirts and scurried from one side of the stage to the other as if playing the mad scene from *Lucia di Lammermoor*. She admitted later to hearing "lone but persistent hisses," from the audience and finally managed to sing, but it was no mellifluous soprano. In Erté's words, it was more like the screech of a cat whose tail had been trodden on. The audience, initially stunned into silence, burst into uncontrollable laughter.

Reports of *Rigoletto* were cabled to the United State, with the *Times* critic commenting that Madame had two singing voices, one soft and one low, both probably pleasant in a drawing room, but not powerful enough for the opera house. He commented: "It was the first time any such singer as Mme. Walska had opportunity to give such a performance and it may be safely said that it will be the last." Erté left the Salle Garnier resigned to foregoing his supper with Ganna and left without contacting her, but was surprised to be telephoned the next morning and asked why he had not kept their

116

rendezvous. He reminded her of the conditions of the invitation.

"So you thought it was a failure?" she asked innocently, and before he could reply, added: "You must have noticed several in the audience were against me, but it was all organized by Prince Yusupov. He's angry that I wouldn't buy his wife's black pearl necklace. So, he paid people to hiss and laugh as soon as I began to sing."

Harold McCormick planned to spend that summer of 1923 with his wife in Europe, but when his mother died Ganna went to America to be with him, arriving in Chicago on July 20 to be greeted by popping flashlights and a volley of questions from reporters, but in deference to the family's loss, there was to be no press conference on this occasion. During subsequent absences on business trips across the United States, Harold kept in touch with Ganna by letters: some matter-of-fact, many loving, several lyrical, and others analytical. A train breakdown on the Wyoming border allowed him to combine all these elements:

"Around are soft hills and slopes and meadows and green grass and plains on which cattle graze - one can look a few feet and many miles. The clouds are hazy and a gentle fall of a few rain drops - Part of the sky is gray and part bright blue - No air stirs but there is ozone everywhere and I feel the expansiveness of this wonderful country. The great joy of living comes over me and the great joy of you to love and think about . . . "

He remained captivated by Ganna despite a nagging jealousy over Walther Straram's influence, fantasizing about his goddess: his "Deevah."

"And again those last days you have told me you love me - many times. I have told you I love you - many times - you have showed me you love me - a few times I have showed you my love for you. And so you have contributed acts and I have contributed words. Oh your acts! You Dear Love. I see the lovely curl of your lips - that outflowing relaxation of safety of confidence, of wanting to give out to me - your lips sometimes speak of me so dearly - That curl I think of which makes rose-leaves simply abstractly pretty but not lovely. I see those eyes sometimes glowing, so large, so fixed, so true. They tell me a story in silence . . ."

Ganna responded with long-distance telephone calls, too busy to write because she had been approached by the general manager of the touring German Opera Company, Theodore Latterman. Walska fully expected to be asked for money but on this occasion her name was the attraction in gaining publicity, and she readily agreed to perform. When the McCormicks were reunited, they went out to

Harold's summer estate at Lake Forest and attended the opera every night during the Ravinia Park Festival, from which Ganna had been banned the previous year as a performer by Edith Rockefeller. She took the opportunity, however, to be coached by the eminent conductor Alexander Smallens for the role of Rosina in *Le nozze di Figaro*, which she hoped to sing with the Germans.

A week before the opening of their tour in the national capital, Walska learned that the company had run into financial difficulties, with insufficient funds to transport the scenery and costumes from the port in New York to Washington, D.C. She didn't have the heart to refuse the $10,000 needed to get the season started, insisting it was only a loan until they reached Chicago, where manager Latterman said all the performances were sold out. When the German Opera arrived in the McCormicks' home city, however, no repayment was forthcoming and an extra $4,000 was needed for their travel to Milwaukee, which was the next venue on the coast-to-coast tour.

When told of this, Madame Walska was hosting an afternoon reception at Harold's Rush Street mansion for General Josef Haller, chief of the so-called Blue Army of Poland, formed in France during the latter stages of the Great War. An orchestra played in the chandeliered ballroom and a large turnout of worthies enjoyed the gay atmosphere, glad of the opportunity to watch Mrs. McCormick carry out her social duties. Then a message arrived for the hostess, informing her that Latterman had given up all hope of taking the evening train to Milwaukee for the next day's performance. The Polish military contingent, looking dashing in their theatrical blue uniforms that might have been designed by Erté for a Ruritanian operetta by Sigmund Romberg, was trying to make the most of the lemonade and grapefruit juice served during this age of Prohibition. They probably wondered why their glamorous hostess had not been able to arrange for some bootleg vodka to remind them of home. All Madame could think about, however, was her poor fellow performers stranded in a foreign country, far away from friends and family, about to lose their livelihood. Briefly excusing herself from the reception, she instructed Harold's secretary to send them the money.

Manager Latterman proceeded to make similar appeals to the McCormicks from almost every city of the long tour. There was a long-distance call to report that the musicians would no longer wait for their back pay and were threatening to strike unless they received immediate settlement. Walska cabled the cash. Then it was the turn of the chorus, followed by soloists: all concocting ingenious excuses for withholding their services, with Walska's bank book ever open to allow the show to go on.

Her determination remained as strong as ever to appear with the company but without giving the impression that she could only sing by being their angel. "I knew perfectly well that as soon as the rumor became public knowledge," she noted, "I would be unable to open my mouth from nervousness." One solution was to appear incognito, and it was a "Miss Brown" who began rehearsals of *Figaro* for a Pittsburgh performance. The assumed name saved her from humiliation when nervousness made Walska's voice disappear again: "After trying a few minutes I gave up and postponed the rehearsal until a later date, pretending a sudden hoarseness and not wishing to admit my stage fright."

Stories began appearing in the newspapers that she was subsidizing the German Opera, which only served to increase her tension at the next orchestra rehearsal when all she managed to produce was a pinched sound in her high register: "The same thing happened at the first performance at Buffalo, for already reporters were running after me to interview "Devah Navarre,' one of the many names Mrs. Cochrane [a medium] had given me and the second name I had used, now that the pseudonym of Miss Brown had been discovered." After the curtain fell, she ran through the back of the theater to avoid the baying hounds of the press to hide in a nearby restaurant for blacks, accompanied by the company's manager who desperately tried to cover with a scarf the incriminating GW initials prominently displayed on Madame's expensive handbag. Mozart's *opera buffa* had turned into high farce for Ganna, but with a serious side because another attempt at launching Madame's operatic career had not succeeded. She sang the Countess Rosina Almaviva at matinées in Louisville, Indianapolis, Buffalo and Albany, after subsidizing the company to the tune of $80,000, with Harold providing an additional $10,000 to defray expenses.

Ganna had yet to find her voice on stage, though she did possess an asset that set her apart from most other women: her physical allure. It was the heyday of silent cinema, having become a respectable medium of mass entertainment - perhaps even a new art form. She had brushed off previous attempts to lure her into motion pictures, but with operatic success seemingly beyond her grasp for the moment, Walska considered an additional career where looks alone might satisfy her penchant to perform. In November, 1923 the Siple Studios, with an office address on Wabash Avenue, Chicago, teamed up with the producer J.H. Harlow - who had contacted her previously - to seek a personal interview to discuss a movie project. She responded almost immediately saying it was impossible, and Harlow came back to her five days later with flattery: "We feel there is no greater box office magnet today than 'Ganna Walska,' and that motion pictures will afford the world at large an opportunity of seeing you. A tentative proposal from us at this time would be $25,000 in weekly payments of $5,000."

Screen test

The company needed to make a screen test before signing the contract, and a property with the unpromising title of *Captain Jinks of the Horse Marines* was suggested as Walska's first starring vehicle, described as, "A story of theatrical life, affording a wonderful opportunity for the display of histrionic ability and photographic possibilities." There was also *Parsifal*: "It is our purpose to give it an adequate musical setting," the letter stated, "adhering to the Wagnerian score and synchronizing the music to the action on the screen." This did interest Ganna, though she queried the fee, which prompted another obsequious response: "Please bear in mind that the offer was made with the object of opening negotiations with you . . . we appreciate your expression with reference to *Parsifal* as a suitable vehicle, and believe that the making of this film with Ganna Walska in the role of Kundry will be hailed as the supreme achievement of the combined arts of motion pictures and mime."

In Walska's world, $25,000 was a niggardly reward for her talents, and she also baulked at making a screen test. "I have no time to loose [sic] on very immature propositions," she castigated the company. "Will make test only as last step before signing contract for your benefit. Hope you understand." This was scrawled in bold, larger-than-life writing on the back of the studio's typewritten letter and handed to her secretary to deal with. Nothing came of these proposals, but her continuing prominence in the press ensured there would be other approaches. One thing was certain, Ganna no longer needed the money after her financial security was consolidated by Harold, changing the trust fund he had set up previously with a new arrangement gifting one million dollars' worth of Harvester common and preferred stock, currently valued at $73 and $109 per share respectively. It meant that his beloved wife would now hold company certificates totaling 27,771 of common and 1,286 of preferred stock, with a combined face value of $2,167,457.

Generous to a fault where singers were concerned, she arranged for a Christmas tree to be set up on the stage of the Manhattan Opera House, where the German Opera Company's chorus sang traditional carols at the end of their tour, and Ganna withdrew from the whole sorry story two days later, when the theater went dark. The money lost was no problem because, with her boosted trust fund, she was convinced that benevolence was the path to self-enrichment. "This philanthropic experience," she would write in her autobiography, "forced upon my easy response to any needy soul, had a great consequence in my development, as the contact with the German Opera taught me discipline, the utmost discipline without which nothing worthwhile can be achieved."

Immediately after the festive season, Harold was hurriedly called away to the West Coast where his brother, still incarcerated at the Riven Rock estate, had become seriously ill. Sitting on the Twentieth Century Limited, he poured out his heart in what he called "an old-fashioned letter."

"A little while ago we just were Ganna and Harold to each other - each in the other's hearts, each in the other's arms - and oh how good it was - you gave me of yourself. I remember once you said to me 'I am so tired of giving I just want to receive - now!!!' That thought of yours weighed deeply with me Ganna and I just wanted to give you all I could ..."

He revealed that two of his doctors had recommended a course of stimulation of the pituitary gland to give him renewed strength and fresh resolve.

Now in her thirty-seventh year, Ganna Walska prepared to bid farewell to her husband and return to Europe where she was sure of a better reception, particularly as a magnificent theater awaited her magic touch to restore its reputation at the center of musical life in Paris. There was a huge throng of passengers and well-wishers aboard the Cunarder "Berengaria" before sailing from New York for Cherbourg on February 16, 1924. The great liner departed punctually at 5:00 p.m. on a favorable tide, negotiating ice in the channel without difficulty, as Madame headed for home, a week away, where a letter awaited from her father in which he complained that he never heard from her and probably would not see her again. He rejoiced in his daughter's fame and quoted a Polish newspaper article which told of Mr. McCormick's purchase of an opera building for her in Paris. Old Napoleon sent greetings from stepmother Helena, brother Leon and half-brother Edward, as well as other relatives and friends, hoping that his Andzia – "my beloved daughter" - would find the time to visit Poland soon.

Diva by Default
1924-1925

Paralyzing stage fright continued to dog Ganna Walska's performing ambitions, and being the wife a well-known American industrialist was equally inhibiting when billed to perform in opera or giving concerts because audiences never knew if impresarios were merely trading on the name, or whether the McCormick checkbook financed appearances. Her vocal potential remained hypothetical, and a cutting quip published in a Chicago newspaper - "Money talks, but you can't make it sing" - was correct in relation to her assets, but ignored the fact that appearances were often bought by singers in those days as a means of getting recognized.

Every day, Ganna's mail contained proposals to capitalize on her celebrity status and untold wealth. The Floyd Stoker Office in New York asked "My dear Miss Walska" if she would be interested in a "short and dignified vaudeville engagement," naming several opera stars who played the circuits without injury to their reputations, "a notable example of this is Madam Calvé." Ganna complained, "People would never believe that I was earnest in my endeavors," unhappy to be regarded as an object of envy. "That is why I felt ashamed of my money. Arriving to my singing lessons in a luxurious Rolls-Royce, I would feel sad when at the door I might meet a wet young girl tired from a long ride in a street car or the subway." She claimed that unequal distribution of wealth had made her realize the injustice in the world and led to a feeling of helplessness: "I was afraid that my expensive fur coat might hurt students in nothing but mackintoshes; and I dreaded the thought that they might envy my daily lessons when they could only afford two or three a week."

For the moment, the best prospect for her artistic aspirations lay beyond the power of Cochran and McCormick money because Madame Walska, the majority shareholder in the Théâtre des Champs-Elysées, continued to be frustrated by not controlling the lease, which had four more years to run. She could rent the main auditorium by the day, week or month from the lessee like any impresario, but being rich Mrs. Harold McCormick meant that the opportunistic Hébertot demanded she pay more than anyone else. Meanwhile, under Walther Straram as her artistic director, conductor, singing teacher and, some suggested, lover, the symphony orchestra she financed, of more than a hundred players, offered Paris *mélomanes* regular concerts in the spirit of France's tripartite national motto *Liberté, Egalité, Fraternité*. There were reduced prices for students, free tickets for blind people, and Walska and Straram also gained considerable kudos for their youth concerts, as well as a series devoted to modern music introducing the works of then little-known composers, such as Schoenberg, Honegger, Bartok and Webern.

The board of the theater's company held their meetings at Madame's town house from April, 1924 when it was agreed that she should seek to acquire the lease in order to gain total artistic control. But Jacques Hébertot, on the point of bankruptcy, held out for an outrageous sum in the millions of francs. "When I indicated that I was not keen about doing this," Walska noted, "he thought he would force my hand by creating so much difficulty for my projected festival that I would be finally forced to accept his conditions." She tried compromise, but the lessee knew that Madame's Mozart season, to coincide with the 1924 Olympic Games in the French capital, was booked and paid for, with no prospect of finding an alternative venue.

This festival included three operas: *Don Giovanni, Così fan tutte* and *Le nozze di Figaro*, together with two concerts: one presenting Mozart's *Requiem*: a rarity in those days. Ganna was to sing the Countess in *Nozze,* Donna Elvira in *Giovanni,* and take the solo soprano part of the *Requiem.* Her musical mentor was kept busy preparing her, though forced to take to his bed with severe stomach pains a few days before the opening and advised to have an immediate appendectomy. He refused, and stoically returned to orchestra pit and podium for the performances

Vital rehearsal time was lost, however, and Ganna's nerves began to fray again, with the only consolation that she would at least look right in beautiful new Erté costumes. By now, she was wise to the musical life of Paris, planning to avoid another conspiracy by engaging an alternative singer for her own roles. Margarete Mazenauer, a Metropolitan Opera regular billed as the world's greatest contralto, would take the role of the Countess in *Nozze*, usually assigned to a soprano, without being announced in advance. The American journalists instructed by their editors to attend the first night and bury Walska were furious when Madame failed to appear, sending cables back claiming that their quarry had quit after a quarrel with the tenor.

Reporters were out in force for the next performance, and, as Walska noted in her memoirs: "Having missed the first opportunity to hurt me, my involuntary persecutors, the gentlemen of the press, came for my next [scheduled] performance when some of my envious enemies tried again - and again - to create a disturbance during the singing." A number of telephone calls had been made to the theater asking who was going to sing that night - Madame Walska or Madame Mazenauer - although the information was not forthcoming and they had to wait until the second act, when the Countess makes her first appearance, to find out.

Harold had just arrived in Paris, and the couple was seen entering a box together before the overture began, though Ganna remained in its anteroom with her cape collar pulled up while others in their party sat in full view of the audience. During the first intermission after the house lights went up, the box was subjected to intense scrutiny by dozens of patrons, and Walska's apparent absence suggested that she was singing that night. The curtain rose on the second act, set in Countess Rosina Almaviva's bedroom, and it was Mazenauer who sang its famous short, but difficult, soprano aria. The music had hardly begun before whistling erupted and once "Porgi amor" was finished the applause was drowned out by booing. Walska, hidden in the anteroom, felt vindicated.

Her performances proceeded without further incident, and even those who had jeered at previous Paris appearances were silenced by her thoroughly professional approach. The director of the Paris Opéra, Jacques Rouché, went to Walska's dressing room to congratulate her, commenting that Walther Straram had worked a miracle with her voice, remembering the only other time he heard her: in the disastrous *Rigoletto*. But Ganna's vocal delivery was not complemented by a confident stage presence, particularly what to do with her hands, which Erté tried to resolve by giving her something to hold for *Don Giovanni*. He designed an accessory said to have been worn by Renaissance ladies on their wrists to deter fleas: a mink bracelet with the animal's head studded with jewels for eyes. He sat watching in horror as Donna Elvira, downstage and in full view of the audience, unconsciously plucked the fur to bits in her nervousness.

Madame's reputation was most at stake, however, not in Paris but Chicago, home of the McCormick clan, where the press followed her activities in minute detail. Following a concert in Berlin, the city's *Tribune* reporter had cabled the lead: "Walska failed to charm the critics," and his racy story told how the director of the Staatsoper, Max von Schillings, walked out of her concert after the first item. In fact von Schillings had previously informed Walska that he could attend for only a few minutes because of a directors' meeting that evening. There were other misleading reports to titillate the readers, including a description of her appearance on one concert platform with glittering diamonds and wearing jewel-encrusted shoe buckles worth a fortune. She had worn no jewelry at all on that occasion, making a point never to travel on a concert tour with valuable items unless giving a costume recital.

Ganna tended to blame the singing teachers for her failure to be accepted as a serious artist, commenting sourly that she was lucky to find one who knew anything about voice production and also happened to be honest. Her daily life in Paris began to be monotonous, waking each morning soon after five o'clock for meditation, reading and writing in her room until seven, when it was time for coffee to be sent up. She waited for the *facteur* to deliver the day's mail, which arrived with the morning papers - a selection of the American, Polish, Italian, French and Russian press for reading before her first lesson promptly at nine. That continued with minimal interruption until midday luncheon: usually one small portion of lean meat with a vegetable, followed by fruit. Walska would rest her voice in the middle of the day for an hour and then started practicing again until four o'clock. "From four to six I go out," she noted. "I always drive in an open car - winter and summer, sun or snow - for only heavy rain forces me to put the top up. In that way I get fresh air while rushing about. At six I sing again until dinner which I usually avoid unless my private life forces me to join my husband in the dining room."

Such a demanding routine must have been boring for Harold, particularly if his wife's self-imposed program of voice development did not progress satisfactorily, when she would continue working after dinner, striving to narrow the gulf between a composer's intentions and her own vocal technique. "You might contend that no voice can stand such strenuous work," she explained defensively, "but I am not giving advice on the correct way to study. I am merely confirming my ardor to learn more and more. After such a day's work it is small wonder that I have to go to bed as early as possible unless I have to go to the opera or a concert, again for educational purposes."

Ganna frequently referred to her "Slavic" nature, blaming it for rarely allowing happiness, with her personal maid instructed never to say good morning because Madame preferred not to speak for the first hour or two after waking. This semi-reclusive, internal existence was in stark contrast to her gold-digger image on both sides of the Atlantic: a dangerous woman who snared rich husbands, and was smart enough to secure the maximum financial benefits from their deaths or divorces.

Madame Walska became a person of multiple contradictions, and in spite of her dark moods, delighted in dressing up and displaying herself to the fashionable world of Paris where she was known for the silk turbans worn instead of conventional millinery, and the black evening gown ordered from Callot Soeurs for her wedding dinner with Alexander Cochran, which continued to do sterling service for a number of years when a woman in her position would be expected to buy a new outfit for almost each social occasion. A fashion rebel, Ganna admitted to being "peculiar about dressing" and suspicious of the famous couturiers "who are obliged to change the style as often as possible to force women to buy new clothes."

Certainly, she rarely looked like other society women, becoming a self-styled pioneer in the field of feminine embellishment by commissioning jewelers to create necklaces, bracelets and rings to display the biggest precious stones they could find. "I never would have thought of wearing tiny diamonds," she boasted, "or an almost invisible string of pearls that cuts the line of the neck unbecomingly and contributes nothing to the beauty of the face." There was no need to compromise on garnets, corals, aquamarines and other semiprecious stones because Ganna could afford diamonds with a name attached to them, perfect pearls, superb sapphires, exquisite emeralds and ravishing rubies to make her stylistic statements. Cartier was the main beneficiary, and, whether in London's Bond Street, on Fifth Avenue in New York, or the Paris boutique on rue de la Paix, Harold's permanent account with the world's most famous jeweler - like Cochran's before him - was kept active paying for his wife's adornment.

Extravagant dressing would become an integral part of Walska's costume performances, setting a trend for other singers by wearing voluminous gowns, like her Second Empire dresses in the style of Empress Eugénie that forced her to enter stages sideways. The novelty caused a sensation with audiences and generated such a racket from photographers during performances that Madame became angry, though the clatter of their shutters might have helped divert attention from her voice. The visual effect was heightened with each change of gown accompanied by a different set of jewels: sparkling diamonds to complement white satin, rubies blending with rich brown brocade, a gold creation adorned with deep green emeralds, and lustrous oriental pearls glowing against a background of lustrous black velvet. These combinations were not likely to win any style awards, but were great show business, and audiences loved them.

Serious opera remained uppermost in Ganna's mind, however, and an engagement for a production of Puccini's *Madama Butterfly* at Nice offered an opportunity to achieve the recognition she so desperately craved. There could be no faulting her preparations; long before bringing the lead role of Cio-Cio San to the stage, she earnestly researched the history of geishas, read about Japanese culture, and, while residing briefly back in New York, nurtured a bonsai garden in her window boxes to provide the right vibrations, which attracted the unwanted attention of neighborhood children who threw stones at their funny shapes. Ganna also studied the body language of Orientals: how they walked, sat and interacted; knowledge of the Far East came from the writings of Claude Farrère (a Prix Goncourt winner who visited Japan) and Pierre Loti (whose 1887 novel "Madame Chrysanthème" was a precursor to *Madama Butterfly*.) The exquisite Musée Guimet in Paris offered a treasure trove of Japanese art and style, and Walska learned dance steps from the soprano, Tamaki Miura, who originated them for her own admired performances of *Butterfly* around the world, and even became familiar with the samisen, a long-necked, three-stringed lute, to accompany dances in the second act of the opera.

Erté played his part by going to great lengths - literally - with her costumes, and having no spending limit, designed exquisite, but heavy, kimonos which she found difficult to handle in following the stage directions. "My wedding gown, for instance," Ganna remembered, "consisted of five superimposed dresses each one longer than the other and each of a different color. In order to put on that nuptial gown at the finale of the first act I had the tremendously complicated task of taking off the four kimonos while singing on the stage." Society *coiffeur* Antoine created shining black wigs to match Erté's rich fabrics, and Ganna's favorite antique dealer in Paris hunted out authentic accessories like a mirror, comb, pillow and doll, as well as a knife for the third act hara-kiri. And to enhance the bitter end of the story, she sought expert medical opinion about the reaction of a dying person to a self-inflicted wound.

Walska was sure she had discovered the perfect operatic vehicle with *Butterfly*. *It* was a "modern" piece premiered in 1904, and Puccini's favorite among his own works; the music perfectly matched its intense drama; action revolved around the title role. She was confident of success with Cio-Cio San where other attempts to convince the world she was a diva had failed. Ganna's image-building included a cover story in the Paris-based *Revue Internationale* which offered its readers, among reports about the Chilean government, future political directions for the Sudan, and China's economy, an incongruous article about Mme. Walska headed "Les Femmes d'Aujourd'hui dans la Vie et dans l'Art." The cover picture: a head-and-shoulders photo of Ganna wearing a silly hat – explaining perhaps her look of embarrassment - reflected the tone of the text which was little more than a mythic account of singing triumphs on two continents.

At this pivotal point in her musical career, she learned of her father's death at the age of sixty-five, with the burial to take place in Warsaw's Powazki Cemetery. After much soul searching, and anxiously waiting to hear about an American concert tour, Ganna made the agonizing decision not to attend Napoleon's funeral. She had corresponded throughout the year with the Russian-born Solomon Isaerich Hurok, who migrated to the United States in 1906 at the age of eighteen, and was now the most powerful artists' manager in the world. Known professionally as Sol Hurok, a list of his clients read like a Who's Who of the concert business, including the leading contralto, Ernestine Schumann-Heink, bass Feodor Chaliapin, violinist Efrem Zimbalist, soprano Alma Gluck, pianist Artur Schnabel and the ballerina Anna Pavlova, as well as a whole galaxy of international orchestras and dance companies.

On the strength of Ganna Walska's public image, the impresario said he would be more than pleased to take Madame under exclusive management and happy to handle all her business on a percentage basis. "I feel that I can promote your interests successfully," he wrote her, "and I know that we shall succeed. You may count on my constant loyalty and anxiety to please you. Please write and advise me what your wishes are in regard to my undertaking your management." Copies of a memorandum of agreement between S. Hurok, Inc. and Madame Ganna Walska were prepared for signature, confirming that her services would be employed for the 1924-25 season in the United States and Canada involving at least fifteen appearances for which she would be paid $600 "for each complete concert." Representation by this prestigious agency was beyond the wildest dreams of most artists, but perversely Madame turned it down, telling Hurok that she was too busy singing opera in Europe to accept his kind offer.

She continued to study the music of *Madama Butterfly* bar-by-bar, note-by-note with Walther Straram and diligently developed the role by playing several minor opera houses throughout France under the name of Anna Navarre – used before by Walska - because the director of the Nice Opera thought it inappropriate for one of his forthcoming attractions to be playing the provinces. According to Ganna, she scored "quite good" critical acclaim there, even if the venues were far from France's musical mainstream, and no influential critics judged her performances.

A fashionable crowd filled the majestic Opéra de Nice on the night of January 28, 1925 during the height of the Riviera's winter season. The portents for Ganna, however, were not good because her spiritual adviser, Mrs. Cochrane, had concluded that two n's in her name stood for negation and produced the wrong vibrations, advising her to adopt the identity used for the recent provincial tour. But it was too late for a change: she had been engaged as Madame Ganna Walska and Nice insisted she must perform with that name. The audience came largely from the local and nearby casinos at Cannes, Menton and Monte-Carlo, including many rich, rootless Americans probably indifferent to the lyric art, though thoroughly familiar with Madame's notoriety from press reports back home.

There was only anemic applause as the curtain fell at the end of the first act, when a reporter for the *New York Times* recorded in his shorthand notebook an ominous silence, and some hissing occurred that must have convinced Walska's personal well-wishers that she was not making many friends here on the Riviera. Ganna was modest enough in her own recollections of the night: "I do not intend to say I sang beautifully for it is all but impossible for a debutante to sing a new part and give as good a performance as an experienced singer doing it for the nth time in the same opera," rating her rendition as better than average. "My interpretation was far more interesting than the customary one, since I tried to portray a real yellow dancing girl, and I looked so different from a fat European, often a generously proportioned Walkuere [sic], disguised at the most in a kimono, often wearing a Spanish flower in her seldom black but invariably curly and much ruffled hair."

The scribe from the *Times* detected an improvement during the second act, even if Walska's voice lacked the necessary strength to stand out against Puccini's powerful orchestration. Erté's costumes looked stunning, but Madame overplayed her mannerisms, prompting outbursts of giggles from a restless audience during the tender moments of the drama, which had acquired the look of melodrama by the third act. The evening ended limply in a mélange of ridicule and lukewarm applause. Ganna had engaged her own publicity agent from Paris, J. Carlisle MacDonald, to feed favorable comments to the newspapers, and he sent eleven glowing dispatches to the Associated Press, representing nearly fourteen hundred subscribers across the United States, and to United Press, with their eight hundred outlets. MacDonald was aware that American papers with correspondents in Nice would submit unfavorable stories, but they were beyond his editorial control.

One of them, The *New York Times,* asked its readers if Madame Walska's career was over because it had been reported that, before going on stage, she told friends if this was a flop, she would end her quest for operatic glory and turn her talents to other unspecified endeavors. The reviews were not all bad, however, except for the Chicago *Tribune*'s - "The World's Greatest Newspaper" according to its masthead - owned by Colonel Robert R. McCormick, its colorful publisher and editor. He came from a separate branch of the Chicago family, related on his father's side to Cyrus, Harold McCormick's father. Suspecting a conspiracy, Walska was sure that the manager of the *Tribune*'s French bureau was preparing publicity for the soprano who would follow her in Nice, thinking it would serve her interests better if he appeared critical of Madame. Convinced of it, she wrote to Colonel McCormick with her complaint and, according to Ganna, the person who wrote the damning review was discharged.

Her contract with Nice Opera included two further performances later on, after singing *Butterfly* successfully in several European capitals, but Ganna was determined to prove her worth on the Riviera, though failing to account for the mayor's concern about his city's reputation. In his opinion, Madame damaged the municipal opera house's artistic status and he decreed that she must never sing there again. When she heard about this, Walska telephoned him to protest against such an arbitrary action, vowing to sue for breach of contract. The mayor responded that she should consider herself lucky that it was Nice and not Marseille where she attempted to sing *Butterfly*. At Marseille, he told her, there would have been a riot.

In spite of the setback in Nice, *Butterfly* continued to open doors for Ganna across Europe, with successes based, not so much on her voice and histrionics, as the striking effect of Erté's costumes together with extensive press publicity preceding each performance. She crisscrossed the continent singing the opera's Italian and French versions, in theaters of all shapes and sizes, including the Festspielhaus at Bayreuth where it was staged under the soft glow of traditional lighting from kerosene lamps. Richard Wagner's son Siegfried was there with members of his family and the McCormicks returned their post-performance hospitality by giving a dinner at which the long-haired Walther Straram implored Ganna not to reveal his identity because he was critical of Siegfried's attempts at composition, suggesting he be introduced to the current Wagner patriarch as a French automobile manufacturer, and not a conductor. The deception misfired because, on shaking hands, Siegfried joked; "It's useless to ask if you're a musician because you certainly look like one."

Walska loved behaving as if she had become a diva through singing this one role and not having to "buy" a single performance of *Madama Butterfly*. She noted in her diary: "Having been re-engaged to make a return appearance to sing at the same opera houses - the best proof of achievement - now I thought it was time to face America." The newspapers there, however, were hounding her over personal problems rather than celebrating European operatic triumphs, by publishing stories about the McCormicks' marriage heading for the rocks. The summer of 1925 saw Ganna in Paris devoting much of her time to the business affairs of her theater - although still not owning the lease - appointing Albert Wolff, the musical director of the Opéra-Comique, as her general director. Harold's business affairs kept him in Chicago, where friends gossiped about his embarrassment over Ganna's independent activities in France and dismay at her conspicuous, even profligate, consumption.

She may have been disgusted by the tone her theater was adopting when a nineteen- year-old African-American dancer with a divine body from St. Louis was a smash hit when appearing at the Champs-Elysées almost naked in a popular revue. Josephine Baker's impact on the French capital was similar in magnitude to the scandalous première on the same stage thirteen years before of Diaghilev's *The Rite of Spring*, and the sensational Miss Baker's cabaret career would flourish in parallel with Igor Stravinsky's in the world of classical music and ballet, consolidated by her saucily sexy "banana dance" at the Folies-Bergère a couple of years later.

Ganna continued to bemoan the twin frustrations of having no control over the attractions at her beautiful theater, and the fact that much of her time was taken up these days on the telephone fending off personal questions from reporters working for the American press. She flatly refused to say anything about divorce, often becoming hysterical when pressed, which only fueled their speculation. Fortuitously, another fling with the movies came along to dispel her annoyance with journalists, making previous flirtations with cinema seem puny. Walther Straram introduced his benefactor to a member of his cultural circle, the brilliant young French film director Abel Gance, and the meeting resulted in an offer for her to play a very different Josephine, with the potential of eclipsing on screen what she regarded as Miss Baker's tawdry fame in revue: Joséphine de Beauharnais, the first wife of Napoleon Bonaparte and, therefore, the first Empress of France.

Walska discussed Gance's interesting proposition for a series of films about Napoléon (*Les Voyages et Les Exploits du Grand General Bonaparte en Divers Pays)* with her French attorney, Charles G. Loeb, and a contract was drawn up for her to receive forty thousand francs ($1,600) in eight installments for the first part, and a million francs ($40,000) for each subsequent production. This was signed on October 10, 1925 in her absence after having left for America again.

Loeb cautioned his client about the director's ability to raise the money offered, but Madame was suddenly star-struck and insisted on proceeding. He then wrote her, "I do not see that you can make any loss by signing this agreement but, on the contrary, under all circumstances only obtain a lot of valuable advertisement." But the lawyer had reason to query the capricious business of film financing because Gance's production company had amassed substantial debts, in spite of a cable to Madame of October 14 giving no inkling of money problems: "*Complete Accord Avec Loeb. Amitiés. Abel Gance.*" She felt sure this was a right career move for her, having sung *Butterfly* successfully all over Europe - with the exception of Nice - and was now signed to play Napoléon's wayward wife on screens all over the world.

In the United States at this time, the manager of the San Carlo Opera, Fortune Gallo, toured a company giving mostly smaller communities the opportunity to enjoy grand opera. A self-supporting venture financed by ticket sales, it was the sort of enterprise Ganna admired: run solely "on the merit of the performances without any sponsorship and especially - contrary to the established tradition of small companies - without accepting a substantial check in exchange for a début." She seemed to be on a winning streak with a movie contract, yet still yearned for serious operatic recognition in America, approached Gallo to let her sing Cio-Cio San in *Madame Butterfly* during his company's season at the Jolson Theater in New York during September and October, 1925.

She insisted, however, that the manager withhold publicizing her appearance, fearing that the press would hound her further about private affairs. They had turned up in force, waiting quayside when the White Star liner "Olympic" docked in New York harbor, with Madame Walska occupying its most regal suite - the Italian Renaissance Rooms - complete with a grand piano. Accompanied by her two maids and Walther Straram, she had announced confidently: "I have returned to prove to the world that I have a real voice, and while I cannot tell you my plans at present in detail, I can tell you that I have chosen New York City, America's most critical metropolis, to make my beginning anew in America."

The 1920s experienced a boom in the cult of celebrity, and the American print media was full of shooting stars, with Madame Ganna Walska epitomizing many of the qualities to attract attention: she was married to the head of International Harvester, with a singing career on both sides of the Atlantic, and flaunted the image of a modern woman with the freedom to do whatever she wished. Combined with her seductive, Slavic beauty, she was

136

perfect celebrity fodder. The fact that Ganna stood aloof from established society, by choice or victimization, only added to the mystique at a time when celebrity reportage filled an inordinate amount of space in newspapers and magazines. Ganna confided to friends that sometimes she felt her life was led in print when visiting the United States.

During a meeting with manager Gallo, arrangements were made for her much-delayed New York opera début. He agreed not to make an official announcement until after a few stage rehearsals, giving him the right to cancel if he thought her performance unsuitable though Ganna boasted that the New York critics would have to eat their words by recognizing true artistry, and stop tormenting her. The influential *Musical Courier* prepared the way with a full-page advertisement illustrated with a striking costume design by Erté, quoting favorable reviews of her *Butterfly* appearances in France, Czechoslovakia and Austria, including a return appearance at the Volksoper in Vienna by public demand:

"We had heard wonderful tales of this Polish-American artist; wonderful jewels; wonderful costumes; and wonderful acting - which is true. Mme. Walska strives to produce an original *Butterfly*, her costumes, her headgear, her 'obi' (girdle) come from faraway lands; her doll-like motions, her bowing, her speech supported by eloquent gestures of her hands are fascinating."

Strangely, the quoted review avoided any mention of the voice.

Signor Gallo may have held unusually high principles for such a precarious business as unsubsidized opera, but the publicity value of having Madame Walska sing with his company was too good to ignore, and he failed to honor his embargo by announcing to the press that the role of Cio-Cio San - taken either by Ganna Walska or Anne Roselle - would be announced three days ahead of the performance on Saturday, October 25. Pressed to reveal more, he explained guardedly that he heard Walska sing at a Paris concert, and, while not an experienced artist in classic style or stage routine, found her sufficiently prepared in Puccini's modern work. Whatever deficiencies Gallo had detected, however, were far outweighed by the exposure surrounding Madame at the moment, particularly reports of playing Joséphine in a series of films about Napoléon, making her, as one newspaper noted, "the latest recruit to the firmament of moving picture stars."

Most movie proposals that had come her way in the past were

from shysters promising to make a star out of anyone who would finance their productions. Now things were different, as she would note in her memoirs. "I had promised myself never to buy my way to any place in the sun of sacred Art. I had no desire for a successful career. I wanted to express my inner being and I knew from earlier experiences that with the help of money this cannot be achieved." But suddenly there was a hitch when Abel Gance's film company crashed and he cabled her in desperation:

"When You Receive This Cable I Have 24 Hours Maximum To Avoid Breaking Up And Complete Takeover Of My Business And Myself By A Bank. Loeb Advises Cabling You About The Urgency And Gravity. If You Can Follow Up Our Negotiations To Participate. Cable Immediately. Yours Abel Gance."

Three days later, another despairing message:

"In The Event Of The New Company Finding It Impossible To Accept Your Contract I Ask You To Please Make Urgent Efforts To Get A Solution Before Wednesday Evening Because I Have Refused To Sign Until Your Response. Sincerely Gance."

He was obviously depending on McCormick money to rescue the project, but Walska had a more urgent problem to fix. Just before the first rehearsal of *Butterfly*, she was informed that permission for her to perform the role from the publisher's representative in the United States, George Maxwell, had not been given. Gallo confessed that he'd been warned previously that Madame Walska might not be allowed to sing Puccini in America, even though the composer's publisher Ricordi in Milan had raised no objection to her performances in Europe.

This provided more pap for the papers on the day before the scheduled performance of *Madama Butterfly,* when a press release issued by the San Carlo company stated that negotiations with Madame Walska had been terminated. It looked like another of her walkouts, with "Walska Quits Again," "Ganna Cannot Sing" and "Walska's Engagement Broken" only three of the resulting newspaper headlines above stories of fierce operatic rivalry and faction-fighting. There was no mention of anyone banning her from performing Puccini, although a journalist had managed to be present at the final dress rehearsal and described what happened when the leading tenor, Franco Tafuro, aborted the tender love duet between Lieutenant Pinkerton of the U.S. Navy and his beautiful young geisha, Cio-Cio San.

138

"Why you turn your head away from me?" he demanded to know. "I must see tears in your eyes."

"Why should I look at you?" Walska queried him. "Couldn't you hear me sobbing?"

"I've been singing this role five hundred times," the tenor retorted, "under the greatest directors of the world, including Toscanini."

"Well, *I* have sung it fifteen times all over Europe. I even went over the stage business with Signor Puccini himself."

At this point, according to the report, Tafuro stormed off the stage refusing to sing another note, followed by a statement issued from the manager's office. It explained that, although the usual "family harmony" of the company was disrupted, Madame Walska remained on "particularly good terms" with Mr. Gallo and it was believed possible that her appearance in another opera might be arranged, perhaps in Detroit. One of the most famous Cio-Cio Sans of the era, Tamaki Miura, performed in her place.

Walska's cherished New York début was doomed, though the widespread coverage attracted another offer. George DeFeo, the artistic director of the French-Italian Opera, told Madame that his company was going to Canada for a short tour under the patronage of Evelyn, wife of the British Governor-General Baron Byng of Vimy. George Maxwell was a friend of the double Great War hero, known to his intimates as "Bungo," and DeFeo claimed that Ricordi's American representative wanted nothing more in life than to receive a knighthood, and Madame Walska singing *Butterfly* under Byng's patronage in Canada might help his chances, if the right words were whispered in the vice-regal ear.

Maxwell told DeFeo that he would probably get into trouble because of promising "a very important person" he would never allow Walska to sing Puccini's music in the United States, but the prospect of an imperial honor upstaged any pledge, and he agreed that *Butterfly* could be performed with Walska in the title role. "Afterwards," he explained, "if I am asked why I allowed it, I will pretend I did not know about it. Naturally, if it were New York I could not be unaware of what was going on. But Canada?!!! "

Ganna would comment sourly on this: "Mr. Maxwell wanted to have his cake and eat it too." But so did DeFeo; after agreeing that she could sing with his company, he revealed that certain subsidies had failed to materialize and suggested that Madame, in return for top billing, might wish to assist in rescuing his opera season with a sizeable check. She, with her new-found spirit of correctness, did not, and the Canadian production never eventuated.

Following this latest debacle, Ganna slipped quietly into Philadelphia to make peace with the San Carlo company, announcing that her long-awaited début would take place the following Saturday in the Berlioz opera *Roméo et Juliette*. She naively expected to work harmoniously with the same group of artists who bitterly resented her presence in the first instance, and after a disastrous stage rehearsal, closed to outsiders, a press release was issued stating that Offenbach's *The Tales of Hoffmann* would be presented on the Saturday night, as originally scheduled. An hour later, Madame Walska was seen boarding a train back to New York, having notched up another non-appearance.

Speculating about the reasons for the humiliation, journalists never discovered the real story behind the ban on her singing *Butterfly* in North America. The "very important person" mentioned by George Maxwell was her nemesis Edith Rockefeller McCormick, who had links with Puccini's publisher in Milan through their American representative, having sponsored English versions of the composer's libretti. Harold's still-bitter, first wife had previously put paid to his second's appearance at the summer opera festival at Ravinia Park, and made similar moves to spike her performances of *Madama Butterfly* in New York. When she learned of this, Ganna commented, with a surprising lack of rancor: "It was a very clever move, for to prevent a soprano from singing Puccini was equivalent to cutting her wings."

When taking take stock of her life by publishing an autobiography, she looked back over her diary notes from this period with disarming honesty. "Naturally I would prefer to keep silent about all my fiascos," she wrote, "which are not constructive, exciting or interesting to read about. However, I will mention them to show how I gathered force to continue after every more or less great failure - to continue and to fail again and again." Following the latest calamity, her hopes of a brilliant career in motion pictures were also dashed when the Société Génerale des Films took control of Abel Gance's business affairs, and the contract Walska had signed with him became void.

By now Walther Straram, who accompanied Madame for much of the current American visit, giving her singing lessons en route, needed to return home to conduct their symphony orchestra in Paris, and there was no time to prepare a proposed concert program for the United States. Ganna decided to leave with him, which infuriated Harold, who was thoroughly disenchanted with the musical mentor's constant attention to his wife. He, too, decided to travel to Europe, but there was a dramatic change of plans at the last minute, explained by one interminably long New York newspaper headline: "McCormick Stays as Walska Sails - Husband Leaves Liner and Goes to Chicago After Starting to go Aboard With Wife - Takes Baggage from Pier - Diva Says She'll Sing in Paris, Then Prove Her Talent Here." There was much more behind that information than met the eye.

Walska, her maids, Walther Straram and Harold were all set to sail aboard the French Line's "Paris" with its passenger list noting she would occupy the luxurious Suite Number 7, and "Mr. Harold McCormick, Chairman of the Executive Committee of the International Harvester Company" in a single room nearby: Number 1. Everyone assumed he was accompanying his wife and Harold confirmed it personally to reporters prior to sailing, while Ganna was being interviewed about future plans, and revealing she was writing her memoirs to tell the world the truth about herself. Then at 9.50 a.m. - ten minutes before departure time - Harold was seen to leave the vessel and make his way from the pier apparently in an agitated state, saying nothing except that he intended to leave for Europe in the near future.

The luxurious liner was delayed, waiting for another ship, the "Majestic" to clear the end of the pier, which allowed the press more time to talk to Ganna and ask why her husband had decided not to make the trip. "Sailing? Why of course he is sailing!" she responded. When it was pointed out that her husband had been seen traveling uptown in a taxicab, Ganna changed her story.
"He will be sailing for France next week."

It was not a satisfactory explanation for hard-bitten reporters, one of whom had checked the steamship passages for the McCormicks and their two maids which were combined on one ticket. Another smart journalist had established that the passports of all four passengers were examined by an official from the Passport Bureau,

141

checking that they contained the correct visas to enter France. Furthermore, in gathering information for their stories, it was confirmed that shortly before nine o'clock, the office of the French Line had been contacted by the freight department of International Harvester in Chicago, which arranged Mr. McCormick's travel arrangements, asking for his reservation be canceled because he would be unable to sail that day owing to pressure of business.

This confusion was, in effect, the couple's attempt to hide a couple of skeletons in their closets: a crumbling marriage and Stanley McCormick's long incarceration in California. When the "Paris" arrived in the northern French port of Le Havre, Walska refused to say anything about divorce, only that she intended to give the French capital an opportunity to hear her voice in *Madame Butterfly*, which she would probably be singing at the Opéra-Comique. Confirmation of Harold's imminent arrival to join her dampened further speculation about marital problems for the moment, and any news of Stanley McCormick's parlous psychological and physical state while incarcerated in California - the real reason for Harold's sudden change of plans - was overlooked. The incident demonstrated that the newsworthy couple was likely to be watched more closely than ever.

Ganna always found time to record thoughts and experiences in diary notes, and now, with enhanced notoriety, she decided it was time to publish them. A chaotic manuscript of three chapters, typed by a succession of secretaries, was sent to a literary agent, Doris Stevens, the recently divorced wife of Madame's New York attorney Dudley Field Malone. Stevens, a pugnacious supporter of suffragist and feminist principles, having become involved with the National Woman's Party (NWP) in Washington, D.C., developed their strategies and had been arrested while picketing the White House in 1917 for which she served three days of a sixty-day prison sentence before being pardoned. A further detention followed during a NWP demonstration at the Metropolitan Opera House during 1919, and the vivid account of her experiences, "Jailed for Freedom," published in 1920, was widely-read. After the Nineteenth Amendment was passed giving women the vote in 1920, Stevens turned her attention to lobbying for the Equal Rights Amendment (ERA) to give legal equality for the sexes.

Doris Stevens was often portrayed by conservatives as "a new woman" who led a shockingly free life with questionable liaisons, but was respected by Ganna Walska for her independence. As an agent, she "straightened out" Madame's text as best she could and rearranged sequences for continuity, sending a copy of her editing for Madame's approval with the suggestion, "If the work pleases you, as I hope it will, just cable me 'Okeh' or one word 'Submit,' and I will understand that this means for me to go ahead and receive offers from publishers. I think the samples are so exciting that I don't see how any publisher could refuse them." Stevens claimed that the *Saturday Evening Post* was "champing at the bit and wants very much to submit you an offer."

A subsequent letter, however, revealed a different response to Madame Walska's literary aspirations. Sample chapters had been sent through Putnam's to the *Saturday Evening Post* and returned with a note saying that the magazine was not prepared to pay a substantial sum for the material. They were seen by the *Pictorial Review*, which found Madame's story "engrossing" but unsuitable for their readership. *Collier's* had not reported to Stevens by mailing date and she had yet to approach book publishers because of thinking it best to sell the magazine rights first. But by May 5, when about to leave for Paris to attend the International Woman's Suffrage Congress at the Sorbonne, Doris Stevens was unable to report any further progress. "It has been most discouraging to both of us," she wrote in a brief note to the author, "since those who might take it will not pay enough and those editors who pay well raise other objections. You will be highly amused at some of them." Convincing herself there would be opportunities later Ganna lost interest in publication for the moment, but continued to record her thoughts and impressions.

Contact with her family in Poland following father Napoléon's death, centered on her younger brother Leon, who made regular visits to Paris on business. Other relations remained remote, and when half-brother Edward had come to study political science in France in early 1925 he tried to make contact with Ganna, and failed. Now, ten months later, he wrote a letter of desperation begging for financial assistance, saying he was living in poverty. It is not known if she sent any money to ease his misery - or was even prepared to see him - because of total immersion in a hectic

143

social life that revolved around her theater and the expatriates of several nationalities living, by choice or circumstance, in the French capital. They included wealthy Americans who had flocked to France after the war, and those who once enjoyed positions of privilege in pre-Revolutionary Russia who escaped with their lives and now found themselves in greatly reduced circumstances following the triumph of Bolshevism. Madame's socializing ranged across the present and former élite of several nations, entertaining them at 14 rue de Lubeck. The Muslim spiritual leader, the Aga Khan, accepted her regular invitations, as did the Maharaja of Kapurthala - the immensely rich and much-honored Jagatjit Singh - who would become India's representative to the League of Nations General Assembly.

Several of Ganna's association with the British, Americans, Russians, Poles, Indians and South Americans resident in Paris, making it the most cosmopolitan of Europe's capitals, came through a new search for spiritual and mystical guidance. A study of reincarnation led her to revisit theosophy through the writings of Annie Besant, the English reformer and activist for women's rights. Rosicrucian philosophy followed, in which Walska immersed herself for a while by studying the Akastric records, the Aquarian Age, and lost Atlantis - little of which led to the spiritual development of her soul because requests for large cash donations always intervened. The person who expounded gospel teachings stationed her husband at the door of meetings to collect fees, giving warning that no progress was possible unless they were received. Another woman trying to augment her income, offered to discover Ganna's previous lives in return for a substantial payment. She fell for this one, only to learn that she had been Cleopatra VII, Queen of Egypt, and sharing the same Ptolemaic heritage with a number of friends who had followed the same procedure.

Walska was on friendly terms with the Grand Duke Alexander, brother-in-law of the last Tsar, whose daughter, Princess Irina, was married to Prince Feliks Yusupov, formerly from one of Russia's richest families and notorious for having participated in the murder of the demonized faith-healer, Grigori Rasputin. The flamboyant and devastatingly handsome Yusupov, accepted in sophisticated Parisian circles as a cross-dresser, was critical of his father-in-

144

law's séances, though he told Ganna how, on fleeing his country he had encountered an old woman living in a cave near Sevastopol who, without knowing his identity, predicted that he would be on the throne of Russia one day. "And," as she recalled their conversation, "the Prince, thinking the old crone was a Saint, believed her."

The Grand Duke communicated by handwritten letters and calling cards sent from his Paris town house on Place Alboni, or a villa in the Haute Savoie, addressing her in the Russian patronymic style as Napoleonovna. He signed himself simply "Alexander" and insisted on introducing her to his medium from the émigré community.

The family, concerned about Alexander's obsession with spiritualism, and knowing Walska's experiences in the occult world, asked if she could convince His Imperial Highness - as he preferred to be addressed - that illusory happiness was pointless. But Ganna had stopped going to the Grand Duke's séances where his medium claimed to put the living in touch with the dead, after being shown a gift said to have materialized from the spirit world. Alexander was told that he had been a Pharaoh in a previous incarnation, and a bronze statuette of him in that guise appeared as if from nowhere on his desk. Ganna examined the object he showed everyone with great pride, discovering under its base the price tag of a well-known Paris department store which sold hundreds of the cheap replicas to tourists.

As if to highlight the plight of many Russian aristocrats exiled in the French capital, Ganna became the owner of one of their former nation's Imperial treasures during 1926. Known as the Duchess of Marlborough egg, the jeweled and enameled Easter egg was created in 1902 under the supervision of Peter Carl Fabergé for Consuelo Marlborough, granddaughter of the American railroad magnate Cornelius Vanderbilt. It was sent for auction after she divorced her husband, Charles Spencer-Churchill, the ninth Duke of Marlborough, following a long and largely loveless marriage.

Flush with McCormick money and buying whatever took her fancy, Walska was asked by Alexander to lend him six hundred thousand francs ($24,000) because his spiritual guide, named Ela, had predicted that Bolshevism was about to collapse and His Imperial Highness the Grand Duke Alexander Mikhailovitch

Romanov - just one of his several titles – would soon be able to return home to reclaim his estates - and any Fabergé baubles that had survived the new régime. She was tempted not to break her rule about lending money, preferring to follow the Shakespearean dictum from *Hamlet*: "Neither a borrower or a lender be; for loan oft loses both itself and friend," but finally agreed, handing over the cash with barely concealed disgust.

Later, when paying it back, Alexander assured Ganna that she would succeed with her singing because he was informed from The Other Side that she was the reincarnation of Angelica Catalani, the celebrated soprano of the Napoleonic era. Ganna was immensely flattered by the suggestion: "As a result I bought and read all the literature of that period I could put my hands on and soon knew the life of that vocal acrobat as well as if it had been my own." Parisian antique dealers experienced something of a bonus as well, selling Madame expensive old prints of Catalani and a large number of books about the diva, but with no discernible improvement in Ganna's vocal technique.

She resolved to end any involvement with psychic phenomena, noting in her diary: "No more spooks, palmistry, crystal-gazing, mind reading, telepathy, astrology, numerology, theosophy, Coeism, seers of vision . . ." That ragbag of questionable concepts largely practiced by charlatans anxious to get their hands on her money, would be replaced by a religious philosophy from the Indian subcontinent first encountered when she was married to Dr. Fraenkel. His musical friends, including the great Russian bass singer, Feodor Chaliapin, and dynamic British-born conductor, Leopold Stokowski, were fervent followers, and Ganna's own library began to contain books on Tibetan philosophy in which she penciled notes and comments. Buddhism she decided was the way ahead for her.

Dollars from Scents
1927-1928

Mingling with Russian émigrés in Paris led to a rich and often satisfying life for this wealthy woman of similar temperament, able to speak their language fluently, while separated for much of the time from her American husband by the Atlantic Ocean. Hers was no simple relationship with anyone, but Ganna could never be accused of being orthodox, in any sense of the word. Approaching forty, living alone, and not bothering with irrelevancies like age, Ganna continued to play the role of a person for whom there were few barriers and no obvious limits. It was a polished performance developed since arriving in St. Petersburg as a gauche teenager more than twenty years before.

The dispossessed Russian élite were forced by their country's 1917 upheaval to abandon great estates and palaces and reestablish themselves in relative poverty, with many coming to Paris. The grand dukes and duchesses, counts and countesses, princes and princesses, barons and baronesses, together with a multitude of minor aristocrats and bureaucrats, had once treated the young Baroness d'Eingorn as an outsider. Now, some of them relied on her as a source of funds to maintain some semblance of their previous lifestyles, and this role-reversal put a smile on the still-beautiful face of the Polish parvenu, continuing to record her day-to-day activities for future publication, including impressions of her social circle.

"I saw much of the celebrated Prince Youssoupoff and his beautiful wife, the daughter of the Grand Duc Alexandre, and Grand Duchess Ksenia (Xenia), the Tsar's sister. They had a house in Boulogne, near Paris, where their cook was a former colonel who received room and living for his work and after dinner took off his white cook's uniform and came to the parlor to play the guitar and sing Tzigane popular songs. Other members of the household were more or less of the old nobility who found themselves without a roof over their heads."

Some exiles were reduced to taking menial work to survive, by washing dishes in restaurant kitchens, dressing up in Ruritanian-style uniforms to act as hotel doormen, and by becoming chauffeurs. The Oxford-educated Prince Felix Felixovich Yusupov, however, had escaped the Revolution with a large bag of jewelry together with two Rembrandts, and, as Walska observed firsthand, was able to offer accommodation to less fortunate compatriots at his house on rue Gutenberg in return for housework to help with the living expenses.

Russians harbored an inherent snobbery about Poles, rather like the British patronizing the Irish, snobbish Australians regarding New Zealanders as inferiors, and today's Rohingya people rejected by Myanmar. Ganna had learned to ignore such cruel taunts at home in Brest-Litovsk, which led to a deep-seated conviction that her people were special, in spite of being characterized and caricatured as bumpkins. "Who's that Polish girl?" they asked when the attractive Hanna Puacz started attending balls and soirées in St. Petersburg, and though Arcadie had shielded her, the boorish behavior was deeply humiliating for her

Madame Walska could be excused for feeling righteous now that the tables were turned. Aristocratic Russians quit the country in a hurry with whatever they could carry; their roubles were worthless, and jewelry became the principal exchange currency. The finest stones and pearls from the Imperial era, set in tiaras, necklaces, bangles, bracelets and brooches offered the means of survival in an expensive foreign land, where astute Parisian dealers sought out the best examples and acquired them, often for a pittance. Collecting fine jewelry happened to be one of Ganna's passions, and moving in émigré circles allowed entrée to those who needed to sell.

With plenty of cash sitting in her bank accounts, she was able to capitalize on a buyer's market in a spirit of opportunism rather than retribution for former derision, by buying precious stones at rock-bottom prices. Sometimes Ganna acted as an anonymous intermediary to make a deal, disguising her identity to obtain small art objects, jewels and silverware - anything that caught her fancy. "I can only offer you this amount because it's as much as my buyer is prepared to spend," she would say in persuading sellers to part with their possessions for a song.

A story made the rounds about Madame Walska alighting from her Rolls-Royce wearing the sable coat Cochran gave her as a wedding present, changing into a simple cloth wrap and ordinary cloche hat, to follow the trail of some special Russian jewelry on foot. She would return to the splendid vehicle, with its *mecanicien* whisking her away from some marginal part of town, taking home her haul to the salubrious *seizième* where she lived. On one occasion when brother Leon was visiting, she stepped out of the Rolls on fashionable rue du Faubourg St-Honoré when her Cartier triple-string necklace caught on the door handle, breaking the thread and scattering priceless pearls like hailstones all over the *trottoir*. Leon immediately bent down and retrieve them, but his sister, needing to keep up appearances on so smart a street knew she might be recognized.

"Don't worry, Lay-on, they're not real," she airily informed him in loud French, pausing to make sure nobody had noticed, then hissed *sotto voce* in Polish, "pick 'em up! Pick 'em up! They're worth a bloody fortune!"

Social life was what she wanted to make of it: at home or on travels throughout Europe. She counted among her friends the Infanta Eulalia, daughter of the Spanish King, who kept a Paris

149

residence and regularly visited Walska's musical *salons* at rue de Lubeck. In return, Eulalia invited Ganna to Madrid to watch a bullfight and she accepted, with reservations. "I was told that the first bullfight often makes such an impression and that if I went a second time I would surely love it for, in the opinion of my friends, I was too much of an artist not to appreciate such beauty." It was a doubtful proposition for someone squeamish about the sight of a single drop of blood, though she was persuaded to watch the celebrated matador, Juan Belmonte, perform his famous *estocada* in the capital's great bull ring to assist in her conversion to the nation's traditional blood sport. But Walska disgraced herself in front of the Spanish monarch by emitting such a piercing scream at the critical moment of Belmonte's killing thrust of his sword that Alfonso XIII turned round in the royal box to find her deathly pale and preparing to leave before the conclusion of the ritual.

Lively conversations with Eulalia, who held unusually progressive views about socialism and the independence of women, prompted Walska to review her four marriages, and she subsequently noted her thoughts in a diary entry: "I need this man for (a) money, (b) social status, (c) philosophic companionship," wondering why these reasons had not given her total happiness. She continued to radiate an aura of devastating charm - both physical and intellectual - to the point where any gentlemen would be ecstatic to have her on his arm, if only for decoration, imagining this beautiful creature adorning his life, stroking his ego and running his home. But Ganna had long ceased to be a mere plaything, having become attracted to the feminist causes espoused by her friend Doris Stevens and the radical opinions expressed by Eulalia in her daring book "The Thread of Life."

Many admirers continued to pursue her, but they often discovered to their dismay, that she was smarter, by taking the initiative, setting goals and achieving them in a man's world. Nearing forty, she was on the cusp of reinventing herself - again - and, as bizarre as it may have seemed to those who lusted after her, Ganna Walska began to espouse feminist principles - or at least turned her mind to the question of women's rights, equality and their role in small 's' society.

She continued to live apart from Harold, regarding him as having "one of the most beautiful souls I ever encountered," while annoyed by his "abnormal sense of what he thought were his responsibilities" and "an entirely misguided idea of what his part should be as an important citizen of his beloved city, Chicago." But Ganna could not afford to be too openly critical of her fourth husband because she depended on income from the trust funds set up by the Harvester Prince, whose company's products she saw and heard whenever she left town, clunking, clattering, rattling and roaring their way across the French countryside, helping to creating an agricultural revolution. International Harvester was literally changing the landscape as farm mechanization replaced human and horse-drawn toil. "During my traveling," she admitted, "if ever I saw in the field an International Harvester machine I always sent to it a feeling of love or with my finger a tiny kiss," recognizing it was Harold's clangorous machinery that provided the steady income allowing her to indulge in *divertissements* like the Champs-Elysées theater.

An endearing side of Ganna's nature was a concern for former relationships. Four years after her divorce from Alexander Cochran, friends in London informed her that he was staying at Claridge's during September 1926, where she contacted her former Alec. He responded:

"It is kind of you to write the letter of friendliness and generosity. And good to know that when we meet there will be no bitter feelings between us. It may be some time before we do meet for I have been laid up by a bit of bad luck. But I do appreciate your writing as you do and I honestly thank you. Yours sincerely Alexander Cochran"

The reference to "bad luck" was chronic ill health caused by his tuberculosis.

Harold's long absences generated considerable press comment. In February, 1927 a French newspaper claimed that Walska was about to divorce her husband in Paris, speculating that a substantial property settlement had already been arranged. McCormick reacted by telling the New York *Sun*: "I know nothing about the divorce rumor, because there is nothing to it," but later modified this to "So far as I know there is nothing to it." Pressed by one reporter wanting to know whether he would be sorry if the rumors were true, he asked:

"Are you married, young man?"
The journalist admitted he was.

"Well, you would be sorry if your wife divorced you - and I would be sorry too."

Ganna preferred to think about their happier times together, like a trip with Harold to Poland, when she sang at the opera in Krakow and her brother's family came to see them. Leon's wife, Marysia, thought she would have to miss the performance because of having to look after her young son. But Harold offered to baby-sit instead, and Hania Tallmadge, Walska's niece, remembered: "When they came back from the theater the hotel room was filled with toys and Harold was sitting on the floor playing with my little brother."

The lease of the Théâtre des Champs-Elysées remained tantalizingly beyond Walska's grip, with Jacques Hébertot restraining her performing activities to the point where the Saison de l'Orchestre Walther Straram of 1926 had to be presented elsewhere, with Madame appearing as a soloist in Mozart's *Requiem*, just before the lessee handed over his interests, without consultation or authorization, to Rolf de Maré, the rich patron of the Paris-based Ballets Suédois. This raised the possibility of her acquiring total control, until the shifty Hébertot then transferred the lease legally to a British-born sportsman named Jefferson Davis Cohn, a stockbroker who owned a successful racing stable in France and was married to the well-known opera singer and screen actress Marcelle Chantelle. All this activity left Ganna as before: owning the controlling interest in the building through her majority shareholding, but having no control of what appeared on its stages.

She studiously ignored the gala première at the Paris Opéra on April 7, 1927, when Abel Gance's silent film *Napoléon* was shown and promoted as the first of six. Running for an epic 330 minutes and employing advanced filming techniques; it was poorly received commercially, partly because the talkies were imminent, although most *cinéastes* treated the coming of movie sound with aesthetic concern. Gina Manès had taken the role of Joséphine that would have been Walska's but for the director's bankruptcy, and missed out in being a part of cinema history (apart from a marginal *Citizen Kane* connection) when, in the fullness of time, *Napoléon* was hailed as a silent movie classic.

Looking for a way of paying for the mounting cost of supporting the musical life of Paris, Walska decided to proceed with a money-making idea she had been developing for some time: a perfume and cosmetics business to compete with the great French *marques* dominating the international market. She may have been inspired by the success of her fabulously wealthy countrywoman, Helena Rubinstein, who, starting from modest beginnings in Krakow, went on to found a small cosmetics company in Melbourne, Australia which mushroomed into a worldwide empire. Many had tried - and most failed - in this fickle business, but Ganna and her backers were confident that her celebrity status would be a commercial asset, particularly in the United States.

After discussions with the lawyers Valois and Loeb about the amount of capital needed for a successful launch, Madame put up $60,000 to start proceedings. They had suggested $200,000 minimum for success in America, but the advice was ignored and the enterprise came into being with Walska transferring $59,000 from New York to Morgan & Cie, Paris, in the name of Société Parisienne de Produits de Beauté Ganna Walska (en formation.)

GW perfume publicity shot

An ambitious range of fragrances and eaux de toilette was planned, bearing the rather racy names of Divorçons, Pour le Sport and a more traditional Blue Ribbon. The company tried

153

unsuccessfully to register Gigolo, and had anyone suggested Femme Fatale, Madame might have vetoed that as far too personal, though Divorçons (Let's Get Divorced) does sound a little too close for comfort, considering the uncertainty surrounding her current marriage. In addition to the perfumes, there were to be eight subtle shades of scented face powder, all-day lipsticks, refined rouges, soap as a combined cleanser and tonic, and concentrated toothpaste containing an anti-pyorrhea mouthwash to freshen the breath.

A full list of proposed products, including cologne for men, seemed endless, with bath salts containing phosphorus in seawater proportions for dispelling jaded feelings in the morning, a shampoo based on honey, milk, sugar and cedar balm intended to revive the hair's natural pigment, and hair lotion perfumed with lavender. An erasing cream would claim to remove facial wrinkles overnight, and there was going to be skin food for the growth and nourishment of derma tissue, a beauty cream that boasted the benefits of a spa treatment, and cleansing lotion for ridding the pores of impurities and recover youthful bloom.

Promoted as ahead of their time, Ganna Walska perfumes "and other preparations for the sophisticated toilette" targeted "the woman of wealth and taste" who, until then, had been unable to buy anything of this quality simply because it was not produced. A measure of Madame's celebrity at the time, which would certainly help to sell her products in the United States, had the *New Yorker* magazine printing a silly little piece in its widely-read Talk of the Town section after she was seen on the street with a miniature poodle. A reporter asks her

> "Is that your dog?"
> "It is."
> "Is that the only dog you have?
> "It is"
> "Well, all I can say is, you are
> damn near out of dog."

Those fortunate enough to be endowed with "fastidious apperceptions," like *New Yorker* readers, were to be targeted by elegant bottles, jars and containers in Art Déco style, with Madame personally approving a color scheme for the packaging in pale turquoise, gold and black. Company letterheads announced "ganna walska cy parfumeurs" in trendy lower-case lettering, with "Mrs.

154

Harold MacCormick, president" misspelt immediately below. The business address, appropriately, was on the rue de Paradis, and a company showroom was planned for the most fashionable part of town, at 2, rue de la Paix. Word spread about the new enterprise during the summer of 1927, when the publicity manager received a request from United Press for a story and pictures to be syndicated across the United States. Notorious for straying from her subject, Walska was cautioned to take care when talking publicly about the company's beauty products.

"Should they ask questions on this subject you should say that you are about to launch the greatest discovery of the greatest European scientist, that is to say, an actual treatment for face lifting which every woman can do for herself without any trouble or danger."

September was judged the ideal time for the launch, immediately following the *rentrée,* France's mass-return from summer vacations. Ganna made every effort to attract maximum attention for her "scent shop," as the American press insisted on calling it, arriving for the opening in her monogrammed open Rolls-Royce wearing a cherry-red velvet dress decorated with gold embroidery and a Russian Cossack hat about a foot high, which stopped passers-by in their tracks and prompted many a wry remark. The long-service Cochran sable coat was draped over Madame's shoulders, and a constellation of sparkling sapphires and emeralds sparkled around the neck, complementing her unique Mogul Mughal emerald, said to be one of the largest in the world. Traffic came to a standstill and gendarmes stood by powerless to do anything about the *bouchon* created on the street, or a crush of *midinettes*, chauffeurs and onlookers gaping from the sidewalk. Finally managing to push her way through the throng to enter the smart new premises, Madame told reporters that the profits would be used to transform her Théâtre des Champs-Elysées into a temple of music honoring the memory of the great French composer Claude Debussy.

Until the theater's lease came up for renewal the following year, she helped aspiring singers and musicians by arranging gatherings at home where they performed for her guests. These *salons* introduced new talent recommended by charitable friends who, as Walska put it, "forced upon me the future Kreisler, Paderewski, Caruso or Chaliapin who only needed a musically frequented salon such as mine that he may come into his own." Louisa Wolf, Ganna's Berlin agent, begged her to give a Russian pianist, already well-known in his country, the chance to display his exceptional musicianship in Western Europe. But she was cautious, having experienced several disappointments with potential stars of the opera house and concert platform, whose rather modest talents were obviously incapable of sustaining professional careers. As a gesture to Louisa, however, she relented and invited the critics - many of whom were also well-known composers - to attend this event as a special favor to her because, as Madame apologized in advance, the young man might not be worth hearing at all.

The cultural élite of Paris turned out in force for the recital, with Maurice Ravel, André Messager, Arthur Honegger, Paul Dukas and Darius Milhaud among them. Walska sat in the front row of her salon next to Infanta Eulalia, having told the composers and music critics beforehand to hover near the door to facilitate escape to the buffet and bar should this particular hopeful prove to be a flop. The handsome young man with raven-black hair, aquiline nose and long, expressive fingers sat down confidently at the keyboard and nobody moved, or hardly dared to breathe, until his program finished to huge applause, so sublime was the music-making. Vladimir Samoylovich Horowitz was on his way to becoming an international celebrity as one of the greatest pianists of the twentieth century.

Following protracted negotiations with Jefferson Davis Cohn, Walska finally gained complete control of her own theater by paying him six million francs ($240,000.) Ecstatically happy at the outcome, she threw a grand reception to announce that she was now the boss. The visionary founder of the Théâtre des Champs-Elysées, impresario Gabriel Astruc, was present and made a speech, as Ganna described it, "glorifying me for what until then had merely been an act of notary business on my part, flattering me to such an extent that I finally revolted at so much insincerity." She quickly put a stop to the adulation with a neat little address of her own:

"I thank you very much dear M. Gabriel Astruc for your kindness but I cannot accept all your compliments as they do not belong to me. It was you who were illuminated with the vision to create such grandeur while [architect] Mr. Perret's genius allowed him to materialize such a conception

that twenty years later it is still up-to-date and had he built it at the present time he could not have improved, so high was his inspiration. As music lovers, we thank you Mr. Perret. And if we will be privileged to hear divine sounds in this frame of beauty in an atmosphere of sublimeness, we will owe it to such a perfect musician as is present with us here, Mr. Walther Straram!"

Her musical mentor's dream of creating an arts center of the top rank through concerts, dance, opera and drama had come true, thanks to the wealth of Madame's husbands number three and four

Running the theater in tandem with developing her perfume and cosmetics company kept Walska busy through much of 1927 and 1928, though she still had time for daily singing lessons with Walther Straram. But it soon became obvious to her business manager that establishing the cosmetics and perfume label in France would be more difficult than expected because of intense competition from well-established *griffes* like Shalimar, Chanel No.5 and Arpège. America was where big money could be made with something new, and they worked hard together for a United States launch, planning to appoint one smart store in each major city for the exclusive sale of products bearing the Ganna Walska name. A marketing campaign prepared the way, with Madame giving interviews to the American press about the difference between cosmetics use in the two countries:

"What is the chief fault I find with the American method of make-up? Well, I would say that its worse offense lies in the fact that it is too obvious and too standardized . . . For it is clear that most American girls make up too heavily and with too little art. They fail to remember that every skin has its own individual nuance of coloring and that you can bring this out only by blending your cosmetics as delicately as possible with the natural complexion and not by covering it up with a thick mask."

It was a perceptive observation, and Ganna's own flawless complexion was full justification for making it.

Seizing the opportunity to combine the roles of diva in music and goddess of feminine beauty, she returned to the United States in September, 1928 for a last-ditch attempt to establish a singing career there, and to establish a New York base for selling her beauty products. Office space was rented at number 9; East 54th.Street and negotiations began with Saks Fifth Avenue to open an exclusive boutique within their store.

Madame's concert tour began in the unprepossessing surroundings of the transportation and manufacturing center of

157

Binghampton, New York State, close to the Philadelphia border, population 72,000. Like a presidential candidate on the stump rather than an itinerant warbler on a one-night stand, she told the local press: "I will succeed in my music. I have struggled ahead like many other singers and now I am ready to place myself before those great critics, the American people, and then let them judge of me as they have judged of other artists in the past." After what *Musical America* described as an informal recital in the city's 500-seat High School auditorium, most notable for Ganna's cream crepe and silver period gown, flappers flocked for her autograph and she, in turn, flung them her bouquets of flowers with a beaming husband watching on.

A couple of whistle stops later, Walska returned to Chicago to be greeted by Harold sprinting along the station platform like a sophomore welcoming his sweetheart home for the holidays. The moment the Capitol Limited screeched to a halt, the glamorous Mrs. McCormick stood standing on the steps of the car, fresh from concerts in Cincinnati and Washington, D.C., waiting to run into her husband's arms. Rotund, bespectacled McCormick, still puffing from his exertions and giving the impression of a shortsighted, middle-aged bank clerk instead of a great captain of industry, managed a wan smile, planted a peck on his wife's cheek and uttered a matter-of-fact "Hello, dear," as multiple flashes from the press photographers' cameras lit up the platform like lightning strikes. Journalists jostled each other for stories from Madame, swathed in a full-length squirrel coat, with a floppy gray felt hat on her head, and clutching a bouquet of wilting roses presented to her by President Coolidge in Washington. She insisted on telling them about her new beauty business, though they wanted to hear more about an incident with a lion in the nation's capital.

Brushing that aside, she told them about going to New York the following week to appear in the United States Customs Court to contest the duty assessed on jewelry and personal property brought over from France. Customs commissioner Camp had just upheld a ruling that she was an American resident through marriage, and must pay duty on all purchases in France. His decision was supported by Secretary of the Treasury Andrew Mellon, prompting Ganna's unequivocal reaction, spiced with feminist overtones: "It is no longer a question of paying duty, or even of residence, but of the rights of womanhood."

The authorities had placed a value of about $2,500,000 on the goods, demanding payment of import duty amounting to eighty per cent on the jewels and seventy per cent on clothing, including the well-traveled Cochran sable coat. In refusing to pay a fine of about a million dollars, Madame said she had decided to fight for her own rights and those of other women. A statement to this effect was issued through Harold's lawyers, and he produced an affidavit corroborating his wife's claim of living abroad. It was the first Ganna knew about a law which determined, not only a wife's residential status, but also applied to the question of suffrage. It incensed her to learn that American women could not even vote in a different state or city from where their husbands lived.

"My object in this world," she told the Chicago reporters, "is to think new thoughts." This impassioned plea fell on deaf ears, but if she would not talk about the leonine interruption to her recital in the national capital, the hard-nosed journalists insisted on knowing if Mrs. McCormick would stay in the city for a while and take her place in Chicago's high society. Ganna refused to be drawn on that as well, leaving Harold to answer them.

"How do I know what she will do?" he responded looking confused. "I hope so, but it's up to you to find out for me if she's going to stay here. America - yes. Chicago? I don't know."

That evening was spent at the Civic Opera, where, across the auditorium accompanied by her acolytes, sat Edith Rockefeller McCormick glowering at Ganna and Harold.

The much-anticipated Chicago début was postponed because of influenza, which sent Walska to bed for three days. The couple spent Christmas together quietly, with her concert rebooked for January 19, 1929. At last, Madame was about to perform as a celebrity in the McCormicks home city after the miserable failure of her *Zaza* engagement some eight years before. A measure of the public interest surrounding the appearance came from cowboy philosopher Will Rogers, whose homespun wit on national radio and in the press debunking social pretensions, made America laugh. While she languished in bed recovering from the flu, he quipped in his syndicated newspaper column that something must be seriously wrong because two days had passed without any news about Madame Ganna Walska.

Orchestra Hall was packed, leading to accusations of Harold papering the house by offering free tickets to anyone who could be persuaded to take them. There were no box holder or subscription lists, which made it difficult to know exactly who attended the afternoon recital, though society reporters managed to identify a scattering of Chicago's socialites. The dignity of the occasion was threatened before the start by a mouse seen scampering across the platform, but no rodent upstart – not even Walt Disney's new cartoon sensation, the anthropomorphic Mickey – could upstage Madame's dramatic entrance.

Appearing in the spotlight wearing a simple white trailing gown with close-fitting long sleeves, whose classic simplicity was emphasized by a total absence of jewelry, Walska's program drew heavily on the German repertoire, all sung from scores with a few French and Italian art songs added for good measure. An encore in English, however, brought the house down. Liza Lehmann's "If No One Ever Marries Me, (and I don't see why they should)" displayed a nice sense of humor for an audience better acquainted with the performer's multiple marriages than the refined pleasures of German lieder. They were warm in their applause throughout, and volcanically so at the end when a procession of uniformed flower bearers carried baskets of roses down the center aisle and Madame gave several encores surrounded by the massed floral display. When it was all over, a crowd milled around her automobile in front of Orchestra Hall.

Most satisfying of all, was next day's press reaction. To Ganna's delight - and Harold's undoubted relief - the critics seemed to be won over at last. The *Herald-Examiner* headlined on its news page: "Ganna Sings, Scoffers Stay To Praise Her" and the paper's music critic, Glenn Dillard Gunn, headed his piece: "Dr. Gunn Lets Out A Secret: Ganna Can Sing!"

"For this woman has something more potent than voice and the fine art of song. She has something more potent than beauty, though of that her dower is justly famed. Her profile seen against any background is a perfect cameo. The harshest critic could not look on it unkindly. Her eager friendliness, her unaffected charm, the genuine kindliness of her smile and the unmistakable sincerity of her lyric address won her public."

The *World's* headline stated:

"Walska In Recital Ends Chicago Jinx.
Forgets Operatic Setback,

Gets Fine Reception."

Praise was heaped upon praise and the Chicago *Post*'s K. Carleton Hackett wrote:

"Ganna Walska at her best in song recital. The voice, however, was much stronger than we had been led to expect ... "

Maurice Rosenfeld of the *News*:

"Her voice is wide in range, it has considerable power ... "

Hermann Devries in the *Evening American*:

"Her first song dispelled any further doubt. Mme. Walska can and does sing. Moreover, she sings artistically."

Ganna was in seventh heaven imagining she'd arrived - albeit late - in the demanding, competitive, ruthless world of professional singing, particularly after a bizarre and much-quoted incident in Washington, D.C. earlier, which had threatened to turn her current concert appearances into a tour de farce.

During a busy round of social engagements in the national capital, Walska had been resting in her hotel suite before attending a dinner at the Polish Embassy when the phone rang.

"Yes?"

"This is the White House calling."

It had to be a joke, and Ganna was on the point of disconnecting when the female voice added, "The President and Mrs. Coolidge would be delighted to have you join them at luncheon tomorrow."

It must be a reporter trying to get an exclusive, she assumed.

"Hello, is that Madame Walska? This is the President's secretary calling from the White House. Are you there?"

The message was repeated while a similar incident sprang to Ganna's mind as she listened. When Charlie Chaplin returned to his hometown London as the most famous star of the silent screen, he was feted in unprecedented scenes of fan worship. One morning, while still in bed, he received a telephone call inviting him to lunch with the Prince of Wales. He regarded it as the ultimate accolade: the former working-class foundling entertained by the future monarch of the British Empire. But it was a hoax.

"Madame Walska, can you hear me?"

"Yes, perfectly well," she replied, making sure not to be naive like Chaplin. "This is Madame Walska speaking and I'm very honored by your kind invitation, but at a loss to know what to say because I'm engaged for lunch tomorrow at the French Embassy."

"An invitation from the President of the United States would normally take precedence."

"Yes, yes, I understand. Only I wonder - you see, this luncheon is in my honor and to meet Ambassador Claudel; the invitations have already gone out." Walska was reluctant to miss this opportunity of meeting Paul Claudel, a distinguished diplomat as well as a towering figure in French literature as poet, essayist and symbolist playwright.

"Just a moment please," the woman on the other end of the line responded. "Please hold the line while I speak with the President."

Ganna was no nearer knowing if the call was genuine or not, but before she could contact the hotel manager, the voice came back on the line.

"As a courtesy to the ambassador, whom he knows well, the President bids me say he does not wish to deprive him of your company and asks you to luncheon the day after instead."

"I'm very sorry," Walska responded, "because right after luncheon at the French Embassy I must prepare for my concert and then leave for Chicago immediately after."

She was put on hold again until being informed that the President had gone to dine and asked if she could be reached at eight that evening. Walska agreed to wait until then, but no return call eventuated, and she felt vindicated by her skepticism. A few minutes later, while passing through the lobby on her way to dinner, she saw the hotel's duty manager and complained that she had left instructions for no calls to go to her room.

"I am awfully sorry, Madame, but as it was the White House . . . "

"Then they may call me at the Polish Embassy if the President decides to ring again," she snapped back and swept out to her waiting automobile.

When Walska arrived for dinner, the Polish Ambassador, Mr. Ciechanowski, was on the telephone speaking to President Coolidge's private secretary. "Oh here is Madame now," he interrupted the caller, handing over the instrument and she heard he now-familiar voice saying that President and Mrs. Coolidge would be very happy to receive her at noon tomorrow before the French Embassy engagement, which would allow plenty of time for her lunch and a rest before the concert. It was not an ideal solution, but Walska could hardly snub the President of the United States.

Next day she spent a pleasant hour at Pennsylvania Avenue, and the President presented her with a huge bouquet of roses on departure. Then, after a stimulating lunch in the company of M. Claudel, followed by a short rest, Ganna arrived at the theater for a rehearsal, where a grand piano and music stand faced the empty auditorium. As her accompanist played the introduction to one of her songs, Madame opened her mouth to sing *sotto voce* when a sound like thunder drowned her out. She let out a scream and was on the point of fleeing the stage when the theater manager appeared in the wings making a calming gesture with his hands to explain there was a lion backstage - safely locked in a cage. The animal was appearing nightly as part of a vaudeville act, and could not be taken away between shows. Walska was assured that the cage would be kept covered during her afternoon performance when the animal usually slept soundly. She was not convinced, but in the cause of art continued rehearsing - and so did the lion. Ganna would recall in her autobiography:

"It was a curious duo in which the voice of the jungle, easily able to cover any Wagnerian *fortissimo*, from time to time accompanied lace-like delicate Mozart music. It might even be said that Mr. Lion was a bit of a critic, for when my interpretation was not right – and His Majesty often considered it was not right – he would start to roar stronger than ever."

This *outré* incident produced several headlines for the evening newspapers: "Lion Outsings Beauty," "Ganna Loses in Voice Duet with Roaring Lion," "Ganna Walska Forced to Quit When Lion Sings" and "Beauty Routed By Bass-Singing Leo The Lion."

Her recital, advertised as "a singer with personality"- perhaps to differentiate her from the impresario's more-established artists like Amelita Galli-Curci, John McCormack, Frances Alda and Mary Garden, went ahead without further incident or interruption. The Washington, D.C. *News* wrote the next day: "The voice is there, a voice of nice timbre and some power," the *Herald*, however, referred to faulty breath control and singing off-key, and the *Post* remarked pointedly that music lovers in the audience had found it more profitable to use their opera glasses than their ears. The beast received the lion's share of the notices with Walska's associate artist, tenor Giovanni Martini, judged the better singer. Beauty, alas, finished a poor third.

Flirting with Feminism
1929

Ganna's oddball experience in the national capital, followed by the Chicago conquest, were left behind, as she prepared for her next public appearance: in the United States Customs Court, New York, contesting the duty charged on fifteen trunks of personal effects brought over from France the previous September. On January 22, 1929, dressed demurely, but radiating an aura of celebrity, Madame enlivened the normally stuffy court proceedings by facing Justices George M. Young and Genevieve R. Cline, informing them through her attorney, Phelan Beale, that the payment of duty was only a secondary consideration. Her fight was against the ruling that her husband, living in Chicago, automatically made her a resident of the United States and liable for duty on goods purchased abroad. Walska testified under oath that, while being on friendly terms with Mr. McCormick, she maintained a separate home in Paris, and came to the United States only for visits, revealing that she had both a city and country residence in France - the latter a recently-purchased château near Versailles - and owned a theater, perfume factory and shop.

Examined by Beale, Ganna explained that she married Harold McCormick in Paris in 1922 and had been in the United States only twice since then. She reiterated that her home was in France and said she had no intention of living permanently in the United States. The government was represented by three attorneys, one of whom cross-examined her. Norris Higginbotham, the Assistant U.S. Attorney-General asked:

"Does your husband contribute to your support?"

"No, I pay all my expenses," Ganna replied confidently, and not entirely truthfully. "I pay the taxes and assessments on my Paris properties."

"When you returned to Paris the first time after your marriage did you tell your husband that you intended returning there to live?"

"I was living in Paris then and I went back. I will always live there because of the interest in my works."

"What are your works?"

"My perfume factory, my country home and my theater,"

"Have you a separate estate of your own?"

"Yes."

After hearing additional testimony, in which Madame managed to promote the concert she would soon give at Carnegie Hall before returning to France, the court ordered the attorneys for both sides to prepare briefs and file them within thirty days.

The attention surrounding her appearance was also a boost for the National Woman's Party (NWP) whose principles Ganna supported as a member through her friendship with Doris Stevens. Eight years before, the NWP began a state-by-state campaign which led to the first congressional hearings on the Equal Rights Amendment (ERA) seeking to give men and women "equal rights throughout the United States and every place subject to its jurisdiction." Stevens had gone to Havana in 1928 on behalf of the NWP, to place the proposed ERA legislation for discussion before the representatives of Western Hemisphere nations to gain official representation at the Sixth International Conference of American States. She succeeded, and the Inter-American Commission of Women (IACW) was created, with Doris Stevens named chair of an influential organization at the forefront of promoting and protecting the rights of women.

By 1929, much work remained to be done by the NWP, their efforts weakened by claiming to represent all women who still faced barriers in a male-dominated society. Madame added her support with radio broadcasts and press interviews, carefully briefed by Stevens and her colleagues, to insist that legislation based on the remnants of common law from pioneering days must be changed. "Such laws did not seem to me compatible with the great freedom this country stands for," she commented.

Her American agents - the Ganna Walska Management Company run by George Djamgaroff, seized this opportunity to issue a publicity release combining their founder's business, political and performing interests. Stressing Walska's support for equality, it announced that she hoped to speak on behalf of the NWP at the state capital Albany, adding the bold prediction "that in a few years from now, after the Equal Rights Bill has passed the various state legislatures, it will be adopted by the United States Congress as an amendment to the Constitution. The company publicity was careful to emphasize, however, that Madame's crusade for women was not all-consuming because music dominated her life, and she was working hard in preparation for a Carnegie Hall appearance on February 12, when she would be giving "the best that is in me."

Many of the audience filling the famous concert hall were attracted by the extensive press and radio coverage portraying Walska as a modern woman, as suggested by her press agent:

"Because of her beauty, her intellect, her tremendous vitality, Ganna Walska belongs to that type of modern women who are dynamic but feminine, women who work hard but remain charming, women who withal retain their sense of perspective and their good sense of humor."

Harold McCormick shared one of the boxes at the concert with his wife's friend from Paris, the Grand Duke Alexander, who was making a lecture tour of the United States speaking about pre-Bolshevik Russia. Critic Olin Downes, who had interviewed the singer in Boston during her previous concert tour, and now worked for the *New* York *Times*, reported that the audience was brilliant, "somewhat in the French sense of the word: in its brilliant and curious assortment of people, many of them distinguished in other affairs, who have nothing to do with music and who seldom or never attend a song recital."

Walska proceeded to delight them by her presence - whatever the motives for attending - and they found her first New York recital an entertaining spectacle. Opinions varied about its musical quality, although there were some reasonable notices for a program including Giordano's "Caro Mio Ben," an aria from Bach's "'Coffee' Cantata" with flute obbligato, Scarlatti's "Le Violette," Schubert's "Die Forelle," Schumann's "Der Nussbaum" and arias from Mozart and Rimsky-Korsakov operas.

"The voice heard yesterday afternoon was sufficiently large for any musical purpose, and it was quite as good at the end of the list as at the beginning."
W.J. Henderson, the *Sun*, New York.

"Mme. Walska disclosed a soprano voice of professional caliber and range, uncommonly sweet and appealing in its native quality. Moreover, her production of tone was conspicuously full and unconstricted."
Pitts Sanborn, *the Telegram*, New York.

". . . a singer who has never mastered the fundamentals of her task, and has leaped for glory before it was sensible or prudent to do so."

Olin Downes, the *New York Times*.

Walska's lengthy sojourn in the United States was further extended by what she regarded as a vital cause: fighting for "truly equal rights for women." It was the one performance she would never dream of canceling, in spite of being anxious to return to France and supervise the decoration of her recently-acquired bijou château, as well as attending to increased responsibilities at Le Théâtre des Champs-Elysées. For the moment, however, Albany had first call on her time.

She traveled to upstate New York on Wednesday, February 20, to join members of the NWP and the New York State League of Women Voters for the new bill's introduction, surprised how young the American politicians looked, "accustomed as I had been to the greybeards of the French legislative bodies." Ganna had a private meeting with Governor Franklin D. Roosevelt, just beginning his term after winning the 1928 election by a narrow margin as a Reform Democrat, and then the women's representatives argued their case in the state legislative chamber for three hours. They urged the adoption of measures to extend jury service to females, permit establishing their own domicile for registering and voting, and allow equal guardianship rights with men. Ganna was unquestionably the star performer in this testimony, supporting the question of domicile: the measure that affected her most. Attorney Phelan Beale provided some elegantly-phrased observations for his client, including:

"The proposition that a wife is an independent thinking being whose wishes are not subordinate to those of her husband is now almost universally accepted as axiomatic."

Members of the Senate and Assembly Judiciary Committees, together with onlookers filling the chamber to capacity, listened attentively to Madame Walska, as if attending one of her concerts, while she explained to them the difficulties of leading a life of separation. "I should like to urge you to amend the bill so that it will include legacy rulings and taxation," she read, with all eyes on her, looking up from typewritten notes from time to time as she punctuated her paragraphs with a flashing smile, which was returned by several of the presiding officers.

"I take the liberty," she proclaimed in one of the best performances of her problematic career, "of bringing my own case before your attention so that I may perhaps show you how unjust is this point of law which forces a woman to reside legally wherever her husband may happen to be."

With measured tone and a modestly theatrical delivery, Walska looked ravishing dressed in a gray ensemble decorated with an apple-green scarf as she continued to read the attorney's text in her cute mid-European accent. Others were waiting their turns to speak, but seemed happy to remain seated until Madame finished. She introduced a concept that was pure Beale in its Irish-American levity.

"It would seem as if this domicile ruling were deliberately trying to deny the old physical law that a body cannot be in two places at the same time. For although I live continuously in my own home in Paris, although I conduct all my business affairs in that city, yet legally I am still living in Chicago. Is that not strange and a bit ridiculous?"

Ganna paused to raise an eyebrow, look around the chamber, and take a deep breath before launching into her concluding remark:

"I have always been eager to see all discriminations against my sex removed, and I sincerely hope that New York will follow the liberal example set by her sister State of New Jersey and abolish this old-fashioned and unjust domicile ruling."

At this time, some of the more progressive reform movements were challenging the policies of the NWP, censuring motives that seemed likely to assist only professional women, who tended to show less concern for their working-class sisters burdened by labor laws and enduring sweat-shop conditions in factories and stores across the nation. Many young women raised in the Jazz Age, with freedoms unthinkable before the 1920s, thought of feminism as old-fashioned, reminiscent of suffragette days, and Madame Ganna Walska must have seemed a strange figure to spearhead such a cause, given her widespread notoriety as a man-eating gold digger, not to mention the foreign accent. But she did look - and sound - like a woman with a mission, confirmed the next day by the *New York Times* headline: "Walska Urges Bill for Equal Rights."

A few weeks later her name appeared again in bold print on their front-page for April 11, 1929: "Gov. Roosevelt Signs Separate Domicile Bill; Ganna Walska Aided Women in Fight For It". The New York *Sun* had already announced, however, "Walska's Albany Fight Is In Vain," because it failed to remedy her original complaint. As finally drafted, the bill allowed women to choose their own domicile only for voting and holding office, and by then Madame Walska was back home in France.

It was April in Paris, with massed tulips in the gardens of the Tuileries, chestnuts in blossom, short, sharp showers alternating with dazzling sunshine, birdsong competing with the honking traffic on rue de Rivoli, and lovers strolling hand-in-hand in air that should have been soft with springtime promise instead of choking exhaust fumes. Every cliché of American popular song lyrics was in evidence as Walska's thoughts turned to a freer lifestyle than the one she'd been leading in the heart of town. Living on rue de Lubeck was a convenient - and certainly swanky - address, a pleasant stroll from her theater and a brief drive to the perfume boutique on rue de la Paix, but she was finding the town house increasingly claustrophobic and missed contact with nature. Her Parisian friends regularly spent time away from the fast and furious capital at their houses on the Côte d'Azur during winter then flocked to Deauville, Brittany or Biarritz for the summer season. There was also the tendency for wealthy Americans to own a château for socializing in the countryside, within easy driving distance of the capital.

Ganna had followed their example before leaving on her recent extended sojourn in the United States by acquiring a property of considerable charm on the edge of the forest of Rambouillet, not far from Versailles in the sleepy village of Galluis, set among rolling wheat fields. This was a serene and settled landscape, at peace with itself, and full of historical connections because of proximity to the former hunting lands of the French monarchy, and near to where the President of the Republic kept his country residence. It was a short drive from Montfort-l'Amaury, the home of France's greatest composer, Maurice Ravel, until he died in late 1928, and not far from the sixteenth century Château du Mesnil-St-Denis owned by Herman Gade of Lake Forest, Illinois, who bought the magnificent building and park during 1929 to entertain his friends with lavish hospitality.

The bijou Château de Galluis (previous page) had been marketed for a reasonable price, and was in such an excellent state of repair that Ganna agreed to buy as soon as she saw the property; admiring its tasteful decoration and the fact that little alteration was needed for her to move in. A formal tree-lined avenue approached the main building, and the extensive grounds would be an intriguing challenge for someone whose only previous experience of gardening had been tending window boxes in Manhattan. Walska planned to spend weekends at Galluis, and she prepared to show-off her new acquisition at a housewarming party during October 1929. In the meantime, she would continue to attend to business affairs in town and take regular singing lessons with the person who had become the most constant man in her life.

Ganna attributed her "musical initiation" from when Alec Cochran first introduced her to Walther Straram, claiming extravagantly that everything she was - artistically, musically and literally speaking - was due to him. "He was certainly one of the greatest musicians and men of highest intellectual attainment I have ever encountered until then," she would state in her autobiography, and she told friends how privileged she felt to own a fine symphony orchestra - named the Orchestre des Concerts Straram – based at the Théâtre des Champs-Elysées which, Walska boasted, was one of the greatest in either hemisphere under the baton of Straram. Certainly, Igor Stravinsky's own recording of "The Rite of Spring" during 1929 confirms that the Champs-

Elysées musicians were top-rate.

The maestro in charge of the players, as well as Ganna's voice, whom she called playfully her *bébé génial,* made sure to convince Madame that she was a considerable *artiste,* while carefully protecting his own reputation by not allowing her to sing too often with his/her orchestra in her/his theater. Walther Straram had a chameleon-like ability to be accepted in whatever he did, and wherever he appeared. With his glistening slicked-back hair, a Toscanini-style mustache and wearing pince-nez, a newspaper reported that he had "gimlet-like boring eyes, a curious walk, long, crooked fingers - an Englishman in England, a Frenchman in France, but whose birthplace was in Syria."

It was whispered around town that, because of his influence over Madame, any friends who dared to say a word against him were ostracized. It was a fate that happened to the cousin of the late Arcadie d'Eingorn, and led to conflict with Ganna's faithful American manager, George Djamgaroff, among others. Rumors said that this musical Rasputin had wrecked Madame's relationship with Alexander Smith Cochran and threatened to usurp her current marriage; it was tittle-tattle that continued to be denied on both sides of the Atlantic, but only added to speculation that Harold McCormick was on the point of suing for divorce because of his wife's omnipresent mentor.

After taking complete control of the financial and artistic affairs of her theater, Walska could have been expected to use such cultural clout to further her own career, but she was sensible enough to realize that operatic fame had slipped beyond her reach and wisely refrained from taking any further leading roles. Acting was different, and on June 1, 1929 she starred in an "historical sketch" commissioned by her and described as a comedy in three acts. *La Castiglione* was staged at the Comédie des Champs-Elysées - the drama theater within the main building - in a charity performance to benefit war orphans. Its subject was the beautiful Italian countess of the title who bewitched Napoleon III - among others - and this costume play of the Second Empire gave Ganna another opportunity to show off her gowns, jewels and acting ability.

The press were briefed that her début as an actress was the realization of a secret ambition. "A singer's talents are not restricted to opera or concerts," she explained to them. "As a matter of fact, a thorough artist in the operatic realm should be perfectly at home in the theater. Good singers always should be good actors or actresses. They generally are." As a feature of the performance, Madame wore a costume and jewels once owned by the real Castiglione, which intrigued Parisian high society and filled the house. They included the celebrity conductor and Ganna's probable lover Leopold Stokowski, and the American screenwriter, playwright and author Anita Loos, whose comic novel "Gentlemen Prefer Blondes," first published in 1925, remained a runaway bestseller. Generous applause greeted Ganna Walska's acting and the success of *La Castiglione* generated talk about taking the show to Broadway in an English translation.

Shortly before leaving the United States after her last visit, Ganna had read in a newspaper that her third husband was seriously ill and living at the Savoy Plaza in New York under constant medical care. They lost contact after she married Harold, apart from a brief correspondence during 1926, but she cherished the time when Alexander Smith Cochran had bombarded her in Paris with endless bunches of sweetheart roses: his way of courting at arm's length. After learning of his sorry state she arranged to send him anonymously a bunch of the same type of roses every day, avoiding recognition by using the less-fashionable florists along Sixth and Lexington instead of the smarter Fifth Avenue establishments, where his name and her custom would have aroused curiosity. He never knew who sent them and died from tuberculosis on June 19, 1929, aged 55, at beautiful Saranac Lake, the fashionable vacation and health care village in New York State. The *Times* announced in a headline "Fortune For Mme. Walska," quoting a statement from her Paris attorney, Charles Loeb that she would now come into possession of three million dollars, which had been written into their divorce settlement. He must have mistakenly added a zero to his estimate, because Ganna would receive only the capital from her Cochran trust fund, and remained doubtful about benefitting at all from the Cochran estate:

"The newspapers erroneously reported that he had willed me three million dollars. I did not believe it. It would not have been like him, for it would have been an indication of human feeling. Knowing that I needed money to give great music the world, he would have been doing a consciously normal

172

act. But, if he had been capable of such a gesture, he would not have died away from me so quietly in life, and I would have mourned him only on his death instead of having done so years before." It was a bitter epitaph, even for a marriage demonstrably not made in heaven.

The winter season at the Champs-Elysées had been a brilliant success while Walska was away in the United States, and she was determined to add her personality to what remained of the 1928-29 attractions before next summer's break. She supervised every last detail of the Bayreuth Festival's visit for the *Ring* cycle - the first time Siegfried Wagner had allowed this production of his father's masterpiece to leave Bavaria. Passers-by on Avenue Montaigne were mystified to hear trumpets sounding the "Siegfried" call from the roof of the theater, personally directed by Walska overcoming her fear of heights by insisting on directing the musicians at just the right moment.

"Uninitiated in the Wagner tradition," she explained to friends, "people on the street would stop and look up as though they were hearing sounds direct from heaven."

Performances began at five o'clock, with dinner for the general patrons served during intermission in the theater's lobby, while a horseshoe table was set up in Madame's private studio for her special guests on the gala opening night. They totaled forty, including the German ambassador, Herr Leopold von Hoesch on her right, and to the left sat the French Vice-Premier and Minister of Justice, Louis Barthou, known as an ardent Wagnerist. Opposite was Paul Painlevé, a former Prime Minister of France with the reputation of being a less-than-successful politician, though nobody doubted his love of music.

Inviting the German ambassador was a daring act of diplomacy on Walska's part because it was more than a decade since the armistice, yet protocol did not allow him to receive members of the French government at his embassy. He had sought Madame's assistance in sounding out the ministers for Justice and War about accepting a formal invitation to a dinner in honor of the Bayreuth artists, and her persuasion succeeded. Barthou had responded by saying he saw no problem, and Painlevé tactfully informed her that he would be delighted to accept the invitation "as a worshiper of Wagner, but not as a War minister!" Thanks to the outstanding production of *Der Ring des Niebelungen* and Walska's social

173

wiles, French government ministers were allowed to cross the threshold of the German embassy in Paris again after an interval of fifteen years.

Her theater may have been an artistic success, but the cosmetics business established to support it, faltered. "Making Dollars From Scents," as an American newspaper headline so neatly described Ganna's enterprise, had been more difficult than anyone anticipated, with sales in Paris disappointing. Things might have been different in America, as George Djamgaroff informed her from New York, if the company increased its working capital and Madame honored a contractual obligation to make a concert tour as publicity for the products bearing her name. The cities where this was needed most urgently he named as Boston, Detroit, Rochester, Dayton, St. Louis, Omaha and Los Angeles - the last-named being the company's best account. Djamgaroff warned that failure for her to appear on stage there and in St. Louis would mean losing more than $6,000:

"Perhaps if you think this over you may realize why I begged you to give me your entire time this fall in order to put over the perfume business as well as to establish you in this country as a serious artist. You will probably not recall that you accepted and then afterwards refused to accept the concert appearances prepared for you. So I hope you will realize the position you are always putting me in."

By October of 1929, Walska and Straram were well into their 1929/30 season at the Champs-Elysées which promised to be more exciting than ever. There would be fifty performances by L'Opéra Privé de Paris, twelve by the Opéra-Comique, an international season including visits by the Pavlova troupe, the Turin Opera, Leningrad Ballet, and Wagner performances by the Dresden Opera. Richard Strauss would direct a festival of his own music with the Straram orchestra, and there was to be a Debussy season conducted by Toscanini. Visiting orchestras were announced as the Berlin Philharmonic, the Boston Symphony and La Scala; there would also be appearances by L'Opéra de Strasbourg, the Dusseldorf Opera presenting Berg's *Wozzek*, and Le Théâtre de Baden-Baden. Recitals, drama and cinema completed an astounding schedule that any of the great performing arts centers in the world would have been proud to present.

There had been speculation in America about Walska's next concert tour to embrace, it was said, thirty or even forty cities over the winter months, including the ones Djamgaroff wanted her to visit for cosmetic and perfume promotion, but Madame vigorously rejected the punishing itinerary, saying only that she might agree to sing at four or five major venues, but a tour of "the provinces" was out of the question. The press caught up with Harold McCormick in California, where he was visiting his newly-married daughter, Mathilde, and denied any knowledge of a tour by his wife. He also refused to comment on the persistent rumors that he'd settled a large amount of money on her and was arranging for a divorce.

His psychotic brother Stanley was still incarcerated - sometimes restrained in a straitjacket - as the prisoner of Riven Rock estate near Santa Barbara. If the press of the time referred to his disability at all, it was in the most general terms as a "madness" because it was accepted as an unwritten rule by journalists that "millionaires don't wash their dirty linen in public," thus suppressing the real story behind the McCormick family tragedy. Harold's visit to see his daughter coincided with preparing a defense against Stanley's long-suffering wife Katharine, who was pressing a legal claim for the right to care personally for her husband, supported by an imposing array of medical experts, but opposed by Harold and his sister, Mrs. Anita McCormick Blaine of Chicago.

Their fight centered on actions to keep the patient under the care of Dr. Edward Kempf, a psychoanalyst brought from New York on annual salary of $120,000, with Harold and Mrs. Blaine asserting that he was succeeding in steering Stanley "out of the shadows." Katharine alleged that she was barred from Riven Rock because of Kempf complaining that her presence interfered with the treatment of her husband's serious condition, described as malignant compulsion neurosis - or in layman's terms, violent sexual mania. Ganna was kept informed of these developments and Harold also sent her details of the live music programs given recently at Riven Rock. "This is the kind of music Stanley listens to," he scribbled in pencil on a list of private concerts, which included several selections from operetta, a medley from *Rigoletto* and the slow movement from Beethoven's fifth symphony.

Ganna's projected concert tour of the United States never materialized, in spite of Djamgaroff's urging, and he was forced to seek a buyer for the ailing American division of the perfume and cosmetics company, while across the Atlantic Madame threw a stylish château-warming party at Galluis. The invitation list included celebrities from the world of music and show business greeted by a fanfare of hunting horns at the imposing main gates of her estate. Guests strolled along the sylvan paths of the park in the company of strutting peacocks to the music of string quartets stationed at strategic points. There was also the rather surreal sight of Isadora Duncan's dance troupe, clad in diaphanous white tunics, cavorting barefooted like Minoan maidens in and out of the shrubberies.

Among the international set greeted by Madame wearing a beige afternoon tea gown with matching hat decorated with ostrich plumes, were her good friends the fabulously wealthy Maharaja of Indore and his new American wife, the former Nancy Anne Miller of Seattle, who were about to sail for India to take up residence there. Also present in the Louis XV salon with its painted piano and crystal chandelier, was Hollywood's archetypal Frenchman Adolphe Menjou, surrounded by a group of admiring female fans. He was taking time out to star in one of the first talkies to be made in France and cut a dash at this gathering, immediately recognizable from his movie image as a boulevardier, but whose acting craft screened his origins as the son of a restaurant owner in Pittsburgh, Pennsylvania.

It was a sophisticated party, full of style, wit and well-being. Ganna was the perfect hostess, making sure that her guests were plied with plenty of food, drink and entertainment to make the occasion memorable. Eleven years after the end of the Great War and almost a third of the way into the twentieth century, the formula for peace and prosperity for all seemed to have been found. But, with so many lifestyles of Ganna's guests based on Wall Street's dizzying ascent, and by buying on margin as if there were no tomorrow, many had unknowingly mortgaged their futures and perhaps the hereafter as well.

A Date with Mussolini
1930-1931

The dizzy succession of plunging stock prices on so called Black Thursday, Black Monday and Black Friday (October 24 - 29, 1929) made little impact on Ganna Walska's fortune because much of it was now in jewelry, property and cash, though her perfume and cosmetics business on both sides of the Atlantic, already in dire straits, would become victim to any prolonged recession. As far as she was concerned what happened was in the hands of Buddha; life would continue as if the storm clouds hanging ominously over Wall Street were only a passing shower. There were other considerations on her mind, with Ganna deciding that the brilliant party in the Arcadian splendor of Galluis should be her social swan song. She complained to friends of being tired of wasting energy on "empty chatter, superfluous repetitions, unimportant statements, low vibrating gossip" which consumed her vital thoughts and diverted creative energy from its proper channels.

She remained fascinated by people in positions of power, perhaps by having four of them as husbands, and admired another who intrigued her more than most. Benito Mussolini was rarely off the headlines these days, raising her curiosity about his motivation. She remembered reading accounts of his March on Rome to form a Fascist government in October, 1922, the bombardment of Corfu Town in August, 1923 and the more recent reports of attempts on the Italian dictator's life, which made her all the more interested in his headlong pursuit of power. "In the early days of Mussolini's reign," Ganna noted in her diary, "stories often appeared in the press of Il Duce's fear of being assassinated. There was also much condemnation of his suppression of newspapers, magazines or books not favorable to Fascism. In France especially he had a very hostile press."

This had less to do with political science: more that here was a big man doing a big job and succeeding. Ganna had paid similar attention to Vladimir Ilyich Lenin, but his lackluster personality never appealed to her like the Italian's charisma. When the American portrait sculptor and socialite, Nancy Cox-McCormack, exhibited a bronze bust of Mussolini in Paris, it set Madame wondering if it was the flattering image of an intensely vain man or an accurate representation of a visionary. She wanted to find out by paying him a visit.

It seemed that every famous visitor to the Italian capital - Hollywood screen stars, prize fighters, artists, authors, press barons, politicians - wished to call on Il Duce for a regulation three-minute meeting, many coming away with good impressions of what he was doing for his country. The busy leader was receiving fewer people these days, however, and getting to see him proved more difficult than arranging an audience with the Pope, which Walska had managed to do two years before, witnessed by Pius XI's signed photo in a silver frame as a souvenir displayed on her piano at rue de Lubeck. She knew Italy's ambassador to France from entertaining him at an Italian festival staged in her theater, and asked him about the possibility of a private meeting with Mussolini. The devastatingly handsome Count Gaetano Manzoni advised her in a formal note from his first secretary:

"You have asked His Excellency Mussolini to receive you on your next visit to Rome. I am charged to inform you that he will see you with pleasure. Please let me know a few days before your trip so I can notify Rome."

Ganna replied that she was ready to depart at a moment's notice, and the compliant Count confirmed the time and date:

"Chère Madame, Next Monday, the 20th of January, at five o' clock in the afternoon His Excellency Monsieur Mussolini will have the pleasure to receive you at Palazzo Venezia in Rome."

Manzoni wrote on his attached calling card, "*ce papier vous facilitera le passage à la frontière.*"

Walska had her maid pack two bags and took along a large selection of newspapers and magazines to read during the overnight train journey from Paris to Rome in a first-class sleeper. Several journals contained articles ridiculing the self-styled Napoléon she was going to meet, and increasingly nervous about crossing the border into Italy, she considered throwing any anti-fascist material out of the train window, as it was sure to be confiscated and her entry to Italy denied. She drifted off to sleep early, expecting to be awakened in the middle of the night for passport formalities, but there were none and she awoke the next morning after a long and refreshing rest to discover the express only an hour or so from the Eternal City.

There were no passport or customs checks at the railway station, either, and Walska noticed that the French socialist and anti-fascist journal *L'Oeuvre* was freely on sale at the Grand Hotel where she planned to stay for a week. In fact, everything seemed perfectly normal: nothing like the rogue state ruled by a posturing Caesar characterized by some of the writers in Paris. She made a mental note to tell her friends at home that they were too quick to judge the Italian political scene without first-hand knowledge. There was a note waiting for Ganna at the hotel informing her that the location of her audience with Mussolini was changed to the Palazzo Chigi, and warned not to be disappointed if it lasted for only two or three minutes because that was Il Duce's limit these days; even ambassadors from nations sympathetic to his régime were only granted a maximum of fifteen minutes.

With a couple of days free in Rome before the meeting, she paid a visit to Baron Fassini, a former diplomat who had once discussed life in China with Puccini and reputedly lent him a music-box playing authentic folk melodies which were adapted by the composer for *Turandot*, his last opera. During dinner with the baron there were long delays between courses, and fearing they would be late for the theater that evening Walska begged her host to hurry the service. Alberto Fassini occupied the ground floor of a *palazzo* in central Rome whose upper stories were rented out: one to the President of the Senate and the other to Benito Mussolini. Those quarters lacked cooking facilities, with meals prepared below, in Fassini's kitchen. That evening, the head of state was dining at the same time, and, as Walska's host had no wish to be responsible for his life in the current atmosphere of assassination threats, the food for each course was vetted by a large dog. If the animal showed no immediate ill effects, it was allowed to be served at the dictator's table.

On the appointed day, Madame arrived fifteen minutes early at the chilly sixteenth-century Palazzo Chigi overlooking windswept Piazza Colonna, and, having been warned of tight security, discovered to her amazement that there was almost none. Fur-coated, she entered the Ministry of Foreign Affairs without being

180

challenged, received half-hearted salutes from the guards on duty, and then found herself alone in a deserted courtyard, with no indication of which flight of steps to take. "It looked like an old abandoned house," she remembered. "I waited a minute or two, utterly perplexed, and then somebody came down a stairway, ignoring me and walking toward the street." She ran after him to ask where Signor Mussolini was to be found, and he pointed back to the building's interior. Walska rushed to an upper level, stepped out along a seemingly endless corridor with her high-heeled footsteps echoing from the stone floor and walls, while uniformed guards stood outside closed doors smoking cigarettes and nodding as she passed. Nobody asked her business, and she finally addressed one of them in Italian, explaining breathlessly that she had an appointment with His Excellency.

"Dov'è il capo del governo?"

He pointed to a heavy door in a dark alcove. Beyond was another gloomy passage leading to a room dominated by dark oil paintings in heavy gilt frames where one of Il Duce's ministers confirmed that His Excellency would see her at five o'clock, as arranged, and Ganna was ushered into the leader's presence a few minutes later.

He got up from an enormous desk to welcome her, pointing to a chair and moving a second one to sit beside her. The first thing Ganna noticed was his apparently unshaven face.

"Mon Dieu, il n'est pas rasé!" But she was mistaken, realizing later: "He being very dark, even freshly shaved, looked black. And he did not use powder after shaving as many men with dark complexions do." Mussolini sat relaxed, with one arm resting on the back of the desk, his dark eyes occasionally fixing on his visitor, and speaking in a soft, almost inaudible voice, which was disconcerting because she had heard that he enjoyed taking the initiative by playing the bully.

Her allotted three minutes stretched to three-quarters of an hour, during which she was dazzled by the man's aura while discussing a wide range of non-political subjects. "I was naturally nervous, excited and spoke too much," she noted. When the meeting came to an end, Walska left the building carrying a signed photograph of Il Duce posing, Napoleon-like, on a horse, and when asked by journalists waiting outside the building what they had discussed, she could hardly remember a thing, so powerful was the impression Mussolini made.

Returning to Paris, Walska received the result of the long-pending U.S. Customs Court claim, learning that the original assessment of around a million dollars had been reduced to a mere $40.20. The Court accepted that most of her possessions were bought in the United States before going to France, and ruled unanimously that Madame Walska should have a distinct legal identity, able to "acquire a domicile separate and distinct from her husband by reason of his misconduct or abandonment or by his agreement either expressed or implied." That should have been reassuring, with Ganna seeking confirmation that in the event of Harold suing for divorce, she would be able to maintain her accustomed lifestyle and continue her cultural activities. Ever patient, but always direct, lawyer Phelan Beale replied to her nagging queries in a detailed letter, confirming that McCormick's trust fund was secure, and she would continue to receive an income of around $100,000 a year from it whatever happened on Wall Street.

He pointed out, however, that the matter was complicated because, if Harold died during Ganna's lifetime, the trust would be wound up and she would retain the principal. At present valuation - even taking into account the erosion of stock prices – its value was about seven million dollars. She would also be entitled to a share of Harold's estate as his widow, though things would be different if she were judged to be the offender in a divorce action. He cautioned his client: **"You must not make a wrong move. You must not antagonize Mr. McCormick because he holds the whip hand, to wit, he can say at any moment: 'Madame, it matters not to me whether you say yes or no. You will come to Chicago and live permanently here, or I will sue for a divorce and the Court will give me one.'"**

Beale advised that Ganna should be the one to sue, but with finesse: **"Harold is being guided by Mr. Walter Fisher. He is a gentleman seventy years of age and impresses me as being austere. You have met him and therefore are able to judge him for yourself. I do not wish to do him any injustice when I express the opinion that he does not regard you in a kindly light and moreover I feel that if he were left to his own devices he would not show you a shred of consideration."**

Meanwhile, the populist press continued to publish speculation about Walska and Straram, with New York's *Daily Mirror* running a story claiming that her mentor, "now rich after ten years' constant association with Ganna has gone to Switzerland." She had to accept that her fourth marriage was nearing its end, leaving it to Phelan Beale to obtain the most favorable terms for a settlement, keeping in mind the advice in his most recent letter: "In any event it behooves to think well before acting."

Whatever suspicions existed about Harold's intentions, his continuing affection for Ganna was enough to arrange a bizarre present in June, 1930. Through the French offices of International Harvester, he arranged for examples of the company's latest machinery to be displayed in the courtyard at the Château de Galluis, so that when his wife awoke on her forty-third birthday, drew the curtains and looked out of her window, she would be greeted "by a whole regiment of robot-soldiers," as she described this extraordinary gesture, "standing there on exhibition and put there during the night that I might be surprised." For someone who had been more accustomed to receiving diamond-encrusted Cartier bracelets on her anniversary, the surreal sight of shiny new trucks, tractors, harvesters, balers and harrows in a wide range of colors sparkling in the morning sunshine must have been quite a shock. Harold's extravagant gesture, however, appealed to Ganna's theatrical nature, noting in her diary that for several days after, word spread around the district, and "the simple field laborers as well as rich farmers were coming to look at those machines with the same admiration that the women would look at an exhibition of rare jewelry."

Somebody suggested she organize demonstrations of the machinery and charge an entrance fee to benefit a local charity, but Walska decided against it because of the unwanted intrusion into her private domain, though it did set her reflecting on the humanitarian nature of International Harvester's products in helping to produce food for millions of hungry mouths across the globe. "In this quasi-religious atmosphere," she decided, "it was easy for me to catch the spark, the feeling of which not only changed my almost disrespectful disdain for the income from commerce but filled my heart with gratitude toward those silent, obedient servants of humanity."

Harold's bizarre birthday present convinced Walska that her concept of commerce should become "spiritualized," and, following the inevitable demise of her perfume and cosmetics ventures as economic conditions worsened everywhere, she determined that, if ever tempted again to be a business woman, it would be idealistically rather than solely with the aim of making money. But Madame's affluent lifestyle continued very much as before, perhaps reassured by President Herbert Hoover's grotesquely premature statement to the American people during June, 1930: "The Depression is over!"

With the whiff of divorce in the air and the need for documentary proof of American citizenship if Harold ceased to be her husband, Ganna had applied earlier in the year to the American Consular Service in Paris for a new passport, which was renewed on March 28 for only an interim period of two months. She assumed that a full version would follow, but the vice-consul contacted her regretting that he had received instructions from Washington, D.C. that no further extension could be granted because of Madame's protracted residence abroad. A false affidavit signed in New York on September 21, 1928, to appeal against the Customs Department ruling, had come back to haunt her because it was the reason for the rejection:

"From the date of my marriage it has always been my intention to reside in Paris, France, and I have never had the intention and have not now the intention of relinquishing such residence and/or becoming a resident of the United States, although, of course, I reserve the right to do so should circumstances contribute to this end."

Marriages to three Americans, and owning property in New York, made it unlikely that Walska would be denied entry to the United States. But without a valid passport to contain visas she might find herself barred from returning to France. She suddenly felt very vulnerable, though her spirits were raised by being awarded the Polish Gold Cross for Merit. Signed by the President of the Republic on November 14, 1930, its citation recognized "Madame Hanna Walska McCormick, Operatic artist, in Chicago."

By the start of 1931, *La grande dépression* was seriously affecting audience numbers at all Paris venues, but Walska managed to keep several productions going at Le Théâtre des Champs-Elysées, including those of L'Opéra Privé de Paris, and she had the uplifting experience of singing briefly with one of Dr. Fraenkel's friends from earlier days: the famous operatic bass, Feodor Chaliapin. He came to her theater to perform perhaps his

184

greatest role, in Mussorgsky's *Boris Godunov*. It was twenty-three years since he first sang it in Paris for the Diaghilev Company, and now returned at the age of fifty-six to thrill audiences with a voice that had lost little of its glorious bloom. Ganna Walska was invited to take the small soprano role of Xenia, Boris's daughter, as *Le Figaro* noted elegantly:

"The great Chaliapin is coming to sing Boris Godunov at the Champs-Elysées and Prince Zereteli and M. de Basil have chosen for this solemn spectacle the very agreeable mistress of the house, Mme. Ganna Walska, to appear with him as Princess Xenia to give this gala in honor of Mussorgsky's masterpiece the aristocratic patronage that cannot, alas, any longer be assured by the elegance of an imperial court, now disappeared."

Much of Madame's life these days seemed to be soured by pending or potential litigation, and it was revealed in May, 1931 that an action brought by her former public relations manager George Djamgaroff had been settled out of court on undisclosed terms. He sued his former client and close friend for fees of $87,000, covering concert, opera and sound picture contracts she failed to fulfill, seeking an additional $100,000 for publicity work, including the aborted English-language production of *La Castiglione*. Another suit pending at this time, brought by Emile D. Gutcheon, former vice-president of Ganna Walska Perfumes Inc., sought $50,000, claiming that his business was ruined when Madame violated a contract to advertise the merchandise by refusing to make a concert tour of major American cities. Apart from her good self, lawyers and musicians were the main beneficiaries of Walska's ready cash, and she must have felt relieved on Monday, June 23, 1931 to give a well-received, sellout song recital at the Champs-Elysées with associate artists, Madeleine Groviez (clavecin) and Walther Straram (piano).

At her château in the ravishing rural countryside of what was then France's Seine-et-Oise *département,* Ganna had plenty of time for introspection, placing above everything else what she called the development of her inner-self and her "Divine Art." This personal philosophy was based on a principle of being usefully employed by thinking she was going to live forever, and acting as if life was cruelly short. It resulted in the town house standing empty for much of the time, with no more gala luncheons where a salon orchestra once played for her guests, and several aspiring artists, such as the now internationally-famous Catalan mezzo-

185

soprano, Conchita Supervia, and virtuoso pianist, Vladimir Horowitz, had proved their worth. This transition to a simpler existence accompanied a lifelong aversion to alcohol. As Walska told friends who asked about her abstention: "Its smell alone would prevent me from touching it," though she was no fervid advocate of temperance, and the wine cellars in town and at the Château de Galluis were kept well-stocked with fine vintages. Ganna drew the line at serving whisky, however, and Madame's servants were told not to mix cocktails "to avoid unnecessary temptation." An alternative low-alcohol cider made from apples grown on her estate was offered to anyone who found it difficult to enjoy a meal without first having an aperitif.

Eclectic style

Two events contrived to deny the happiness she sought: the illness of Walther Straram, which forced Walska into running the theater's complicated affairs virtually single-handed, and divorce. Her only real surprise was that her unconventional fourth marriage had lasted so long. "Perhaps I could have made Harold happy," she pondered in a diary note, "but it would have been to the prejudice of my own soul's development." She was convinced now that the

186

potent influence of Jung and Freud had conspired to deprive him of developing his mind's potential. "By keeping everything to himself, he automatically condemned frankness in others around him and reduced even me to silence." Ganna complained that Harold always made huge problems out of minor incidents, like remembering her birthday and brooding for days over its date, never questioning if these deficiencies affected his performance as the head of one of the world's largest corporations.

According to her, Harold's pampered childhood was the reason, becoming a hypochondriac at an early age and never allowed to be "natural." She claimed that all his boyish flights of imagination had been suppressed in the same way that his growing body "had always been covered with socks, mufflers, sweaters, snow-boots, scarves and gloves. When he was allowed to go out, he was so hermetically covered that he could not possibly have any contact through the great quantities of woolen garments with the fresh air, nature's most vivifying elixir."

Walska had always wanted to help Harold "find himself," but after leaving the United States after her last concert tour it was now too late because his attentions had turned to another singer. Betty Noble of Los Angeles became McCormick's musical protégée, showered with gifts and the promise of a brilliant career. During January, 1931, Thomas Lowrie Fisher (acting for McCormick) and Phelan Beale (Walska's attorney) reached agreement on a financial settlement, allowing Harold to divorce his wife on the grounds of desertion. She would receive approximately a quarter of his International Harvester stock, leaving her richer by about six million dollars, but forego the principal of her trust fund in the event of his death. This cleared the way for an uncontested hearing in the Chicago Circuit Court on October 10, 1931 in a room so crowded with litigants that few recognized the son of the Reaper King was obtaining his divorce.

When the news broke in Paris, Walska lectured the press that the state of marriage must not interfere with a woman's career. "It seems to me," she told reporters, "that a woman after marriage should have the same right as a man to pursue a career. I had hoped Mr. McCormick would take the same view, for he is a splendid man and I admire him very much. Even if we have reached the parting of the ways on this question we, nevertheless,

187

remain good friends." One newspaper speculated that Walska would now marry "that fiery little orchestra leader, Walter [sic] Straram, who is revealed as the 'Svengali' of her strange career." It suggested that the strange hold over his Trilby was based on hypnotism, and his total domination of Madame was the reason for her belief that she was a great prima donna. The failure was because he could not hypnotize the audiences as well.

Straram

He was suffering from throat cancer, and returned to Paris after treatment in Switzerland, to recuperate at Galluis. By now, the dire economic circumstances cut deeply into most aspects of French life and performances at the Champs-Elysées were reduced for the 1931-32 season, though their quality remained high, to be graced by the Ballets-Russes de Monte-Carlo, a festival of Polish music and appearances by four reigning giants of the keyboard: Horowitz, Landowska, Paderewski and Rubinstein. The main auditorium, with its excellent acoustics, was now being used as a recording studio, with the number of sessions for the Columbia company increasing during 1931. An annual Grand Prix du Disque was introduced, and Walther Straram's recording of Debussy's

188

symphonic poem "*Prélude à l'après-midi d'un faune*" won.

Ganna Walska experienced little sense of freedom following her divorce, continuing to search for what she termed "real love, love of the first magnitude," admitting to herself that she was to blame for her apparent reputation as both a *femme fatale* and an uncaring woman, but insisting it was a creation for her self-defense. Women friends judged her as independently-minded, always needing to question relationships and rarely letting her heart stray in the direction of romance, while most of them flirted constantly. Cheap compliments were anathema to Walska and being in the business of promoting the performing arts tended to attract some rank opportunists.

A well-known poet lavished attention on her, though he had just published letters received from another woman madly in love with him There was a distinguished violinist who professed to adore Ganna, but revealed that while playing the Brahms concerto he counted the empty seats, calculating how much money he'd lost. A famous painter claimed that his adoration would inspire him to produce a masterpiece, though Ganna knew he only wanted to paint her portrait and exhibit it for publicity. For a while, she endured the attentions of a handsome ambassador, "whose love for me was so great," that at any diplomatic or political gathering he would jealously monopolize her, so that next day all Paris would gossip about his tactics. But Ganna knew it was only window dressing because he was a well-known homosexual.

Instead of serving an individual, and having failed at that four times in marriage, she now had it in her power to use the theater to foster harmony between political parties, and even nations. At this stage of life - middle aged, but ignoring it - she dreamed of saving a world embroiled in economic chaos and political discord, through music:

"It has no nationality, only its servants, the musicians, have one. It is not limited by any frontier. It vibrates everywhere. It is free as the waves are free, and no one has power over it. Man can forbid listening to the universal waves but it is not in man's power to stop the waves themselves."

The depths of the Great Depression were plumbed when the Dow Jones Industrials index registered a low of 41.22 points on July 8, 1932. That, as well as mounting political tensions in Europe generated by Hitler's rise to power and the spread of Mussolini's fascism, prompted Ganna to help international relations by inviting the representatives of France and Italy to a musical luncheon. The French foreign minister, Philippe Berthelot was no admirer of Il Duce and his policies, but he agreed to sit at the same table as Count Gaetano Manzoni, the Italian ambassador. At the end of a cordial meal, blue Chinese porcelain finger bowls were placed in front of the guests, each containing a gardenia flown over from London that morning. It was the custom for a man to present his flower to the lady sitting next to him, but to everyone's surprise, Berthelot rose to his feet, picked up his bloom, stretched across the table and handed it to Manzoni. His courtly action was accompanied by a few well-chosen words about its fragrance symbolizing lasting peace.

During the 1932-33 season at the Champs-Elysées, Walska sang some Mozart arias with Walther Straram conducting their orchestra, and she returned to the opera stage for one of the best performances of her checkered career, though being a private appearance there was little publicity surrounding the event. She took the leading soprano role in Debussy's only work for the stage, *Pelléas et Mélisande*, noting in her diary after the performance:

"On this memorable evening, my friends seized the occasion to express with flowers their appreciation of the beautiful music heard in our theater. The result of their thoughtfulness was that the scene where Mélisande dies was transformed into a gorgeous garden because, around the bed where a short time before I had given up my life, there were more than 160 floral arrangements, in huge baskets for the most part. I couldn't help thinking, mischievously, that they were giving me a first class funeral! But I was the only one who could understand the irony of it, as I knew the flowers were sent to me as a hostess, a patron of the arts, a friend and not at all as an artiste."

Parisian music lovers fully expected the 1933-34 season at Madame's theater to be frugal, reflecting a world in the grip of the Great Depression, but Ganna continued to support many attractions with her own money, knowing that box office receipts would never cover expenses. She contracted forty-nine dance performances from leading companies such as the Ballets Russes de Monte-Carlo, the Nijinska dancers and Les Ballets Joos. Lotte Lehmann, Lili Pons and Heifetz were engaged to perform in the grand auditorium, and there would be a series of seven concerts conducted by Toscanini. Walther Straram managed to help compile the schedule, despite a worsening throat condition which led to his returning for further treatment in Switzerland.

During that winter, Walska herself developed severe laryngitis which forced curtailment of her daily vocal practice with a dire warning from the doctor that she might be unable to sing "for weeks, months or maybe never again" if his advice to rest was ignored. She decided to take a vacation by returning to St. Moritz, last visited soon after the turn of the century when Arcadie was a rebellious sanitarium patient.

Ganna joined a group of friends for winter sports, hardly recognizing the fashionable resort under its blanket of dazzling white snow. She noted in her diary: "Could that ugly barracks be the luxurious Palace Hotel where I had stayed before?" She unwound there away from the stress of attending to the endless details of running her theater and worrying about Walther. "I was as carefree as a lark," she admitted. "I had come for ten days but already by the end of the second day of jumping in the snow in my ski costume my cheeks got rosy and my friends were flabbergasted to see such a quick change, which I suppose must have come from a relaxed mind." Her only regret was that the winter days were so short; it was dark by four in the afternoon, when she retired to the welcoming warmth of Hanselmann's Conditorei und Cafehaus for

191

pastries and hot chocolate.

Charlie Chaplin was staying at the Palace and she enjoyed his attention, flirting with "the handsomest man Great Britain has produced," listening to his witty conversation, laughing at his pranks and spending time together on the ice rink. "He skated badly," she recalled, "but his skating suit was so becoming to him!" Ganna at forty-five was a couple of years older than Chaplin, who was still enjoying the worldwide popularity of the 1931 movie *City Lights*, his first sound feature, though it was silent cinema in most respects. She lunched outside in the dazzling sunshine at the exclusive Coriviglia Ski Club high in the mountains "where the proximity of the sky and the entire world below made me forget all the intrigue and petty gossip."

In the exhilarating air of the high Alps, it mattered little to anyone if a Bourbon prince was the guest of a rich parvenu, or that the Duchess of Alba suddenly switched her affection from a stunningly beautiful Russian girl to an angular Englishwoman. Sexual intrigue among the European aristocracy that would have been considered risky in Paris, counted for little here, where Walska lunched many meters nearer the "Cosmic World," as she called it, stripped down to a sleeveless pullover and ski pants, only worrying about getting her nose sunburnt.

She questioned herself about taking singing too seriously and whether to call a halt to the daily torture, once her throat was better. At bed time, the moon shone through the windows of her suite, illuminating the scene outside as if it were day, and, heavy with fatigue, she felt beautifully drowsy, her eyes refusing to stay open to read the Paris newspapers. They could wait for tomorrow and tomorrow's papers could be read at some other time.

After a few days in the mountains, Ganna's total relaxation was almost complete, watching a heavily-pregnant Gloria Swanson who might give birth right there at the inn. "*Patratras, ça y est!*" she wrote, "La Gloria rises and before she actually moves, her stomach protrudes to such an extent that it seems to take the first step. Probably she is going to her carriage to borrow the horses' hay to lay the little Swanson in like an infant Jesus." But no, the fading cinema star only fetches her vanity case from the sleigh to powder her nose, and Ganna sighed with relief not to be enlisted for midwife duties.

One afternoon, she encountered Lady Mountbatten, realizing how beautiful, how British, she looked, and wondering if her pearl earrings were genuine because, being enormous, they would be terribly heavy, knowing from experience that even the slightest weight could pull painfully at one's ear lobes. "If they are hollow inside, they must be light and they are so becoming!" she thought. "But can it be that an heiress such as [the former] Miss Ashley could wear imitations?" Walska would learn later that they were fake pearls: Mrs. Jacques Cartier, of London's Cartier confirmed it.

There was a gala dinner for thirty people where she was seated next to Chaplin and opposite another wildly attractive Englishman who flirted with her. "Good! That way I could see his handsome face and enjoy speaking to Charlie," was entered into her diary, and in this liberating atmosphere, she prepared to succumb to something not tried since her first year in America: to dance with "my Britisher." Her black, figure-hugging Chantilly gown looked most becoming, and after visiting her room briefly Ganna was about to descend to the dance floor for a carefree evening when the phone rang. It was Dr. de Reynier, Walther Straram's physician, calling from Leysin, two hundred kilometers away, to let her know that he would be conducting an urgent, perhaps fatal, operation on his patient the next morning. Hurriedly, Ganna shed her lace gown, put on traveling clothes and caught the last train for a long, fractured journey to be with her mentor, leaving the gaiety of St. Moritz far behind.

De Raynier's experimental surgery took place with her half-watching squeamishly from the next room as he inserted "a dynamo into the affected throat of my teacher." Further procedures followed and Ganna anxiously awaited the result of each, "realizing that the patient might choke to death at any moment." Fortunately he didn't, and over the next weeks she would shuttle by train between Paris and Leysin, sometimes repeating the exhausting journey several times a week, "when Dr. de Reynier would inform me by a long distance call from Leysin that the next cauterization might be fatal, especially if the patient were not inspired by my presence." Straram said he preferred to die rather than not breathe the same air as she breathed. Eventually, she took him back to the Château de Galluis for convalescence, where he spent most of the spring and summer months of 1933, too weak to play any active role in the theater, his conducting days over.

GW with Straram

As autumnal mists began to gather at Galluis with the year approaching a *triste* conclusion, Walska was informed by her New York housekeeper, Mary Placek that some pipes had burst in her Park Avenue mansion and needed urgent attention. During Walska's long absences in France, the property was under the protection of a patrol company and Mary discovered water in the cellar during one of her regular visits, probably from the leaking pipes. Madame decided it would be better to supervise any repairs in person rather than relying on cabled instructions and transatlantic telephone calls. She traveled to New York, where repairs were completed during a whirlwind week's stay, before hurrying back to France on the fast North German Lloyd liner "Bremen," scheduled to depart on November 9. The visit was so brief and unannounced, that reporters only caught up with Ganna on the point of departure, intrigued by such an extravagant journey simply to fix a few leaks.

Wearing a squirrel-lined, green-plaid cape and blatantly *décolleté* beneath, Madame chatted to journalists in her shipboard suite surrounded by masses of orchids and gardenias. It was like old times as they pressed her to comment on a recent breach of promise action brought against her former husband, claiming $1,500,000 damages. After divorcing Walska, the American press had followed Harold McCormick's amours closely, and by all accounts he had been a rather active sixty-year-old. He first squired the Californian singing hopeful, Betty Noble, then Baroness Violet Beatrice von Wenner, an internationally-known portrait painter who, besides having a talent with her brush, was also an accomplished harpist, accompanying Harold at his virtuoso whistling recitals for the entertainment of friends. The baroness's sitters included Lord Robert Cecil, Otto H. Kahn, Count Ferdinand von Zeppelin and McCormick himself, with one of two portraits by her hanging at Rush Street, where Violet was expected to become the new chatelaine. But she was replaced in his affections by divorcée Mrs. Rhoda Tanner Doubleday, the former wife of Felix Doubleday, son of the famous New York publisher, at thirty, half McCormick's age. Apparently, after a two-year friendship and at least fifty ardent love letters indicating his desire to marry, he made a firm proposal, and then went back on his word.

Walska was in a playful mood, enjoying being the center of attention again, telling the press that personal experience told her that America provided good husbands, and if she ever married again it would be to an American.

"But I am not on the witness stand for my former husband," she insisted, refusing to comment about Harold, "nor for the lady who is suing him." They asked about her house repairs, and she remarked that American houses were so well-constructed that none of her paintings or pieces of furniture was water-damaged by the burst pipes. "America builds good houses and provides good husbands," Ganna proclaimed, as if they were both self-evident truths.

Walther Straram clung to life until shortly after her return, dying at his Paris home on November 24, 1933. He was fifty-seven, and left as a legacy the 1933-34 season at the Champs-Elysées which, in spite of dreadful economic conditions, promised to keep the theater alive at the forefront of the performing arts. But his passing heralded the end of an era, and a few days later Madame Walska wrote a letter of resignation as president of the company. To some it sounded like ingratitude for Straram's years of devotion and hard work, as his body was interred in Passy Cemetery, close to the tombs of three French composers whose music he had conducted on many occasions, or played as Ganna's accompanist: André Messager, Gabriel Fauré and Claude Debussy.

The truth was that Madame was exhausted after battling mounting costs and declining audiences, seeking a future free from those restraints. She had attempted to touch all aspects of expression: love, art, philosophy, politics - anything except sport - but with the passing of her mentor (or lover, *éminence grise*, manipulator or Svengali, depending on the gossip) found it difficult to find a replacement vocal coach. Her performing career had stalled since the last American tour more than four years before, though Ganna retained a blind faith in her ability to sing, not any more in opera but certainly on the concert platform. Contact with a dedicated musician like Walther Straram, she declared, had made her soul richer and bigger as she set off for America yet again.

This time she took along twelve trunks of costumes for a series of dress recitals, together with a cache of show-off jewelry. There was billowing black taffeta and corals to complement Beethoven, a pure white ensemble with diamonds for Brahms, and various eye-catching changes to match the musical moods of other great composers. The *Concert Guide* printed an article headlined "Ganna Walska Claims Modern Singers Do Not Protect Their Natural Gifts," in which the "noted Polish soprano, here for a recital tour," declared that many great voices are "sung out" in a brief period. Published in New York a fortnight before her Carnegie Hall appearance, Walska told the *Guide* that the biggest stars, the greatest artists, were never sure of themselves: "They realize they must work and study always." The publicity stated that singing remained her passion and that she had spent years in the perfection of her art, though the first audience of the tour in Philadelphia might have been excused for regarding it as a lost cause. *Time* magazine reported that she appeared unable to sing without clutching music scores, and each song in a thin, warbled tone tended to sound the same as the last. Yet, with the scantiest encouragement, the magazine's critic noted, Madame Walska returned beaming to the platform to teeter through an encore. The

196

Philadelphia *Record* was more brutal: "Madame Walska's art is that of a little child. She should be seen and not heard."

She arrived in Chicago just after the possessions of Harold's first wife, Edith, who had died in August, 1932 in her suite at the Drake Hotel, were sold off at public auctions. After all the recent fuss over McCormick's love affairs, Ganna was taken aback to be asked by a reporter on stepping down from the train if a reconciliation with her former husband was likely.

"Eet ees not a question of that," she replied. "We are good friends: that ees all. I am very happy always to see Meester McCormeeck." She was told that Harold had tickets for her concert. "Eet ees very like heem," was the response, with a twinkle in her eye.

There was a message waiting at her hotel, and shortly after, Ganna was seen walking to the McCormick mansion where she lingered over a two-hour luncheon with Harold and, no doubt, enjoyed a rather interesting tete-a-tete.

Almost five years since she last sang to a capacity audience at prestigious Orchestra Hall, a much smaller turnout in the Auditorium Theater made up in enthusiasm what it lacked in numbers, with the applause led by Harold, apparently still one of her greatest admirers. He sat prominently in the middle of the house and no one seemed to enjoy the recital more, but his former wife's hooped gowns of the Second Empire and modern dresses for encores, her wigs and jewelry - so valuable that everything was guarded by two detectives during the performance - served to deflect attention from the singing. A robust reception failed to disguise the fact that only ten of the fifty-six boxes were occupied, and many of the main-floor seats remained empty. In three years Ganna would be fifty and could still win hearts with her looks, but there seemed to be no future for her thin little voice.

She would disagree, for the moment at least, deciding to add to what was already written for her much-delayed autobiography by analyzing the subject dearest to her heart:

"Singing is the greatest of self-expressions because it is complete in itself and if perfect must be free from any outside help. Without a piano, the best of pianists falls from a genius to an ordinary mortal. If a shipwreck brings Fritz Kreisler to an isolated island he would find himself in the same position without his violin, while a singer on such occasions could still charm the savages through a God-given voice."

The Carnegie Hall recital, scheduled for January 29, 1934 was postponed because of a severe cold, and finally given on the Friday evening of April 6, billed as a "Song Recital in Costumes of The Second Empire," which rather set it apart from the usual fare offered at New York's leading concert venue, home of the mighty Philharmonic. Seat prices ranged from $1.10 to $3.30, matching the level of the greatest singers and instrumentalists of the day, which deterred many from attending. Consequently, Madame Walska and her accompanist, Stuart Ross at the Steinway, faced an audience of curiosity-seekers more interested in her mode than the melody and must have sensed a zaniness about singing Hugo Wolf lieder wearing Second Empire drag in the hallowed surroundings where the great Tchaikovsky himself had conducted part of the inaugural concert in 1891.

Walska stayed on in the United States for another month before returning to Europe, and there was added excitement in the air on the morning of May 5 when the "Ile de France" made ready to sail from the port of New York with the man Mussolini dubbed "the world's most famous conductor" on its passenger list. Arturo Toscanini, a former Fascist parliamentary candidate and now the fiery little musical dictator of the New York Philharmonic Orchestra, he was a cult figure on both sides of the Atlantic, famous for relentless pursuit of perfection across a wide range of orchestral and operatic works. He flatly refused to allow any shipboard press photos, though he did pose for two schoolboys by the gangway who asked for his autograph. Madame, on the other hand, was only too eager to talk about his forthcoming concerts with the late Walther Straram's Orchestre Symphonique at the Champs-Elysées between May 25 and June 6. She told journalists that she founded the ensemble some ten years before, had borne all expenses, and the Toscanini concerts would be dedicated to the memory of her former musical director. Asked if she found a new romance during her stay in the United States, Ganna responded: "Romances are not made to order. I still believe in them, however. One may overtake me at any time."

Home in France, still grieving for Walther Straram and with time on her hands after the excitement of Toscanini's galvanizing presence, she made a conscious effort to move away from overt materialism in line with withdrawal from social life, vowing that her former extravagances were a thing of the past. She declared there would be no more *champêtre* (garden party) galas at Galluis with *riz à la grec* to titillate the palate of the Duchess of Kent's father, Prince Nicholas of Greece; no further feasts of riabthik (a gourmet bird from Russia) stuffed with the finest caviar flown to Paris from Romania. This dish had been a special favorite of the American Tony Montgomery, Ganna's interior designer, who transformed the stables at the château into comfortable guest quarters with infallible taste. But she could never forgive his unforgivable *faux pas* when, on tasting riabthik *farcie* for the first time, he congratulated her chef, who had been a colonel in the Tsar's hussars, with the comment: "Your caviared chicken was a masterpiece!" The cook's reaction, she recalled, was to be "frightfully shocked."

No longer would her overworked kitchen staff prepare elaborate luncheons *à la russe*, starting with a vast selection of hors d'oeuvres followed by the major-domo announcing an hour later: *"Leurs Altisses Imperiales et Royales sont servis,"* causing consternation among the guests assuming the myriad hot and cold specialties already offered - and heartily consumed - *were* the buffet luncheon. Henceforth, Walska would not spend hours in chic boutiques selecting individual gifts for her women friends to be distributed from Sicilian carts in the château grounds by the Isadora Duncan dancers, or concern herself with the minutiae of decoration, where the bounty from the château's *potagère* - tomatoes and celery, pomegranates and figs - was artfully incorporated in elaborate table settings, with the hostess dressed to match the autumnal leaves of a centerpiece by wearing a striking Chanel creation in gold fabric bought specially for the occasion. Ganna had been famous for her seasonal dinners, particularly those of the paschal celebrations of the Russian Orthodox Church, and wrote for her memoirs:

"Adieu to the Easter table bearing suckling pigs, Russian, English and Prague hams artistically dressed in white sugar. Adieu lamb, colorful pastries, the gigantic chocolate egg decorated with a huge ribbon and almost touching the ceiling, which was later the delight of the village children. Adieu the beautifully painted paper eggs with a surprise inside that gave everyone so much pleasure to open.

In her late forties and comfortably wealthy in spite of the Depression, her former svelte figure easing to a fuller waistline and more generous bosom, Walska was on the point of leaving behind what she acknowledged as having been a brilliant, but superficial, period of her life. "Occasionally I saw a few intimate friends," she noted, "and only those who were interested in the line of my conception, unless it was those who needed my assistance." Continuing the struggle to release her voice from its mystifying restraints was harder than ever, though she refused to accept the generation gap that allowed young students to succeed where she had to wrestle with endless technical difficulties.

Over the years, Walska had been tempted by a multitude of cults and fringe religions, and, abandoning her former social excesses, decided it was time for a new foray into mysticism. The motivation came from an elderly American woman who lived in an eleventh-century priory at Saint-Benoît-sur-Loire, not far from Galluis. Grace Gassette, formerly from Chicago, and passionately devoted to art and the occult, had once exhibited her paintings at the Junior Salon in Paris during 1910. She lent Walska some books to read by the English writers Alexander Erskin and Alexander Cannon, both advocates of hypnotism, with Erskin having caused a stir by asserting that deafness and blindness were able to be cured by hypnotic suggestion. Ganna felt that she received renewed hope from these sources and, more significantly, a new interest that compensated for the drudgery of daily singing lessons and the lull in her life, after withdrawing from the day-to-day affairs of her beloved theater. The Champs-Elysées would see no more seasons under Ganna's personal management.

Soon after resigning her presidency of the company in April, 1934 - but retaining a majority shareholding - the French government made an offer to lease part of the building for the national radio service, leaving Madame Walska to depart the scene with a recognition she cherished above all else: the Légion d'honneur. The application to receive the award was made to Louis Barthou, Minister of Foreign Affairs, on May 27, 1934 from eight influential personalities in French music, and was almost as satisfying as the ribboned medal itself because it reflected how the profession appreciated her contribution to their art:

"We have the honor to seek your kind approval for the nomination to the order of Chevalier de la Légion d'honneur of Mme. Ganna Walska, founder of the symphony orchestra of the Concerts W. Straram. Since its

foundation, consolidated over several years, this orchestra has never ceased to be one of the pioneers in the promotion of French music here and abroad. The programs have always been graced with an obvious desire to present to the public, not only the great classical works of our musical heritage, but also introduce us to the works of young French and foreign composers. It is thanks to Mme. Ganna Walska, whose name is found among all forms of artistic support that this association has been and continues to be her work of great and valuable promotion."

The metaphysical writings of Alexander Erskin intrigued Walska and she wrote to him care of his British publishers, waiting for a reply that never came because he had died a few months earlier. Dr. Alexander Cannon endorsed Erskin's theories and she resolved to see him instead. Miss Gassette, as proprietor of a small publishing company called Les Editions du Prieuré, happened to be in contact with Cannon, having proposed translating his book "The Invisible Influence" (1933) into French. When next she wrote to the author, she asked if he would see a friend in need of help, and received a positive response.

Walska knew only what Miss Gassette told her about Cannon, but delving a little deeper, would have revealed his split personality, as a serious academic and well-known showman. A qualified psychiatrist, he was the senior author of the well-regarded reference book "The Principles and Practice of Psychiatry" (1932) as well as a volume of popular psychology, and another about hypnotism. But he also gave lectures with demonstrations of psychic phenomena to large audiences around Britain, billed as "Alexander Cannon, K.C.A. (Kushog Yogi of Northern Thibet.") He embellished his sessions with so-called Colour-Music, in which the audience was asked "to pay attention to the different colours used for the various types of music and its variations," to put them in the right mood for what followed.

The women departed from Le Bourget, the aerodrome just north of Paris, famous as the landing site for Charles Lindbergh after his historic solo transatlantic crossing seven years before, and it was still quite an adventure in 1934 for these two, setting off to fly to London's airport at Croydon for a medical consultation. The meeting was to be at the consulting rooms of a Dr. Jensen, who allowed his colleague to use premises because Dr. Cannon was employed by the Mental Hospital Service of the London County Council, and not allowed to practice privately. Crossing the entrance hall, Walska noticed a silk top hat on a stand.

"Dr. Cannon obviously has not arrived yet, although there is someone here with a top hat," she commented to her companion. Alexander Cannon was the hat's owner, and the rest of his attire looked as if he had stepped out of a Dickens novel. He was a small, rotund individual with a florid complexion, shiny bald pate and small piercing eyes peering through metal-framed spectacles perched halfway down his nose. To complete the Pickwickian appearance, he sported a winged collar under his cutaway morning coat and wore spats. The image thoroughly confused Walska, though Miss Gassette seemed perfectly at ease with this man, who claimed to have been an explorer in some of the most inaccessible regions of the world.

Cannon had written about sending messages from Tibet by a form of telepathy, yet here he was, the caricature of a nineteenth century Harley Street physician, squinting through a pair of cheap glasses. Ganna herself had experienced poor eyesight since childhood, unable to focus on small print without the aid of what she regarded as disfiguring reading glasses, reserving those for home, and using a monocle in public which doubled as a fashion accessory. Cannon, noticing her disapproving stare, apologized for his eyewear, which he said he explained was worn on his distant travels as a protection against the evil eye.

He took Madame into another room where she was introduced to a female medium to find out what was wrong with her. Dr. Cannon declared that this plump young woman was the finest diagnostician in all of England, while his colleague, Dr. Jensen, hovered in the background ready to take notes of her prognosis. Ganna allowed the scene to play out, but felt increasingly uncomfortable about the procedure. "When this new type of Aesculapius could detect no more ailments in me," she recalled, "I was dismissed, but not before receiving orders to see Dr. Jensen the next morning for a more detailed medical examination, a thing I had not undergone in all the years of my life."

Although highly skeptical of the methods employed, she went along with them, and during the second day of the London visit met a different medium who was hypnotized and then questioned about her ailments, while Cannon repeated everything that was said, adding the fact that the patient had been born in Paris. Walska corrected him, explaining she was Polish, at which point he stared at her for a few moments over the cheap spectacles, which had now slipped to the very tip of his sharply-chiseled nose, and then addressed her in a patronizing manner, as if his patient was a naughty child speaking out of turn.

"I am certain the medium is right," he confirmed smugly. "She is always right. Once someone was told by her that he was born in America, but the gentleman in question was positive that he had been born in England. A year later, however, he wrote an apology saying he had just discovered that his mother had been visiting America at the time of his birth: a fact he had never known until that moment."

Dr. Cannon ignored Walska's incredulity, announcing that it was time for her to be hypnotized. She agreed, but after several attempts failed he said it was not unusual because there were people who could not be put into a trance at all, and some only succumbed after several sessions. He persisted without success, trying to convince his patient that she was already under his spell. "For Justice's sake," she noted later, "while the modern Mesmer continued telling me I felt nothing, nothing at all, not even the touch of my hand or feet or anything I imagined I felt - I pinched myself to see whether it hurt. It did - and how! I most certainly felt all those sensations in spite of his suggestions to the contrary. Finally, I could endure no longer the hypocritical comedy."

In spite of his foibles, Cannon continued to interest Ganna after learning more about him. She was familiar with the American social élite - the famous Four Hundred – for whom she was an outsider in spite of marriages to two of America's wealthiest men - also with the blue bloods of Europe listed in the Almanach de Gotha, together with British nobility in Debrett's and the aristocracy of Burke's Peerage. But this man was something else. Added to the other titles and qualifications on his calling card - AK.C.A, M.D., Ph.D., D.P.M., M.A., Ch.B., F.R.G.S., F.R.S., TROP M&H" - was "Master the Fifth of the Great White Lodge of the Himalayas." He revealed in the greatest confidence that this was one of the most secret organizations in the spiritual universe, but he would allow her to have the names, addresses and telephone numbers of other members, including Master the Fourth, who lived in America.

Ganna's patience wore thin after a final, unsuccessful consultation, when instead of admitting it was impossible to hypnotize her because she was such a strong personality, Cannon warned the two ladies - presumably to earn an extra consultation fee - against flying back to France the next day as planned, because he foresaw a terrible air disaster. On the day of their delayed departure, with no news in the morning papers about any crashes, a bill from Dr. Jensen was delivered to Claridge's because Cannon could not charge directly for his services, and the amount was so breathtakingly enormous that Madame wondered if she could leave London without cabling her French bank for assistance.

She arrived home safely with a pile of notes about improving her health and singing, including a list of sentences, mostly in the style of "My postilion has been struck by lightning," that needed to be repeated to improve her diction, using what Dr. Cannon called the "inverted megaphone tone," always keeping in mind that she must be aware of the space between the teeth on enunciating her "o" vowels:

"The old motorist on the lonely road scolded his frozen chauffeur for not noticing the hole in the hopelessly old motor.

"Rose told Joe Boles not to throw Tony's note away till he phoned Sophie's home."

"With the handing over of Roosevelt's note to the British by Wendell Wilkie, his onetime political opponent, the romanticizing of the political situation by society, gave way to cold and sober calculating.

The women sent thank-you notes to Cannon and he replied to Walska's: "It was a great pleasure to see you. The result of the mental determining which you are not conscious of, but is working effectively upon your conscious mind, will bring you a success and a happiness and a state of good health which you have not previously enjoyed."

The day his letter was posted from England - October 9, 1934 - Ganna learned about the death of the French Minister for Foreign Affairs, Louis Barthou, assassinated in Marseille by a Croatian separatist while accompanying King Alexander of Yugoslavia, who was also struck down by the bullets and bled to death. Jean Louis Berthou, aged seventy-two, was a former prime minister, and a good friend. With his passing, Walska not only lost a staunch supporter for her patronage of the performing arts, but the whole of Europe was affected politically because Barthou had been working tirelessly to reinforce France's ties with the Balkans, Italy, Poland and the Soviet Union, with the aim of forging alliances to counter the growing threat of Nazism. He was the primary figure behind the Franco-Soviet Treaty of Mutual Assistance signed, after his passing, in 1935.

There seemed to be little justice in Walska's world at the moment - either personally, or for her adopted country. She was shattered by the Barthou news and frustrated by experiencing few benefits from Alexander Cannon's treatment, cabling him about her concerns. He replied by letter, claiming to know exactly what was wrong:

"It shows that you have not carried out fully the advice given to you by the trance subject as regards swimming, and carrying out WITHOUT FEAR but with faith all those exercises I gave you to do. You also were to go somewhere which was peaceful, not Paris. Go down to Miss Gassette and live there for three months whether you like it or not. THIS IS YOUR WAY TO A CURE. Believe in God and His power to heal you. I have sown the seed but if you allow the 'chaff' to grow up it will strangle the seed I have sown and your visit to London would then be wasted."

The restless Ganna did not relish the prospect of leading an ascetic life in Miss Gazette's ancient priory, despite Cannon's assurance that only there would she find "God, Peace, Contentment, Happiness and YOUR VOICE!"

Instead, she travelled to New York aboard her favorite ship, the French Line's "Ile de France," on Christmas Day, 1934, too late to entertain her traveling companions to a traditional Polish Christmas Eve dinner, having made no prior arrangements for her stay.

She took with her the address of Master the Fourth of the Great White Lodge of the Himalayas and made contact, remembering Dr. Cannon's instructions to address him always as "Master" and when they met to give the secret sign on a mystic triangle he gave her to wear around her neck.

She kept in contact with the Master by inviting him to dinners in town and seeking his company for theater and opera visits, but found his insistence on knowing exactly how much he owed her for each outing to be very plebeian behavior. They corresponded frequently and he was revealed only as Mr. D. in diary entries.

Ganna also indulged in other mystical and religious exploits during her stay, including instructional sessions at New York's Baha'i Center on West 57th Street given during February 1935 by Madame Barry-Orlova, a lecturer and writer from London. She also attended lectures by the handsome American evangelist, Manly P. Hall, during his return engagement "by popular demand," to give ten different presentations whose subjects ranged from "Memory of past lives as proof of reincarnation" to "The first principles of Occult Philosophy."

Madame returned to Paris to attend to the financial affairs of her Champs-Elysées theater, which had been closed in early 1935 with an outstanding debt of 400,000 francs (the equivalent of $16,000) in back taxes. She wrote to an influential New York friend, Felix Warburg, the banker and philanthropist, seeking his help in raising the amount, asking that he regard the request as an art enterprise and not for any personal reasons. Warburg replied that keeping her orchestra playing and backing theatrical productions did not interest him because he was already obligated in many relief schemes as a result of the Depression, "Nor could I encourage you to try to keep these two activities going indefinitely, for you have had your own experiences there and they are identical to what we have had over here." Ganna tried to imagine a future without her beautiful theater and fine symphony orchestra, but could not escape the fact that she must economize during these terrible times. Back in 1932 she had declared $200,065 as net annual income to the United States Government, paying $71,830 in tax. By the following year, with the Depression deepening, her income had fallen to $84,909; in 1934 she declared $72,064 and this was reduced by another $5,000 for 1935 when she signed the Treasury form 1040D as a departing alien. Ganna remained in a comparatively comfortable financial state, backed by considerable assets, if not nearly as much cash-in-hand, but decided that she could no longer support the performing arts with her own money.

Reduced income had little effect on Walska's travels, and while attending the International Music Congress in Venice, a woman came to whisper something in her ear.

"I am Alma Mahler."

She was, in fact, a couple of family names on from that, having being widowed by the great composer's death in 1911 and divorced from her second husband, the celebrated architect Walter Gropius of Bauhaus fame in 1920. Alma was now married to the Austrian novelist Franz Werfel, which made the nuptial scoreboard for these two great *femmes fatales* of the twentieth century: Walska 4 - Mahler 3. They became firm friends, with Alma calling Ganna her soul sister, and Madame noting for her autobiography:

"There was never any rivalry between us, but perhaps she never realized to what degree her passage in the Doctor's life [Joseph Fraenkel] was a tragedy for me, for I unfortunately realized only too late the reason for the trembling of the Doctor's hands when he first shook mine, and his rather sudden proposal of marriage the next time I saw him - an act not easily comprehensible coming from a serious-minded European thinker of his stature. The explanation was simple, if cruel to me - I looked very much like Frau Mahler, and the resemblance made him believe he loved me."

Ganna Walska seemed incapable of living without causes - preferably with mystic overtones - like so many women of independent means at a loose end during the Great Depression. One of her missions was deep concern for the enigmatic Thomas Edward Lawrence. The much-mythologized Welshman known globally as Lawrence of Arabia, war hero, writer and former spy, was the second-lieutenant popularly thought to have single-handedly championed the cause of independence by riding into

Damascus at the head of a victorious army and rescuing the Arab revolt against the Ottomans. He led a very different life now in retirement, dominated by speedboats and motor cycles, and, with a track record of associating with some of the wealthiest and most influential men in the world, Ganna reasoned that she should capture his attention.

"Arabia," she mused: "so far away, so *Ballet Russe*."

Lawrence, however, suffered an accident while riding his powerful machine, having swerved to avoid colliding with a young cyclist on a country lane near his home. The radio reported that King George sent his personal physician to aid the hero, which confirmed for Ganna that he had been much more than a mere spy, if the British monarch was trying to save his life. She entered in her diary: "Before I had loved him only to fill the emptiness of necessary desire to love at any cost, to worship an ideal," but now decided to act before it was too late by going to England. While making travel arrangements, however, the radio announced in solemn tones on May 19, 1935: "Colonel Lawrence died last night without recovering consciousness." Ganna sat down to write, histrionically: "The foundations of my tranquility, made solid and firm during these years, tumbled and crashed. Emptiness entered my heart again."

As a personal tribute, to Lawrence of Arabia she read his "Revolt in the Desert" (1927) reissued in an abridged edition after his death.

Restless after the advice she received from gurus and mystics failed to fix her health and singing problems, Ganna Walska sailed for New York again, where the superficial pleasures of dinner parties and theater visits with friends soon palled. She soon turned to Mr. D. in Weehawken (Master the Fourth) for a new astrological chart, and sought solace from another book. This one was "Unveiled Mysteries" by Godfré Ray King, published in 1934 about an encounter with the mystical Saint Germain, Chohan of the Seventh Ray: the violet ray, of freedom, alchemy, justice, mercy and transmutation – the sponsor of the United States of America and hierarch of the Age of Aquarius. Walska heard that the writer and his wife, Edna Anne Wheeler Ballard, were lecturing to large audiences on theosophical matters and the occult under their professional name of the Ballards, and she simply had to meet them. Discovering that they were in the national capital and could be contacted at the Roosevelt Hotel, she impulsively took the train to Washington, D.C., and accepted an invitation to a Thanksgiving dinner with friends of the Ballards.

Expecting much, Ganna convinced herself that divine guidance had led her to an inspirational experience from these "Sole Accredited Messengers of Saint Germain," known across the United States through radio broadcasts, publicity campaigns, books and public meetings of their spiritual organization known as the "I Am" Activity. To end the session she attended, Edna played some harp music Walska thought she recognized as an old Polish melody heard in Brest-Litovsk as a child; it brought tears to her eyes, and returning to her hotel room she fell on her knees to give "humble thanks for the light that my soul had received. I was purified and felt an exultation I had not felt since my first communion in my very girlish years!"

She visited the Ballards just before their departure for the West Coast, learning that they regarded themselves as Chicagoans, having been married there, and knew all about Ganna's struggles for singing success, assuring her that more and more performers were discovering God in themselves, naming the movie star Mary Pickford and operatic soprano Amelita Galli-Curci as examples. The couple said they had been waiting for Madame Walska to discover them, and were sure that the spirit of Saint Germain himself guided her. It was, of course, exactly what she wanted to hear: "For the first time in my life," Walska recounted in her autobiography, blissfully forgetting all other moments of revelation, "I had found the Truth! At last! I had an answer to all my troubles."

It was a fragile certitude, however, based upon a shadowy eighteenth-century figure known as the Count of St. Germain, regarded variously by followers and skeptics as a courtier, musician, alchemist, inventor and charlatan. Probably not a real count - and certainly no saint in the Roman Catholic pantheon - Germain became a prominent figure in several strands of occultism, leading to fringe religions and the New Agers' cult of the Age of Aquarius. He came to dominate Ganna's thoughts, and his influence prompted a resumption of singing lessons, though she soon found that fulfillment was harder to attain because the urge to succeed increased her vulnerability.

Walska's New York voice teacher, Frank La Forge, an accomplished pianist, composer and recording artist for the Victor Company, as well as accompanist for many famous singers including Marcella Sembrich, Lily Pons and Ernestine Schumann-Heink, tried to convince her that improvement would come if she studied for long enough and swam regularly in New York's public pool to improve her breathing. "I tried hard to learn and swim gracefully," she noted, following La Forge's advice, "but could not succeed because I could not let go." Ganna drove to Connecticut at weekends for extra tuition, admitting: "After singing with my throat choked in unswallowed tears, frozen morally and physically from driving two hours in terrific snow, singing two hours, then two hours' drive back I was quite a pathetic figure." It reminded her of the time a decade before when, equally frustrated, she had discovered that singing at the top of her voice in the Central Park tunnel made it sound much fuller amplified by the echoing resonances. Perhaps Madame suspected, deep-down, that she was one of those people capable of giving a prima donna performance only while - metaphorically speaking - soaping herself under the shower.

For market watchers, Monday, December 16, 1935 may have been seen as a pivotal moment in the fortunes of the American economy emerging from the long, dark tunnel of the Depression. Madame Walska's main indicators, however, were not rising stocks on Wall Street, or even smaller dole queues on the streets, but the inauguration of the grand opera season at the Metropolitan Opera House under a new era headed by Edward Johnson. He had succeeded the authoritarian Giulio Gatti-Casazza as manager, promising to recapture some of the glamor that surrounded Met openings in the past. Ganna would be there over the next few months, among the well-dressed throng, meeting old friends and hearing great performance. It was now acceptable to be seen sitting in the orchestra seats, even on opening night, though she did occupy a box with her guests for this glittering gala, though one of them, Alexander Markey, an admirer with Polish connections, was unable to attend because of being absent from New York on a business trip to Canada.

Around Walska's box, caught up the air of excitement and expectation - not entirely generated by Verdi's *La traviata* with Lucrezia Bori, Lawrence Tibbett and Richard Crooks in the leading roles - was the cream of New York society seated in the famed "golden horseshoe" and parterre boxes. Reporters filled shorthand notebooks with minute details of the finery on display, with Mary Elizabeth Plummer, a staff writer for Associated Press, busily recording that Princess Stefanie, "who boasted a close kinship to a Czar," and the American-born Princess Thurn und Taxis married to a Hungarian, both appeared in pearls, diamonds and red velvet, while "ropes of emeralds clanked on Ganna Walska, the singer, former wife of Harold McCormick of Chicago."

Details of operagoers' extravagant outfits and priceless jewelry filled the syndicated social columns of hundreds of newspapers from coast to coast, as diverse as the Milwaukee *News*, the Santa Fe *New Mexican*, the *Christian Science Monitor* in Boston and the Youngstown, Ohio *Vindicator*, with New York's *Evening Post* selecting Mrs. William Goadby Loew and Ganna Walska as

211

symbolizing the opening night's splendor. To make the occasion complete for Madame, her unable-to-attend admirer, Markey, sent a message from the Royal York Hotel in Toronto: "Please do not try to be anything but your choice self, which I find a cosmic delight to contact," signing it "In perfect rhythm, Alec."

The unsatisfied urge to sing remained a barrier to Ganna's rationality, and plenty of people were prepared to guide her down the path of self-delusion in return for fat fees. Ever generous, she sent the Ballards a Christmas box to Los Angeles containing an expensive white cape for Edna, which was extravagantly acknowledged: "I shall wear it and feel your love enfolding me and shall send back to you our love and the Blessings of the Ascended Masters." The couple was holding classes related to their popular "I Am" cult - an offshoot of theosophy - at the Shrine Auditorium during January, 1936 but Madame was too occupied on the East Coast to attend them.

That winter, she was a familiar sight at many musical events in New York as well as gatherings connected with the teaching of what she referred to as "Ancient Wisdom." At one of them, Ganna listened to a Dutch woman propounding a theory about the use of color in healing, by artificially replacing chromatic deficiencies in one's aura. Dr. Cannon and Sri Sukul had mentioned this technique before, and, willing to try anything, Walska sang for this "mannish" person who diagnosed an apparent absence of two or three hues which severely inhibited her voice development. The woman suggested visiting her in Europe, where she had the right equipment for treating the problem, and, in the meantime, suggested that Walska see her master, a mystic known only as Mr. L. who lived in Chicago. They went together, with Walska traveling incognito, and registering under an assumed name at the modest Pearson Hotel on East Pearson Street, after being more familiar with the residential comforts of Rush Street or Lakeside Drive in the past.

Mr. L. proved to be sympathetic, worldly and approachable. But during a conversation about teaching philosophy and religion Walska told him about meeting the Ballards and was shocked to hear the saintly man's opinion that her new best friends were perpetrating a gigantic psychic fraud by living a life of luxury on the proceeds of their lectures, books and broadcasts. Mr. L.

revealed that only that a few years before, Godfré Ray King had been a painter, and, from the tone of voice, Ganna could only assume that he meant artisan rather than artist. Those four days in Chicago led her to believe - not for the first time - that her life had changed irrevocably for the better through meeting this mystic-master, and just in time, because she and her maid were due to return to Europe and there were a hundred-and-one things to do before that: attempting to get a new passport, attending to her American income tax declaration, packing and closing down the New York house.

There was disquiet in the air about the political situation in Europe, with the League of Nations imposing sanctions on Italy for invading Ethiopia, the specter of German rearmament, and gathering political chaos in Spain - to mention only three of the world's many trouble spots. As a consequence, the United States government had adopted a policy of not issuing travel documents to nonresident citizens for fear of having to rescue them in the event of emergencies overseas. Walska's own passport expired several years before when the State Department refused its renewal, and since then she had voyaged back and forth across the Atlantic on American consular papers issued in Paris, together with documentation from the French consul in New York. Always at the back of her mind, however, was the threat of being denied entry to either country - and more so now.

Her attorney, Phelan Beale, with excellent connections in Washington, tried everything possible to change the State Department's stance, though Madame castigated him for failure to have her case treated as a priority, threatening to dispense with his services. His response, addressing her uncharacteristically as "Mrs. McCormick" to show his displeasure, stated: "It is entirely agreeable to me that you inaugurate your passport undertaking through another attorney. May I say to you in real friendship that in the matter of your passport you cannot blow hot and cold at the same time."

He meant that once her application had been refused, she could hardly expect to retain the status of a nonresident and at the same time procure a passport, assuring his client that it was not a denial of citizenship because only the courts could do that. He was going to Washington, D.C. soon for a senatorial investigation and promised to take up her matter, if she so wished. Madame did.

True to his promise, Beale sought the assistance of the Secretary of State, Cordell Hull, who called on the chief of the passport bureau, Mrs. R.B. Shipley, but to no avail. The official view remained that Madame Walska retained only minimal ties with the United States, having no family or kin in America, and no business interests. The fact that she owned shares in a large corporation (International Harvester) did not require her presence, and ownership of a town house in New York was not in itself evidence of residing because she also owned a house and a château in France, together with a business (the theater), which indicated her true allegiance.. This infuriated Ganna, who was used to getting her way by buying whatever she wanted, except, of course, a great singing voice, spiritual fulfillment, and an American passport - even with assistance from the Secretary of State himself.

Her search for the meaning of life continued by visiting Mr. D. in New Jersey, who continued to ply her with astrological analysis. Ganna also kept company with Alexander Markey, madly in love with her and desolated that he could not be her partner at the recent gala opening of the Met season. Ganna was wary of male approaches these days, particularly when they looked like becoming serious, having made a pact with herself that she could never again live with a man - and certainly not entertain the thought of a further marriage. Approaching fifty, she played hard to get like a flirtatious teenager, resulting in a flurry of amorous notes from Markey, like: "My soul weeps to have seen hurt in your eyes. We belong to each other, and nothing you or I can do - neither Heaven nor Earth, nor fire nor water can keep us apart."

But he was not her only admirer currently. Antoni Jechalski, who lived in Poland, was a longtime friend, and they had spent time together over the years in Zakopane, Warsaw, New York and Long Beach, and he visited the Château de Galluis. Jechalski - unlike Markey - seemed reluctant to commit himself to Ganna wholeheartedly, which probably made him more appealing, and they exchanged letters and cables expressing their love for each other. He called her "Dzi" - the Polish rendition of the letter G (for Ganna), and she used the second-person familiar (like *tu* in French or *du* in German). While Markey tried to win her over with prurient pronouncements, Jechalski tended to cable words of affection and she responded, unusually frankly, by saying that her body longed for him.

Madame's heart may have beat a little faster from their attention, but her soul continued to belong to music, deciding it would be helpful to record some of her favorite art songs for study purposes. That way she could critically evaluate her own voice and perhaps make the progress her teachers so often failed to deliver. Hiring a studio at the National Recording Company on West 46th Street, she engaged an accompanist and recorded a selection of her favorite songs and arias ranging from Schubert's "Die Forelle" and Schumann's "Die Nussbaum" to "Morgen" and "Die Nacht" by Richard Strauss, "Depuis le jour" from Charpentier's *Louise* and Gounod's arrangement of "Ave Maria." Pressure of time became obvious toward the end of the sessions, with tiredness creeping into the voice, resulting in excessive vibrato, and the recording engineers could have been excused for wondering how the famous Madame Ganna Walska earned the reputation she had, if this was the best she could do.

No company had ever asked her to record, and now nobody seemed interested in hearing her voice in any capacity, though she did find herself in demand from various religious groups, including one of the most prestigious: the World Fellowship of Faiths. This global organization, described as "a continuous parliament of religions," sought to foster peace and brotherhood through mutual understanding among peoples of all faiths, races and countries, and to oppose evils such as the Nazi threat to the Jews, the segregation of blacks in America, and extreme nationalism wherever it happened.. Herbert Hoover was honorary chairman of their American National Council, and with distinguished men of the cloth and from public life heading groups in Britain and India it was just the type of cause to attract Ganna's sympathies, as well as her generous donation. She entertained one of the founders, Kedarnath Das Gupta, at her New York home and agreed to participate in a banquet to celebrate the diamond jubilee of the International President, the Maharaja Gaekwa of Baroda, on January 28, 1936 in the Grand Ballroom of the Hotel Biltmore. It was where Ganna had made her New York concert début two decades before with Caruso, hoping for a brilliant career ahead. But this appearance, eighteen years later, was no more demanding

215

than speaking a few words in support of the Fellowship and singing a single, simple Polish folk song.

Mr. L. proposed coming to New York for a few days to give advice about facing the summer in Europe, though at the last minute he was involved in an automobile accident, suffering a deep gash in the throat. Walska thought it inadvisable for him to travel while recuperating, but "with an angelic devotion, my newly discovered but old friend still insisted on coming." She agreed that if his doctor sanctioned the journey, there were many questions she wanted to ask him personally. One was about his Dutch apostle who had fervently expressed her love for Ganna, which was disconcerting to someone unaccustomed to lesbian approaches. Male adoration had been part of her life for the past thirty years or more, and she was deeply shocked by the aggressive approach, dismissing such women as "freaks of Nature" by following misguided instincts.

Reading one of L.'s daily letters, Ganna's heart sank ever deeper on learning that he could not come to New York, after all. "Being God's soldier, ever doing a soldier's work I must on my Master's command be in Chicago," he wrote. Next morning, she received a small wooden packing case containing L.'s portrait of his Master which Walska and the Dutch lesbian had admired during their visit to Chicago. She told her maid to put it down anywhere, and when asked if it should be opened, her irritable response was, "No. I will take it to Paris unopened."

This "inspirational portrait" (actually a photograph) was kept in her room until the moment of departure on April 3, and then, in spite of its cumbersome packaging, she insisted on carrying it personally to the "Ile de France," departing from Pier 88 in the North River. A Western Union telegram was delivered to her suite from Alexander Markey (discreetly signed "A.M.") saying that the very best of him went along with her and promising "A Love Beyond Mere Words." When all visitors had gone ashore, Walska improvised an altar in her stateroom with the picture as its centerpiece, lit a seven-day candle – also from L. - and arranged flowers around it sent to the ship by several well-wishers, including an extravagant bouquet from Harold McCormick.

216

Doldrums
1936

Madame soon reverted to habitual routines on arrival back in France: attending to business affairs, entertaining brother Leon and close friends at Galluis, taking singing lessons, and reading spiritual subjects. Some ready cash was raised by selling pieces from her extensive jewelry collection, with *Paris-Midi* reporting that the former Barbara Hutton, now Barbara Hutton Haugwitz-Reventlow and known as the Woolworth heiress, paid $1,200,000 for a set of emerald jewelry given to the Countess de Castiglione by Napoléon III, including a diadem, double-necklace, earrings and bracelets. The *New York Times,* quoting the French report, reminded its readers that Ganna Walska's collection was first revealed publicly when the United States government sought to levy a million dollars in duties on jewelry and clothing she brought to America in September, 1928.

She made her usual visit during high summer to the Salzburg Festival, first attended when honeymooning with Harold fourteen years before. Ganna exchanged greetings and smiles with familiar faces in the festival theater, nodding formally to each other like members of an exclusive club, knowing that she cut a sad figure among them, and confiding to her diary: "For an artist at heart - as I certainly am if I am anything at all - it is a small tragedy to be unable to create and to have instead only a seat in the first row of any opera house of both hemispheres." This private suffering was inflamed by realizing how the world of the arts had become dictated by commercial considerations. Now, instead of deciding the artistic policy of her theater, she was condemned to sit in the audience "helpless to contribute a fresh spark, except by paying endless bills."

Ganna's visit to Salzburg with a young Parisienne named Madeleine held few pleasures, except to see the delight on her companion's face when hearing the finest interpretations under the musical direction of Arturo Toscanini and Bruno Walter. Walska also enjoyed some good theater, stimulating what she called "a healthy American feeling" which was gradually replacing her Slavic tendency for introversion. But there were too many ghosts of the past at the Salzburg for peace of mind, with constant reminders of former happiness at the festival on meeting the Austrian poet and playwright Hugo von Hofmannsthal, who wrote the text for Strauss's *Der Rosenkavalier,* and the theater director, Max Reinhardt, one of the festival's founders. She had been entertained by Richard Strauss himself and presented with a signed portrait of the great composer to join her gallery of silver-framed celebrities on the grand piano at rue de Lubeck. But now, the discomforting summer heat in the Austrian Alps demoralized her, and the performances in Mozart's birthplace disappointed because of inadequate singing. "Nowadays the artists seem to be less perfect than during my first visit to Salzburg," she complained in her diary.

By the end of the first week, a bored Ganna Walska found the social proprieties as oppressive as the mountain humidity, no longer able to face the daily prospect of greeting "all of New York" in the hotel lobby each morning, "seeing all of Paris" for lunch, and meeting everyone again on the street. She would have run a mile in the opposite direction to avoid most of these people on their home ground, and it was just like a transatlantic voyage: "How-do-you-do to the right and How-do-you-do to the left, empty conversations, useless questions, not always sincere compliments, snobbish criticism of last night's performance, sympathetic enquiries about my voice."

Ganna decided to quit the festival early, reserving sleeping accommodation on the night train back to Paris, and then spent part of her last day in the Tyrol listening to some singing students. One of them praised her teacher's method, remarking that even if she were awakened in the middle of the night, she would now sing correctly because of having absolute voice control. Walska wondered if this was the lost chord in her own long and bitter struggle. "One day I can sing well and the next - for no apparent reason - I cannot sing at all," she told herself, reasoning that it must be control she lacked, not technique. With hopes raised again, she cabled the teacher in question at her holiday home in south-western France where she was running a summer school, asking to

218

work with her during the following week. That night at the Festspiel, Ganna watched and silently sang along with the three leading female roles in *Don Giovanni,* which she knew well, becoming Donna Anna, Donna Elvira and Zerlina for a few precious hours.

At the buffet during intermission she met an acquaintance, the American socialite Mrs. Cornelius Crane, who revealed that she had been trying to contact Ganna for the past couple of months after discovering an extraordinary singing teacher who was also a mystic, claiming to have received messages from her Tibetan mentor to contact Madame Walska and help her with the voice. This was a sudden *embarras de richesses* because next morning, teacher Cécile Gilly sent a favorable response from France, and during the afternoon Mrs. Crane telephoned St. Moritz from where Madame L'Orsa, medium and voice teacher, said she would be delighted to meet Madame Walska. Two long train journeys, halfway across Europe and back, followed in quick succession: the first from Salzburg to Paris, where Madame stayed long enough only to take Madeleine home, drop off her maid, and change luggage. Twenty-four hours later, she was on the Simplon-Orient express approaching what she fully expected to be "the realization of my life's purpose."

On the way to the Cranes' house, she and Mrs. Crane's brother remained in the car while the hostess did some shopping and he expressed curiosity about Walska's visit to Madame L'Orsa because he'd thought she talked too much for a teacher and seemed to have an inflated respect for money. Ganna had heard comments like that before and, "unless the young man was completely mistaken - and I did not feel he was - my opinion of Madame L'Orsa was already formed." As they neared her chalet, Ganna had the familiar sinking feeling of being taken for a ride: the victim once again of her own faulty instincts. In the afternoon she met the formidable teacher, who was preoccupied with a legal wrangle over the ownership of her property. "I met this fighting lady," Walska noted, "took a half-hour lesson for an enormous price and did not change my opinion." She left for Paris on the next train.

The fall of 1936 was shaping up to be extremely hectic for her, with acceptance of Cécile Gilly's offer of lessons. "Back at Galluis," she wrote, "I no sooner changed my luggage again than I

219

was off in my old Rolls for another experience. How many I had, only to meet inward disaster which gradually diminished my hopes!" Ganna could, of course, have stayed at home surrounded by the sylvan splendors of the château, planning the development of its gardens – finding horticulture an increasingly pleasurable pastime - but needed first to satisfy her curiosity about Madame Gilly and her teaching method.

A long drive across country to the Gers *département* on the rough roads of aptly-named *La France profonde* was neither pleasant nor comfortable, with problems along the way somewhere in the Limousin region when a leaking radiator caused her old Rolls to stall under a searing sun without a single tree nearby for shade. Her chauffeur stubbornly insisted that he knew the way and refused to seek directions as a matter of professional pride, getting hopelessly lost. They finally reached the sleepy town of Eauze late at night, to stay at a modest commercial hotel with the misleading name of the Grand, where she was offered the establishment's best room, whose primitive facilities harked back to a former era. In the absence of a bath or even a washbasin, the exhausted traveler went straight to bed, only to suffer the agony of a loudspeaker across the street blaring out the soundtrack of the Friday movie, which screened and screamed late into the night.

Next morning, Walska discovered to her dismay that she must wait until five that afternoon before Madame Gilly was finished with her students, deciding not to stay a moment longer than necessary in Eauze, a pretty little place for lingering, with a population of about 3,500, an interesting Roman past, and a reputation for producing some of the finest Armagnac from grapes grown in the surrounding vineyards. She would return to Galluis after a trial lesson, preferring an all-night drive to having her ears assaulted again by the Saturday cinema and her body attacked by hordes of stinging flies. At five o'clock she shook hands with Cécile Gilly, they took tea, and afterward she sang.

The teaching methods were explained and they coincided with Ganna's expectations: "I actually saw the reflection of my intuition in her explanations," she stated in her autobiography. Gilly was the wife of the well-known French-Algerian operatic baritone, Dinh Gilly, who performed leading roles at the Metropolitan in New York for five years, and was also a favorite of audiences at the

Paris Opéra and the Royal Opera House, Covent Garden. Cécile knew all about vocal technique, advising her new client not to endure the drudgery of morning and evening lessons any longer: a half-hour would be enough - and not necessarily every day. Ganna was eager to know if the critics were right in saying she was not meant to be a singer. "I was waiting for some concrete indication," she recalled, "begging my soul to give me proof that I was wrong, that I had taken the wrong path, that I had played the wrong cards." She was assured of her artistry and offered further lessons.

Walska left on the long and winding trip back home, as uncertain as ever about her future, and when Madame Gilly stayed longer than expected at Eauze, her daughter took over the lessons in Paris. During one of them, while singing Beethoven's "Ich liebe dich," all the right tones fell into place in a way she could only dream about, having to stop herself from kneeling and praying on the studio floor for an apparent miracle. As soon as the session finished, Ganna stood alone in the music room repeating, "Oh God! Oh God!" and to avoid anyone seeing her in this embarrassing state left the house to seek the privacy of her waiting car. But it was nowhere to be seen. Becoming confused, trying to imagine where the chauffeur could be because he was instructed always to be early, "I put my music case down in the middle of the sidewalk in front of me and waited, unable to do anything else. I saw a radio shop next door. I went in and asked the time but my voice disobeyed me. People looked at me curiously. Again I struggled to repeat my question. I heard funny words coming out of my mouth. I heard them as if from a great way off, as if that voice did not belong to me."

It was four-fifteen, the Rolls should have been there at four, and Walska stood helplessly waiting until the vehicle finally drew up. She was driven to her next appointment - a milliner's - spending an hour trying on the latest hats and graciously accepting flattery from the staff. "I saw myself in the mirror - deeply beautiful with the reflection of the glorious inner sunshine. Any hat seemed suitable to the perfection that was in me that day." She allowed the assistants fussing around her the satisfaction of thinking that her radiance was due to their creations: the hats being responsible for a new luster in her eyes and a glow to the cheeks. They displayed model after model, gushing in their *vendeuse* vocabulary, and

Walska reflected later: "Truly if they had put the ugliest stew pan of a hat on my head - a sacrilege to my sense of beauty in ordinary circumstances - they would not have been able to disturb the glorified peace, the mighty sublimity of my inner being." She never knew how she arrived home at rue de Lubeck, where a woman friend waiting for her, exclaimed "You look eighteen, darling!"

A young Dutchman named Sam Waagenaar was one of Cécile Gilly's students at this time, and noted Madame Walska's difficulty, as a mature-age student, to mix with young singing hopefuls. "On the ground floor, across a corridor," he remembered, "was a room where the students waited for their lessons, which usually lasted for half-an-hour. But when Ganna had hers, we were forbidden to be there because she didn't want us to hear. Waiting was then outside in the garden." He also recalled Madame being driven in her open car from Galluis into Paris to watch performances at the theater "clutching a *coffret* on her knees containing various sets of necklaces, earrings and hairpieces in rubies, diamonds, sapphires, and emeralds, deciding which to wear after reaching her *loge* dressing room.

The continuing sorrow of L's disappearance from Madame's spiritual life was eased when a friend phoned to ask if she would entertain Shri Meher Baba, a well-known Indian mystic. This self-proclaimed second Christ had a host of mainly female followers, and, if he wished to grace her with his sanctifying presence, how could Ganna refuse? She had first come across him when reading Paul Brunton's "A Search in Secret India," where Baba was represented somewhat ambiguously; later, Rom Landau in his bestselling "God is My Adventure" (1935) depicted him as something of an impostor. One of Baba's most ardent devotees was Princess Norina Matchabelli, the former Italian stage and screen actress Maria Carmi, who created with her late Georgian husband, Prince Georges, the American perfume and cosmetics company bearing his family name. He had once confided to Walska that Baba was responsible for stealing his wife, making him the laughing stock of Paris.

The princess visited the French capital during 1935 - the year her divorced husband died - and became a good friend of Ganna's, who was touched by her total adoration of Baba. Norina later wrote from New York saying she had pledged the Indian mystic her life and possessions, including the $250,000 proceeds of selling the successful Matchabelli company which she inherited. Norina cabled in late 1936 that Baba and his entourage were coming to France:

"Baba Will See You Paris Ninth [of November]. Stays Overnight. Would You Then Keep Up Your Invitation Extending Him And Five People Hospitality." This posed a problem for Walska because the converted coach house used as guest accommodation at Galluis was already shut for the winter, and the central heating in the main house had a fault. But despite some skepticism about the celebrity ascetic, she was prepared, for Norina's sake, to open up some rooms and pretend to be a disciple.

Princess Norina's instructions were followed to the letter, providing a bedroom for Baba "and two boys," together with two other rooms for the rest of the group. There was to be breakfast for the *ménage à trois* in the master's room at 8.30, with tea, cream, toast, butter, jam, porridge and fruit; meals for the others would be taken in the dining room, "or wherever," with lunch to be served at precisely one o'clock for the spiritual master and his boys, taken in their room and comprising two vegetables, rice, curry, salad, sweet and fruit. Far from conversion - if Ganna had felt moved to seek it - there was to be no conversation with the holy man because he had taken a vow of silence, using an alphabet board or complicated hand gestures to communicate. The chatelaine was rushed off her feet trying to satisfy the demands of fourteen visitors. "I was busy every second," she noted, "running from the kitchen to Baba's disciples, from the garage to the housekeeper who complained that our cook had lost her head - *et pour cause!* - while my secretary in the meantime was suspended on the telephone for the master's orders."

She thought that the Indian, aged forty-one, acted like a capricious prima donna, "and his disciples played the parts of typically enslaved accompanist, secretary and maids," while Norina was in her element as a beautiful impresario. Everyone was terrified of displeasing the mere wisp of a holy man, with dark features, long and wildly flowing hair, dressed in a white Gandhi-style robe. His effeminate manner suggested to Ganna more mistress than master, with his acolytes constantly on-call. "They waited at his door," she wrote in her diary, "like a dog sitting on the floor, on the stairs - in order to respond more quickly at his call. And when a call came, they rushed in quickly in military style that I trembled for any antiques that might be in their way."

Next morning, the entourage had just sat down for breakfast, when the master rang and they rushed to answer his demand, leaving brioches and croissants to be reheated several times over until they were too leathery to eat, with their coffee becoming bitter and undrinkable after standing too long. Worse was to follow at luncheon, whose starting time was changed eight times and finally brought forward from the original one o'clock to eleven-thirty, with the inevitable result that the food failed to meet the usual high standards of the château kitchen because Walska's harassed cook had no hope of preparing an unfamiliar vegetarian menu at an hour's notice. The unreasonable demand was because Baba had decided to attend a movie matinée to see a new musical based on the life of an American showman, *The Great Ziegfeld*, starring Dick Powell, Myrna Loy and Louise Rainer.

Familiar with the sometimes tyrannical behavior of opera stars, Walska was not unduly upset by the antics of the visiting mystic, who reminded her of the distraught diva in another recent motion picture, *A Night at the Opera*. But that was where any resemblance to the Marx Brothers ended, except perhaps for Harpo, because Baba was a mute messiah, having uttered not a single word for the past ten years, according to Norina. After a hurried meal, the whole group was transported in several automobiles to the nearest movie theater and Ganna sat down in its darkened auditorium telling herself that in another three-and-a-half hours she would be delivered from these visitors: "I beg your pardon - from Baba's saintly presence!"

The supporting feature on the double-bill was a cheap Western; with so much shooting that the over-amplified sound gave her a terrible migraine. And her estimate of how long the session would run was wildly optimistic because the main attraction - which would win the Academy Award for best picture of 1936 - had the distinction of being the longest Hollywood talkie made to that time: three hours.

Recovering from the bizarre visit with its Marx Brothers overtones, Walska's life achieved a degree of serenity not experienced for years, with only one niggling concern for an inveterate transatlantic voyager: no current passport. Having let the situation slip, she instructed Phelan Beale to press her claim once more, and he wrote to Secretary of State Hull to find out if it would now be in order for a passport to be issued to Mrs. Ganna Walska McCormick, as she continued to be known post-divorce. The authorities remained intractable, however, with Ganna almost giving up in despair, assuming she could continue to use the American visaed affidavit that had served her for years. The attorney advised, however, that as the department had her previous documentation on file, she should make a formal application, and Ganna reluctantly agreed to a new affidavit being prepared.

The information, intended to prove her suitability, included details of city, state and federal taxes paid over the past ten years, together with Beale's calculation that Madame lived in the United States for six-and-a-half months during 1933-34, five-and-a-half months in the period 1934-35 and about four months in 1935-36. He confirmed that Walska's residence was of serious importance: "that she is a good American citizen and that she regrets that she ever conceived the idea of living abroad." The document added that his client needed to spend a portion of each year in France because of considerable property interests which she was unable to liquidate because the affairs of the Champs de Elysee [sic] theater were in a confused state due to tax liens, mortgages "and other complications." The text ended with a dangerous statement that could ruin the application if its veracity were challenged:

"And for whatever value my views may merit, I further believe that the said applicant, Ganna Walska McCormick, wishes in all sincerity to return to the United States and to reside permanently here and to discharge in good faith her duties of American citizenship; and that this she will do, never thereafter leaving the United States except when it is absolutely necessary so to do for the final liquidation of her property interests in France or to make an occasional brief visit for pleasure purposes as American citizens so frequently do."

That statement would prove to be strangely prophetic, though Madame's travel plans at the moment favored going east to India, rather than returning west to the United States. As for taking up permanent residence there: it had never entered her mind.

225

Cause and Effect
1937

With confidence regained after Cécile Gilly's singing lessons, Ganna Walska faced the New Year regarding herself as mistress of her actions, desires and movements. She was a slave only to one almost wild cat at Galluis that shunned all other human contact, "who did not like to be fed but by myself and who, whenever he saw me putting on a hat, hid himself under my bed, so sad that I was leaving him." She would have taken lessons seven days a week, but Gilly, a strict Roman Catholic, never worked on a Sunday, and her oldest student used that day "to hear any lecture on metaphysical subjects that happened to be announced."

One weekend she learned about Rudolf Steiner, the Austrian-born scientist, social reformer, editor and founder of Anthroposophy, a Christian movement based on the principles of theosophy, which attempted to find a synthesis between science and mysticism. Steiner's broad vision had led to the development of schools for physically disabled and mentally retarded children, as well as participating in a modern art movement known as Der Blaue Reiter ("The Blue Rider"), established by Wassily Kandinsky and Franz Marc in Munich during 1911, with its expressionist concept of a colorful universe. Friends interested in art and mysticism invited Walska to join them on a visit to Dornach, near Basel, where Steiner had worked.

She spent only ten hours in the Swiss memorial village, admiring its ambiance and attending a performance in the beautiful theater called the Goetheanum, designed by Steiner to house all the arts. "There was no mundane atmosphere whatsoever," Ganna noted in her diary. "One felt no embarrassment in finding words when meeting new people. The special characteristics of those seeker-workers who are practically anonymous (even the program does not mention the actors' names) are quite visible even to a materialistically inclined eye. They have an utter lack of egoism." Life in the spiritual-cultural community greatly appealed to

Walska, impressed that no artist or artisan sought personal credit or acclaim, though she did think that certain of Rudolf Steiner's most loyal followers might be reproached for being *"plus royaliste que le Roi."* She would claim that this brief visit resulted in a spiritual uplift and an improvement in her singing, the former through associating with "real people" and the latter from a technique derived from the actors she heard speaking "outside the lips in a special manner." Ganna invited one of the Dornach drama instructors to Galluis and struggled for weeks to form her vowels and consonants as he directed.

She decided to stop thinking about technique for a while and search for a new soul mate: somebody to serve as a cause, like she had hoped to do with T. E. Lawrence. A perfect opportunity presented itself when the newspapers announced the death of Ignacy Jan Padarewski's (second) wife, the former Helena Gorska also known as the Baroness de Rosen. The name of the much celebrated Polish pianist, composer, diplomat and politician was synonymous with keyboard virtuosity, making him perhaps the most famous pianist of his day - certainly among women - and Walska's immediate reaction, noted in the diary, was "Now I will marry him." She imagined herself as half the age of the "sick, spoiled and moneyless" long-haired genius, who had served as the prime minister of a reconstituted Poland for ten months in 1919 before returning to the concert circuit. In fact, she was forty-nine and he seventy-six. Ganna had been approached by some American friends to help pay the tax arrears on his two thousand-acre vineyard property called Rancho San Ignacio on California's central coast. This was a normal act of generosity for expatriate Poles, based on the bonds of nationalism, and Walska admired the fact that the great man had given away his own fortune amassed from performing, and since the war had played in Europe only for charity. "He cannot play much longer," she reasoned. "Even now his undying spirit is more powerful than the elasticity of his mortal fingers. *I* will take care of him!"

Her close friend and long-time admirer, Dr. Josef Orlowski, a Polish journalist based in the United States, who planned to write a book about her, visited Padarewski in Morges, a small community in Switzerland's Vaud canton situated on the shore of Lake Geneva, and told her of the pianist's financial difficulties.

Responding, Ganna sent a written proposal for a union between herself and Paderewski through his companion, Ernest Schelling. "After all," she reasoned, "I merely desired to give to that great soul, to that imposing personality, to that man already old, broken in health, and without future, my years of remaining youth, the unrestricted richness of my generous nature as well as my earthly possessions for his service."

Ganna's unfettered benevolence knew no limits where it concerned one of Poland's greatest sons born, like her, in the former Russian Empire. Paderewski might now be regarded as a featherless eagle, with arthritic fingers, long-faded political expertise, and bygone celebrity, living lonely and lost on a mortgaged Swiss estate, but she had the power and the money to change all that: to make him feel that the world still needed his spirit. Herr Schelling, however, blocked Madame's ambitions by suppressing her letter and nothing happened.

Walska continued to take lessons with her usual dogged determination trying to learn by example from the singers she admired the most. She wrote in justification of this: "A very important question enters my mind as to who is the greatest artist - the genius or one who acquires his ability through hard work, strong will power, perseverance and unshakeable determinations." She thought about the career of one of the supreme sopranos of the nineteenth century, Adelina Patti, concluding: "I am sure that today in these times of terrific speed when people want to hear, see, be deeply touched and expect to find all these things combined in one person, Patti with her gifted voice alone could not have the same phenomenal success she had with our grandfathers."

She also reviewed Enrico Caruso's contribution to the lyric art, taking comfort that he was pilloried during his early career: "Demonstrations were so hostile against him in Italy every time he sang that he wanted to quit a thousand times. Through heroic perseverance, however, he became the idol of the world." Ganna never understood why her own progress had not followed the same paths as Patti and Caruso, sometimes taking out a yellowed and much-thumbed magazine clipping during moments of doubt, to read over and over again to recharge her confidence:

"If there are any so foolish as to think that because of several rebuffs by critical audiences Mme. Walska will be delivered from pursuing her

musical career, they show very conclusively that they are decidedly unfamiliar with the caliber of the lady's courage. Besides, is it not recorded in musical annals that the celebrated Jenny Lind was once hissed off the stage? And did not the Swedish Nightingale become one of the greatest divas of her time? Such is the truth and with such a precedent what may not Mme. Walska expect?"

Walska was very attached to the frayed, unattributed and undated clipping, showing it to friends whenever they asked about her unwillingness to perform in musical comedy or operetta, where her light soprano voice might have been heard to better effect. Roles such as Anna Glawari in Lehar's *The Merry Widow* or Rosalinde in Johann Strauss's *Die Fledermaus* seem to have been tailor-made for her personality, but they were classed as operettas and of little interest to a potential prima donna. Others tactfully suggested that she should continue giving concerts in costume, by displaying her outstanding jewel collection combined with a repertoire reviving old, forgotten songs. Some advised her more realistically, to sing only at home for a few close friends who would be generous in their response.

These well-meaning souls were the most annoying because they never understood Ganna's motivation, unable to comprehend which dream lived on, and what urge possessed her: "They could not even imagine that if all the operas in the world were wide open to me, I would not take advantage of it if I felt that I could not do it up to my standard of singing." She never questioned her stars, only to make fallible human interpretations of them, because being at one with the cosmic world meant she couldn't fail. "If I should be unable to express myself through my voice, it would only mean that my mission lies elsewhere and my search in the field of singing was only part of the process of preparing my soul for something bigger." That was precisely what the celebrity evangelist Manly Hall told her several years before.

The Château de Galluis provided much of the harmony Ganna now needed. Strolling its park-like grounds and through the developing gardens wearing a simple gray woolen dress and no makeup, gave a sense of being at one with her idealized world. The rural tranquility was often shattered, however, by the buzz of activity because improvements were always taking place. Decorators' scaffolds cluttered the main house, plumbers modernized bathrooms, a wooden summer house on wheels was constructed under the trees, and gardeners dug new flower beds. The estate was a manageable size, matching what the French called a bijou château, not at all ostentatious, though some visitors thought it looked rather sparse inside.

On the ground floor, off a stone-flagged entrance hall stood the large dining room leading to an ancient chapel. The annual Christmas tree was erected there, with Madame, dressed up as *Père Noel* emerging to distribute presents to the excited village children who had never known anything like it. There were two salons with shiny parquet flooring, each dominated by a grand piano - one white, the other black – and a scattering of antique furniture, several wing chairs and long tables always displaying lavish floral arrangements. Three bedrooms were situated on the ground floor, together with a bathroom showing a typical Walska flourish of enormous sea shells converted to washbasins. Along a corridor at the back stood the large open-plan kitchen.

A grand staircase gave access to the upper levels where there were another four or five bedrooms, with Madame's own spacious quarters occupying a corner suite looking down on ornamental ponds and flower beds, and beyond to the trees and lawns of the estate. An adjacent apartment and office accommodated Mlle. Albertine, her secretary, and under the roof, several attic rooms were used mainly for storage.

Away from the main house stood what Walska called *Le petit château*: separate guest accommodation in the ivy-clad converted stables, where Walther Straram had spent much of the summer of 1933 convalescing after his throat surgery. Another building in the grounds, probably an orangery in earlier times, displayed striking décor of fantasy figures clad in sea shells, their long flowing hair picked out in red and brown corals.

Though she reveled in the calm of the countryside, Ganna never quite managed to escape the demands of day-to-day living that drew her back into the real world of Paris. With her poor eyesight, she was obliged to wear glasses for reading and signing checks, two of her more frequent activities in the city. Declining vision was a normal condition of aging, but personal vanity dictated that she avoid wearing glasses, even when the eye specialists she consulted in New York, London and the French capital assured her there was no alternative: she must expect to need ever stronger lenses. Walska claimed that one day an inner voice had told her "Stop wearing these glasses!" and she obeyed by abandoning countless pairs scattered throughout the château, in the Rolls, at rue de Lubeck, around her theater, giving away the Cartier platinum *face-à-main* (lorgnette) inlaid with diamonds previously used for evening wear.

Walska wanted to share her current karmic joy with all, insisting that everyone could have "the same certitude in their hearts as I now have in mine," pointing out that she'd never heard of a happy man in power: "Certainly no king, no dictator could say that he found his heart's desire while envied so much by the whole world." She cited Napoléon Bonaparte's miserable life, and thought that Edward VIII's abdication in November 1936 to marry Wallis Simpson was because he had accepted the unreality of power. Several well-informed sources in New York and London assured Ganna that Mrs. Simpson was "mystically inclined" and a strong influence on the king, insisting that he forego his hereditary obligation as monarch, visualizing his mission elsewhere.

In the tide of tittle-tattle surrounding Britain's abdication crisis, Madame would have been surprised - and not a little shocked - to hear that her former spiritual adviser, Dr. Alexander Cannon, had secretly attended the monarch during his brief, uncrowned reign. The Archbishop of Canterbury, Dr. Cosmo Lang, heard about it from an informant, who assumed it was something to do with Edward's mental health or alcohol, after Cannon had boasted publicly about treating the king by hypnosis. It was a time when mysticism was all the rage within the cocktail party set, and the archbishop became alarmed, alerting prime minister Stanley Baldwin about his concern that Edward VIII was being adversely influenced.

The British press reported none of this, but *Time* magazine in America wrote about Dr. Cannon's role, calling him a "Miracle Man" who counted fascists among his patients, including Sir Oswald Mosley the newsworthy leader of the violently anti-communist and anti-Jewish British Union movement. When this story surfaced again more than seventy years later in a BBC radio program, the king's official biographer, Philip Ziegler, told the *Daily Telegraph* that he thought drink was an unlikely reason for the secret treatment, but he may have received advice from Cannon about a sexual problem. This seems to confirm a persistent rumor, covered-up for many years, that Edward suffered from premature ejaculation. It was certainly not a subject that Madame Walska would have discussed in polite society, except perhaps in an oblique way when making diary notes for possible publication about Harold McCormick's erectile dysfunction before and after his "monkey-gland" operation in Chicago.

These were confusing times, with Germany and Japan signing an anti-Comintern pact and agreeing to cooperate against international communism, as well as recognizing Japan's brutal régime in Manchuria and General Franco's iron-fisted rule in Spain. A Rome-Berlin axis was proclaimed by Benito Mussolini to form an alliance between Fascist Italy and Nazi Germany, while millions worldwide continued to suffer the aftershocks of the Depression, with speculation now rife about war in Europe. Ganna Walska, however, remained serene in spirit and comfortably bestowed with worldly wealth, allowing her the luxury of querying the notion of possessions and concluding that if money could buy health, emperors and Hindu potentates would live forever. "Alas!" she philosophized, "they are as subject to maladies as any factory worker, probably even more because the laborer is not acquainted with the indigestible *paté de foie gras* and other expensive foods that are poisons to our systems." She accepted as fact, questionable statistics suggesting that rich people died younger than the poor.

In addition to smoking and alcohol, another of Walska's obsessions was the killing of defenseless animals for sport or fashion, though she had not been averse to wearing a sable coat and various fox-collared garments. Galluis was close to the great forest of Rambouillet, just north of one of the prime hunting grounds of France, and she abhorred the practice of visiting politicians and heads of government being invited there on shooting parties, and then proudly displaying their trophies for the press. Living in a rural area where *la chasse* was in the blood of its people, meant that her opposition to hunting and opinions about animal welfare tended to fall on deaf ears, though Ganna insisted that shooting was strictly forbidden on her own property. "Skeptics," she wrote, "may easily mock and say that according to my way of thinking all one has to do to become good and go directly to Heaven is not to give one's wife a mink coat for

Christmas, not to have a steak for luncheon and not to go to the nearest woods on the first day of the hunting season to shoot partridge." She added, by way of summing-up her feelings, that those who were unwilling or incapable of killing a rabbit certainly would not consider killing a human being.

For once, there was some good news concerning the Théâtre des Champs-Elysées. Completion of the auditorium for the Paris World Fair of 1937 was delayed by striking construction workers, creating a desperate situation for organizers who needed access to a large assembly hall. The City of Paris made a deal with the theater's controlling company, agreeing to write-off its tax arrears and pay for refurbishment in return for its use during the period of the fair. Madame was also approached by the Royal Opera House, Covent Garden, to lend scenery from her private production of Debussy's *Pelléas et Mélisande* to the Beecham Opera Company during a special season to celebrate Britain's forthcoming coronation.

The Mad Inventor

Springtime London was bursting at the seams with visitors from all over the world for the rare spectacle of a coronation to take place with solemn ritual at Westminster Abbey in the presence of the British establishment, though its ancient symbolism permeated all levels of society. The capital was in party mood, perhaps sensing better times ahead, as artillery in Hyde Park and at the Tower of London boomed out ceremonial salutes to honor King George VI at the start of the stuttering monarch's reign by default, unexpectedly thrust upon him by constitutional obligations. Stability had returned to the House of Windsor following the royal rupture caused by the abdication of George's elder brother Edward, who had relinquished the throne after less than eleven months' rule.

Hotel rooms were impossible to find at any price and Madame Walska's regular patronage made no impression at all on managements of the swanky establishments usually delighted to receive her: Claridge's and the Ritz. Over-booked, they politely turned her away and she was glad to accept the hospitality of friends. Several in London shared her passion for fringe religions and the occult, among them Mrs. Barry-Orlova, known as Gita, of the Baha'i faith, and Joan Lestock Reid. Soon after arriving, Ganna was entertained at the Authors' Club by Gita and introduced to a man who was taking a course of spiritual lessons with her. The name Harry Grindell Matthews meant nothing to her and he made little impression until escorting the ladies to their car when, as a parting comment he said "God bless you!" This intrigued Walska, who asked if he might like to see *Pelléas et Mélisande* the next evening because she had an extra ticket.

It meant that Grindell Matthews would have to sit apart from them in the Covent Garden auditorium, and, after arriving early, the two women found him already there, suggesting he might like to join them for a chat before the performance began. Walska recalled: "When the conductor took his place in the pit and the lights dwindled, he left to look for his [own] seat. Something urged me to let him stay with us. But already he was up and logic told me that it was better to go before the orchestra started."

During the first act, with her Champs-Elysées set splendidly adapted and lit for the Royal Opera House stage, with delicate strains of Debussy rising from the orchestra pit under the direction of Giorgio Polacco, followed by some fine singing from Roger Bourdin and Maggie Teyte in the title roles, the seat next to Walska remained empty. She thought it almost sacrilegious for someone to miss the first three scenes of Debussy's masterpiece, but understood it was coronation time, with the city crowded and London's traffic in chaos because of a transport strike. But nobody came, and during the first *entr'acte* Grindell Matthews, noticing that the place next to Ganna remained unoccupied, discreetly returned to sit beside her and was able to stay for the rest of the performance. She thought to herself: "The house is sold out, not an empty seat anywhere, not an unoccupied chair in the boxes - yet the place next to mine remains vacant . . . Is it destiny?"

Grindell Matthews

235

Aged fifty-seven, but looking considerably older, Harry Grindell Matthews was a professional inventor whose career revived when war with Germany seemed likely. This gentle man - a veteran of the Boer War, pioneer of cinema sound, developer of wireless telephony techniques and weapons guidance systems – was quite a celebrity in Britain, having been dubbed "Death-ray Matthews" by the populist press after news that one of his devices had killed a cow at two hundred yards during its first War Office tests.

Behind a nondescript appearance and retiring manner, he was a man with a mission - and Walska was always attracted to noble causes. Grindell Matthews belonged to a small band of boffins (backroom researchers) often caricatured as bumbling, untidy eccentrics, peering at the world through thick lenses, and totally unconcerned about their appearance. With the looming threat from Germany, these men sought to develop new weapons and strategies for the government; many were ingenious, some approached genius, others remained in the realm of science-fiction. Most never went into production because of failing to win official backing, though there were a few exceptions, like Hubert Scott-Paine, a powerboat engineer who designed fast craft for the Royal Navy. One of his vessels capable of fifty knots was rejected by the Admiralty because of failing to meet strict contract specifications, and Scott-Paine took his design to the United States where it would become the motor torpedo boat - the famous P.T. - destined for distinction in the South Pacific campaigns of the Second World War. Most British boffins could only dream of success like that.

After Walska returned to Paris and Grindell Matthews went back to work at his remote mountaintop laboratory in Wales, a curious relationship began to develop between them, though noticeably one-sided at first. The inventor called by long distance telephone to declare his love for Ganna, claiming to have heard her sing years before in New York, following up this unexpectedly bold approach by asking, "You believe in me sincerely, don't you?" She noted in her diary: "In the back of my mind I kept wondering why this question, as generally sincere people do not mention the fact of their sincerity."

Madame's London friends regarded Grindell, as he was known to them, far too eccentric for her because the very nature of his work and lifestyle gave an impression of the archetypal mad inventor of comic books and science-fiction. She, on the other hand, imagined him as a faithful soldier to science, on whose altar he had sacrificed the sight in one eye when an experiment went wrong. Checking his entry in "Who's Who," Grindell's career looked distinguished enough on the printed page, revealing that in 1911 at the age of thirty-three he demonstrated a wireless telephone for ship-to-shore communication off the French coast, and subsequently sent Britain's first press message by radio telephone from Newport in Wales to the *Western Mail* in Cardiff. This, of course, was rather small stuff when the man known as the father of radio transmission, Guglielmo Marconi, had established a regular transatlantic radio-telegraph service and Caruso with the famous Czech soprano Emmy Destinn took part in the first experimental remote broadcast from the stage of New York's Metropolitan Opera in 1910, marking the birth of public radio broadcasting.

Grindell Matthews' work at the time was on a smaller, more social scale, like giving a command performance of wireless communication between motor cars at Buckingham Palace for Her Majesty Queen Alexandra and Princess Mary. But the list of his subsequent inventions was impressive, including an automatic pilot for aircraft, a device for steering boats at night by means of searchlight beams, an early form of radar detection, wireless-controlled torpedoes, and electric stabilizers for airships. He had also played a significant role in the development of talking pictures for Warner Bros. in the United States during the 1920s.

More recently, newspaper readers throughout the British Empire became familiar with his name through a stream of stories linking the inventor with mysterious sea trials to perfect the detection of enemy submarines, as well as his plan for an aerial defense cordon of London by means of rockets spraying a metal curtain in the sky, the projection of rays to kill cancer germs, and even the development of a rocket airplane able to travel at two miles a second and capable, the papers speculated, of manned flight to the Moon. There were colorful descriptions of Harry Grindell Matthews' heavily-guarded hideaway on land owned by the Duke of Beaufort a few miles from the city of Swansea, where the solitary scientist carried out his experiments in a newly-built laboratory protected by double barbed wire fences, with a landing field nearby. This bespectacled figure with a patch covering his damaged eye and dressed in an open shirt and plus-fours, lived on his hilltop in comfort with electricity, telephone and hot water supplied, luxuries denied the Welsh sheep farmers, his immediate neighbors

The only passions shared by "Death-ray Matthews" and Madame Walska seemed to be curiosity about the metaphysical world, together with a love of nature and music. Whatever the attraction - and in spite of Ganna admitting that she was annoyed with herself at feeling this way - she could not dismiss Grindell from her mind. "What does the coming into my life of this man mean anyhow?" she asked her diary. "Especially since he has come at a point when I no longer expect a personal expression of love. Can it be a temptation? - I have none. Is it a trial - a trial to see how much I can stand without losing the spirituality I have acquired, without descending to the lowest regions? Or is it to be a stepping-stone to as yet unattainable summits? I wonder."

Her personal philosophy, now steeped in Buddhism and seasoned by countless spiritual and mystical experiences, told her that she no longer needed the company of a man. But in Grindell Matthews she saw one at odds with the world: the victim of an epoch of jealousy, injustice and hate. He was a martyr no less, unappreciated in his own land; a great inventor who was about to save humanity from wars and disease. A primal urge to support his work prompted her to invite him to Galluis, initiating almost daily contact between them by telephone and telegram. Her offer was frustrated when he cabled on June 18, 1937:

"Deeply Touched By Your Gracious Invitation. Because Of Immense Pressure Outside My Control For The Next Two Or Three Weeks Impossible To Seek This Paradise. This Is The Goal Of My Dreams And They Will Be Fulfilled."

In the meantime, Gita became a matchmaker, keeping Ganna informed about the inventor in letters from London. "Last night," she wrote in one of them, "Grindell Matthews dreamed a dream about you that thrilled him greatly. He has invented a musical instrument which he calls the Lunafone. [Luminaphone] It has never been exhibited except in his home on Long Island where his wife sang with it." According to Gita, Grindell saw Walska in his dream standing on the stage of a great theater in a white dress "with exquisite light playing about you from another invention of his which picks up the vibrations of a voice in colour, out of the ether."

He needed to save the sight in his good eye, but could not make time for an operation because of constant journeys by plane, train and automobile between Wales and London, suggesting that Ganna visit him instead:

"Impossible Leave England. Entreat You Come To Me. Destiny Calls Us Both. Love Grindell."

She found it difficult to reconcile her feelings, not so much about his cause, but the poor impression of him gained from their first, brief meeting. "His hands trembled so he could hardly lift his glass of vermouth to his lips from which a cigarette eternally dangled." Alcohol and smoking happened to be habits she loathed. "His hair was untidy because of the black elastic eye-patch which squeezed his head mercilessly and gave him atrocious headaches. His forehead was irregularly shaven because of his poor eye but why he shaved it I never understood." She had never accepted untidy men, justifying this change of heart by gazing at his youthful photo in the British edition of "Who's Who," convinced that he looked like a thinker, reminiscent of Goethe. Walska's opinions of her unlikely lover's personality blew hot and cold, noting that science had turned his soul into "Self- accommodating clay."

Ganna agreed to meet Grindell in England on July 11, a couple of months after they first met, when she flew from Le Bourget to Croydon to be greeted at London's airport by the waiting inventor. Reporters were there as well, tipped-off, she suspected, by Grindell's need of publicity for his inventions. After being bustled through customs, Madame was asked if her visit was in connection with Grindell's work.

"Perhaps," she replied enigmatically, flashing an engaging smile. "Perhaps," declining to comment further, except to confirm that he was in talks with high officials at the War Office and the Admiralty about his wonderful developments. In their reports next day, several newspapers described her as "the French millionairess."

What should have been a pleasurable time of getting to know each other, turned into a nightmare when Walska discovered that Grindell became madly jealous of anyone who approached her -

male or female. She noted in her diary: "When I pointed out to him that this characteristic was rather small and unworthy of such a big man, he became so depressed and sad and worn looking that I was afraid he would not survive the night in those low spirits. Grindell spent a sleepless night sitting in his car outside the Ritz in Piccadilly, sending his driver into the hotel to warn that if she left he would collapse and die. Taking the threat seriously, Ganna rather warmed to the idea of such devotion: "Genius is like a child," she told herself. "Like a child he could not live if I were not there to bid him a smiling goodnight."

The inventor had vital work to finish, however, and she returned to France, which prompted a letter from Gita a few days later. It asked: "What in the name of heaven have you done to H. Grindell Matthews?" She described a man approaching her at the theater, and, had it not been for the telltale eye patch, she wouldn't have recognized Grindell. He had been speaking to Ganna on the telephone, and said she did not care for him anymore. Gita explained that the inventor's difficult personality and intense insecurity were rooted in his mother, "and until he lost her there was no other woman but her. Then he married the very beautiful and gay Mrs. Archie White of New York who gave him a terrible whirl for two years, then refused to give him any time for his work, and haunted him, and tortured him with sarcasm and witty remarks at his expense so that he had kept away from women ever since he left her."

On July 20, 1937, Grindell's idol died, and Walska wired:

"Am Taking For Granted That Your Attitudes, Thoughts And Feelings Towards Marconi's Memory Are Noble And Based On Spiritual Law"

He replied:

"Deeply Shocked Sudden Passing Away Guglielmo Marconi. I Lament Fellow Pioneer."

Walska realized that, apart from any other character traits, she was dealing with a highly envious person: "He was especially jealous of those in his profession," she noted, "always believing that [French radio pioneer] Branly, Marconi and others took his ideas as well as the credit for them." Mistakenly thinking it would interest him, she read out articles over the telephone about inventions described in the French and American press and magazines because Grindell was unable to read small print with his one failing eye: "But the idea that someone else could achieve where he failed upset him to such an extent that even two or three days afterwards he would still be in such low spirits that I stopped giving him information about this vital work."

In late July, Britain's *Sunday Referee* newspaper reported under the headline "Submarines Can Be Spotted 12 Miles Away" that Grindell Matthews would be taking a "mystery cruise" during August to carry out experiments in underwater detection. "He claims to have perfected an electrical device which it is hoped will make Britain invulnerable from attack by submarines." The article stated that two wealthy yacht owners - one of them a member of parliament - had put their own craft at the inventor's disposal.

While Grindell prepared for sea trials by installing himself and his assistant in the Gloster Hotel on the Isle of Wight, Ganna invited Gita to stay at the Château de Galluis during early August. Impressed by the importance of the inventor's work for a national cause, her visitor revealed in the greatest confidence that the real reason he could not visit France was because of being told he would be killed abroad by enemies who had reason to wish that his invention would never see the light of day. Relishing this cloak-and-dagger suggestion, Ganna noted: "In London he was not allowed to take two steps without being escorted for the sake of protection by a Major in the Intelligence Service." The inflated view of Grindell's importance was nurtured by Gita, reassuring her hostess that AGM is quite safe as Scotland Yard men are guarding him [at] his laboratory."

The anti-submarine invention was a moment of destiny, according to Walska, quoting the inventor's "keeper," the retired Major Lestock Reid. The forthcoming demonstration of Grindell's "fond child, which he had nursed for seventeen long years," would make or break him she believed, "if only he could hold out for two more months! But his health was very poor and it was feared he might have a nervous breakdown at any moment which could have been fatal with his defective heart aggravated by the sleepless nights since he fell in love with me."

She went off to the Austrian Tyrol for the annual Salzburg Festival, deeply worried about the events taking place beyond her control. Grindell, too, continued to be anxious about their future as the trial yachts, named "Unity" and "Lorna," docked in

Southampton and he implored Ganna to come to the Isle of Wight to help him "create." Increasingly ardent sentiments flew between them in a regular exchange of cables, like an early form of e-mail. From the Isle of Wight:

"Deeply Touched By Your Wire. Your Happiness Counts More Than Anything So Shall Long And Live For September . . . I Adore You."

After a performance of a Mozart mass in Salzburg Cathedral, Walska wired him:

"Heard Mozart Mass This Morning Between 11 And One And Was Allowed To Raise Your Highest Thoughts . . . You Made Me Extremely Happy Writing Last Three Words - I Adore You."

Everyone had been far too optimistic about the anti-submarine trials because there were delays and frustrations, with eyesight problems for both the inventor and his assistant, though, at first Grindell remained philosophic, telling his Ganna:

"You Are Turning Me To Divine Vibrations And Are Helping Me Tremendously Today. Cannot Express My Feeling On Wire. Too Sacred."

Then, gloomily:

"Experiment Held Up At Least Two Months. I Must Take It On The Chin Dear Heart."

Turning to long, rambling conversations on a crackly telephone line between the Gloster Hotel in Cowes and the Salzburger Hof, where Walska was lodging, the couple made plans to meet in London during September. It was an unsatisfactory means of communication, with frequent interruptions, missed words and lost nuances, and Ganna preferred to express clearer thoughts by wire:

"Now You Got Greatest Opportunity To Show Strength Of Your Indomitable Spirit And Quality Of Your Affection For Me."

Medical consultants had insisted that Grindell's failing eyesight would lead to blindness unless he had an operation soon, and all she could do, in the face of the inventor's stubbornness about surgery; was to pray. In return, he talked about dark moods, and wondered if he could continue to work without her promising to marry him. It was emotional blackmail, and Walska reacted rationally for once by mentally reviewing her record at the altar: "Marry? I had never thought of it! Not for anything in the world would I marry again. Never!"

Accepting the Chaucerian concept of "never" as meaning an extended time, she persuaded herself on reflection that she needed an emotional investment that would bring quick returns, begging

Grindell to allow her to help him carry on his work. Among a wide circle of friends in London was the Polish-born art historian and writer on comparative religion, Rom Landau. His books about developing detachment from personal disappointment, and in particular "God is My Adventure" from 1935, influenced Walska at this time, mentioning to him that she might be obliged to marry again as a duty to help a genius who was trying to save humanity. "Why?" he responded. "For selfishness?"

Grindell's sea trials were a disaster and he blamed everyone but himself, as well as the notoriously unpredictable waters of the Solent where they had taken place. With winter approaching, any further experiments were out of the question until the following spring, and Walska noted that he was broken in almost every way, except spirit, "for nothing could diminish his self-assurance, he did not know even the meaning of the word humility - and nearer a nervous breakdown than ever before, while the pain in his eye maddened him with constant suffering." She offered what encouragement she could during flying visits to London, complemented by long-distance telephone conversations and cables, citing some of the great geniuses in history who failed first before succeeding. After much soul-searching, Ganna came to the decision quoted in her autobiography: "I must consider it as a divine privilege to save this man for God's work! I hesitated no more . . . I decided to marry him."

In Chicago, the *Tribune* announced "Ganna Walska and 'Death Ray' Expert To Wed," and Cardiff's newspaper, the *Western Mail*, published a headline, "Mr. Grindell Matthews to Marry Baroness," describing their union as a romantic fusion of science and music. London's *Evening Standard* trumpeted: "Ganna Walska to Marry 'Death Ray' Inventor" and the London *Times* in its stuffy old way, noted, "Mr. H. Grindell-Mathews and Madame Ganna Walska. A marriage has been arranged, and will take place shortly, between Harry Grindell Matthews, of Tor Cloud, Clydach, and Ganna Walska of Château Galloise [sic], Paris."

The *Western Mail* sent a reporter to interview the inventor in his laboratory, and Grindell confirmed that he was indeed engaged, explaining,

"We met for the first time at the Covent Garden opera three months ago, but I had heard her sing in New York two or three years ago. Since we have

met she has been coming over every weekend because I am still at work. She is very sympathetic towards my endeavors and is anxious I should not lose any time in continuing my work until it is completed."

The Chicago *Tribune* elaborated on the death-ray connection in its story, informing readers that Grindell Matthews was the former husband of Mrs. Archibald White of New York (the former Olive Moore of St. Paul, Minnesota.) Walska's four previous marriages were listed and her age given as forty-five. She was still a beauty, though it might have surprised the State Department to read this, while deciding whether or not to issue her with a new passport, because their records contained a variety of ages for Madame: many of them older.

The forthcoming marriage was warmly welcomed by the couple's friends in London's spiritual circles, though Walska's New York attorney received the news with bemusement. In a letter, Phelan Beale offered legal advice on her future citizenship, and the need to have a prenuptial agreement drawn up, suggesting she lose no time in visiting the American consul in Paris and explain that she wished to retain her status as a naturalized American national through three of her previous marriages. Addressing Ganna skittishly as "Young Woman," he warned of probable grim times ahead:

"You know as well as I that a great war in Europe is only a few months or a few years away from us. Indeed, no one can tell whether or not an incident will develop within the next thirty days that will cause an immediate war. There is no way in which either England or France can escape being involved."

Beale recommended sending her International Harvester stock certificates to the United States for safe-keeping in a deposit box.

Within the space of one working week in early October, 1937, he sent off three long letters, warning that marriage to a foreigner would not alter her income tax commitments in the United States, also mentioning that he had known the inventor and his wife socially when they were living in New York. "But Ganna," he cautioned, "he is an inventor. All inventors are temperamental and 'cracked-pots' in one way or another, otherwise they could not possess the genius necessary to invent things." Beale added with a fine touch of blarney:

"This is not intended as a criticism of Mr. Matthews - on the contrary, it is a compliment when I call him a genius. But the point of this letter is that

244

you are temperamental yourself and given to wild rages and temperamental moods. Both you and Mr. Matthews must have a tremendous amount of courage to think that two temperamental artists will get along like two bugs in a rug."

It was the sort of friendly advice that Walska needed, but came too late to change her mind. Returning to the safer ground of legal opinion, her attorney advised signing a mutual ante nuptial contract:

"Bear in mind that when you surrender an interest in Mr. Matthews' estate both during his life and after his death, you are probably engaging in merely a gracious gesture because inventors rarely have any estate or property, whereas you have a very substantial property."

He added, a final, haunting phrase:

". . . nothing herein is intended to be a reflection on Mr. Matthews, but still no man can read tomorrow's dawn and we know not what the future holds."

Walska invited Major Lestock Reid, Grindell's "keeper" and his wife Joan, to spend a couple of days at the Château de Galluis and thought it would be nice if her husband-to-be joined them, but he remained reluctant to travel. The Reids had a wonderful time, though their conversations were dominated by discussing Grindell's unpredictable moods and how Ganna might cope with them. This motivated her to fire off an angry cable about her fiancé's reluctance to come to France, prompting a conciliatory cable from him:

"Darling What Has Happened. Small Differences Of Opinion Must Not Affect Our Deep Feelings. We Should Be Above Such Things. Talk With Major Has Disturbed Peace Of Mind Still Further. Just Off To Mountain To Arrange Affairs Prior To Entering Nursing Home."

Walska was incensed because she already knew from Major Reid, following his return to England, that Grindell was about to have the operation to save his sight. A specialist had diagnosed the problem and Reid asked Ganna to be understanding because Grindell was in no condition to think clearly or to make sensible decisions. She remained deeply hurt, however, by not hearing first about the operation from her husband-to-be and admonished him once more:

"I Remind You That You Gave Solemn Promise Not To Do Anything About Your Eyes Before Consulting Me. And Even Without Such Promise I Ought To Be First Person To Know Of Your Going For Operation Instead Of Learning Of It Casually."

Reid managed to persuade the inventor to put aside his work for a short time and forget about the forthcoming surgery to visit Galluis for a couple of days before his surgery. The couple's brief time together was like the calm after a storm, discussing arrangements for their wedding and plans for his future research, perhaps based at the château. Ganna pledged to place herself at Grindell's service as a debt to humanity, recording in her diary:

"I fervently hoped that I was chosen to be instrumental in saving the world from the calamities of wars, for the [British] War Minister, Duff Cooper, said that with those two inventions, on which Grindell was working, in hand he would proclaim their existence to the world and distribute them to friendly countries so that no enemy would be Don quixotic enough to invite suicide."

A letter from Major Reid, written at the Cavalry Club in Piccadilly, informed her that Grindell had two consultations with his doctors, who were now confident of saving the sight in both eyes. He added: "GM himself is in great form, very pleased at the doctors' optimism as to the results of the operation and his own good state of general health as revealed by their examination - but, above all, I venture to think, delighted with memories of his visit to Galluis!"

The faithful Major wrote again next day saying that the telephone had been cut off to Grindell's private room at the fashionable Lady Carnarvon's Nursing Home in Portland Place, London, to cushion him from worries of any kind, ending his brief typewritten note:

"He is very cheerful and says he feels better already. The only thing that worries him at all is how to communicate with you, which he considers the most important thing, so I do hope you will send him plenty of nice cables - he was particularly thrilled at the one he received this morning."

Saving Britain

Ganna Walska prayed regularly in her chapel at the Château de Galluis as she waited anxiously for news from London. Behind the imposing ornamental gates and high stone perimeter wall, the chatelaine would stroll aimlessly across dew-spangled lawns bathed in soft, end-of-year sunshine between borders of massed chrysanthemums planted in readiness for the observance of Toussaint. She lingered beneath trees decked in vivid autumnal tints and wandered over to the grotto stopping to watch the play of sparkling water in her Goya fountain, then went to admire the still-blooming rose garden. Ganna was pleased to see some apples remaining on the trees in the orchard, while the rest of the crop lay fermenting on the ground, filling the air with a pungent smell of cider.

Since purchasing the property, she had spent considerable time, effort and money in developing her country residence, and the results spoke for themselves. Walska was immensely proud of her antique Spanish, Portuguese and Dutch tiles inside the house - she thought they were the best private collection in Europe - and there were extensive displays of crystals and coral, as well as flamboyant Italian mirrors among the furnishings. She made plans for her new husband's recuperation by having a space cleared in *Le petit château* for fitting-out as a laboratory, where he could continue his experiments.

Ganna felt like a new person, full of enthusiasm and energy, attributing it all to Grindell:

"Galluis, which until then had been an Eden here below, was to become a celestial haven which Inspiration has chosen for its dwelling - where wild, hungry and sick cats together with pheasants and hares that escaped the huntsman's gun found refuge, Galluis was to hear now such heavenly sounds as its birds had never created and to see color never before seen by ordinary human eyes - and these sounds and color combinations would annihilate any dreadful disease."

But before Grindell Matthews could continue his work on a cure for cancer through experimental sound and color therapy, there was delicate surgery to be done on his eyes, and time hung heavily until the phone rang to shatter the rural tranquility of the estate on October 25, 1937. It was Major Reid calling to say that GM's operation was over and apparently a success, though the patient would have to remain in total darkness for at least a week. Shortly after, a more encouraging cable arrived from the matron of the nursing home:

"Operation Successful. Eyes Saved. Patient Doing Well And Cheerful."

While Grindell rested in limbo and Walska waited for the moment he would be fit enough to travel, arrangements went ahead on both sides of the Atlantic for their marriage. In New York, Phelan Beale drew up a prenuptial agreement between Harry Grindell Matthews, "a subject of the British Empire, residing in England" and Ganna Walska McCormick, "a citizen of the United States of America, residing temporarily in France." In several hundred words of legalese it stated, in effect, that neither party would have claim on the other during their marriage nor after - whether dead or divorced - except through their wills. Beale had emphasized the importance of this agreement to his client because, as a resident of New York State, she would have to surrender one-half of her property there if Grindell should survive her.

Madame enjoyed a little light relief from these legal matters on receiving Frances Alda's just-published tell-all autobiography "Men, Women, & Tenors," finding it a frank exposé by a great prima donna who had rivaled Nellie Melba in the pantheon of all-time great sopranos, but became overshadowed by her powerful husband, the almost legendary opera administrator Giulio Gatti-Casazza. His long and influential career as boss of La Scala, and then the Metropolitan Opera, had stolen some of the limelight from his straight-talking New Zealand-born, Australian-raised wife, until they divorced in 1928. Alda's ghosted life story redressed the balance by allowing her no-nonsense personality to shine through. Colorful anecdotes included the occasion when her lace knickers slipped down to the ankles during a performance, and Caruso made play of picking up the garment from the stage and stand waving it triumphantly like a trophy to the shocked Metropolitan audience.

Alda also recalled the time when a vicious New York critic (W. J. Henderson) wrote that she "came from the land of sheep and bleated like one." Highly critical of the current trend for opera stars to sign fat movie contracts, she claimed never to have been seduced in that way: "There's no art in singing in movies," she wrote, "Damn it, out in Hollywood, you don't need a good voice. You need a good microphone." There was juicy gossip about Caruso, Lawrence Tibbett, Lucrezia Bori, Edward Johnson and many others, including Madame Walska, mentioned as a former social friend who was never regarded kindly as a singer. Alda claimed to have spent "one whole summer in Europe" for a fee of ten thousand dollars trying to instruct her in the rudiments of singing, "But work as I did, I could not teach Ganna Walska to sing. 'No, no, no,' I'd say to her, 'you're singing like five million pigs!'"

Grindell was allowed to leave the London nursing home a fortnight after his operation, discarding the patch he'd worn for years over his damaged eye - which had made him look like a prototype for the famous American advertisements for Hathaway shirts. He was nervous about what had gone wrong with his submarine detection device during the summer's sea trials, though the prospect of a return to Galluis buoyed his spirits a little. The château and its grounds were ideal for convalescence, and the couple discovered a mutual interest in the trees on the estate. Ganna always regarded them as living entities and could never pass by without liberating them of dead limbs or broken branches, imagining they suffered like human beings. Grindell shared her sentiments, and much to the amusement of the gardeners, set to work energetically clearing all the dead wood he could access, sparing only the parasitic mistletoe, explaining to his bride that the Iron Age druids were wary of separating its growth from the host for fear of bringing bad luck .Walska recorded this idyllic time in her bulging notebook, including the couple's quirky passion. "Being, tall, skillful and with the experience that he gained on the Welsh mountain where he had built his laboratory, he freed hundreds of Galluis trees from the heavy weight, thus bringing many again to life so that I no longer had the feeling of walking on the battle field."

She was thrilled with Grindell's transformation after the surgery: "Now he was in good health, not the smallest detail escaped his eyes - he could even drive a car if he so desired - his hands trembled but little, he looked fifteen years younger and he could work under the best possible conditions without any worry about financial problems." Time, however, was the inventor's enemy: he needed quick success because the Admiralty would be more generous with the threat of war intensifying. "He deduced he would then become Lord of something-or-other," Walska revealed, already calling her Lady Grindell, and unable to understand why she was not excited by the idea of a title. But during an eventful life in and around the top echelons of society, Walska claimed that she had been offered the opportunity to become the wife of a Grand Duke of Russia, an Archduke of Austria, an Infante of Spain, an important ambassador, a European prime minister, a Monaco Grimaldi, or one of the wives of a Hindu potentate - all of which were turned down.

In fact, acceptance of Grindell's anti-submarine invention was so pressing that the peace and beauty of Galluis could not detain him longer. After a stay of little more than a week, he exchanged the Arcadian pleasures of rural France for his bleak Welsh mountaintop. It was little consolation, in the light of his abrupt departure, for Ganna to be congratulated by Major Reid, writing that not only he, but everyone who had met the inventor on his return, was struck by the marked improvement in his looks and spirit. After a round of business meetings in London, including lodging a will with his solicitor made in Walska's favor, Grindell Matthews took the train back to Wales, leaving her miffed from spending so little time in his company, and no prospect of the château being used in the near future as his laboratory. Doubts clouded Ganna's thoughts as Christmas 1937 approached, with the tension reaching a climax in another flurry of exchanged cables. To Grindell on December 14:

"If Your Heart Knows Absolute Sincerity Towards Mine, You Should Never Feel Upset For Then Nothing Can Come From Me To Make You Unhappy."

December 14 from Grindell:

"Nearest And Dearest. Am Utterly Sincere But For That Reason Am Disturbed By Your Unfounded Suspicions. They May Destroy That Happiness That I Have Sought All My Life And Found At Last In You. Longing To See You."

December 15 from Walska:

"If This Happiness Can Be Destroyed So Easily It Couldn't Have Been Real

Happiness. You Didn't Even Phone To Find Out If I Am Not Ill, Down, Discouraged, Feeling Useless To Myself And Everybody. Unable To Make You Happy. Even Handicap Your Convalescence. Wondering If Not To Leave Everything To Disappear. Who Cares."

Major Reid added to this expensive traffic by telling Ganna what she already knew: that Grindell was terribly unhappy about their situation, and suffering badly from a lack of sleep. She tried to humor her inventor by describing Galluis "Dressed In White For Christmas," sending regards from the trees on the estate and greetings from the cat, which had just produced "Five Sons." It was a desperately sad festive season, though Walska sent off telegrams under their joint names looking forward to marital bliss as "Mr. and Mrs. Grindell Matthews." She also remembered her attorney in New York, divorced from his second wife six years before, and now joking that she should consider marrying him, if her present plans fell apart. Ganna responded:

"Merry Xmas Happy New Year Dear Phelan. Still Free If Your Proposition Still Holds as Letter Suggested. Be Careful I May Take Lawyer To Sue You For Breach Of Promise."

Another cable was sent to Harold McCormick at 675 Rush Street, Chicago:

"May New Year Help You Find Peace And Happiness As You Found Your Place At Our First Christmas Dinner."

It indicated perhaps that Harold, for all his faults, was the only man she had really cared for.

The year 1938 dawned with Galluis shrouded in freezing fog, transforming the estate into a winter landscape of delicate shades of gray like a delicate Chinese watercolor, as the world faced mounting uncertainties. Britain postponed a scheme for the partition of Palestine, the Spanish Civil War was in full bloody flight, and conflict between Japan and China continued with no sign of a settlement. In Germany, the Nazis now had a stranglehold on most aspects of national life and war seemed imminent. As he had hoped, the situation worked in Grindell's favor with the Admiralty and Air Ministry, while his financial backers, anxious for returns on their investments, pressured him to complete his inventions.

The ever-attentive Major Reid kept Ganna informed of developments, though not at liberty to give many details. But he did indicate that as the result of an interview at the Air Ministry with Grindell present "it should greatly facilitate our work in giving them what, they tell me, they most urgently desire." Ganna was more interested in hearing something to boost her confidence at a low moment and received Major Reid's assurance: "In all this you have played a great part and I think that in a comparatively short time you will be able to congratulate yourself on having helped to change the course of history.".

A Paris newspaper reported that Ganna Walska was about to marry the inventor of the Death-ray in spite of recent gossip suggested that Madame was preparing to take the veil. On being asked by a reporter if she had really given up her religious vocation, Ganna replied "Perhaps God will wait for me - men do not wait!" Reservations were made at the Carlton Hotel on Pall Mall in the heart of London's club land, and the American vice-consul returned Walska's duly authenticated documents, clearing the way for a civil ceremony. On Friday, 21 January they were united in a brief registry office ceremony with a minimum of fuss, and Harry Grindell Matthews became Ganna's husband number five.

Newspapers across the United States covered the event, with New York's *Herald Tribune* headlining "Ganna Walska Weds Inventor of 'Death Rays,'" giving the groom's age as fifty-seven and the bride's as forty-five, although she was now in her fifty-first year. *Time* magazine recorded the marriage of "Ganna Walska d'Eighnhorm [sic] Fraenkel Cochran McCormick," describing the bride as the "Polish-American opera singer, perfumer, feminist." After reading about the ceremony, Phelan Beale cabled Ganna: "Felicitations Ganna But Remember If Things Go Wrong I Am Waiting At The Church." There was no honeymoon for the couple because ministry officials insisted on visiting Grindell's laboratory immediately after the ceremony to inspect the progress of his work, and Madame returned home alone to France.

She expected to be joined by her husband at Galluis in the near future, telling Associated Press in Paris they planned a delayed honeymoon trip during February to "some winter sports resort." In the meantime, Major Reid continued to feed her information about Grindell's work. "It seems, like the politics of the world which it will so greatly influence, have reached a rather critical stage and it will need perseverance and determination on your husband's part to pull it through." The inventor himself was confident that he could tear himself away from his laboratory, and Reid thought a break would be beneficial for him. It was wishful thinking, however, and failed to eventuate.

At first, everything – except their separation - seemed normal enough for the newlyweds. Four days after the ceremony Grindell wired from London, before returning to Wales: "Just leaving Paddington Full Of Wonderful Thoughts." Ganna replied, like a love bird: "Almost Wishing For A Storm To Offer You Shelter." After that his communications declined, although hers continued: "God Bless Work Entrusted To You By Higher Powers Today And Ever."

And then: "Again Sunshine Three Quarters Of Which I Am Sending To You And To Your Work."

Regular remittances were sent from France to cover her husband's far-from-modest lifestyle, with the amounts in dollars, going into his London account with Coutts and Co. in the Strand. On March 4 Ganna bought him a brand new motor car - a black Terraplane saloon manufactured by the Hudson Motor Car Company of Detroit, Michigan.

With Grindell absent, Walska turned increasingly to her garden for consolation, compiling a detailed planting record of the flowers and shrubs around the principal buildings of the château, perhaps creating subconsciously in nature what she had failed to do in art with her voice. She wrote a note for her Polish gardener, Leon: "Would you please plan for lots of wallflowers, yellow and brown, in large clumps for the path in the middle of the kitchen garden. For the little wood near the garage would you add to the crocus already indicated. Very rustic, they can come up anywhere. Even if they won't grow, we can always try them." She also added more pages to her memoirs, hoping to publish them soon under a title she liked: "Always Space at The Top."

Galluis became Ganna's spiritual home where she felt completely at ease in the small, caring community of about four hundred people comprising little more than the Mairie, a church, general store, bakery, village school, her château and Mr. Dalseme's large farm, together with workers' cottages. A regular visitor to the estate was Jerome Dalseme, aged seven, who ran errands for Madame to buy bread, newspapers and milk, leaving them beside a flower garden massed with red and white tulips during springtime - the national colors of Poland. Jerome was rewarded with one franc for his efforts, and used to buy children's magazines in the village *épicerie*. Later in life, he remembered Walska's singing practice emerging from the open windows of her upstairs apartment, not so much for its quality, which to his boyish ears seemed terribly shrill, but because the chatelaine always wore white, like an acolyte before the high priestess of her muse.

Jerome made sure to protect a privileged place in the face of rival claims from his siblings. "She loved children," he recalled, "and for some reason or other I was Madame Walska's favorite boy, so I was very fortunate. I think my brother and sister were a little jealous of me because of that." Galluis was known as a *bourgeois* château, in the sense of being middle-class and conventionally respectable, with none of the disparaging overtones of that term in English. The locals Walska mixed with were proud of being *bourgeois*, including the Dalsemes at Galluis, the Bormans, with their son André and daughter Sophie, who lived and farmed in the adjacent commune of Méré, and a couple of families in the neighboring town of Montfort-L'Amaury.

The composer, Maurice Ravel, had lived at Montfort from 1921 and Jerome Dalseme remembered having his hair cut on the first day of each month, sometimes in the company of the great man of French music. Ravel died in a coma during December, 1937 from what was known as a chronic wasting disease, probably resulting from a serious head injury sustained a few years earlier when getting out of a taxi. He had long been reclusive and was never part of Walska's social circle in Paris; though he did attend a few of her musical matinées at rue de Lubeck during the late 1920s. She appreciated his song cycles, but was no admirer of the operatic works, and loathed his most famous composition, the vulgar *Boléro* ballet, choreographed by Bronislava Nijinska, which Walther Straram conducted at its première to sensational success in November 1928 at the Paris Opéra. Her mentor subsequently played the music as an orchestral showpiece far too many times for her liking, and maybe the composer's as well, because Ravel was said to have described the composition (perhaps in referring to its balletic origins) as "a piece for orchestra without music." Mrs. Dalseme was English and a gifted musician, having studied at St.

254

George's Chapel, Windsor, where she played the organ occasionally for the royal family and now gave concerts for the *bourgeoisie* around Galluis. The Bormans - he was Latvian, his wife Polish - brought new strains of cereals from Latvia, farming at Méré and leasing some of the Dalseme land at Galluis to produce crops of hybrid wheat and barley which found a ready market.

Having been forced out of his native land by the invading Russians, Mr. Bormans was understandably anti-Soviet, but tended to be pro-German, knowing Herman Goering well enough to invite him to shoot wild boar in the former royal hunting lands south of the Loire, known as the Sologne. Walska probably met Hitler's designated successor and head of the Luftwaffe at a local social occasion, because Jerome Dalseme remembered seeing a signed photograph of Goering on one of the grand pianos at Galluis, sharing the crowded space with autographed pictures of other notables she had met. They included Benito Mussolini, and less-threatening luminaries like Enrico Caruso, the Wagner family, Pope Pius XI, Claude Debussy, Feodor Chaliapin, Fritz Kreisler, Lauritz Melchior, Franklin D. Roosevelt, Arturo Toscanini, Leopold Stokowski and Richard Strauss.

Ganna immersed herself in this healthy, but often solitary, life as contact with her new husband - barely half a day away by air - lapsed to occasional telephone calls, sporadic cables, and regular dollar transfers to his London bank. He spent the summer of 1938 obsessively involved with inventing and his cables seem to accept that their relationship was ending before it was even given a chance to flourish:

"I Shall Always Cherish The Glorious Hours We Have Spent Together And Dream Of What Might Have Been And Strive To Do Everything I Know You Would Wish. Now I Tell You Goodnight And God Bless You Always."

And three months later:

"Divine Spark In Danger Of Being Completely Extinguished By Breath That Might Have Kindled It To Great Flame."

To which Ganna replied pointedly:

"Nothing Divine Can Be Extinguished. Divine Is Only Good And Eternal."

Christmas 1938 came - and went - and another year began with everyone asking not if, but when war would break out. President Franklin Delano Roosevelt sought huge funding from Congress to defend the United States, while the British prime minister and his foreign secretary visited Rome for crisis talks as Italian troops assisted Nationalist forces to take Barcelona - the last major stronghold of the Republicans in Spain. Europe was in turmoil and time was running out for Grindell Matthews. On the day that Hitler dismissed the president of the Reichsbank for opposing the Fuhrer's plans for massive expenditure on rearmament, he sent this brief cable to his wife:

"Happy Memories Of A Year Ago Today."

It was a starkly moving reminder of their first wedding anniversary. She replied:

"In Memory Of That Anniversary I Pray That Soon You May See Real Value In Life Based On Divine Foundation."

Grindell, unable to convince the British authorities that his inventions were viable, saw his backers drift away. Major Reid quietly retired to his Berkshire home, and Walska was left to finance a husband whose mental state and heart condition were in a parlous state. The inventor's sole champion was a journalist who had just finished writing his biography. In early 1939, with Britain and France about to recognize General Franco's Nationalist government in Spain, Ernest Barwell assumed the role of Grindell's intermediary, or amanuensis, writing to Walska from Swansea:

"GM has spoken so much about you that I seem to have known you for years, and I know that you will be interested in the completed manuscript of "Spirit of Place." GM is particularly anxious that you should read the last two chapters and I am also awaiting your verdict on these. I think you will appreciate the fact that had I written what I wanted to write about you it would have been out of place in this record of GM's inventions, for it would create a diversity of interests."

Barwell suggested "with some trepidation" that Walska might consider writing her own story titled "Musical Memories," which she ignored because of receiving further interest in her memoirs from elsewhere.

Her friend, Albin E. Johnson, the European Commissioner for the New York World's Fair of 1939, had good publishing contacts and discussed Walska's book with Lincoln Schuster of Simon & Schuster, who expressed interest in seeing some of the manuscript. Johnson also promised to show the material to Earle Balch of Geo. P. Puttnam's Sons, confident that he, too, would want to consider it. But Ganna dithered about being ready to publish, deciding to wait "until the big work in my life is ready for it."

Europeans spent the fateful golden summer of 1939 waiting for the inevitable to happen. In August, the British Prime Minister, Neville Chamberlain, warned Hitler that Britain would stand by Poland and an Anglo-Polish treaty was signed in London. At the end of the month, attempts by French Prime Minister Deladier and Chamberlain to negotiate with the Fuhrer failed, with children beginning to be evacuated from Paris as the nation prepared for war. The families living around Walska at Galluis began shutting up their houses and she arranged for her most precious paintings, silver and small valuables to be packed into crates and buried in pits on the estate. Following Mrs. Bormans death from cancer, Ganna had wanted to adopt her daughter, Sophie, whom she adored, and take her to the safety of America, but the girl chose to remain in France with her brother and father.

Meanwhile, in the midst of this mayhem, the chatelaine of Galluis calmed her nerves by planning a planting schedule to greatly enhance her château's grounds in the future - if there was to be one. She instructed gardener Leon: "Forsythias - plant a hundred close to the gate, along the drive to the main entrance and in the little forest . . . Forsythias to be planted in the little forest near the Goya fountain . . . Think of Forsythias for Madame Gilly . . . Plant Spanish broom - I adore yellow - plant snowball bushes."

News of Nazi intentions reached the peaceful small community from an unexpected source. Mr. Dalseme had engaged a Paris architect to design a new *vacherie* for his pedigree milk herd, and this man, André Zigot, had a girlfriend who worked for British intelligence in London. Little-by-little, he learned from her that Galluis would be in grave danger if the Germans invaded: the English would be arrested - that meant Mrs. Dalseme - and most likely any Poles. Then it was announced on the radio that Germany had invaded Poland, immediately annexing the free city of Danzig, and two days later - as threatened - Britain and France declared war on the aggressor. By the end of September Warsaw surrendered after a violent three-day bombardment, with Marshal Sikorsky forming a Polish government-in-exile in Paris, and Walska learned that her birthplace of Brest-Litovsk was in German hands. It was time for her to leave France, as she had under similar circumstances twenty-five years before, fleeing what became

257

known as, but demonstrably was not "The war to end wars."

Ganna became a rich refugee, like a few of her aristocrat Russian friends fleeing the Revolution of 1917, gathering up her most valuable jewelry, depositing what was unable to be carried in a wall safe, and left Château de Galluis in the care of a local *maçon*, Roger Eudes. She obtained an emergency travel document from the American consulate in Paris on September 23, added it to a newly-issued French identity card, and paid $375 for a ticket from Lisbon on the Pan American World Airways flying boat operating the southern transatlantic service on a three-day flight between Europe and the United States, via the Azores.

In a frenzy of organization, Walska telephoned Grindell to inform him of her plans and then took long and exhausting train journeys west through Spain and into Portugal. Making an overnight stay in Lisbon, she thought the authoritarian rule of the country's dictator, Antonio de Oliveira Salazar - now in the seventh year of his régime - was a resounding success. The superficial assessment was based on her conviction that the world needed more strong leaders like Salazar in these unsettled times: "For only a spiritually powerful man [like Salazar] can bring about the absolute impossibility of war." At the hotel she discovered there was no safe large enough to hold her enormous jewel case, which was just about all she carried, and the desk clerk suggested she leave it somewhere in the lobby. "No one will touch it," he assured her, "we sometimes have millions of dollars' worth of jewels just left on a window sill." Understandably suspicious, Ganna nevertheless followed his advice, noting later: "And it was the truth, for my limited fifty pounds weight [allowed on the Pan Am flight] of emeralds, diamonds, rubies and pearls were safely on the window sill open to the street when I returned late that night." Next day, she boarded her flight in Lisbon harbor clutching the heavy jewel case and shortly after, the Boeing 314 Clipper fired its four massive motors and took off westward into the sunset, leaving everything else Walska possessed in Europe to the winds of fate.

Arriving at New York's Port Washington terminal after a deafening and seemingly endless flight, Ganna informed reporters that Paris was gay again despite the war, with cafés, cabarets and theaters reopening after being closed for the month since France declared war on Germany. Depending on which newspaper you read, she was described as a "songbird," "former songbird," "ex-opera diva," "former opera singer," "a one-time opera singer" or simply "singer." They were all accurate descriptions - except for diva. The syndicated gossip columnist, Alice Hughes, wrote:

"Who should turn up among us but Ganna Walska?! Remember? The dashing woman who wanted to be an opera singer, but couldn't, but who did succeed in marrying four men, two of them millionaires. Walska's another refugee from Europe's boom-boom. Now she'll pig along on Park Avenue somehow."

Grindell Matthews was left to fend for himself in Britain for the third major war of his sixty years. Walska, on the other hand, had achieved an escape that Houdini might have envied: distancing herself from a desperate situation that most Europeans were forced to stay and endure. In fact, she had managed to avoid many of the most threatening world events of her fifty-two years: the Great War (as it was known before they started being numbered in the style of British monarchs or Americans with dynastic pretensions), the Russian Revolution of 1917, the Great Depression, and now the Second World War. In these chaotic times, her confused husband lost track of her. After cabling Galluis, and waiting for a reply that never came, he repeated his wire to New York, wishing Walska every happiness for Christmas and the New Year. She replied from Park Avenue:

"Sent Three Telegrams Since Wire Communication Was Established With England. Last One Before Leaving Galluis Giving New York Address. Merry Christmas And May 1940 Be Your Year Of Realization."

It was signed rather bluntly - as if Grindell knew any other person of this name - "Ganna Walska." He responded in the same vein:

"Affectionate Thoughts. May The New Year Be All Happiness For You. Grindell Matthews."

They faced the 1940s far apart, in every sense, with Madame back in the comfort of her New York City home, "mentally lost for a while as I usually am when I am not working on my voice." She had not expected to be in America again until ready for another concert tour in costume, "But alas! I was far from being prepared to herald the Divine Tone, for in those last months in Europe I worked even less than usual, first because my teacher took a vacation and then because the mobilization came . . .There could not be any singing . . . My chauffeur had gone . . . Gasoline was restricted and my Rolls drank plenty of it."

- 20 -
Mecca of Equality
1940

Thoroughly disoriented by her dramatic exit from Europe, Madame Walska was at least comfortable in a substantial Manhattan mansion, with servants, a new chauffeur, secretary, and wealth enough to maintain a lifestyle of privilege. The Buddhist faith allowed her to accept whatever happened to the properties and possessions in France, and she was free of the self-imposed mission to help Grindell Matthews save Britain from war, now that the hostilities were hotting up. It was time to refocus on where she had to live, sensing that America could become the new guardian of Western art and culture. But Ganna was at a loss to know how to fill her days in New York's dynamic atmosphere, after the rural charms of Galluis which she had accepted as her home.

She took long, meandering walks in Central Park wearing the Cochran sable coat against winter's chills and remaining mentally adrift until one of Harold McCormick's Chicago friends, the free-thinking Juliet Rublee, wife of lawyer George Rublee, an adviser to the Wilson and F. D. Roosevelt administrations, invited her to a yoga demonstration by one Theos Bernard at the Hotel Pierre. The name sounded familiar to her because when married to Joseph Fraenkel, Ganna once met a Dr. Pierre Bernard, known in the press as "Oom the Omnipotent." This colorful character living in Nyack, New York State was variously a bank president, avid baseball fan, prize fighter and realtor, as well as an occultist and guru who delighted in staging bizarre publicity stunts; one, she remembered reported was dancing with a baby elephant.

There was, however, a more serious side to "Oom the Omniscient," as he was more respectfully known from a Tibetan prayer-wheel mantra chanted by his followers, because Bernard owned an extensive Sanskrit library and had the ability to teach the more complicated principles of yoga in simple language. Mrs. Rublee, widely-known for championing the controversial birth-control movement, and also passionate about film, world religions, art and dance, became interested in Pierre Bernard's nephew, Theos, as the result of a recently-published bestseller. His "Penthouse of the Gods" described in words and pictures a spectacular journey from India to Lhasa, where the author had lived with Tibetan priests, and claimed to be the world's first White Lama. A nationwide lecture tour in late 1938 brought his story to wide audiences, and his visual records of secret ceremonies from a remote society on the roof of the world attracted considerable attention from newspapers and magazines, including the mass-circulation *Family Circle,* which had published a serialization of the book.

During the years of the Great Depression, the public had eagerly embraced the concept of Shangri-La as a Himalayan Utopia through James Hilton's popular novel "Lost Horizon," first published in 1933, followed by the movie version of 1937 directed by Frank Capra and starring Ronald Coleman. This haunting tale of paradise found - and eventually lost - cast a potent spell on readers and cinema audiences eager to believe that mythical Shangri-La was the remote and mysterious region of Tibet. For many of them, Bernard's "Penthouse of the Gods" confirmed it.

Ganna accompanied Juliet Rublee and Princess Zalam-Zaloski (the former Mrs. Leopold Stokowski) to a demonstration of yoga exercises by one of Theos Bernard's pupils, to be followed by the yogi-author himself introducing sixteen-millimeter film he shot in India. She could hardly fail to notice that the White Lama lived in considerable luxury in the seven hundred-room hotel constructed during the 1930s, with its club-like atmosphere and outstanding views over Central Park, which perhaps explained his nickname: "the Dalai Lama of the Pierre." After the yoga demonstration, the ladies were guided to front-row seats facing a screen with about twenty others present, the lights dimmed and Ganna would describe what happened next in her diary:

"One of the young helpers - in a dinner jacket that looked as if it had been rented for the occasion and whom I took to be a waiter - began to give an explanation. Interested in the striking-looking pictures, I did not pay attention to the common-looking narrator with his still commoner English when I heard 'From this plateau we moved . . . 'We?' Oh, then he too belonged to the expedition of bearded Theos Bernard."

Then it dawned on her that this narrator must be Bernard himself, without the scruffy beard and filthy Tibetan rags depicted on the cover of "Penthouse of the Gods." She had yet to read the book, but having glanced at the pictures inside, was not impressed:

"I was studying him further as he spoke. Unfortunately I was unable to change neither my intuitional nor my visual opinion of him. His voice was monotonous, without force or character and his English was that of uneducated man far from scholastic experience."

Ganna was probably being hypercritical of this charismatic person, twenty years her junior, because of resisting warm feelings for a man again after the dismal experience of marriage to Grindell Matthews. She had mixed with Europeans for such a long time that Theos Casimir Bernard might have shocked her with his lack of Old World formalities, though his achievements were far from ordinary. Born in Tombstone, Arizona, in 1908, his ambition as a child was to be an athlete but ill-health led him in other directions. After high school, Bernard studied law, gaining both an MA and LLB at the University of Arizona. He was influenced by his celebrity uncle Pierre on the East Coast, and a visiting guru who instructed him in a system of Hatha Yoga - a form of physical purification through muscular discipline and respiratory control. After law school, Theos went to India for further studies.

Yogi Theos Bernard

262

The peripatetic Bernard journeyed on to Tibet with his cameras and notebooks, arriving at the holy city of Lhasa - only the third American ever to visit this beacon for foreign Buddhists, he claimed - to be hailed as a reincarnation of the saint Padma Sambhara. This gave him the rare privilege for a foreigner of participating in religious ceremonies and to visit some of the leading Lamas at monasteries normally closed to outsiders. He immersed himself in the Tibetan language and subsequently described his adventures in the spiritual-travelogue diary "Penthouse of the Gods," with a forthcoming British version retitled "Land of a Thousand Buddhas" (1940). The author's ambition then, he told his friend Don Brown, a professor of religious studies at the University of California, Santa Barbara, had been to propagate a wider understanding of Eastern philosophies by establishing a Tibetan institute to bring scholars together for research and study. Brown recalled their Hollywood meeting in the late 1930s with Bernard "bubbling over with enthusiasm over future plans and possibilities . . . [he] planned to get some Lamas to come over and join the Institute."

Madame Walska admitted to being in a vulnerable state after leaving France, having neglected her body for the past ten years through being obsessively concerned with singing, and accepting that a God-given allure for men had brought her mostly misery. Now she was alone in New York City responding irrationally to this young yogi, a good-looking guy in an all-American way, interested in the things she was, and with a gift of the gab - a quality identified by Professor Brown when reminiscing about him: "What a talker!"

She decided to get back into shape by signing up for daily lessons with a "Mrs. R." at Bernard's studio, discovering that she was a demanding teacher. This slavery, as she called it, continued throughout the winter of 1939-40, during which she never sighted Theos Bernard again: not even meeting him accidentally during visits to the Pierre. Then, learning that he held private classes on Wednesdays, she enrolled for these informal half-talks, half-lectures and question-and-answer sessions. Bernard mentioned that some of his students rented the hotel suite for him, each contributing $250 toward its upkeep. Walska thought it a rather steep price to pay for a few evenings of informal conversation, and he hastened to point out that not everyone could afford to pay, which she took as a cue to write her check for $500, joking to friends that the generous fee was for the right to a double portion of curry served at the end of the sessions, which came from an Indian takeout.

Still restless, Ganna Walska thought that now might be a good time to publish her memoirs while she attempted to settle back in the United States without the support of a rich husband. Her notebooks and diaries, however, contained many thousands of words needing professional editing, after a succession of secretaries had tried - and failed - to turn them into a readable form. She had engaged an attorney named Maurice J. Speiser, with offices on 5th. Avenue, to find her a rural property in New York State, and learning of his contacts with publishers and authors - including representing Ernest Hemingway for Hollywood screen rights - he agreed to help in placing Madame's memoirs.

Speiser warned his client tactfully that, in addition to editing, and revisions, her book would have to be "Englished," but Scribners were not interested in the material, and the chaotic manuscript was forwarded to Simon & Schuster, with Speiser meeting their representative for a working lunch during which the sixteen chapters were analyzed, resulting in a breakdown of content, page-by-page. This revealed that personal material represented sixteen per cent of the word count, the occult accounted for fifty per cent, and random philosophic thoughts another sixteen per cent. With proportions so heavily weighted in favor of the mystic, Simon & Schuster decided not to touch it. Then in quick succession Hearst's International Cosmopolitan rejected the proposal, as did the Macmillan Company, suggesting it was better suited for magazines, such as *Saturday Evening Post* and *Cosmopolitan* - which previously rejected an earlier version. Madame's literary ambitions seemed to be following her singing career.

Spring arrived in the city, with Central Park acquiring its annual mantle of new greenery, much appreciated by Ganna on brisk daily walks, delighted to see the massed daffodils, budding shrubs and watch the frolicking squirrels. It made her think of gardener Leon's extensive planting at Galluis the previous autumn, and to wonder nostalgically how it fared. She fretted about her family in war-torn

Poland, but apart from the stark reality of her brother, his wife and their children being caught up in the dreadful events she heard about every day on the radio and read in the newspapers, war news from Europe, filtered by time and distance, might be from another planet. Walska hoped that the Galluis tulips would bloom as brilliantly this year in their vivid red and white as a defiant symbol of the spirit of her homeland so brutally bludgeoned by the Nazi aggressor, and she thought about her beautiful Champs-Elysées theater, presumably standing empty and gathering dust while waiting for the Germans to occupy Paris. On March 23, Grindell cabled from Britain: "Monday's Thoughts For Easter. Would Be Happy To Know If You And Family Are Well."

Ganna replied, knowing that "family" was code for her cats: "Happy Easter To You. Am Quite Well. Family Also. But In Galluis. May God Bless you. Ganna Walska."

She continued to take yoga lessons with Bernard's assistant, and while discussing diet, ventured to ask if the White Lama ever ate red meat. Mrs. R. burst out laughing. "Oh yes! And how!"

"You mean Mr. Bernard eats steaks?"

Ganna had assumed that a holy man with an ascetic lifestyle would be vegetarian, though it was revealed that her guru had a hearty appetite for all kinds of food, together with a lively appreciation of popular culture. In his private lectures he constantly associated himself with yogis, monasteries and eastern scholarship, but his assistant disclosed that he went to the cinema frequently, and action movies with plenty of blood and guts were among his favorites.

Soon after this conversation, and without explanation, Mrs. R. was packed off to California to continue Bernard's work there - whatever it was - and Theos invited himself to visit Madame at her Yonkers country retreat in upstate New York, where she was renting a house for the summer while hoping to find a suitable property to buy. He declared that from the first evening they met at the Pierre, when seated directly in front of him, he fell in love with her and tomorrow being the full moon he wanted Ganna to marry him. This followed the instantaneous marriage proposals she had received from Dr. Fraenkel, Smith Cochran and Grindell Matthews. "Naturally I was speechless," Ganna noted. "If I could give way to my sense of humor I would have laughed but I felt it was utterly out of place owing to his extreme solemnity."

Theos showed no surprise at her negative response, but fell into a rage of uncontrolled fury when told bluntly that she was in no mind to commit bigamy.

"You're married?" he wanted to know, as casually as if asking the time of day.

She nodded affirmatively.

"Then ask for an immediate divorce. It's the least he can do for you!"

His anger smoldered unabated until she handed over a copy of her typewritten memoirs so that he could find out more about her.

Although horrified at the time, Walska regarded the marriage proposal in her memoirs as perfectly reasonable: "A few hours later while telling me goodnight he unexpectedly and very gauchely wanted to take me in his arms and when softly and delicately I pushed him away, he collapsed into an armchair like a lump and heartbreakingly sobbed out: 'Every time I fall in love this happens to me!'"

Summoning up maternal instincts from deep inside her, Ganna said that she bent over, lifted the arms covering his face to dry away the tears, and saw he was sleeping like a baby. "From that day on," she wrote, "I only knew that I must help him." She had found another cause to pursue.

The Fleming H. Revell Company returned the Walska manuscript with a rejection slip, and by the end of 1940 the names of only three companies remained on Maurice Speiser's list of possible publishers: Harper's, Greystone Press and Julian Meisner Inc. He suggested that it might be better to make the editorial revisions he had recommended earlier before resubmitting the book, knowing of someone who could start to "English" the material. Walska agreed to meet this editor, Mrs. Jere Knight, who lived with her husband in a rural backwater of Pennsylvania called Pleasant Valley, liked her, and suggested she get on with the job right away.

With Theos Bernard, Ganna Walska had found a mission to replace Grindell Matthews' abortive attempts to save his country from the Germans, though the new man in her life was as much a mystery as the person who remained her lawful husband. Theos revealed little about himself: nothing at all about family, marital

266

status, birthplace, childhood, youth or education, and she refrained from asking. During a heat wave in May, 1940 when Manhattan became stifling, Ganna invited him to spend the weekend at Yonkers.

On the Sunday morning, after receiving no response from knocking on the door of the guest bedroom, she entered to find Theos "seated as always *à l'oriental* - cross-legged typing, typing, and so eagerly, so absorbed that he detected my presence only when I was already standing near him."

"Blessings, blessings, beautiful lady!" he greeted her, "I'm so happy! It's the first time since I left Lhasa that I feel again as I did in Tibet. I feel that I belong here. Again I feel at home . . . Such a calmness . . . no telephone . . . no interference. I can sit here and write and write. Oh I'm so happy! May your heart be enlightened for giving me this heavenly weekend I will gather enough vitality to enable me to go back to that horrible hotel."

Walska fell for his applied charm in spite of her intentions, suspecting that what he really wanted was, "Some place, perhaps in his beloved California, in his adored desert where he feels so near to God, alone with his books, his work!" The manipulative Theos, knowing he had a rich and receptive audience in Madame Walska, continued to enthuse about the Golden West, comparing it to Sikkim, Darjeeling and other parts of India and Tibet that he had visited. He described California's seasonal beauty with glowing intensity: the golden sunsets, mountains in April covered with lilac followed by the flowering yuccas of May and June. She noted: "His description was so vivid, so contagious that I too began to share his imagination for California." When Ganna's New York singing teacher was called to Hollywood for work in the movies, it was the perfect excuse for her and Theos to take a trip there: it would avoid interrupting her singing lessons, and she could share his bubbling enthusiasm for the Coast.

Their transcontinental flight touched down at Tucson, Arizona in a flaming desert sunset, and after a few days in the area, they drove to the movie capital of the world, which made a big impression on Walska:

"Veni, vidi, vici! Oh! Those six weeks I spent on the Blue Point over the shop in a rented-for-the-occasion-from-a-painter tiny apartment. At night the lights of the terrestrial sky surrounded me and as far as my eyes could

reach. **Whenever I am asked to give an account of my extensive traveling in the new and old worlds, which made the greatest of all impressions - without hesitation I would always answer: 'My view of Hollywood at night, lit by billions of artificial and real stars.'"**

Theos Bernard kept his distance by checking into the Beverly Hills Hotel at her expense with "a friend" who, she noted cynically, "made his physical appearance invisible to me," departing the following day because the bustling establishment, much favored by the movie crowd, was too noisy for him. She imagined that Bernard's buddy must be "a young man, perhaps a schoolmate eager to see his childhood pal, wanting to learn about traveling in the East, perhaps interested himself in a study of Oriental spirituality." Theos said they could work together on his new book if he were to take a house instead of staying in a hotel. Ganna was more accustomed to being in places like the Paris Ritz, the Carlton in Cannes, London's Claridge's, or the Palace at St. Moritz, but agreed to pay for their accommodation at many times the rent of her modest apartment. She also bought an automobile for Theos because he complained about the distances to be covered in Los Angeles, with taxis only available outside the big hotels. Walska engaged a Filipino cook as well as a valet, and Bernard's exigent companion moved in with her guru, though she never set eyes on him.

If Ganna called by the rented house, Theos always appeared at the front door the moment her car drew up, and when she was invited for dinner, his colleague happened to be out for the evening, only returning home only after the last guest had left, or as she suspected, waited in the bushes until all visitors were gone. "A criminal, an escaper from Sing Sing prison could not behave differently than this mysterious friend," she entered in her diary. The situation became so bizarre that when Theos was teased about it, his reaction to innocent jibes was decidedly frosty. These came from Ganna's friends like "soul sister" Alma Mahler and her husband Franz Werfel, who had escaped Nazi persecution in Austria by making their way on foot through France and Spain, then taking a ship to the United States, and were now living in the Hollywood Hills. Werfel was completing a German novel, *"Das Lied von Bernadette,"* that was to make him famous through its English version, "The Song of Bernadette" (1942*)* and a movie of the same name starring Jennifer Jones, who would win the Oscar for best actress at the 1943 Academy Awards.

Despite spending an enjoyable time in the movie capital during one of its studios' most productive eras, Walska faced returning east after learning that new taxes were biting into the incomes of the wealthy. She fully expected her French property and possessions to be in German hands now, following the Nazis' triumphal entry into Paris on June 14, and her future in America, far from war-torn Europe, now seemed less secure, with Britain pressing the United States to join the Allied cause. Furthermore, Grindell was in a desperate state, having run out of support for his projects, sending off a cable to New York on June 28:

"Work Nearly Complete. All Means Now Exhausted Can You Help. God Bless You. Grindell."

He waited more than a week for a response because Ganna was still in California, and then dispatched another:

"No Reply To Last Weeks Cable. Hope You Are Well. God Bless You. Grindell Matthews."

The messages were relayed to Walska by her secretary and she replied to them, rather incoherently:

"I Did My Bit. Cannot Do More Without Forcing Situations. Forcing My Sincerity."

Defeated, Grindell brought to an end this short burst of transatlantic communication by cabling to where she was staying, care of Madame Sedes, 6377 Brynmawr Drive, Hollywood.

"Quite Understand. Please Cable When You Have News Galluis. God Bless You. Grindell Matthews."

By Independence Day 1940, Walska had received a rough draft of the first sixteen pages of her book from Jere Knight, together with a promise to work on the remainder of the manuscript over the summer.

This wasn't quick enough for the impatient author unable to understand why editing took so long, suggesting that perhaps they meet for a few days at Yonkers during September, when she returned from the Coast. Knight sent more corrected pages and Ganna responded to them by letter:

"I received the first article and was extremely happy about it because you understand just what I want. But once in a while, probably because of my bad English, you seem to get the opposite meaning of the one I wish to convey. Such small things as "but" instead of "and" sometimes change the whole phrase. It is for this reason that I thought we could do the work

faster and better, with less rewriting, if we could get together and collaborate."

Home on Park Avenue, Ganna's thoughts were far from Grindell and Galluis because of focusing on her guru's mission, in spite of being wary of Bernard's general demeanor, observing "meanness" in him, "hateful eyes" and "closed tightened teeth." She failed to understand what was wrong at the time, but would comment later, "I realized only irresistible desire to hurt, to insult . . . And at midnight when I finally fell asleep with a heavy heart I was awakened by the telephone ringing to hear his desperate voice: 'I love you! I love you!'" There was no mention next day of the night's disturbing behavior; no apology, no explanation, no expression of regret for his dark moods. "Still, the maternal instinct, deeply rooted in every woman's heart, dictated that this man needs me," she thought, accepting his conduct as a type of mental illness.

Jere Knight was reluctant to leave the rusticity of Springhouse Farm, Happy Valley to be with Walska in Yonkers or Manhattan editing her memoirs:

"It hardly seems possible that the summer is almost past. There are so many things to be done on a farm such as this is, that the end of a season means numerous chores of preparing for the next. And so I have been happily busy putting up food in glass jars so that the extra supply of fruit and vegetables grown during the summer can be kept and used the following winter. It is the life of a farmer's wife - a rich and full life. Especially as my mornings are devoted to working at the typewriter."

She suggested that Madame might like to stay "in the real country," by visiting her at Bucks County, Pennsylvania:

"You see, we lead a real country life at our farm and it would require some planning ahead to absent myself so spontaneously for so long."

Walska declined the invitation, forcing herself to be patient as Knight continued the thankless task of making new chapter divisions to give the muddled text some cohesion, and in the process coming across countless inconsistencies that needed to be explained by mail, because the Knights' farm had no telephone. In the meantime, Maurice Speiser contacted other possible outlets for the autobiography and received a letter from Richard R. Smith, a New York vanity publisher, who showed interest - if Madame would finance the entire cost.

Ganna cabled Mrs. Knight from Yonkers (making a boo-boo

by calling her June instead of Jere) saying she would meet her on the first of November to discuss the revision, though getting together proved difficult for these women leading totally different lives. A cold prevented the editor from traveling, and when it developed into influenza, she was forced to take to her bed, delaying further progress. They did manage to meet just after Thanksgiving in New York, with Knight predicting that her part of the job would be finished early in the New Year after retyping the corrected manuscript.

The White Lama
1940-1941

For weeks, the American newspapers were full of stories about the Blitz, that relentless sequence of air raids by the Luftwaffe on the British capital, resulting in widespread death and destruction from dropping incendiary and high-explosive bombs during fifty-seven consecutive nights of attacks. London did not suffer alone; on the night of 14-15 November waves of German aircraft targeted armaments factories around Coventry in the English Midlands, devastating the city center, demolishing its medieval cathedral, killing nearly four hundred people and injuring more than eight hundred. Press reports of the suffering, together with listening to graphic commentaries on the radio by Edward R. Murrow, made Ganna feel guilty about abandoning her fifth husband, and, having heard nothing from him for weeks, sent off a cable:

"If Possible Let Me Know How You Are. Where Are You. God Bless England. Ganna Walska."

His reply came eight days later:

"Well And Happy With Cable Just Received. Shall be Glad Of Any News Of Dear Galluis And Family. Returning To Tor Cloud Tomorrow. God Bless You Always. Grindell."

On December 24 she wished him "A Peaceful 1941" and then celebrated the festive season at home in Polish style with a few close friends, beginning on Christmas Eve with the traditional meatless vigil feast known as the Wigilia. According to custom, an additional seat was kept for a stranger at the supper table as a symbolic reminder that Joseph and Mary sought shelter at the inn. On Park Avenue the chair was filled by Theos Bernard.

Mrs. Knight worked on Ganna's memoirs until the end of January, bemoaning the fact that it left her no time for winter sports, hoping to enjoy them all the more when her task was finished. In Manhattan, Maurice Speiser negotiated the terms of a publishing contract with Richard R. Smith and hired three typists to prepare the manuscript, anxious to get the hundred remaining pages completed. He took on the combined roles of managing editor and libel lawyer by suggesting some changes to avoid litigation over personal remarks about a number prominent people.

"Forgive my persistence in suggesting again that the chapter on Paderewski, upon re-reading, could well be edited. While it shows frankly your desire to sacrifice yourself, it does still use the names of two persons, Mr. Paderewski and Mr. Schelling, without their permission or desire and it strikes me that the last paragraph on page 236 takes liberties with discussing Padereweski's 'out-of-date conceit' and references to 'It was my beautiful guiding spirit.' Both of these in one paragraph would be considered a gratuitous reference to the disadvantage of Mr. Paderewski."

Speiser explained that the assumption of her philosophy being the right one and Paderewski's the wrong, could be considered presumptuous.

Ganna's switch of loyalty from Grindell to Bernard forced her to think about living more prudently to protect her assets, the loss of which would be for her a fate worse than debt. She also wondered about the safest place to avoid war if the United States became involved in the conflict - or worse – invaded. Madame had intended to buy a country property in upstate New York, but found nothing suitable, and now reasoned that if the Germans attacked, it would be on the East Coast and she would be in the firing line. "I was certainly one of those to be prepared for any such eventuality," she noted, "and while the charm of California still rang around my heart, I considered a plan to acquire a self-supporting ranch, so that if the worst would come and my possessions would be liquidated for me by the hands of world events, I could always retire to such a farm in that already beloved part of the States."

Theos Bernard, with ambitions to bring Tibetan Lamas to California, grasped the opportunity of realizing this with Ganna's money, while she began studying the real estate columns of the Los Angeles newspapers. He knew that Madame Walska had little idea of California's geography or climate, and generously offered to give up his valuable time by flying out to the Coast and inspecting what his friend there recommended. She thought it a splendid idea and happily paid for the expensive trip. Soon, enthusiastic wires and telephone calls began arriving from Theos, who needed extra mobility for his searches:

"As For Cars Found Brand New Cadillac Beautiful Red Body Asking Twenty Six Hundred. Recommend Selling Two New York Cars And Taking This One."

And the next day:

"Nature Getting Ready Here For Springtime Rehearsal. Have Uncovered Several Prospects Which Our Practical Friend Highly Recommends. Suggests Your Coming Earliest Convenience To Make Final Decision. Our Karma Seems To be Unfolding As Does The Day."

He could be both lyrical and charming, even in the restrictions of a cable, particularly when he wanted something badly. The prospects he mentioned ranged over a wide area from coastal Avalon to the Santa Ynez Mountains, with the possibility of renting if owners were not willing to sell. He managed to extend his searches during three rainy months at Walska's mounting expense, accompanied by his anonymous friend and traveling as far as Arizona and San Francisco. In mid-February he revealed:

"Cable From India Brings Tibetan Blessings. Lamas Are Ready To Come To Carry Out Great Work. They Will Advise Me Departure Date As Soon As I Instruct Them. And So Our Karma Unfolds."

For long periods Theos remained incommunicado, and Walska worried where he was, which resulted in an explanatory letter:

"I am sorry that I have failed to let my girl know, for never do I want her to be distressed for a moment, but I forget she is not familiar with our train routings etc. Just keep after me and eventually I will learn, for it is not from any lack of feeling in the heart, but pure thoughtlessness, feeling that my girl will figure it out. Hourly I dream of her, with each move I contemplate a message, but details are always blotted out by flooding torrents of feeling which is impossible for me to write down when I am constantly surrounded by people , people, people in hotels, lobbies, writing desks etc. And now I am trying to get passage to Santa Barbara to wait for my girl – I hope there is no need to say why."

He then reverted to sending brief cables to "his girl."

"Just Down From The Garden Of The Gods. Rains Continue Harder Than Ever. When Are You Going To Come. Someone Wants You."

In mid-April he said he was negotiating with two people named Knapp and Clarke - about buying or renting their properties, and at the end of the month sent a telegram from the Hotel Leamington in Oakland:

"I Can Leave On Moments Notice And Meet You At Burbank Airport Whenever You Say."

While Bernard was away with his open brief to find a secure hideaway for Ganna, which could also be used for his proposed Tibetan institute, Walska remained in New York, attending dinner parties, the opera, concerts, theater and cinemas - the usual social rounds. Her favorite movie house was the RKO Palace at

274

Broadway and 47th Street, which premièred a new film by a show business *enfant terrible* named Orson Welles. When still only twenty-five, he had attracted overnight fame in October, 1938 with the notorious Halloween stunt of broadcasting live his version of H. G. Wells' novel "The War of the Worlds," presented as breaking news. Its realism convinced many listeners that Martians were invading New Jersey, leading to some scenes of hysteria and massive press coverage. It was a strange irony that his near-namesake - the literary source of this extravaganza - had once dismissed radio broadcasting as fit only for "very sedentary persons living in badly lighted houses or otherwise unable to read."

Welles was the creative force behind the Palace's latest screen attraction *Citizen Kane,* as its producer, director, joint writer and star, which opened on May 1, 1941 to unalloyed praise by the influential *New York Times* critic Bosley Crowther as "close to the most sensational film ever made in Hollywood." It told, in flashback, the story of the fictional newspaper tycoon, Charles Foster Kane, a titanic egomaniac consumed by his own terrifying self-interest: a character regarded by many as a barely-disguised caricature of the real-life press magnate William Randolph Hearst, though the screenplay by Welles and Herman J. Mankiewicz was developed from a stage play written by the former when a precocious teenager. The title role was probably based upon an amalgam of three almost legendary tycoons: newspaper man Hearst, the electric utility baron Samuel Insull, and someone Walska had clashed with previously: Robert McCormick, publisher of the Chicago *Herald.*

In spite of Crowther's review, others were not as enthusiastic about the movie's qualities, and patronage at the Palace was unexceptional. Walska never said if she saw *Citizen Kane* during its brief run there, but if she did, the picture might have suggested certain similarities with her own life, particularly the role of Kane's second wife, named Susan Alexander in the film and brilliantly played by Dorothy Comingore. On screen, the fictional Kane builds an opera house in Chicago to showcase the flaky talents of his new bride, and Welles, an inveterate cigar man, would have heard smoke room talk in what he regarded as his home town about Walska's famous failure, as a would-be prima donna and never-was diva, to sing *Zaza* with the Chicago Opera as

275

Harold McCormick's protégée.

Many years later, when *Citizen Kane* regularly topped international polls as a seminal movie classic, Robert Wise, its editor (and later top Hollywood director), was convinced that the opera sequences referred, not so much to William Randolph Hearst, as Harold McCormick and his ineffectual championing of the woman he wanted to marry. At the time of its production under a working-title of *John Citizen U.S.A.*, Orson Welles regarded Susan Alexander as the pivotal character of his screenplay, sending a telegram to composer Bernard Herrmann with background information about the "Suzie" role. It read, in part: "A Small But Rather Good Voice. This Is The Ticklish Part Of It. Even 'GW' Had Something Of A Voice." Those initials could only refer to Ganna Walska, though the person parodied in *Citizen Kane* remains a matter of conjecture. Susan Alexander was also likely to have been a composite figure: of William Randolph Hearst's mistress Marion Davies, and Ganna Walska. Madame, though, seems to have remained blissfully unaware that her miserable singing career was mythologized in such a brilliant and enduring way.

Theos Bernard continued to be optimistic in his cables and letters from the West Coast, and Ganna found his lyrical descriptions seductive, particularly when narrowing the search to two properties and insisting it was time for her to look at them. She flew out to California with high expectations, not realizing at the time - and reluctant to admit later - that Bernard was taking her for a long and expensive ride. The places he selected were earmarked for his long-planned Tibetan institute, not primarily as Ganna Walska's security against a Nazi invasion of the United States. One was owned by a wealthy member of the British aristocracy who was deeply interested in Bernard's cause and the other by an even richer former industrialist who shared similar Buddhist interests.

Before Walska came on the scene, Theos had kept in touch with his academic friend, Professor Don Brown of UC Santa Barbara, University of California, writing to him from time to time, and phoning from New York during 1939 asking if he would see Sir Humphrey Orme Clarke, a young Englishman of means, aged thirty-three, who was buying a place near Santa Barbara to be used for Buddhist studies. Clarke had found a neglected thirty-seven-acre estate named Cuesta Linda, bought it for $35,000, and went to live there with his beautiful wife Elizabeth. It was rumored locally that Theos had an affair with Lady Clarke, and, whether true or not, she unexpectedly departed for England, leaving her husband in residence.

Brown received another phone call from Bernard in early 1941, not long-distance this time but from the top of a mountain in the nearby Santa Ynez range. As he recalled, Theos had flown out to the Coast planning to live there permanently, and invited him to drive up straight away to see his "Tibetan monastery," giving instructions on how to get there.

"I drove up Refugio Pass road and turned right at the summit until I came to a left turn off some miles along the Camino Cielo. After the low chaparral of the coast side of the mountain, I was astounded on driving over the crest to find myself suddenly in a forest of giant pines growing in a lovely basin of considerable size."

Bernard - all smiles - greeted him, striding out of a spacious building built from huge logs. Inside, his visitor was astonished to find an enormous living room dominated by a stone fireplace, with tiger skin rugs on the floor and empty bookcases arranged around the walls. Theos sprang a further surprise on his friend when a Chinese cook appeared from the kitchen to announce their meal was ready. A variety of delicious oriental dishes was served for lunch, culminating in an almond dessert accompanied by fragrant Chinese tea.

"Bernard certainly did things in style," Brown noted.

Afterward, he was taken along a boardwalk to a lookout giving spectacular views of the entire Santa Ynez valley and the distant San Rafael range. "The mountain dropped steeply away below the lookout so that it seemed you were looking out of an airplane."

The estate was called El Capitan, owned by George Owen Knapp, who described it as his mountain retreat, which he wanted to sell. Holding out the possibility of finding a purchaser for him, Bernard persuaded Knapp to rent it in the short term to Madame Walska. At a height of four thousand feet, the property was not nearly as lofty as Lhasa, but rarified enough for use as part of a proposed Tibetan institute; it was "The Garden of the Gods" Theos referred to in a recent cable to New York.

When she arrived to inspect the Cuesta Linda estate on the

coastal plain, Walska was disappointed, regarding Sir Humphrey Clarke's property, nestling dramatically beneath the serrated blue mountain range and close to the ocean in exclusive Montecito, as something of a white elephant. The owner had been called away for war duties at the British Embassy in Washington, D.C., having owned the estate for little more than a year, leaving behind some poorly maintained Italianate gardens, two enormous swimming pools - one of them heated with its bath house large enough for use as a dwelling - and in the middle, the faded splendor of a large Californian Spanish mansion It looked nothing like the simple farmhouse Madame Walska had in mind when thinking about moving to California. There was an adjoining commercial lemon orchard whose income, Theos assured her, would help pay for running everything. But she knew that Cuesta Linda did not suit her purposes: "Naturally it was everything but a self-supporting farm, this seigniorial domain that required great quantities of servants and several luxurious gardens necessitated a whole staff of gardeners, without mentioning the fact that I had not the slightest idea how to run a lemon business."

On hearing her reaction, Theos immediately offered something better than citrus growing near the ocean, by reminding Ganna of his other discovery up in the mountains.

"If you get that property," he pointed out, "then in addition and gratis would be given to you a really God-chosen divine retreat from where you can see all the Pacific and China, and where you cannot help but feel one with the Infinite." They went up into the mountains to view El Capitan, driving along the precipitous roads Professor Brown had described, through a rocky wilderness with hairpin bends confronting a chasm on every curve. Their driver refused to give warning blasts on the horn and Walska shuddered to think what would happen if they met an oncoming vehicle: surely hurled to an instant death. She wrote later:

"After an hour-and-a-half - to me it was an endless period of time - we finally arrived at our destination. We went to a glass tower à la Hitler's Berchtesgarden, where one actually was lost in the immensity of space."

Installed in the wild mountainous terrain, she saw a heated swimming pool, tennis court, with an organ inside the house that could fill the mountain air, as she put it, "with the sublime sounds of Bach." But a pragmatic streak told her that this impressive place commanding an unbelievable view would also need a resident staff to run it.

Surrounded by the dense Los Padres National Forest, the El Capitan complex comprised a dozen buildings: the lodge itself, an unfinished three-storey lookout, three guest cottages, caretaker's accommodation and workshops. Ganna knew it was too big and far too remote, preferring Cuesta Linda, if a choice had to be made between the two. But Bernard's contagious enthusiasm and the intoxicating pure mountain air combined to make up her mind to rent the property for his special work:

"The place must have been created especially for me, for us, the destined place where the monks from Tibetan monasteries would gather for translating the sacred manuscripts that Mr. Bernard brought for this purpose from the Forbidden City of Lhasa. No one could resist such an exaltation! No one could throw icy water on such divine inspiration by speaking of impracticability by reminding this youthful knowledge-seeker that it is not a self-supporting farm! I know I could not."

After agreeing on the rent, the lodge soon received a name-change, becoming known as Penthouse of the Gods, after Theos Bernard's bestseller.

In fact, Ganna Walska was persuaded to buy both properties he selected, ignoring the cost by convincing herself that she had enough money to live comfortably with funds that, had it not been for her forced departure from Europe, would have been spent on the expensive upkeep of her theater, the Château de Galluis and Paris town residence, or sent to her family in Poland. Contact with them was now impossible, and, although the cost of living in New York was rising, the income taxes she paid in America were still prewar taxes. Ganna's head said she must not be so extravagant, but her heart told her otherwise. She toyed with the idea of selling the Park Avenue house to finance her Californian purchases, but lawyer Phelan Beale vetoed it, insisting that she needed a domicile in New York for legal reasons. He also approved the publishing contract with Richard R. Smith, allowing the project to proceed without further delay. Three thousand copies of Walska's story would be printed initially, with thirty-two pages of illustrations, and the author agreed to pay $4,000 in two equal sums for the privilege. The proceeds from the first edition were to be divided between author and publisher 60-40 percent, which meant that if 2,500 copies were sold at the proposed retail price of $3.50,

Walska might just recoup her investment.

1940s

She became owner of the Cuesta Linda estate in June 1941, intending to change the name and call it Tibetland in honor of Theos, without realizing it strange - or even coincidental - that the sellers of both properties - diplomat Sir Humphrey O. Clarke and philanthropist George Owen Knapp - were Tibet enthusiasts and thoroughly familiar with Theos Bernard and his work. Knapp had often referred to his mountaintop complex as "the Potala," after the Dalai Lama's great palace in Lhasa, and Clarke wrote to her from the British Embassy in Washington, D.C. on July 4, revealing his own interest in her guru's welfare:

"I suppose by now you are settled at Cuesta Linda and enjoying the restful calm of Santa Barbara after the hectic fever of New York. I take it too that Theos is installed and able to proceed with his work undisturbed. I hope that he has somewhere suitable where he can put all his books: these have been in store for far too long and it is high time that he have them all out and start the essential work of compiling a catalogue of them."

Instead of a modest, self-sufficient farm, Ganna Walska had acquired a piece of Santa Barbara history with Cuesta Linda. The original ninety-eight-acre homestead grant of 1877 changed hands several times during its first few years, probably because the challenge of clearing a dense cover of live oak trees and choking chaparral became too daunting for successive owners. Englishman Ralph Kinton Stevens made the first real impression on this wild patch in 1882 by settling on the estate, which his wife, Caroline Lucy Tallant, named Tanglewood, for obvious reason. Stevens was an adventurous, well-educated person with the ambition to become a nurseryman, after working as a ranch hand and on survey teams throughout California. His special interests were citrus and palms, though he faced a struggle to establish them at Tanglewood because of an erratic water supply. Dams and reservoirs were built, but there was never quite enough for proper irrigation and more than half of the original property was sold-off in an attempt to make the remainder viable.

Stevens built a substantial sandstone and shingle house for himself, his wife and three children, and the enterprise flourished as he became friendly with the local plant men, with his lemon nursery providing the stock for many of the commercial orchards being established around booming Santa Barbara. With no formal horticultural training, Ralph Stevens installed a notable array of plants, trees and shrubs around the house, and had started landscaping the grounds when he died of a heart attack in 1896, at the age of forty-eight. Widowed Caroline was left to look after her brood by renting the main house to winter visitors, operating a guest ranch, and leasing the property to a school. She managed to keep going until 1913, when Tanglewood was sold to George Owen Knapp, who became known as one of the Hill Barons of Montecito because of his extensive land holdings in the area, including a beautiful estate known as Arcady. Knapp was the founding vice-president of the Union Carbide company, and when he purchased Tanglewood was the chemical company's president.

He kept the property for only three years, too busy on other projects to do much work there, and sold it in 1916 to Erastus Palmer Gavit, a wealthy New Yorker in the gas and electricity business who traveled to California each year with his wife Marie and daughter Marcia Ann to escape the eastern winters. He renamed the property Cuesta Linda (Pretty Hill in Spanish), demolished the Stevens house and engaged the Pasadena architect, Reginald Johnson, to design a spacious Mediterranean-style villa of six bedrooms and four bathrooms, together with outbuildings and extensive servants' quarters.

1920s

With its Italianate gardens, Cuesta Linda became known as one of the area's finest properties, and from 1926 was included in the Summer Garden Tour raising funds for the ambitious Santa Barbara Plans and Planting Committee. When presidential candidate Herbert Hoover made a campaign stop in Montecito in 1928, it was one of the four grand estates he visited. Marie Gavit died in 1937, having survived her husband, and Cuesta Linda was sold to Sir Humphrey Clarke in 1939.

During the summer and into the fall of 1941, Ganna Walska busied herself in preparation for Theos Bernard's use - or "fixing up the place," as she was reported saying when the local newspaper learned that "the colorful Polish-born soprano" was purchasing the property. There was much to do inside and out, with the garden needing urgent attention after being left to nature's own devices for too long. She was told that Lockwood de Forest was the best landscape architect in Santa Barbara and decided that he was the man for the job, becoming her estate director. His itemized accounts, from mid-1941, show how seriously Madame regarded the formidable task ahead.

Charging several hundred dollars a month for his professional services, de Forest arranged labor, bought plants and shrubs from local nurseries, supervised repairs and maintenance, arranged soil treatments and planned the installation of a new orchard. His June statement totaled $2,349.29; the July figure rose to $3,778.32, and during August soared to $4,701.15. These were considerable sums at a time when a good laborer could be hired for five dollars a day. Among the multitude of jobs needing urgent attention, de Forest initiated work in the palm grove and the lower garden, planted cacti around the main house, cleared and planted around the swimming pool, renovated the old lawn, attended to the principal drive and arranged for pest eradication.

Meanwhile, Madame was rushed off her feet trying to arrange the Lamas' accommodation at both the renamed Tibetland and at Penthouse. The first to arrive was to be Geshe Chhophei, and $700 was remitted to Calcutta through the American Express Company in Los Angeles to buy his ticket, though nothing more was heard about the travel arrangements for weeks after. Sir Humphrey Clarke had suggested that these holy men would greatly help in the classification of Bernard's collection of Tibetan books. He warned Madame Walska in a letter from the British Embassy: "I hope that the necessary financial arrangements have now been made. If they are to come, they should come now before an extension of the war makes travel from India impossible." He also hoped that she would be able to provide a place where "La Varnie" could continue his experiments. He turned out to be her guru's invisible Californian friend - a man with a French-sounding name who apparently specialized in chemical formulae.

Theos packed the car once a week with what Ganna called "enough food for an over-run European country," taking it to La Varnie, who lived somewhere over the mountains. She steeled herself to be "utterly uncurious," never asking questions while watching the red Cadillac's cavernous trunk being loaded with hams, wine, chocolate, vegetables and jerry cans of fuel. When Theos returned after one of these excursions, he asked laconically if she would "do something" for his friend, who was in poor health; it was his coded way of inviting him to occupy one of the

283

freshly-painted cottages on the estate. A few days later Tibetland's first visitor arrived and Walska met the mystery man at long last, not through any formal introduction, but coming across him strolling in the garden. He appeared much older than she had imagined - perhaps around sixty - with gray hair and a prominent nose as the only distinguishing features of what she described as a forgettable face. Added to this was an awkward demeanor that made communication difficult, though he sounded totally American and not French, as his name suggested.

Ganna assured him that the privacy of one of the Tibetland cottages would be far more pleasing than living the life of a hermit somewhere out in the scrubby desert wastes. But she was wrong. A few days after moving in, Theos told her that La Varnie was returning to his simple shack because he found the cottage damp, and it was impossible to sleep there. She was happy to see the end of their lugubrious visitor, but Bernard became so depressed at the prospect of his leaving that she suggested he move into the main house instead, taking one of the airy rooms on the upper floor with an enchanting view over the treetops to the Pacific Ocean.

Theos described La Varnie as the greatest living chemist, but was currently unable to practice his genius without a laboratory. Walska responded generously by offering to locate a workshop for him in the former stables, a spacious brick building with a large fireplace and vivid mountain views through enormous picture windows. There was an adjacent bedroom, bathroom and well-equipped kitchen, as well as bookcases enough "for all the literature of the world." Remodeling was finished in record time, after the builders were offered cash incentives for early completion.

Theos called La Varnie to inspect the finished work, while Ganna stood at the gate of the stables' own garden separated from the rest of the estate by a picket fence, proud of her achievement. "Both men were approaching," she recalled, "walking as if they were following a funeral. I opened the door and gave the key to Mr. La Varnie, saying that it was up to him to keep it. We entered that beautiful studio . . . to show them around. When two or three minutes later we left, our charming personage had never opened his mouth and never changed the sour expression on his sour face as we returned in silence."

Sir Humphrey Clarke had cautioned her about him in a recent letter: "He is no longer young and it would be a pity if he took his knowledge to the grave before being able to impart it to others." The laboratory remained unused, however, and Ganna was reminded of her similar experience with Grindell Matthews at Galluis. She still had no idea who this man was, or what strange hold he had over Theos, and Clarke revealed nothing more in his letter, referring instead to Walska's own role in an unfolding drama, which, he said, was preordained:

"In brief, whether you realize it or not, you have been granted an opportunity in this lifetime such as is granted to few women. I trust that you will not have to reproach yourself later with having let it slip. The cause that Theos serves far outstrips any of our personal ambitions and desires."

That, too, matched the comments from Gita and Major Reid about Grindell Matthews' work. Then, like a bombshell, a cable arrived from her husband's Welsh housekeeper, Lilly Morris. It was dated September 11, and was all the more poignant for its brevity:

"Mister Grindell Passed Away This Morning. Any Special Arrangements."

Before Ganna could compose herself and answer it, another one came - collect - from Richardson, Grindell's solicitor in England:

"Grindell's Last Will Appoints Me Sole Executor. No Funds Available For Funeral. To Prevent Burial At Expense Of State Approximately Fifty Pounds necessary.

There is no record of a response, but Ganna learned a little more about her fifth husband's demise from the New York *Herald Tribune* of Friday, September 12 in a sober account of the inventor's career, including the dispiriting comment: "But, as far as the public knows none of his lethal machines has ever been employed in the present war." The final paragraph made the only reference to a wife - and none too kindly, considering she was besotted with another man promoting a different cause: "When he married Mme. Walska in 1938 the inventor said he was too busy working on his aerial torpedo invention to go with her on a wedding trip. Mme. Walska went to Paris alone."

A letter arrived from Ernest Barwell in England, and where the previous cables were brutally brief this was deeply disturbing in its details:

"Grindell, at the time of his death, had just completed arrangements to come over and join you in America. He wanted to surprise you, and to

apologize for certain remarks. He told me that they were only made in the heat of the moment, and because, although he was disguising it from you, his heart was actually giving him trouble . . ."

The biographer added that Grindell had sold his Welsh bungalow for £575, though the money had not been received and it was left to executor Richardson to settle his outstanding financial affairs, which were in a woeful state. Apparently, it was planned to give half to Miss Morris as compensation for receiving nothing for her domestic duties over the past two years, and the rest was to buy a ticket to the United States to see his wife.

Barwell said he rushed to Grindell's Welsh mountain home as soon as he heard of his death and found things there "at sixes and sevens." The body was sent to Pontypridd for cremation and he took the ashes away to be scattered. On a brighter note, he announced that arrangements had been made for publishing his biography of her husband with a revised title, "The Death Ray Man," and a film company was showing interest in making a movie based on his extraordinary life. These events, so far away, had little immediate impact on Walska in the throes of organizing a new life with Theos in California, until she read a message from the mayor of the city of Swansea enclosed with Barwell's letter, which moved her to tears. It provided a bizarre epitaph for a doomed relationship:

"Please extend to Madame our deepest sympathy as a town in the death of a brilliant husband. We had hoped to have the honor of hearing her sing in our magnificent Brangwyn Hall. Will you please issue the invitation for her to come as the guest of the town after the war, so that we may hear her? We will welcome her for herself, as well as for the genius who was her husband."

Neither Swansea - nor anywhere else - would hear Madame Ganna Walska sing again in public.

She had promised to deliver the finished manuscript of her autobiography by July 1, 1941, and failing to meet that deadline, admitted that she was ashamed of herself. The contract was amended, and three months passed before Richard T. Smith queried the whereabouts of the material, hoping to receive it in time for publication during the spring of 1942. Similar hitches plagued the plans for bringing Tibetan Lamas to California. Letters passed back and forth between Pauline M. Finlay, Walska's secretary at Tibetland, and American Express in Los Angeles, trying to discover what had happened to the remittance sent to Calcutta months before. No allowance seemed to be made for the fact that it was not the best of times for international money transfers, particularly when the company's office in Calcutta had been instructed in wartime to arrange travel for a senior religious figure from Darjeeling and then find an onward passage for him to the United States. All that could be established was that $400 was forwarded to Calcutta, but an American visa had been refused for Geshe Chhophei's visit.

Soon after her fifth husband's passing, Ganna learned of the fourth's death from a cerebral hemorrhage at his Beverly Hills residence on October 17, aged sixty-nine. Harold McCormick was chairman of the board of the International Harvester Company at the time of his passing, and his third wife, Adah Wilson McCormick, who he married in 1938, was at the bedside together with his two married daughters and son. The residue of his fortune was valued at $9,412,765 after estate taxes of $3,165,437 and Illinois inheritance taxes of $580,257, and went to Adah and the children. Harold's death prompted Ganna to check some sentiments she had written about him for the forthcoming book, to make sure they rang true:

"While we were married I wanted him to give me the same quality of feeling that I gave him. Now, being above personal feminine vanity and selfish desires for my own happiness, I can touch his beautiful self and overlook completely those differences that separated us in an earthly way. I can love him now in a much nobler sense."

She decided not to change a word.

Love and affection were uppermost in Ganna's thoughts at this time: besotted by Theos for what he could achieve in a spiritual sense, and flattered by the attentions of one of the most glamorous personalities in the world of music, lusting after her perhaps for a different reason. English-born, Antoni Stanislaw Boleslawowicz, known to the world of classical music and beyond as Leopold Stokowski, had lived in the United States since 1905 and for most of that time, between 1912 and 1938, was director of the mighty Philadelphia, one of the world's greatest symphony orchestras. He tended to scandalize musical purists with his flamboyant, no-baton conducting technique, while ruffling others' sensibilities by programing the latest atonal works. Nobody could deny his ability to communicate with audiences, however, and achieve sumptuous sounds from his players. Women adored him, and Stokowski the lover was notorious for his affairs with some of the richest and most famous beauties of the age, including a widely-publicized fling with Greta Garbo. He'd found Ganna Walska irresistible when they were first introduced more than twenty years before during a soirée at Dr. Fraenkel's house, and, sharing an interest in Buddhism, they met up again in New York soon after Ganna's forced flight from Europe, when their long-term attraction for each other was rekindled. In between those meetings, Stokowski continued to send her passionate love letters:

"Little child come quickly to our nesting-place because I can't wait - I am thinking of you all the time - in a new way - and sometimes I nearly choke with impatience to see you. Send me a telegram the moment you arrive because I want to come straight to you - I am thinking always of your kiss - you said it would all happen this way and it has."

That hastily-scrawled, undated note on White Star Line notepaper probably came from the early 1930s after he conducted with great success at Le Théâtre des Champs-Elysées and enjoyed a passionate fling with the owner.

During 1940, Stokowski started building a house in the hills behind Santa Barbara, close to Tibetland, while working in Hollywood on his most famous project *Fantasia* - Walt Disney's audacious idea of combining the high art of symphonic music with the popular culture of animated cartoons, pioneering technical innovations like multi-plane cameras and multi-track stereo sound. The conductor happened to be in New York while Walska was in residence at Tibetland when he wrote her again, less flamboyantly than before, about their lasting mutual passion, which happened to be Theos Bernard's as well:

"I really would like very much to see you because I think we are both searching for the same thing and both have partly found it, but as it is infinite in its range, we shall be forever searching. Since I last saw you, I have been twice to India and once to Tibet, and these experiences have enriched my life beyond all telling. Halfway up to the mountains near you I have built a simple but most beautiful place hidden in the trees where no one can see it. I would like to take you there if it would interest you. It is a kind of Ashrama."

Ganna returned east to find another letter from Ernest Barwell waiting for her, sent following a British court hearing to settle Grindell Matthews' affairs. "Please do not distress yourself any further over clearing up Grindell's debts, and the construction of a memorial to him down at Clydach," he told her, having taken the matter into his own hands: "I realized the difficulties with which you were faced 'over there' and explained this in court." The judgment had gone against her late husband but the London editor of an American news features service was present in the courtroom and approached Barwell with a proposition. "As you may perhaps know," the biographer told her, "Grindell kept a very candid diary, and the American offered five hundred pounds for the details relating to his last romance [with Ganna] and for the messages that passed between the bungalow and the château." Barwell thought this offer would settle the affair because "neither of us wants to leave Grindell's name sullied, or any other unpleasant reflection on you in your helplessness so far away - and I have given them a tacit agreement to hand over the documents on January 1." He trusted this would meet with Madame's approval.

It certainly did not. Since arriving in America, she had been reluctant to send any more money to London in chasing a lost cause, but this was the first she heard of a candid diary, and the thought of having it sold to an American news service horrified her. Before she could contact Phelan Beale for his legal advice, however, Madame was spared any embarrassing revelations by the intervention of world events.

On the quiet Sunday morning of December 7, 1941, wave after wave of Japanese aircraft launched a surprise attack on the naval base at Pearl Harbor, and that infamous act in Hawaii jolted the United States and Britain into declaring war on Japan. No revelations of a failed boffin and his celebrity wife - however titillating - were likely to interest anybody now.

With Ganna back in New York, Professor Don Brown was staying with Theos Bernard at Tibetland that terrible weekend, and they listened together to the news broadcast announcing the Pearl Harbor attack.

"That does it!" Bernard exploded in frustration. "That's the end of my Tibetan institute plans 'till after the war. We can't hope to get any Lamas over here now."

During her absences from California, Walska had been told about wild parties that took place up at Penthouse from her housekeepers there, and it was clear from the monthly accounts that large amounts of food and drink were ordered - far more than Theos and La Varnie could consume on their own. This had caused her to have second thoughts about buying the lodge, particularly after her guru and some of his friends had damaged the contents of the still-rented property. Ganna asked the Knapp family to refund her deposit of $9,500, but they refused, insisting that Madame had made a firm commitment to purchase. A reduction in the asking price was negotiated and she acquired the title deeds, together with furnishings, for $17,500, in September, 1940.

A repetition of Theos' irresponsibility had compounded her nervous state over the possible publication of Grindell's secret diary, but her heart began to flutter again at the age of fifty-four after hearing from Stokowski. Ganna sent a stern warning to Bernard threatening to withdraw her support for his projects, and he responded by cabling her in New York:

"Your Message Relating Grave Situation Just Received. Apparently You Are No Longer Interested In Going Ahead With Plan To Establish The Tibetan Academy Of Literature Which Was My Sole Purpose In Coming To Santa Barbara. Under The Circumstances If You Will Merely Say The Word I Will Leave Immediately. It Is A Matter Of Importance That I Continue With The Original Plan Here Or Elsewhere So Please Let Me Have Your Final Decision. I Trust There Will Always Be A Friendly Feeling. Theos Bernard."

The Japanese attack of December 7 torpedoed Theos Bernard's plans for his admitted "sole purpose" Tibetan Academy, leaving Walska in a quandary. Should she persist with her young, charismatic guru, or search for destiny with the attractive old maestro?

After much reflection, she decided that life without her spiritual advisor and his fervent Buddhist convictions was too bleak to contemplate. Leopold Stokowski, aged fifty-nine, moved on to be associated with other famous women, including marrying "Poor little rich girl" Gloria Vanderbilt, forty-two years his junior. Walska's lifted her threat and invited Theos to share the festive season in Manhattan. He replied with a cable signed "The Hermit Of Tibetland:

"Very Happy To Accept Your Invitation To Spend Christmas At 94th Street Retreat"

Tibetland
1942

1942 dawned with Theos Bernard making his way back to California, having completely won over Madame Walska. Now, during the depths of winter, she sat in the comfort of the Park Avenue corner mansion, looked after by Mary Placek who had returned to full-time service, agonizing over "the extreme irony Hitler's invasion made in Europe, while my simple taste and the realization of hunger and privation the people are enduring - or are not able to endure and die - in inflamed Europe." She used only part of her extensive New York property in order to economize, but continued to run her two Californian estates, "the upkeep of which demanded more than my income allowed me to spend." Life became focused again, even though Ganna protested that events were moving too fast and beyond her control, caught up in a whirlwind of organization, planning a Tibetan museum, library and temple for Theos.

His demands would have been considered extreme in any circumstances, but were outrageous with America at war, insisting on using a powerful automobile because it offered better protection in case of accident (a yogi should never risk his precious life) which resulted in his driving around Santa Barbara, or out into the desert and up to the mountains, in the gas-guzzling Cadillac.

Bernard's living quarters were kept heated at all seasons of the year, with him claiming that divine inspiration came more easily in a cozy atmosphere, no matter at what cost or whether the coal miners were on strike. The temperature of the outdoor swimming pool in the cooler climes of Penthouse, four thousand feet above sea level, was maintained at a constant ninety-four degrees because no war was going to interfere with his comfort.

Walska was well-aware that he was allowed to lead a pampered life in California, and she would melt on reading:

"Just a note to say hello and let you know that there is only one thing missing out here and that is you; so do not stay away too long. I will busy myself with the details of the work that is planned so the time will fly by."

She had organized an expensive refit for Penthouse of the Gods to make the property more suitable for year-round living, and Theos went up there to see it under the season's first canopy of snow. "It was truthfully a sight for the Gods, an inspiration hardly to be surpassed," he wrote her. But the heavy snowfall made the track to the dam supplying the lodge's water impassable, and the installation of a new pumping system was delayed until workers could negotiate the treacherous roads with heavy vehicles. Back in the temperate climate of Tibetland - only a few feet above sea level - he noted the first, tentative signs of spring:

"The fruit trees are beginning to blossom, the oaks are putting out their new leaves, even the turtle is beginning to move around a little. The pussies, well they own the place, you have to ask them for permission to come in. If you will come soon, all will be perfect - please don't keep us waiting."

Ganna mailed boxes of candy for her guru's sweet tooth and carefully studied every word he wrote, underlining expressions of affection and adding scribbled comments: "Love!" "Nature and love." "Love and return." She finalized plans for travel to the Coast by train, which brought another of his tender typewritten missives to make her heart beat faster:

"I wish I could make the time fly faster. Your boy will be waiting for you at the station in Los Angeles on April 3, so that you will not have to waste a single second getting back to Tibetland and I will be able to be with you from the very moment of your return to California."

Theos noted that the weather could not have been more perfect, allowing him to sunbathe in the nude every day and to take long walks in the sunshine.

"My one prayer is that the lilacs will hold out so that my girl will be able to see them, for it is one of the truly inspirational sights of nature."

He signed this letter "Much love from your boy," blatantly designed to ensure that Ganna' checks kept coming to pay for his idyllic lifestyle.

While basking in the glow of being on the path to true spiritual fulfillment, the publication of Madame's memoirs was further delayed by comments in the manuscript about her fourth husband's sexual proclivities. The ever-cautious Maurice Speiser thought she had gone too far in her intimate remarks about Harold McCormick:

"Your statement to me concerning them was very frank, quite understandable and would have, if published during his lifetime been of questionable taste, if not libelous. I am not suggesting that the entire matter be eliminated, but merely that with your usual grace and tact it be curtailed

to slight references and to very tactful language, so that you yourself will not feel that you have in any way desecrated the memory of one who has passed on."

Knowing that Walska was impervious to criticism where her writing was concerned, he suggested a more tactful alternative:

"Harold's importunities for marriage were persistent, unfortunately they were not justified, as he knew that no consummation was possible and never was possible in spite of his hectic efforts to make it so. My concern was, therefore, based upon our mutual understanding that our matrimonial state should be limited to a platonic companionship based on the sincere and actual love and respect we bore each other."

Stripped of ambiguity, the statement was certainly more to the point than Madame's rose-colored rambling, but she rejected it outright. Speiser reiterated that her description of their intimate life was in poor taste, and the standoff led to further delays. Printing expenses mounted, with Richard Smith hinting that he might have to revise his original quote because of rising labor and material costs. He advised that the soonest "Always Room at the Top" could be on sale was six months, and only then if his editor received the completed manuscript at once. The change of title may have come from Speiser's appreciation of the prodigious British author, Arnold Bennett, whose 1914 novel "The Price of Love" had quoted a luxury cinema advertising itself as: "There is always room at the top."

The main reason for the current publishing delay was not crude comments about a former husband's sexuality, but the fact that Ganna had yet to finish the concluding chapter. "Always Room at the Top" was not an autobiography at all, rather a collection of Madame's non-linear jottings mostly about the sanctity of singing, her quest for spiritual enlightenment, and frequent criticism of spouses, with reams of personal philosophy inserted for good measure. Her original account ended at Galluis during the fateful summer of 1939, with the assumption that her future was based there. The sudden forced flight from Europe opened up new vistas which required additional chapters, covering Walska's return to the United States, meeting Theos Bernard (though never mentioning him by name) and being coerced to purchase the Californian estates to fulfill his ambitions.

This was dense, difficult-to read material, full of fustian phrases, with Ganna's cute - though faulty - English needing extensive polishing for publication. Jere Knight did her editorial best, but there remained a further revision from Eileen J. Garrett of Creative Age Press, which would publish the book on behalf of Richard Smith. A six-hundred-word introduction was also called for, incorporating Walska's disclaimer for readers who might find it heavy going:

"If my reader finds it difficult at times to follow all my experiences, it will be because his soul has not passed through the same labyrinth of thoughts and feelings as mine and therefore he will be unable to identify himself with the phases of life I have lived through."

The surprising thing about all the extra effort was that, being vanity publishing, everyone seemed so concerned about propriety, content and style.

In the additional material, Walska described the new, unnamed man in her life as "an old soul dwelling in a young Arizona boy, who already had time in the flower of his youth to gather much knowledge in India and Tibet." Harking back to when she had urged rights for women with the National Woman's Party - and perhaps because of her bouquet of bridal breakdowns - she added a feminist message that seems misplaced from someone who had sought what she wanted out of life by allowing herself to be represented as Woman - the Supreme Prize. It was certainly out-of-step with the times when America's war effort relied increasingly on a female workforce, and certainly no tribute to the work of Elizabeth Cady Stanton and Lucretia Coffin Mott who launched the women's rights movement at Seneca Falls, New York almost a century before, calling for reform of discriminatory practices that perpetuated sexual inequality.

Instead of a rallying cry to her sisters from a former NWP supporter, Ganna's call to arms sounded more like her *cri de coeur*:

"There is not a man who prefers the physical expression of love to the sublime feeling of the godly nectar that is living in him and if Don Juan constantly changed the object of his attention it was only because he could not deposit the beauty of great emotional power in the soul of one woman."

Writing as someone who had been put through the hoops, she urged her female readers:

"Woman! Give man a chance and he will bring you a bit of heaven and all these things shall be added unto you, even in the form of such earthly possessions as a mink coat or a few carats of diamonds . . ."

The manuscript ended in a paean of praise for America's Golden West, predicting a bright new future for herself there, and was handed over to Richard Smith on April 15, 1942 with his hope that it might now be produced within the original budget if printed the old-fashioned way - from type, instead of plates. Electrolytic plates were made of copper, he explained, and the government's restriction on the use of the metal - except for war production - imposed strict limits on the time they could be retained. Compounding the uncertainty, however, the editor, Mrs. Garrett, returned the manuscript to Smith a week later with a note saying that she did not find herself in sympathy with the contents, and could not see it through to publication.

During those early months of 1942 the Japanese crossed Thailand to invade Burma, and British troops defending Malaya withdrew to Singapore which subsequently surrendered to the imperialist forces in what Winston Churchill described as the worst disaster and largest capitulation in British history, conveniently forgetting his disastrous Gallipoli campaign of the First World War. Even Australia, previously thought immune to attack, was bombed in February, 1942 by hundreds of Japanese aircraft, with the northern city of Darwin and its port shattered by more missiles than had rained down on Pearl Harbor two months previously. With these grim scenarios on the other side of the world, there was no longer any possibility of Tibetan lamas reaching the United States, and Miss Finlay wrote again to American Express demanding a refund of Madame Walska's original remittance. Finally, in May, 1942 - almost a year after moves were initiated to bring a holy man to California - she was informed that her employer could expect a refund of $248.92 from the original outlay of $700. It had been a costly exercise in futility, but Ganna spared no expense where Theos Bernard's interests were concerned.

A dearth of lamas, however, failed to deflect plans to install facilities at the two estates according to his wishes. Walska's bills increased as fireproof safes were bought to store his precious documents, and she busied herself from morning 'till night with Theos' welfare, though tested to the limit. Her daily routine is recorded in the diary:

"Generally I like to meditate and write and read in bed - my day in the

country starts a little after four - instead for his sake I had to dress and run to the kitchen in order to cook his eggs, to choose his berry, to spy on the cook to see if everything was perfect and often to carry myself a heavily loaded tray from the kitchen, situated at the side of the main house, to his pavilion because he would not come to the house to eat. He did not like to see faces in the morning!"

Ganna believed that Bernard's two main irritants - sea fogs blanketing Santa Barbara and poor radio reception - were the only things she could not control for the benefit of her hypersensitive man. In addition to following his every whim, there was work to be done on the estate which, due to California's generous climate, began to take on the appearance of a jungle in some of the neglected areas, with the Montecito Fire Department ordering brush to be removed before it became a summer fire hazard. She also needed to study and approve Lockwood de Forest's 1942 planting notes:

> "Cantua buxifolia
> Lilium humboltii
> Dragon Palm for Oasis
> Get tulips spread around
> Move up Bananas and cover
> ground with Periwinkle
> Move pink Watsonias from Iris
> Garden. They are to go
> to the right of the Cascade
> where brush has been burned
> Take out Bay Laurel on lawn by
> the house. Replace with
> Curly-Leaf Willow . . ."

The meticulous de Forest had planned and planted separate gardens around some of the estate's outbuildings, including the garage, music studio, and the Green and Rose cottages. He also drew up designs for a new swimming pool, lotus pond, house garden, as well as rose, bamboo and cactus areas. Reflecting Walska's lack of horticultural knowledge, but knowing what she wanted through coaxing nature into a kind of open-air stage set - as she had started to do at Galluis - de Forest established a "Blue or Silver Garden" with blue flowering plumbago, ceratostygma, lilies and delphiniums. Tibetland, with vastly different climatic and growing conditions to northern France, allowed Madame free-range to develop her innate sense of color and form.

Equally demanding, in her own way, Walska kept the director

296

rushed off his feet, asking him to look out for mature and unusual cacti to soften the bare facade of the main house, explaining:

"Born in Poland where the severe winter climate does not allow the growth of evergreens, I immediately was attracted by the fantastic cacti strangely looking like Salvador Dali's untouched-by-any-man forms. I made a rare and expensive collection of those as well as assembling all sorts of plants, trees and vegetations."

Santa Barbara's nurseries received an unexpected windfall at a time when many estate owners were absent or resisted parting with their money in wartime. The reputation of the chatelaine of Tibetland as a big spender spread through their businesses like a canyon brush fire, though she was tight with cash and usually offered less than the asking price, becoming known in the business for securing purchases at "Walska rates." She also turned her attention to Tibetland's interiors, providing welcome work for local interior designers. The whole of the main house was to be furnished and decorated in Tibetan style "with the objects that were to be placed in the future Tibetan museum building which was abandoned with the beginning of the war for priority reasons."

La Varnie agreed to come and live on the estate during the summer of 1942 on condition that he never met anyone else there. On one occasion, however, when the three residents were lunching on the terrace overlooking the broad expanse of the main lawn, Walska saw Lockwood de Forest in the distance, and, having something important to tell him, called him over. La Varnie jumped up like a frightened rabbit.

"Who is that?" I don't want to meet anybody!" he barked, throwing down his napkin and preparing to run. Ganna explained that it was her chief gardener and headed-off Lockwood's approach. With such trivial incidents, day-to-day life at Tibetland became top-heavy with tension. War restraints urged on the general community were often ignored by the two men, and, having let go her butler and a chambermaid, Ganna had to perform unfamiliar household chores like dashing to and from the kitchen carrying the dishes for their meals and being rewarded only with ingratitude. "Those two great intellects would never move a finger to help me," she noted, "but constantly they would make me feel badly by pushing their plates away with sarcastic remarks if luncheon did not suit their tastes."

There was also growing friction with Lockwood de Forest. He was annoyed by Madame's constant demands on his time, finding it demeaning for a respected landscape architect to be regarded as a head gardener. Ganna complained about his costs and absence of detailed accounting, which resulted in his letter of resignation explaining that nothing was charged in searching for particular materials and plants - or for his office time. De Forest offered to continue advising Madame, but reminded her that he had many clients "who, during these days, only call me in for a consultation of an hour or so."

Life *à trois* at Tibetland descended into guerilla warfare of the mind, and Ganna needed to call on her inner strength to survive. She complained to her diary of being subjected to a total violation of manners, including the filthy habit of spitting on the terrace mat during dinner, which violated Emily Post's recommendations on etiquette. But that was nothing compared to the mental anguish resulting from dinner table conversations when La Varnie reacted to news of war disasters by remarking that the millions of dead would ultimately rejuvenate and consolidate the European soil by serving as fertilizer. "Pieces of meat in my mouth would choke me," Walska reacted. "I was actually paralyzed and unable to move, especially as always in these cases, too frequent alas! I tried to hide my feelings by pretending a lack of appetite."

La Varnie owned a rented house at La Crescenta in the Los Angeles foothills which had become rundown, and when it was vacant he mentioned that if he had the means to make repairs, he could live there quietly working on his chemical formulae. Happy at the prospect of getting rid of Bernard's odious friend, Walska offered to help. Much to the surprise of the neighbors, La Varnie's house was painted Tibetan red and furnished with Buddhist objects from Tibetland, together with carpets, linen, silver and glassware. Curtains were fitted, lamps purchased, pictures acquired to decorate the walls, a radio bought - anything that contributed to comfortable living, including a housekeeper and gardener, hired locally. But a week after moving in, he started complaining that everything was wrong, including La Crescenta being too hot, and the live-out housekeeper finding it impossible to reach him early enough to prepare his breakfast.

He took the easy option by returning to the comfort of Tibetland, providing an occasional moment of black comedy to relieve the habitual stress. One happened on an evening by the light of a full moon accompanied by sweet-smelling incense, when the men prepared the lady of the house for an important announcement. Theos took a deep breath to disclose that, after a careful study of Ganna's character, they had decided that she was now worthy of their full confidence and confessed, "as if he would have been a presumptive heir to the throne of England," she noted, that Theos's friend was, in fact: his father.

After this extraordinary revelation, La Varnie's corrosive presence began to permeate every aspect of Tibetland life, and Walska needed the assurance that there was a place for her in Bernard's future work. After much soul-searching, she reluctantly accepted that the only way was to accept her guru's earlier proposal of marriage, seeking advice from a Los Angeles lawyer, James W. Mack, who drew up two copies of a prenuptial agreement. It was the same arrangement recommended by Phelan Beale for marrying Grindell Matthews, though Walska wanted to leave her two Californian estates to Bernard if she were to die before him so that his sacred mission could continue.. Her immediate concern as a serial bride about to take a sixth husband was to avoid the publicity. Mack acknowledged that secrecy was a problem for "prominent people" and could only suggest taking simple precautions.

Pre-Strip Las Vegas was famous for runaway weddings, and was mentioned as a place where the county clerk might be persuaded to issue a marriage license in a prearranged location, with the ceremony performed by a justice of the peace. But license applications required the bride and groom to state if they were previously married, and, in the event of being widowed, that must be revealed as well. If divorced people were involved, information was needed about when, where and on what grounds a decree was granted. The application also required their names, ages and place of residence, and the information was available for public inspection. Madame Walska became worried.

James W. Mack was a smart operator, however, persuading Mr. Payne, the county clerk of Las Vegas, to have the ceremony performed at his home on Monday, July 27 at 9 p.m. A justice of the peace would be present and Mr. and Mrs. Payne could act as witnesses. "If you travel by automobile," Mack asked Ganna, "can precautions be taken so that you will not use either your car or your friend's car? Otherwise, it will be very easy for any curiosity seeker to find out the identity of the parties from California." He said he had portrayed his client as so timid that she would be embarrassed by the presence of third parties and had received assurance that no one would be there except himself, the justice of the peace and Mrs. Payne.

To cover every eventuality, the attorney made similar arrangements with the county clerk of Kingman, Arizona, the site of a large U.S. Army Airforce Base, about the same driving distance from Santa Barbara as Las Vegas. He advised that both clerks were anxious to please, but would expect "handsome compensation for the extra trouble and service rendered by them." Ganna opted for Las Vegas, and, instead of a long and boring automobile ride, preferred to fly there, though warned that due to war demands, civilian passengers holding reservations on commercial airlines often had to yield their seats at the airport to military and government personnel.

After these thorough preparations, there were no delays, no complications and, most significantly, no reporters to reveal the secret marriage of Ganna Walska to Theos Bernard. After travelling to Las Vegas for the brief ceremony, the couple returned to Tibetland to carry on their lives exactly as before. The efficient Mack forwarded his itemized account five days later, and, considering the amount of time, effort and expertise he invested in the successful arrangements, a fee of $1,500 was not unreasonable – except to his client. Unaware of Madame Walska's perverse dealings with lawyers and financial advisers - including the sharp comments sometimes heaped upon her faithful New York attorney and friend Phelan Beale, or the standoff with her former agent and business adviser Djamgaroff - he could not have been prepared for Madame's response. Mack, Beale, Speiser, Djamgaroff, and many others, tended to stray beyond the call of duty in their desire to please Madame, only to face the consequences of being treated as mere functionaries. She wrote Mack:

"As you know, I am not a business woman; I do not understand anything about accounts but I am quite able to arrange all my business because I can always grasp ideas pretty well. As to the technicalities that I never

300

understand I protect myself or rather I protect my budget by never doing anything blindly and asking always in advance the amount of cost."

Soon after the wedding, Professor Don Brown from UC Santa Barbara, University of California, drove up to Penthouse to visit his friend Theos, who asked him a surprising question.

"Did you ever hear of Ganna Walska?"

"Of course, the wife of Harold McCormick."

"Well, I just married her."

"What did you do that for?"

Theos had always insisted to Brown that he was too busy and too involved in his work to marry again. Walska knew almost nothing about her guru's previous marriage to the pioneering social psychiatrist Viola Wertheim, who became Bernard's acolyte and boosted his grand design for Tibetan religious and cultural studies in the United States. Now he was boasting to the professor that his new wife's great fortune made possible the realization of his dreams.

In September, Lockwood de Forest announced he would be leaving Santa Barbara on war service to join the Camouflage Battalion associated with the Air Corps, whose main task was to hide the appearance of airfields and military aviation installations. He suggested that her estate gardener, Joseph Klefenz, should take over at Tibetland, which would result in better care of the property and economies for Madame. Contractors could undertake any specific tasks she wanted, and his office would help if required. Just before his departure, de Forest staked out every one of her fuchsias that needed to be moved. "I am sure that the effect will be excellent," he wrote, and, as a parting comment added: "You are wonderful! I never would have thought of using cactus at the front door or many of the other plantings you suggested. They are very handsome and I congratulate you."

Returning to New York for the winter, Walska realized that she could help her husband by separating him from direct paternal influence. Theos was eager for a doctorate, and a neat solution was to join her in New York while writing a thesis for Columbia University. That settled the son's side of the problem, leaving La Varnie, now back in his house at La Crescenta, in a disgruntled state. Walska suggested he sell it, invest the proceeds in war bonds and live in Green Cottage at Tibetland, which could be heated for the winter. Mr. Glen Agassiz. Bernard, alias G. A. La Varnie, went back to the deserted estate, and Walska, delighted that separating father and son had succeeded, sent him a cable:

"We Are So Happy To Know You Are Back Home. May Good Health And Great Inspiration Be With You. With Much Love From Children."

This tongue-in-cheek message initiated a lively correspondence during the winter months, with La Varnie (as he preferred to call himself) asking about progress of his son's thesis; becoming concerned about Theos's health; confirming the arrival of food parcels and promising not to eat himself sick; acknowledging birthday greetings while admitting he was a stranger to such kindness; complaining that air letters could take twenty-five days to reach the coast in bad weather - and giving profuse thanks for Walska's regular checks.

Mr. and Mrs. Bernard lived in separate parts of the Park Avenue house, with Theos working on a thesis, intended to form the basis of a book about Hatha Yoga, which he had studied in India. But the domestic turbulence experienced at Tibetland soon migrated to New York, with Walska never knowing if she would be greeted with a smile or a snarl when they met. One evening she went to his room to be greeted by a barrage of insults, paralyzed by their ferocity. When he made to attack her physically, Ganna rushed to the elevator, praying that he would not catch up before there was time to press the button and descend to her own quarters. She locked her doors and threw herself on the bed, shaking like a leaf in a gale, only calmed by the serenity of the slow movement from Mozart's *Jupiter* symphony playing on the radio. Ganna tried to justify these "moments of madness," as she would call them, were involuntary because her new husband was not responsible for his actions.

On another occasion, walking together along Broadway to the movies, Theos developed an ugly mood while criticizing a mutual friend, and she responded: "I don't think it's right for you to say that . . ." The sentence was cut short when he halted abruptly, glowered at his wife, and began shouting insults, grabbing her arm with one hand and clutching his walking cane with the other, fighting to retain balance. Panicking, Ganna pulled herself free and ran into a side street, stumbling along in shock for half a block, knocking into people. She stopped to look back and there was no sign of her husband, knowing he could only move slowly since injuring a leg in a ski accident several years before - one of the reasons for his not being drafted into the military.

Walska walked toward the famous RKO Palace Theater, searching for his tall figure, assuming he had gone home, and decided to stay away for a while. She bought a ticket for the movie, taking a back-row seat, and then noticed Theos sitting a few rows in front of her. "My anxiety changed to bewilderment when I saw him almost bent in two, laughing, loudly laughing, innocently laughing, as only his inner youth and exuberant vitality would allow, laughing at something funny on the screen."

When the picture ended, she watched him rise slowly and painfully from his seat. Walska waited in the lobby while he put on his coat with difficulty while leaning on the cane, then approached from behind and whispered softy in his ear.

"May I help?"

He turned with a blissful look in his eyes, and, unaware of the people all around, joyfully embraced her.

"My girl! My girl came to see me! My girl came to help me!"

Walska's memoirs remained in a production limbo, though the question of paying Maurice Speiser's fees arose. He suggested $1,500 as appropriate recompense for his legal and literary services which had the effect of unleashing her vilification, complaining that his demand was almost half the entire cost of publication and offered to send a check for $1,000, with the reservation that she regarded this, in view of the circumstances, "very high retribution." Letters flew between them, with poor Speiser attempting to save the situation by adopting a conciliatory tone. "I am a lawyer who has been practicing for thirty-seven years. I have the honor of representing a great number of writers and playwrights among whom as you know are Ernest Hemingway, Hans Habe, E.E. Cummings et al." On the question of the bill, he stated (as James Mack had done for looking after her marriage arrangements) that professional fees were never matched by physical work, but related to the amount of time expended and the importance of the task. Speiser meekly accepted the reduced amount Ganna offered, agreeing that it would cover his past and future services until the book finally appeared.

23-
Life with Yogi
1942

Christmas 1942 was as joyous an occasion for Mr. and Mrs. Theos Bernard that personal and wartime circumstances allowed. La Varnie sent from California a present of a group of ceramic figures, which amused Walska, while she mailed him an umbrella from Saks Fifth Avenue, and when he failed to acknowledge the gift was worried that he might have been embarrassed to receive something unnecessary for the climate where he lived - although he had complained about a spell of wet weather in a recent letter.

Ganna arranged a series of public lectures for her husband in the Park Avenue mansion, starting on January 7. They were a continuation of the previous fall's gatherings designed, she said, to cure Theos of an inferiority complex, which attracted "people that had nothing in common with me, with my ideals, my way of life, people not interested in music, religion or philosophies, mostly those who go to bed at the hour I get up, those that breathe the smoky rooms of night clubs." It was an inconvenient moment to open the house to strangers, with the risk of exposing her life to the predatory press she still held responsible for distorting the facts about her singing success, and now persisted in representing her as an aging opera-mad socialite. It was a small price to pay, however, when she could see Theos benefiting from the response, which made him consider writing a second thesis.

At first, Walska baulked at financing a further degree, but Bernard's persuasion won her over after she accepted that his academic achievements would help humanity. This petite, far from robust, woman assumed the role of her husband's personal porter, carrying his bags weighed down with books because the doctor advised against any physical exertion that might be detrimental to his health. Ganna became, as she admitted, his redcap, though all outward signs suggested that Theos was as fit as a fiddle, continuing to swim and dive, play the occasional game of football, and passionate about throwing boomerangs: all activities that seemed to conflict with his dependence on a walking cane.

Walska devoted most of her time to her husband that winter, concerned about his physical well-being and trying, wherever possible, to help his academic advancement by courting favor with the professors at Columbia by inviting them to smart lunches at Park Avenue. She also paid for private lessons in Sanskrit, Tibetan and Bengali, as well as French and German after Theos insisted it was necessary for him to know these languages better in order to translate the ancient documents in his possession. War or no war, Bernard demanded his daily breakfast bacon, Dundee marmalade or strawberry jam - a jar of which used up the food coupons that deprived her cook from getting butter for a whole month.

In one of her letters to La Varnie, Ganna complained that they were experiencing "the same seemingly monotonous life" in New York. "My work is progressing very well and very fast," she explained, referring to her latest singing lessons, "only I am like a guinea pig, experimenting from time to time with new things." At an age when many divas would be thinking about their final, farewell curtain, followed perhaps by opening an exclusive singing academy, she was in no position to consider a performing future, but the rigorous discipline from decades of practice had made singing lessons addictive, like religion or drugs.

A further call on Madame Walska's time came from the New York Chapter of the American Red Cross, inviting her to become chairman of their newly-formed American Polish Section to raise funds for the 1943 war charities campaign. It involved soliciting money from companies and individuals for contribution to an ambitious national target of nearly thirteen million dollars. She proudly accepted the honorary appointment, making an impassioned speech to "My dear people" at the inaugural meeting:

"I am told, direct from Red Cross headquarters from Washington, D.C. that fifty-six thousand packages are being sent to the Polish prisoners now detained in Germany. That is only part of the picture. Only last week a ship loaded with supplies left Philadelphia under the American Red Cross supervision and protection on its way to the warring areas. This week they are loading another ship in New York. There is much more I can tell you, however, the most important thing is that your dollars will help to carry on this work. With that one thought in mind, I appeal to you to give as generously as you can."

They donated unstintingly: the Witkowskis and Borzeckis, the

Paterackis and Smyklas, the Glebockis and Mroks - more so when radio stations across the United States broadcast a recording of Madame's impassioned appeal:

"Our fatherland is dying and cannot give bread to its children. The Easter holidays are approaching. The beautiful spring holidays of resurrection. Think about those in Poland! How many tears are flowing? The Polish nation has suffered much, how much torture and tyranny. The weak could not go on. They succumbed, but only the very strong and enduring are waiting for the resurrection of Poland. Help them!"

Easter came and went with decisions about the autobiography still pending, and its appearance in the bookshops seemed as far-off as ever. Picture captions needed to be completed, spellings checked, and a dedication delivered: "To all those who are seeking their place in the sun." Walska was asked to decide on the color of the binding cloth, whether her full or only the last name should be on the spine, and design of the jacket. Richard Smith could give no idea of a completion date because war conditions cast a pall of uncertainty over everything, though he was able to offer a small ray of hope with the text being printed. By May, Walska was getting anxious about her return to springtime California, wanting to see publication first, but she could do nothing about the binder being short-staffed.

She was eager to get on with the development of both Tibetland and Penthouse of the Gods, though little could happen without her presence, and Bernard's health rather than publication became the main reason for remaining in New York for longer than anticipated. He had become listless and more irritable than ever - if that was possible - and made an appointment with his physician, Milton J. Raisbeck, at his rooms on Park Avenue. The society doctor had treated him principally for monitoring an irregular heartbeat, and after a thorough examination was able to present a general summary of Bernard's condition by comparing consultation notes over a five-year period:

"Between 1938 and 1942 there were minor fluctuations, but in general the heart size remained within the normal limits. Now, in May 1943, there is an increase above the normal, not quite as large as in 1936, but nearly so, and this I consider unfavorable, due largely to general hygiene."

The diagnosis stated that everything else appeared satisfactory: no major problem with circulation, leakage from the aortic valve relatively slight, and an excellent electrocardiogram. Only the size

306

of Bernard's heart was something to worry about. A recommended revamp of his patient's general lifestyle was accompanied by a series of instructions which, Raisbeck said, "I hope you will take to heart and endeavor to follow." They included being in bed by 10 p.m. with no reading for at least five nights a week, and to rise at a reasonable hour. The doctor also proposed some hydrotherapy, relaxing after meals with minimal physical effort, and taking a short rest during the afternoon.

After settling into this new rhythm, Theos and Ganna were able to leave for California in early June by rail because of the continuing restrictions on private air travel. As soon as they arrived, she wrote Speiser complaining that the journey had left her "dead tired," and in reference to the suggested design of the book jacket studied during an interminable trip, Walska informed him tersely: "Yes, certainly accept this jacket. As a matter of fact, accept from Mr. Smith anything. I do not want to give him any excuse for delay again."

The atmosphere at Tibetland quickly reverted to its previous state, with tensions between father and son ruling the household. Happily for Madame, they preferred to spend much of their time at Penthouse of the Gods, where Professor Brown and his family visited occasionally. He remembered driving up the challenging Refugio Pass road of an evening, with wild pigs running in front of the car through the winding switchbacks. They arrived to Chinese tea and snacks, followed by conversation with Theos late into the night while stretched out on hammocks strung between the towering pine trees just outside the lodge. Brown recalled: "His stories of Tibet and India were endless and spellbinding." The family loved the large pool there, enjoying hours of pleasure swimming, with the children hurtling down a slide catapulting them into the sparkling water.

With her men away in the mountains, Ganna could concentrate on developing the Montecito estate, delighted with the visual effect of the cacti Lockwood de Forest had planted around the entrance to the main house, together with other improvements he introduced. But his absence and wartime restrictions continued to hinder progress, though her way of life, and that of the men she supported, remained relatively unaffected by the raging conflict in the world outside. By the time Walska was comfortably installed for the summer of 1943, there was some encouraging news for the Allies on the North African and Pacific fronts, but sickening reports had come from Poland on the discovery of the Katyn massacre by the Germans, when thousands of Polish officers were murdered and thrown into mass graves by the Russians near Smolensk. That tragedy was soon followed by the uprising in the Warsaw ghetto and the Soviet Union severing diplomatic relations with General Sikorski's London-based Polish government over the alleged blame for Katyn. There was no news about Madame's properties in France, but the creation of a National Resistance Council under Jean Moulin gave hope that the nation might free itself from the Nazi yoke one day.

Contact with Walska's family in Poland continued to be impossible, which left her wondering if they had survived the horrors printed in the newspapers and heard on the radio every day. Ganna recalled lines from her radio broadcast: "Everything requires money. A lot of money is needed to destroy the insane enemy that has taken over the world. Money is needed to speed the day of victory . . ." But those exhortations were the opposite of the life she was leading - or forced upon her by the Bernards, father and son - that made her utterances about the dispossessed and dying of Europe sound vacuous. Ganna had emoted over the airwaves: "We cannot quietly lead our lives, knowing that our people are suffering deprivation and sickness in terrible captivity, endure terrible things and wait for us to help them," while apparently more concerned with pleasing her husband-guru, and making sure that his parasitic father with the curious dual identity lacked nothing he desired. Her heart-rending references to children "dying like flies" came over the radio with sincerity, but the personal sacrifices made by the members of this odd trio, amounted to little more than Madame pretending to live more frugally than before by keeping her Rolls-Royce in its New York garage for the duration of the war, while the Bernards complained endlessly about food rationing and government restrictions on travel and finance.

More to the point, Ganna had not been able to proceed with Tibetland's development after Lockwood de Forest went off to war and there was no other source of professional advice until she learned that Santa Barbara's superintendent of city parks, Ralph

Stevens, had been born and raised on her estate. His father settled there in 1882, and it retained several features from his childhood, including the towering Monterey cypress dominating the main lawn and some imposing Chilean wine palms scattered throughout the gardens. Now aged sixty-one, Ralph Tallant Stevens offered to assist Madame Walska, while continuing to be in charge of the city's parks and gardens with a war-depleted staff. Falling under her spell, he promised to help in acquiring plants, shrubs and cacti for Tibetland and to supervise their installation.

The strain of living *à trois* erupted again as soon as the Bernards came back from Penthouse of the Gods, with Walska suffering a physical attack from Theos while he was engaged in the routine task of changing a light bulb in the library. Alerting him to possible electric shock, Ganna advised taking care: "It was a trifle, such a tiny trifle, that even after the incident I could never remember what it was all about." Theos had taken his wife's comment as personal criticism: "I learned all those strange peculiarities only after the terrifying experience of his jumping on me, catching my throat with his two outstretched hands, pushing to choke me against a wall." Shrieking insults, Theos tightened his grip, but Walska was able to tear herself away and rush out through the French windows into the garden, not daring to venture back inside the house for several hours. Returning to the privacy of her pavilion in the early evening, she passed by Bernard's room undetected, noticing he was calmly reading a book. Next morning Ganna handed him a written note telling him to go, which he accepted without question, although later in the day she had a change of heart, remembering a promise made to his mother that she would care for her son.

At long last, on August 17, 1943, Ganna Walska saw herself in print on receiving an advance copy of "Always Room at the Top" from Richard Smith, cabling him immediately: "Beautiful Book Just Received. Thousand Thanks," and to Maurice Speiser: "Initial Volume Received. Very Beautiful. Million Thanks." It looked splendid; substantially bulky with 504 pages, dozens of illustrations, and an elegant dust jacket incorporating a flattering photo of the author. Many of Ganna's friends were surprised and delighted to know that she had written an autobiography, but critical reaction was as mixed as it had been for her singing, with most little more than short notices, like the *Herald Tribune*'s:

"Engraved on Ganna Walska's stationery is the phrase *"Malgré Tout,"* and no summary of her career could be shorter or more to the point - in spite of everything. Astrologers have told her that she is a Jupiterian type, with Napoleon's star - the sign of tremendous uplift but also the indication of vertiginous fall."

From Nashville, Tennessee to Washington, D.C., Salt Lake City, Utah to Yonkers, N.Y., press comment trickled into Richard R. Smith's office, some of it complimentary:

"It's a vivid picture, her book, of an age that will never repeat itself. There are numerous excellent illustrations throughout the autobiography." - The Yonkers *Times.*

"Seldom has there been a more searching, more courageous autobiography than *Always Room At The Top.*" Chicago *News*

"Here is a fascinating 'I confess' book by Ganna Walska, the famous Pole - It is the book of an artistic and literate woman who was obsessed with the Demon of Perfection." - Washington, D. C. *Times Herald.*

"In the book are many other figures out of the pseudo-intelligentsia of Europe and Asia in a bygone day. The author has the saving grace of an intense personal religion which, when she writes about it, indicates conclusively that she has done some intelligent thinking for herself, after all." - Nashville *Morning Tennessean.*

The most percipient piece appeared in *Newsweek* - in its music column - headed "Ganna Walska's Calvary," meaning her burning ambition to become a prima donna which became the cross she had to bear, or, as the reviewer put it: "the Calvary upon which she crucified her soul." There was the usual catalog of husbands, accounts of failed attempts at divadom - "Mme. Walska was referred to by the press as one who should be seen and not heard" - and her unfailingly magnificent appearance was appreciated. But it was the quest to find out why she could not sing, when "she explored every sect under the sun," that received the most attention. The writer noted that a parade of astrologers, palmists, telepathists, theosophists, numerologists, reincarnationists, and every other sort of -ist, were interested in the Walska wealth before the Walska soul, though she kept bouncing back for more.

The book trade followed the old advertising adage of any publicity being good publicity, and what was written about "Always Room at the Top" should have led to brisk sales. But trade surveys were slow during the war, and results would not be available for many months. In the meantime, an overstretched Ralph Stevens promised to keep an eye on Tibetland's gardens during Walska's sojourn in New York during the winter of 1943-44, while Theos Bernard chose to remain on the West Coast, indulging in extensive travel to New Mexico, Arizona and around California. She made her usual social rounds, spent time and money acquiring what dealers assured her, hand-on-heart, were genuine Tibetan art objects, and attended the opera and theater, including a visit with friends to the smash-hit musical by Rodgers and Hammerstein. Theos reacted rather snootily to this in one of his letters:

"You are so right about those plays and the entire world of entertainment. It serves a rightful place in society, but it is not for us; however I am glad to know my girl saw *Oklahoma!* Occasionally one sees an inspiring play, but even then it is no substitute for the inner life. I would rather go to a Trans-Lux with my little one - it is at least a simple recreation . . ."

In February, 1944 he set out for New Mexico in the red Cadillac, using precious gas coupons issued for medical reasons under the signature of his New York physician, Dr. Milton Raisbeck, and kept "his girl" informed of the trip in a series of brief cables:

February 11 - "Found A Little Bit Of Paradise Here In The Desert. My Plans Still Unsettled. Will Let You Know As Soon As Possible."
February 12 - "Wonderful Being Home In Desert Again."

February 15 - "Desert Is Grand But Sunday Is Lonesome. Sagittarius Longs For Home. Hope You Will Come As Soon As Possible."

From Tucson, Arizona:

February 17 - "Going San Francisco Monday. Will Go Home To Santa Barbara Soon. Feel Need To Be Working For Richer Inner Life. Come Soon."

February 21 - "Leaving Land Of Sunshine For S.F. Looking Forward To Returning To Tibetland. Come Soon - Much Missed."

From San Francisco:

February 24 - "Leaving Monday Evening For Tibetland. Arriving Tuesday Morning To Await Your Arrival."

February 27 "Contemplating Return To Tibetland With New Mood Brings Much Joy. Fruitful Karma For Work Ahead Is Certain. Please Know I Do And Come Soon."

He also dispatched long, lyrical letters describing the scene at Penthouse of the Gods:

"We are seeing another aspect of Nature's beauty as it reveals itself in this hidden paradise, for it has been raining, sleeting, hailing and snowing all at once and then suddenly everything is calm and the sun will almost break through the fog bank that is pouring in. With all its fury it makes for scenes most inspiring. Then this morning the ground is frozen solid and all the puddles of water left by the passing storm are turned to ice. From the tower one could never hope to see a more beautiful picture than the sunrise on the distant hills covered with snow and the valley below sparkling like a three-ring circus. It is not much different than the view seen from Gantok in Sikkim – so it truly is Tibetland."

Ganna responded with long-distance telephone calls, which had the effect of receiving ever more descriptive pages from him:

"After talking with you over the phone, I went to the tower for my evening's meditation. There I watched the sunset and the full moon ascend with the heavens above. As its effulgent glory lighted up the shadowy valley below, it awakened in my heart an ever increasing
desire to be of service to you."

On the first day of spring; when a young man's fancies traditionally turn to thoughts of love, Theos eagerly awaited her return:

"A few hours in this environment and the rest of the world fades from memory. I have breakfast out-of-doors absorbing as much sunshine as time will permit. Again, in the middle of the day, I steal away from my work for a sun-bath. The air is so filled with inspiration that it is truly difficult to remain indoors. It is that time of year when one is impelled to go into the country to tramp through the fields or climb mountains. Do not stay away too long. You are much missed; come as soon as an opportunity permits."

The first publisher's statement for "Always Room at the Top"

312

was issued on February 28, 1944, and showed that during the first four months, 556 copies were sold and paid for, another 690 were reported sold but as yet unpaid, 222 free copies were sent out for review and 1,539 remained in stock. By now, however, Walska had lost interest, yearning to be in California enjoying the early springtime weather so glowingly described by her husband. The atmosphere there, however, had turned decidedly chilly because the staff detested looking after La Varnie and had the perfect excuse to ignore him when he installed a mistress in Green Cottage at Tibetland.

Ganna feared the worst when told about it by her housekeeper, but discovered on arrival that the woman - a sculptress named Jill - was good-looking, Madonna-like, well-dressed, with an artistic sense, and in no way a gold digger. She liked her air of serenity and apparent angelic disposition, which had the beneficial effect of calming La Varnie's abrasive restlessness. Walska thought that Jill was performing something of a miracle on Mr. Bernard Sr., though reality soon reared its ugly head when he expected his woman to cook and scrub for him like a servant. This inflamed Madame's feminist sensibilities, and she invited Jill to move into the main house for protection. But La Varnie would not hear of it, ordering her back to the cottage where he said she belonged, and begging forgiveness for his wanton ways. But it proved to be no recipe for harmony, with Walska noting in her diary that the atmosphere remained "daggers drawn."

Unable to stand any more abuse, Jill soon packed her bag and departed, telephoning Ganna and asking never to give La Varnie her new address because he tried to pursue her, and she changed domicile three times to evade him. Theos was working on a new book and needed to consult his father each day about technical and linguistic details, as Walska noted: "But [La Varnie's] severe criticism, due to his bitterness, paralyzed his son's effort to such an extent that he was unable to write at all. He became more depressed than ever before and finally, in a state of complete collapse, he begged me - he who knew only to be obeyed - to arrange so that Mr. La Varnie would leave."

This wretched situation forced Walska to act because a long summer lay ahead with several friends invited to visit and her depleted domestic staff could hardly look after them all in such a large house, particularly when alienated by Bernard senior and his boorish ways. She mustered the courage to tell him to quit the estate in a long letter dated May 18, 1944 - one of the most difficult she ever had to write. It read, in part:

"Mr. La Varnie, you are not happy here. You hate your cottage, the climate, everything. And by always being dissatisfied, criticizing and condemning everybody and everything, always negative, cynical and ugly in your whole attitude toward life - you make me very low in spirit and in such an atmosphere I cannot advance my life's work - my artistic and my spiritual work."

He was gone within a few days, renting a house in the Los Angeles suburb of Northridge, though, true to his nature, he soon found it unsuitable, and within a month returned to his old haunt in the San Fernando Valley. Calm came back to Tibetland, with Theos returning productively to his writing, Ganna welcoming several singing teachers, and taking other guests up to visit the glories of Penthouse of the Gods

GW Pavilion

One way of surviving the highly-charged atmosphere surrounding her, was for Walska to retire to her spacious and well-appointed pavilion, sit down at the desk, and record incidents and

314

memories in her diary-notebooks. It was something she did regularly since the early 1920s, with and many of her jottings finding their way into "Always Room at the Top." Now she toyed with the idea of describing her tempestuous time with Theos and his objectionable father in another book, already having a title: "My Life with Yogi." This lifted her spirits at a low moment by letting Maurice Speiser know:

"Just a few words to thank you for your letter and to ask you – hold on to yourself so as not to fall down - to find for me an editor because I have started a new book. I do not want Mr. Smith anymore, but I suppose he could not be there in 1970 because with his sweet character the bile that is in him will have eaten him to the ground long ago. So different with you and me – we will be young and fresh – so please look around for a newcomer editor that is comprehensible and sweet, especially comprehensible because when I am writing I do not understand even myself."

Walska had only just heard from Speiser that 1,500 copies of "Always Room at the Top" remained unsold - about half the print run - but he agreed to seek a new publisher for her next book, as requested: "one that would be sympathetic and understanding." There was no hurry because, according to Madame's schedule, a whole quarter-century would pass before they needed to start thinking about producing the second volume of her autobiography. By then she would be in her eighties.

- 24 -
Burbank Blues
1944-1946

During the late summer of 1944 Ganna Walska left the Bernards to their own devices on the West Coast with the father languishing in smoggy San Fernando Valley and his son enjoying the fresh air of the Santa Ynez mountains at Penthouse. She would have stayed longer, but wartime made it impossible for any significant progress in the garden at Tibetland, and, being a woman of action, she chose not to sit on the terrace idly watching the grass grow. With a reduced staff, Ralph Stevens was rushed off his feet coping with the demands of Santa Barbara's extensive public parks and gardens, finding only a few moments to serve Madame's horticultural ambitions, asking her to deposit planting instructions with him before departing for New York. Theos continued working on his Tibetan grammar, while La Varnie busied himself with developing formulae for a new range of cosmetics. Ganna kept in touch with her husband mostly by telephone, and with his father through letters sent with the regular monthly checks.

Over the next few months she heard from the chemist genius that he was hard at work on a new liquid makeup, while continuing to lead the life of a hermit. He was ever grateful for her assistance, which included sending gas coupons to keep his car on the road, and parcels containing "fruit, sweets and eats," as he called them. La Varnie's mobility was greatly reduced these days in spite of the coupons - which he sold on the flourishing black market - and only went into the city by train if absolutely necessary. Walska complained in one of her letters to him that she was stressed, both physically and financially, though heartened by encouraging war news. The Russians reached her hometown of Brest-Litovsk in the biggest Soviet offensive of the war to date, and perhaps there would soon be news of her family, she speculated, as Allied forces landed on the south coast of France, Roosevelt and Churchill approved plans for the advance into Germany, and Rommel committed suicide rather than face a court martial for implication in a bomb plot to kill Hitler.

With the prospect of returning to what she regarded as a normal life, Walska's Rolls-Royce was taken off its blocks, dusted off, polished and put on the road again, to be driven by her black chauffeur named Troy. La Varnie responded to this news: "I have limited myself to the very least of life's ways," claiming he was now poverty-stricken, "and at this time of high rents, the excessive cost of food and other necessities, there is little chance of me conserving in this manner. And again my automobile is acting up and if I do not get it into the shop for an overhaul ere long I am certain to find myself stranded for keeps."

During a season of sorrows on both sides of the continent, Walska worried about the state of her health, and, taking the advice of her milliner - a society darling known professionally as Mr. John (John P. John) - she made an appointment with a young physician who recently set up practice in Manhattan. Dr. Herbert Koteen, aged thirty, could hardly fail to notice the overdressing when Madame flounced into his newly-painted rooms one day, and being unfamiliar with foreigners and their ways, he found her accent hard to place: perhaps French, Italian, or maybe German. Whatever her nationality, he was rather shocked when Madame adopted a coquettish manner when asked her age: "Oh doctor! A gentleman never asks a lady how old she is." He knew little about his new patient except a few comments in the populist press concerning her multiple marriages. Walska had recently provided her own personal profile for Phelan Beale in support of another passport application, but it would have been little help for a physician: **"My maiden name was Anna Puacz. I was born in Brest-Litovsk, Poland on 26th June 1892. My personal description is - Sex: Woman (I suppose you know!), Complexion: Fair, Color of Eyes: Blue Gray, Color of Hair: Brown, Height: 5 feet 3 inches, Weight: 130 pounds, Race: White (I suppose you know!)"**

It was accurate enough, apart from the incorrect date of birth that would have made her almost five years younger than her actual fifty-eight, and was medically misleading.

Dr. Koteen's professional pride challenged, he felt it necessary to explain that he was first and foremost a physician - not a gentleman - and must know Madame's real age if he were to offer correct advice. She continued to prevaricate in a playful manner

317

and he had to guess that she was early to mid-fifties before proceeding with an examination to check her heart and lungs under a fluoroscope.

"Please remove your beads, Madame."

"Beads! Beads? These are not beads. They are sapphires, emeralds and rubies. You may be an excellent doctor, as recommended by my dear friend Mr. John, but you don't seem to know much about anything else!"

When asked to shed her clothes for a routine pelvic examination, Walska flatly refused, and Koteen would reveal many years later that in all his forty years of practice, only two women ever denied him such an examination. He was confused by Madame's almost pathological modesty, and stung by the sharp remarks, but managed not to show it, asking her to step onto his scales.

"What's *this* cheap contraption?" Ganna demanded to know, and he became resigned to losing a patient so early in his private practice. But Ganna warmed to his youthful style - if not the basic medical equipment - and made a further appointment.

On her next visit, she asked if Dr. Koteen knew where Santa Barbara was, complaining that the doctors there were poorly trained and suggesting that he would find it a good place to work. He dismissed the idea, responding that teaching was too important for him to leave New York.

"But Troy could drive you to the medical school in Los Angeles three times a week." He wondered why she was being so insistent. "Come out and see. You can stay with me."

The ambitious young man was adamant about staying put, recalling: "I'd been teaching at Harvard, Johns Hopkins and Cornell, and the idea of Los Angeles was ridiculous." But once Madame's mind was set she didn't give up easily, continuing to describe the charms of Santa Barbara until she needed to know the time. The doctor turned his nondescript desk clock in her direction.

"How *can* you have such a thing?" she reacted in mock horror.

He shrugged his shoulders, pride preventing him from explaining that it was a simple matter of cost to someone setting-up a practice - as with the cheap scales. A few days later, Tiffany's delivered a handsome replacement timepiece to his rooms, initiating a string of expensive gifts from his new patient, including a gold thermometer case, also from the famous Fifth Avenue jewelry showroom.

Members of the armed forces in beribboned dress uniforms were much in evidence in the Metropolitan Opera's red and gold tier, formerly known as the Diamond Horseshoe, when Madame Walska attended the start of the 1944-45 season. The management offered free seats to service personnel in recognition of their war effort, and several hundred were expected to be entertained each week, sharing boxes with members of the Metropolitan Opera Guild Club. Those lucky enough to be invited to this glittering first night may have looked forward to Gounod's *Faust*, but the Opera's most spectacular annual production - on or offstage - was the display of unabashed affluence that had continued as a social ritual right through the war.

The gaudy spectacle, known by regulars as "the Big Show," may have changed its cast of celebrity characters over the years, with production values stripped of some of their more expensive features, but the Met's ballyhoo retained much of the spirit of its first night in 1883. The widely-syndicated Cholly Knickerbocker newspaper column reported:

"The gold that once glittered is brass, but it shines just as brightly; the photographers' bulbs are as rockets bursting in the air every 10 seconds, as another social celebrity arrives; and the fashion and society editors work themselves into a positive tizzy of excitement over the whole thing."

Ganna Walska had been a regular first-nighter for a quarter-century now, and wouldn't miss it for the world: to see and be seen, though she deeply regretted not having been invited to sing on the venerable old stage.

New York's weather turned icy, while relations between Ganna and the two men who dominated her life thawed a degree or two, as they tended to do for the dysfunctional trio when at a distance. Jars of La Varnie's potions arrived regularly at Park Avenue, presumably with the idea of marketing them one day, knowing Ganna's connection with cosmetics years before. Night creams, complexion toners and color powders were accompanied by detailed instructions for their application.

By the beginning of 1945, with American marines landing on Luzon in the Philippines, the notorious Burma Road reopened by the Allies, and Soviet forces discovering the abomination of the Nazi's Auschwitz concentration camp in Poland, Mr. Bernard senior had softened his previous appalling opinions about the

319

drawn-out war, and now hoped that the world would soon see the end of "the evil Karma which has visited the people of this Earth." Letters passed between them in which Ganna described her New York rounds of dinner parties, theater, opera and cinema visits, together with her continuing singing lessons, while he continued to be grateful for generous remittances and newsy information, glad to know that the publisher Snider had accepted his son's latest manuscript: "Philosophical Foundations of India" by Theos Bernard, MA, LL.B., Ph.D.

Keeping in touch with his wife, Theos sent brilliantly descriptive letters describing Montecito's winter weather:

"Since you have never been here during the rains, it is hard to picture the grandeur of Tibetland during this celestial house-cleaning when nature purifies the air and washes the gardens every day with 'liquid sunshine' - it is just like having a glimpse of heaven during a nightmare. For me all the beauty of this environment is magnified a million fold by each rain drop that comes from above. You see, here I even have a symphony, for every evening there is a Mozart concert made up of uncountable tiny voices coming from the lotus pond and swimming pool, and all day the drizzling rain rings in harmony with music of the celestial sphere – so you see it is not so bad – in fact there is really nothing bad in Nature."

It was difficult for Walska to set a date for returning to California because she and Mary Placek were both under Dr. Koteen's care, with Madame stressed-out, and her longtime personal assistant suffering from a heart condition. It would be another six weeks before they were ready to face the demanding coast-to-coast rail journey, but the prospect of their arrival delighted Theos when he sent off a cable to New York on May 25:

"Grand News To Know You And Mary Are Coming. Will Meet Super Chief Thursday May 31 Union Station. Until Then Much Love. Theos
And three days later:
"Impatiently Waiting For Thursday. May Full Moon Bring You To New World And Flood Your Life With Joy. Much Love. Theos."

For the first time in four years, the emotional climate at Tibetland was calm and Walska was able to expand her Southern Californian horizons beyond the boundaries of the two estates, to appreciate the city on her doorstep. Santa Barbara revealed itself as a compact, somewhat isolated community, capitalizing on an unrivaled location between the mountains and the sea, facing south, and blessed with a benign micro-climate. Much of its architecture had a Spanish look, influenced by the nation that originally discovered this beautiful coastline only fifty years after Columbus arrived on the other side of the Americas.

Around the end of the nineteenth century, the city and surrounds, with a fine mission complex from 1782 - but ignoring the welfare of its original inhabitants, the Chumash Indians - became a winter playground for the rich from the Eastern states and the Midwest. Santa Barbara developed a reputation for producing a race of bronzed sybarites, and luxurious hotels such as the Arlington and the Potter welcomed the wealthy on vacation. Some visitors decided to stay, buy land, and build extravagant mansions just east of the city in an unincorporated area known as Montecito.

America's fledgling cinema business established a cultural link when the Flying A Studio became the largest movie lot anywhere in the world, with D.W. Griffith among dozens of directors working there, and for a brief, flickering moment Santa Barbara became the silent film capital of the world. But it was never quite the Eden it seemed because there could be trouble in this paradise. Certainly, the sun shone generously for most of the year on its orange and lemon groves, and made the ocean sparkle with a Mediterranean luminosity, etching the bold backdrop of the serrated Santa Ynez mountain range against an azure sky to remind well-heeled travelers of the Côte d'Azur. To them it was like living in the south of France without a language problem.

But Santa Barbarans could never really relax because fierce summer winds had the nasty habit of fanning wildfires that leapt canyons and left hillsides scorched. Winter rains could bring widespread flooding in town, and sudden storms endangered coastal shipping, battering the palm-fringed foreshore to leave it looking like a battle zone. An even greater menace lurked beneath people's feet, with the city sitting foursquare on the Pacific plate of the notorious San Andreas Fault, responsible for severe earthquakes in 1806, 1812, 1857 and, most notably, the widespread destruction of 1925.

When she purchased Tibetland, Ganna Walska ran against the tide of fortune for Montecito's great estates, many of them developed in Santa Barbara's boom years 1911- 1919 during an era of minimal taxes, low land prices, and cheap labor. After the depressed 1930s, many of the larger holdings requiring unfettered fortunes to maintain faced subdivision into affordable lots. The war severely curtailed the supply of garden workers, domestic staff and nursery suppliers, leaving several of the extravagant essays in grand living under-managed and overgrown. By the end of hostilities, Montecito's flamboyant estates seemed out of place in a new world order, but Ganna Walska never paid much attention to what others were thinking - unless they were music critics. She was determined to develop her Tibetland to match those of Montecito's golden era, when George Owen Knapp's Arcady, Henry E. Bothin's Piranhurst, Lolita Armour Mitchell's El Mirador, Major Max C. Fleischmann's Edgewood and other estates with evocative names like Casa Dorinda, Las Tejas, Casa Bienvenida, Riven Rock, Val Verde and Glen Oaks, could boast of lifestyles that were the envy of the world.

In the early 1940s, when she first acquired Cuesta Linda and El Capitan, seeking to distance herself as far as possible from an enemy invasion, Ganna was unaware that just a short distance away, Camp Cooke would become the most extensive military training area on the West Coast of the United States. A large services hospital was established in Santa Barbara and a prisoner of war camp set up at El Capitan beach. But none of this mattered much anymore during the summer of 1945, with prospects for a speedy return to peace after General Jodl signed Germany's official surrender in early May. There remained only Japan to deal with, and a secret new weapon of mass destruction was being prepared to deal with that.

Walska's war had been a singular kind of conflict, based largely on battle of wills between three conflicting personalities, but now a sense of calm permeated Tibetland and Penthouse, reflecting global optimism. Ganna leaned more heavily on her New York physician for advice about the real or imagined ailments that continued to vex her, making long-distance telephone calls from Santa Barbara to Herbert Koteen concerning the most trivial problems, including checking that any local medical advice she received was correct. This even extended to contacting him during the family's summer vacation at a remote cottage in the Adirondacks, cut off from the world without a phone.

One morning, the doctor was out in a canoe enjoying the mountain scenery when the sound of an approaching siren echoed through the hills, shattering the sylvan tranquility. With lights flashing, a police vehicle ground to a halt beside the lake in a cloud of dust and two officers got out, attracting Koteen's attention with gestures to return to shore immediately. He had committed no crime to warrant such attention, and the only explanation could be a medical emergency, perhaps involving his wife or son.

Paddling furiously across the mirrored surface, he reached the shore to be informed that the police had received an urgent call from a Madame Walska in California who needed to speak to him urgently about a medical matter. Greatly relieved that it had nothing to do with his family, Koteen speculated that Ganna's assistant must be experiencing a recurrence of her heart problem, and still breathless drove to the nearest public telephone to call Tibetland. A distraught Ganna answered, and through her sobs and difficult-to-understand English, combined with drop-outs on the line, it was impossible to understand what was wrong. He suggested tersely that she calm down and explain the situation to him very slowly.

The patient was revealed as Ganna's pet parakeet, which kept falling off its perch. Herbert Koteen could hardly believe what he was hearing, but knew this was not the moment to complain about an unwarranted interruption to his precious vacation. Ordinarily, he would have suggested Ganna get off the phone, call a local vet and not bother him because he was familiar with only one disease in birds called psitacosis, caused by a virus-like bacterium and transmissible to humans as a form of pneumonia. He prescribed a half capsule of tetracycline - a new broad-spectrum antibiotic - to be taken in water, hoping that Madame's bird would be able to swallow it somehow. He learned later that after this call, her parakeet squawked, then flapped to the floor and died before any attempt could be made to administer the recommended dose.

Back on the eastern seaboard for the winter, Walska accepted that she must wait until the troops came home before embarking on full-scale development at Tibetland, when her life could be divided conveniently between winters in the East, enjoying New York's unique culture, and summers in California, perhaps in the company of her closest relatives: brother Leon, his wife and their daughter from Poland - if they had survived. With La Varnie out of the equation, living with Theos had become uncommonly placid, but with the war moving to its conclusion, he was restless, already

323

talking about making a return visit to Tibet.

This gave Ganna an excuse to plan her own future, though it never occurred to her for one moment abandoning their *mariage blanc*, as she called it - the French euphemism for marrying without consummation - leaving Theos uncared for, unprotected, and without money. She noted for her next book:

"I always shielded him from want, to ensure his independence and to give him possession of the 'Penthouse,' his beloved (as much as he is capable of loving anything) place in the mountains, together with the necessary income to run this expensive estate, as well as to enable him to voyage freely to India or Tibet - or any place that his restless nature desired – in the hope of finding the peace he desired."

Madame's outfit for the Met's gala opening this year provided one of the extraordinary sights of the 1945-46 season resulting in syndication of her picture across the nation's newspapers. With hair piled on the top of the head and a bare midriff exposed to the chilly November night air, she caught the photographers' attention in an outfit decorated with beaded spangles that would have dismayed her former designer, Erté. *Time* magazine reported that she generously exposed her midriff in a Lakmé sort of gown. Evening sandals and harem pants were held up by a silver belt adorned with jangling trinkets and offset by a ruched bra-like garment, the whole ensemble topped by an open, knee-length fur cape with matching criss-crossed ties across her ample bosom. This outrageous outfit, which might have been called hippy later, suggested a fashion victim rather than a wife questioning the future direction of her marriage, though the latter was probably responsible for the former.

While they were separated, Theos continued to send letters professing his love, which made it increasingly difficult for Ganna to know how to regard their future: together or independently. He offered an explanation for his feelings:

"I am just not made to run in the herd of the socially minded. This also holds true with friends - they desire that I have every comfort, but once the pleasantries of a visit are over, I grow weary when I cannot recede into my chamber of solitude to live in the inner world that nourishes everything I have found to be of value and everlasting; so there must be a little Cancer in your boy, or perhaps it's the love I hold for one who gives me understanding and patience, those virtues so much needed to nourish the richness of human relationship."

She analyzed every word, underlining this particular paragraph

324

and marking it in extrovert scrawl "He needs me." When Theos exposed himself in this fashion, Ganna tended to fall to pieces.

"Just keep after me, and eventually I will learn, for it is not from any lack of feeling in the heart, but pure thoughtlessness, feeling that my girl will figure it out. Hourly I dream of her, with each move I contemplate a message, but details are always blotted out by flooding torrents of feeling which is impossible for me to write down …"

In early May of 1946 he sought to confirm the date of her return to Santa Barbara:

"You will arrive on the Constellation Wednesday the 29th at 11.45 in the evening. Is that correct? I will be there waiting for you regardless of what hour it arrives, so have no worry if it should be late. I will be ready to drive you on to Santa Barbara immediately."

The schedule was changed and he cabled:

"We Are All Joyous To Learn That You Are Arriving On The 21st. I Will Be Waiting For You At Burbank. Theos."

Ganna called him, begging not to be met at the airport, preferring to take a taxi to Tibetland, but he insisted on welcoming "his girl" in person after months of separation, saying he would not be bored reading a book or two while waiting. The night before she and Mary left New York, he telephoned to say he was waiting impatiently, and when they arrived at the airport there was a wire waiting at the check-in desk, wishing them a good flight and happy landings. It gave Walska a warm, forgiving feeling to know that her husband was mellowing at long last.

The noisy trans-continental flight took all night, arriving on schedule, and as she came down the steps of the Constellation into the blinding brilliance of a Burbank morning, Ganna thought she glimpsed Theos in the welcoming crowd.

"There's Dr. Bernard," she told Mary.

But a man suddenly blocked their way.

"Excuse me, are you Madame Walska?" he asked.

Ganna's first instinct was to deny it, assuming he was a reporter and she was certainly in no mood to be interviewed after a throbbing, restless night in the air. But taken by surprise, she confirmed her identity with a nod.

"May I have a few words with you?"

She didn't want to keep Theos waiting any longer than necessary and tried to fob off this person, whoever he was.

"Why do you want to speak to me? I can't stop now because

someone's waiting for me."

"There is nobody waiting. That's what I'm trying to tell you."

He shepherded the two women away from the bustle of the arrival hall to explain.

"I have a subpoena for you, Madame."

Neither Walska nor Mary understood what he was saying, looking at each other with raised eyebrows.

"I'm serving you with divorce papers," he explained.

Ganna still failed to comprehend, thinking it must be a practical joke, perhaps perpetrated by Theos. "I know you can be served breakfast" she thought with an inherent sense of the ridiculous, "I ate mine on the plane half-an-hour ago. But serving papers - what is this?" The man, soberly dressed and looking more like a bank clerk than a member of the press, now that she examined him more closely, waved a document in her face.

"This is from Dr. Bernard. A suit."

"Dr. Bernard! What's happened to him? An automobile accident?" she asked him anxiously.

Ganna remembered that when she first met her guru he talked about his fear of being killed on the highway. He was always driving too fast, too recklessly, but she reasoned that he couldn't be in hospital or dead because he was there in the waiting crowd. He had waved to her. Or was her poor eyesight playing tricks? The process server waited a moment before thrusting the papers into Walska's hands.

"Dr. Bernard is suing you," he said.

Passengers were collecting their bags and leaving the airport as the women stood outside the terminal, squinting in the harsh sunlight, utterly confused by the turn of events.

"Suing me?"

"For separate maintenance."

"What is this maintenance? "

He studied her blank look, impatient with this comedy of misunderstanding.

"Dr. Bernard wants a divorce."

Later, Walska would describe this moment of revelation as if confirming the veracity of the old English saying Wedlock is a Padlock:

"My heart began to sing Alleluia. A tremendous weight suddenly fell from

my mind and I felt so happy, so happy I could have danced there, I could have kissed this ugly man whose business was a sort of spy and bringer of misfortune. I could hardly maintain my usual calmness, my *savoir faire . . .*"

The anonymous process server was sympathetic to the situation, however, asking Madame if she had a lawyer and offering to drive the ladies into Los Angeles. But Ganna would no hear of it. Ensconced in a hired car, with her bags filling the trunk and piled up on the front seat beside the driver, she was able to relax a little, and only then noticed Mary's face, which was deathly white. She tentatively asked her mistress what had happened to Dr. Bernard.

"Mary, Dr. Bernard wants a divorce."

"Surely he wouldn't do such a thing after all Madame has done for him?"

Walska was in no mood to discuss it, needing to be left alone with her thoughts as she closed her eyes.

Although half-suspecting that both Bernards had conspired to engineer this situation, Ganna expected to find everything at Tibetland as she had left it the previous fall. The vehicle swung into the familiar tree-lined gravel drive and she felt elated to be back among the flowers and greenery of her magnificent estate, looking prettier than ever in the springtime light. But on stepping through the front door, it was obviously no longer the Tibetland she knew. The rooms where her Tibetan collection had crowded the walls were bare, with only their fixtures left hanging. Shelves were denuded of books, and her precious rugs were gone from the floors exposing the dusty boards beneath. When she finally looked in the garage, the Cadillac and Packard were missing as well. Upstairs, desk drawers had been emptied of their contents, and closets stood ransacked with their doors wide open looking as if a gang of well-organized burglars had methodically pillaged the place.

Freedom!
1946

Ganna Walska would want to forget the summer of 1946. Instead of going full-speed ahead on schemes for Tibetland's development after restrictions on labor and materials were being lifted, much of her time was spent closeted with attorneys discussing the divorce. Habitually suspicious of the legal profession and their ways, she was affronted by her team's insistence on besmirching the reputation of Theos Bernard in order to contest his claim for unspecified support. Julian Francis Goux and Byron C. Hanna were engaged to represent Walska, and, according to her, could see nothing but the naked facts as interpreted by them to mount the defense. "They were translating my words in entirely different ways," she noted, "doing their utmost to deliberately reject anything good in my opponent." She found it incomprehensible that the lawyers refused to accept her relationship with Theos Bernard was not built upon the three-dimensional formality of conventional marriage, and infuriated by their inability to believe she had willingly become a slave to support him without being blinded by passion.

When the Santa Barbara press announced that Madame was to be the defendant in a divorce suit filed by Theos Bernard, most of her Montecito neighbors were surprised to learn that she and Dr. Bernard had been man and wife - in a manner of speaking - for nearly four years, so remote from the community were the rarely-seen residents of what many locals continued to call called Cuesta Linda. A notice of intention to take Walska's deposition was filed for June 3, to answer Bernard's complaint for separate maintenance, charging extreme cruelty. Theos contended through his lawyers, the Santa Barbara firm of Robertson, Shramm and Raddue, together with T. H. Canfield, that he was physically unable to support himself, and his wife as "a person of substantial means . . . is able to pay the plaintiff a reasonable sum monthly for the support and maintenance of the plaintiff."

Ganna was determined to pay no maintenance at all, and while the attorneys representing both sides prepared their cases, news of the impending litigation attracted a bunch of unsolicited mail offering some bizarre advice to Madame. One letter signed "Alpha Lux," the pen name of Dr. Adolph Oosterveen of Los Angeles, stated: "I feel like I know how to deal with such characters as Bernard very effectively through the understanding of the inner powers," He said he was familiar with the Yogi and Tibetan systems - "know their greatness as well as their weakness" - and offered help in frustrating Theos's "evil and selfish plans." Oosterveen described himself as a metaphysician, claiming that nothing would give him greater pleasure than to exchange mental powers with the White Lama on Madame's behalf, with no mercenary or selfish motives attached.

This reminded her of a letter she received a year or two earlier signed by "A sister who suffered from these crooks," warning of the grave danger facing her from evil influences, including black magic. It had been kept on file, and, on reading it again, now wondered if the sensational claims were based on more than a few grains of truth about the Bernards and their associates.

"This guy Theos you have around you is in cahoots with a bunch of crooks to skin you alive for all they can get out of you. They are a bunch of crooks of the worst type using religion to cloak their nefarious dealings with helpless women to gyp them of all they can. You are down on their books as the biggest sucker they have come across. I have been gypped good by these gangsters and know from bitter experience. His ex-wife was taken in for seventy-five thousand dollars and when he couldn't get any more out of her, she was canned and left in the cold and nearly went overboard ..."

This scurrilous information, couched in cheap crime-thriller prose, was obviously from somebody familiar with Theos Bernard's past, and implicated several of the White Lama's buddies.

"This guy Clarke is a member of the gang and was used as a blind for you to buy the property ... Your friend the fake count is in it for a slice of the bacon. They have decided that you took your bank roll from Americans and that it is OK for them to take it from you by hook or by crook. The swindler said that you are dumb but a hard nut to crack and as soon as they get all they want you will be disposed with in the swimming pool or with bitter tea."

Walska had dismissed this as malicious gossip at the time, but now, on studying the context more carefully, she realized that the sender had known more about Theos Bernard's life and motives than she ever did. Could it have been written by the embittered Mrs. R., his assistant, who had been banished to California soon after Ganna came on the scene several years ago? There was no way of knowing because she was woefully unfamiliar with her guru's past, except that his first wife, Viola Wertheim, was a niece of the patriarch of the wealthy and influential Morgenthau family, their famous son Henry Jr., a longtime friend and political ally of Franklin D. Roosevelt, who served as his Secretary of the Treasury for many years. Viola, she remembered, had divorced Theos in 1938 and was said to have founded Columbia University's Department of Community Psychiatry, engaging in pioneering work by providing psychiatric care for black children.

Then there was the smooth-talking British sportsman-turned-diplomat, the Eton and Oxford-educated Sir Humphrey Clarke, who acquired the Cuesta Linda estate in 1939, made a few minor alterations to its interior (though none to the grounds) with the apparent intention of living there with his family, but needed little encouragement to sell it to Madame Walska in 1941 for Theos to use as a center for Tibetan studies. It was a subject close to his heart, confirmed by his correspondence with her in the early 1940s.

As for the "fake" Count S. Colonna Walewski; he was a dealer in occult and mystic objects who may have assumed a false title, but that was nothing unusual for migratory Poles, and Bernard certainly knew him long before meeting her. It suddenly dawned upon Ganna that this cast of apparently unrelated characters - who might have come straight from an O. Henry (William Sydney Porter) short story - shared a common quarry: her.

Madame's deposition was delayed for a month until July, 1946, with talk among the legal fraternity of her being a rare case of an internationally-known woman being sued by her husband for alimony. Bernard claimed that he had informed his wife he was born a white child into this world, endowed with the power to be the spiritual savior of mankind, and that he was the spiritual and physical reincarnation of Padmasambhava, an ancient Buddhist saint of Tibet. He further revealed in sworn evidence for his maintenance claim that he was a duly consecrated White Lama, and, if assisted by his wife, could have used his powers to advance and perfect the spirituality of his own soul, of the soul of Mme. Walska and of mankind in general.

Her answer and cross-complaint asserted that Theos was well able to support himself, asserting that Bernard removed himself from Tibetland along with his father, Glen A. Bernard (who was also named in the suit) to Penthouse, "which has been misused well-nigh exclusively for the materialistic enjoyment of the plaintiff and in utter disregard for the purposes for which it was to be used." The court was asked to find the plaintiff not entitled to support and maintenance; that he must leave Tibetland and Penthouse; surrender her valuable Tibetan library and documents; and be restrained from molesting Madame Walska.

The Bernards were said to be confident of winning their case, but took a foolish step too far which lost them credibility. A telephone call from La Varnie in Los Angeles asked Ganna if he and his son could visit her to collect their remaining possessions. She agreed, and they arrived at Tibetland in the company of a third person, and were received politely in the denuded library by Madame wearing a smart day dress, as if preparing for a Montecito tea party. She steeled herself to show no emotion, and managed to suppress the feelings she had about their execrable behavior. But instead of tea, she offered whisky, and the Bernards' companion was introduced as a Los Angeles attorney, who handed over a calling card bearing the name Jerry Giesler, criminal lawyer.

Ganna had read stories about this man, a household name known in the business as "Get Giesler." He numbered Clark Gable, Alice Faye and William Powell among his current crop of Hollywood clients, and was famous for having represented Errol Flynn in an action for statutory rape, for which the actor was acquitted. The sixty-year-old Giesler explained to Ganna that his presence was to advise Theos in seeking an out-of-court settlement of the maintenance claim against her, thus avoiding the need for a courtroom battle with its inevitable publicity which, he understood, Madame wished to avoid.

Walska kept calm, knowing she was at a severe disadvantage without her own lawyer present, and, thinking quickly, excused herself briefly from their company.

"I've promised to call a friend who is having a birthday today. I'll return a few minutes."

She left the room while the men stood sipping their scotch and talking among themselves, returning fifteen minutes later to announce she had also spoken to her financial adviser in New York about a settlement.

"He's unable to give me any idea of my position at the moment. I'll know by tomorrow, so why don't you gentlemen return around the same time and we can talk about it then."

The unsuspecting trio agreed, but found the atmosphere totally changed when they arrived at the estate the next day. No hospitality was offered, and Madame Walska was well- briefed to take the initiative in a performance as good as any she gave on stage.

"Gentlemen, I actually spoke yesterday to my New York attorney Mr. Phelan Beale of the firm of Bouvier Beale while you were here enjoying a drink. He happens to be a member of his local Bar Association - in fact one of the senior office holders - just like Mr. Giesler in Los Angeles I understand - and has asked me to give you a message."

Picking up a single sheet of paper, Ganna put on her reading glasses with a flourish and read out the contents, directing them to Giesler.

"Mr. Beale says please feel free to sue for any amount you wish, and in return my client will respond by suing Mr. Bernard for twice the amount. The moment you take any such action, however, you will be referred to the American Bar Association with the aim of being disbarred for unprofessional conduct in subjecting a defendant to unacceptable pressure."

Following a pause for her words to register, Ganna made a prearranged signal by scratching her left ear, and a man entered the room wearing a silver badge of office, identifying himself as the county sheriff.

"Until this moment, gentlemen," he told the astonished visitors, "you have been guests in this lady's home. Now you are trespassing. I will allow you ten minutes to collect your rightful possessions and then escort you to the gates, and ask you not to return."

The scene might have come straight from a Hollywood B movie, and left Ganna continuing to worry about her own attorneys' treatment of her adversary. "Above all," she noted, "they did not believe that Dr. Bernard was mentally ill." She was convinced that her team thought she was still in love with Theos by raising the question of her ability to face the coming ordeal in court. "Their decent desire to see a villain punished made them ask almost daily if I wanted to continue my case." Byron C. Hanna, in particular, could not disguise the fact that he regarded Bernard as a parasite living off Madame's money, but pointed out to Ganna that in blaming mental instability for his character, the case would collapse. If a husband were to be declared insane, the wife must continue to care for him; it was no basis for her defense because Bernard would be unable to sue for divorce if he admitted mental incapability - and neither could she.

Order-to-show proceedings were made in Santa Barbara on July 12, when Walska learned for the first time details of Bernard's first marriage as she sat in court, demurely dressed and looking considerably younger than fifty-nine. The plaintiff testified that his former wife, Viola Wertheim Bernard, had financed his education and a two-year trip to India and Tibet, where he studied Oriental philosophy, gathered material for his books and was further assisted by Sir John Woodruff and the Maharajah of Darbunga. He confirmed that Viola continued her support on his return to the United States with a financial arrangement, after she began divorce proceedings. He told the judge that he was instructed not to answer any question about the size of the settlement and insisted he would continue objecting to questions intended to suggest that he might be attempting to defraud Mme. Walska. Her defense attorney, J.F. Goux, rejected this: "We're entitled to know how much he got from his first wife and what he has left."

Bernard smiled smugly, as if convinced he was smarter than the combined wisdom of those in the courtroom, reiterating that he would not answer the question. He proceeded to testify that he first met Walska when she enrolled for lectures in his studio at New York's Hotel Pierre in 1939, saying she became interested in his attempts to found an institution for the study and furtherance of Tibetan literature and culture, and purchased their present estate on Sycamore Canyon Road [Tibetland] a few years ago. He certified that he had been classified 4-F in the draft because a rheumatic heart made him unfit for military service.

Bernard's self-confidence persisted throughout the sultry Friday morning and looked set to take up most of the day - possibly extending into Saturday - until a dramatic turn of events occurred late in the afternoon, when he was forced to admit by Judge Westwick that his first wife established a trust fund of $40,000 for him on their divorce eight years earlier. His suit for separate maintenance from Madame Walska contended that he was unable to support himself, but disclosure of the Wertheim fund and other assets - including approximately $5,000 in war bonds - amounted to perjury. The case collapsed immediately, with Bernard's team left to pick up the pieces, and Walska's attorneys filing a cross-complaint seeking divorce.

Both parties agreed there was no community property involved, that Madame Walska owned her estates, and agreed to hand over the few books and manuscripts that Bernard had left in her Tibetland library. A previous arrangement to pay Theos $1,500 providing he left the Penthouse estate would stand, together with a generous voluntary gesture of $5,000 for his attorneys' fees, instead of the $2,500 already agreed upon. Following this, Judge Westwick announced the decree granted, and Walska, finally accepting that her marriage number six had not been made in heaven, noted in her diary: "Miraculously, almost in a twinkle of an eye I was vindicated. I got rid of such a dreadful individual without even any financial cost," overlooking the unstinting $6,500 payment to her former husband and her own considerable legal expenses. "I did not need any longer to care for him, not because I did not want to but because he himself gave me that unexpected undreamed of Freedom!"

In later, more commercially-minded years, the name Lotusland might sound like a botanical theme park featuring water lilies, but in 1946 it was a perceptive name-change chosen by its proprietor for a property that, in seventy years since its foundation as a government homestead grant, developed under three memorable identities: Tanglewood, Cuesta Linda and Tibetland. None was as evocative as the name of Lotusland because there had been Indian lotus lilies planted in an irrigation lake by Tanglewood's first owner around 1890, and they continued to flourish.

Chon Tun, an eleventh century Chinese poet, wrote about the aquatic lotus:

"How stainless it rises from its slimy bed. How modestly it reposes on the clear pool - an emblem of purity and truth. Symmetrically perfect, its subtle perfume is wafted far and wide, while there it rests in spotless state,

something to be regarded reverently from a distance, and not to be profaned by familiar approach."

The sacred lotus was an inspiration for the people of Egypt, India and Asia in general, who saw its annual emergence to seek the nurturing warmth of the sun as a symbol of spiritual renewal and growth. To ancient Egyptians the aquatic plant represented creation, life, immortality and resurrection, while Indians recognized spiritual transcendence, beauty and purity. In Hinduism, deities were depicted seated on lotus thrones, and the lotus posture in Yoga became the most suitable sitting position for religious meditation. By rising from its muddy roots, the lotus represented Buddha's quest to conquer the darkness of illusion, and victory in the light of perfect understanding. For Madame Walska, at another tangential point of her life, this exquisite flower reminded her of past convictions and future aspirations. A personal motto *Malgré Tout* ("In spite of everything") had once headed her notepaper, and she adopted the new name for her estate to reflect her stoic determination to overcome life's difficulties and create, like the lotus, a perpetual source of beauty.

Lotus pool

Agreeing with a saying from proverbia that marriage is a lottery -

to which she would never again subscribe - Walska yearned for a sense of family that had been largely absent from her life since leaving Brest-Litovsk at the beginning of the century. With this in mind she planned to provide a cottage on the estate for her closest relations, brother Leon, Marisya and Hanka Puacz, after receiving the joyous news that they had survived the horrors of war in Poland.

Ralph Stevens now had more time to attend to Madame's estate needs, and the double gates he designed and installed in 1946 were the first of many major improvements at Lotusland. A concern was the condition of the swimming pool and bath house, designed by George Washington Smith and installed in the mid-1920s. When Walska bought Cuesta Linda the pool was leaking and she asked Lockwood de Forest what would need to be done to make it functional again. His answer was not encouraging and she saw it as an excellent site for a water garden displaying lotuses and lilies, planning a larger, more modern swimming pool nearer the main house. That would be Stevens' next big project.

But all this - and much more - was going to be expensive. Madame Walska's two Californian properties employed seven people on a permanent basis, with others engaged on regular contract work. Without local taxes, utility charges and Ralph Stevens' fee, she was paying about $2,000 a month just to keep everything running, and, with ambitious plans for building and planting, expenditure was sure to rise in line with her limitless vision. Having decided that Penthouse of the Gods must go, Ganna was told by Santa Barbara realtors that it would be a difficult property to sell. In addition, she had the expense of maintaining her New York house, and uncertainty over the château, town house and theater in France. Fortunately, three of her husbands provided a secure financial base that had seen her comfortably through two world wars and the lengthy Depression.

A combination of trust funds and stock holdings meant that Walska's position throughout the 1940s had remained remarkably stable: 1942 net income $205,939 - income tax paid $155,866; 1943 net $243,127 - tax $181,765; 1944 net $271,068 - tax $213,169; 1945 net $259,151 - tax $224,682. There was little to suggest that the pattern would change, because additional to annual income and taxes, the California and New York properties were valued at more than $200,000 and her total assets at this time were estimated by Phelan Beale at between three and five million dollars.

The phone rang at Dr. Koteen's consulting rooms in Manhattan and he assumed it was another patient seeking advice at his fast-growing practice, but it was Madame Walska needing to speak to him urgently. He prepared for a real or imagined emergency involving herself, Mary or another household pet, but it was to cancel a consultation. She was going to Paris for a few days and while away wanted to offer him the use of her opera subscription and automobiles, together with the services of Troy, the chauffeur. "I protested to no avail," Koteen recalled. "I had never seen her cars, but six foot and three inches of Troy I knew well because he was also my patient."

He thought nothing more about it because he lived in upstate New York and used the train and subway each day to reach the hospital where he was teaching. Then Troy phoned him to ask what time his train arrived in New York City. "I traveled with a group of friends most days," the doctor explained, "and mentioned that a car would be waiting to pick me up at Penn Station for the next week or so. This intrigued them, especially when a towering chauffeur, dressed in black and wearing leather driving gloves, stepped out of an old Rolls-Royce and recognized me.

"Doc, your ca-aar is waitin'."

This became pleasurable routine for a week, until the chief of surgery needed to discuss a patient with him, and, about to leave the hospital for the day, suggested they share a taxi downtown. Koteen said he had a car waiting outside. "He looked at me in surprise, asking how long I'd been in practice, and at that moment Madame's huge Cadillac pulled up, Troy jumped out and opened the door.

"Doctor Ko-teen, you ca-aar's ready, Sir,"

The two men got in and a blanket was spread over their legs.

"Remind me, Herbert, how long have you been in private practice?" the chief asked, halfway to the station.

"Just a few months."

"That's what I thought!"

Koteen tried to explain the situation but was cut short by his colleague.

337

"No, don't say a word, Herbert. I know you're a very good doctor - and obviously a very successful one as well!"

Walska went to France because she learned that the caretaker of her château had located some valuables hidden there at the start of the war. "Her gold clock, art work, silverware, and other items were buried before the Nazi invasion," Dr. Koteen said. "Apparently, an enormous hole was dug and filled with heavy canvas bags containing these treasures, the soil replaced and then several feet of manure added as a deterrent. Ganna told me that the idea to outsmart the enemy was her own." Jerome Dalseme, son of the gentleman farmer at Galluis, who later founded the Excelta Corporation in California - an internationally-known supplier of precision hand tools for all types of industry - confirmed that his family also deposited their silver, paintings, and some furniture in crates, hiding them from the Germans in pits on their farm property.

Visiting war-torn Europe was a chancy experience for anyone in 1946, particularly as there were only two flights a week from New York's La Guardia airport to Paris, though Ganna's single-minded purpose was to find out the state of her properties after almost six years absence, then return to the United States as quickly as possible. She noted: "I went with one [flight] and returned right away five or six days later with the other plane," finding the Théâtre des Champs-Elysées virtually unscathed but full of dust and her Paris town house intact. But Walska hadn't the heart - or time - to visit Galluis, being told that the château still stood, though in need of urgent repairs, with its park and gardens totally neglected. Jerome Dalseme, an eyewitness, recalled: "The château deteriorated during the war and was not livable afterward."

On her return, Madame was reluctant to speak about the whirlwind visit, finding postwar Europe too depressing for words, mentioning only that almost everything she owned there was safe and arrangements were made for furniture from the château to be shipped to Santa Barbara. If there had been no war, most probably she would have remained a resident of France, running her theatre and developing the grounds of Château de Galluis.

According to Léa Dankiewicz, daughter of her housekeepers at Galluis during the 1930s, "Many years of Madame Walska's work and joy were destroyed, abandoned, turned upside down. The

338

château was occupied for a short time by the Germans and by different groups of children from the Paris suburbs escaping from the threat of bombing." Hania Tallmadge, Ganna's niece, who visited Paris with her parents as a small child before the war, gained the impression from later conversations "that all the furniture stayed in the château, with Aunt Andzia taking only her best jewels." Sam Waagenaar, who studied singing with Cécile Gilly during the thirties and got to know his fellow student well, corroborated these accounts, adding: "Enric Straram took care of Ganna's belongings during the war. He had removed all antique furniture from the building and put a large collection of valuable jewelry in a safe, built into one of the walls. The Germans occupied Château de Galluis, and afterward the liberating G.I.'s were there, and it was evident to Enric (whom I knew quite well) that soldiers of both these armies had been trying to open the safe, but with no luck. After the war, Enric, who had the key, found all the jewelry present!"

Her rushed trip to Paris exhausted Walska and she called Dr. Koteen for a checkup. During a house call at the Park Avenue residence he noticed her extravagant portrait by Victor Stemberg from Imperial Russian days hanging on the wall.

"Madame, you were a very beautiful woman," he remarked.

She playfully slapped his face.

"*Docteur*, remember this: I *was* a beautiful woman, I *am* a beautiful woman, and I will always *be* a beautiful woman!"

By now, she had given up much of her social life, with the exception of the Metropolitan Opera's annual opening of the season, adding a new page to its glittering history - and peripherally to Ganna's. With the United Nations Organization preparing to adopt New York as the site for its permanent headquarters, there was little of the military gold braid in evidence that had marked the previous opening night. Instead, the city was overflowing with international diplomats in suits or national dress, adding a cosmopolitan touch to the annual parade of wealth and glamor for the opera. Regulars with long memories said this opening resembled the start of the thirty-fourth season on November 11, 1919, when the war-weary audience put on a huge display of ostentation, just like the repeat performance for this year of peace, 1946.

Fashion writers for the press agencies noted a return to elegance, with Madame Walska's picture splashed across the pages of many newspapers coast-to-coast, showing her stealing the show in a simple white jersey off-the-shoulder gown and cape. Gasps of admiration came from onlookers in the auditorium as her parure of diamonds, extending from a glittering, jewel-encrusted headband and sparkling pendant earrings, down to her deep *décolletage* displaying a multifaceted necklace, turned her into a one-woman light show. Last year she had worn an unflattering mishmash that seemed designed to shock. This time, feeling as free as a bird, there was no self-conscious bare midriff - as the papers noted - just sheer, feminine elegance.

This was an audience more interested in what happened socially in the crowded foyer than dramatically and musically with *Lakmé*. As the press observed, the crowd stayed with the opera during its first act, when Lakmé falls in love with a British officer - as no Brahmin maid should do. But after the first intermission allowed an extended visit to the second-floor bar, there were many deserters as the next act began: some stayed drinking, others wandered back late. At the end, when Lakmé ascends to a celestial life after taking poison, on realizing that her Englishman will never decide between duty and love, there were only four curtain calls for the excellent cast. As Jack Gaver, United Press staff writer, wrote, "It seems that opera goers must get most of the applause out of their systems during the show. I know that the palm-beating at the end was scarcely more than polite, with everyone in the orchestra running for the exits, and even a Broadway dud gets a better hand at the close."

Ganna was less concerned with these trifles, still subscribing to Seneca's maxim about never being too old to learn, while at the same time regretting she was not in the same league as Lily Pons, whose bravura performance in the title role had been thrilling. But Ganna was grateful to have sat and marveled at the beauty of fine singing in Léo Delibes' operatic masterpiece, with its overtones of Oriental mysticism, which reminded her of the symbolic lotus, and the brilliant future she planned for her newly-named estate.

Life without Yogi
1947

In March 1946 Britain's wartime Prime Minister, Winston Churchill, delivered a speech at Fulton, Missouri declaring that Stalin had lowered an "iron curtain . . . from Stettin in the Baltic to Trieste in the Adriatic," warning his academic audience that the Soviet Union was aiming for infinite expansion of its power. It was the start of the Cold War, when an ideological curtain fell to divide the nations of eastern and Western Europe, upsetting Ganna Walska's plans to bring her brother and his family to the United States. Her singing student friend, Sam Waagenaar, had managed to contact the Puaczs on her behalf from Holland in late 1945 and confirmed their survival, but with Poland under Russian domination once again, the free movement of its people became restricted. What had been assumed during the euphoria of victory over Japan as a simple matter of signing a check and bringing her family to California, turned into Madame's own Cold War crusade.

The job of fixing the problem went to Phelan Beale, who, as her attorney for a quarter-century, should have qualified for some sort of campaign medal for service beyond the call of duty. Ganna turned to him for advice about her family, as she had in matters of marriage and divorce concerning several of her husbands, together with his eternal attempts to obtain a United States passport for her.

During the winter of 1946-47, he made enquiries through his Washington, D.C. contacts and was referred eventually to America's ambassador to Warsaw, Arthur Bliss Lane, who agreed to speak unofficially to the Polish Foreign Ministry about obtaining travel documents for the Puacz family. The most direct route to the United States was by passenger ship from Gdynia to New York, but there was little likelihood of American consular representation there in the near future, and Lane suggested that Leon, Marysia and their daughter Hanka go to Stockholm, where an American consular office existed, and travel on from there. It was a complicated solution, and the   attorney could expect no further help from Lane because he was about to be recalled when relations between the two nations reached a low ebb after the new Polish ambassador to the United States was rebuked by President Truman for his country's politics while presenting his credentials at the White House. There was the added problem of Leon Puacz leaving his sister in America to make all arrangements, prompting Beale to comment pointedly in a letter to Walska: "I cannot understand your brother not trying to help himself in this matter. He is not like his sister."

Lane acted quickly before his recall, helping to obtain passports from the Polish authorities to permit the Puaczs to exit Poland, assuming that the American consul in Sweden would issue the necessary immigration visas for onward travel to the United States. The attorney needed advice about the next move because the family might be required to wait months before they could get the documents - and the waiting period could exceed the time the authorities allowed them to remain in Sweden. Such were the complexities of travel between East and West during the early ideological struggles of the Cold War.

Beale then learned there was no American quota for Polish immigrants, telling his client, "I do not know what more we can do to help your brother," explaining that the practice of American consuls abroad handling immigration matters was a delicate subject.

"It is a situation that is loaded with dynamite and no one wishes to touch the matter. I say loaded with dynamite for the reason that America consuls are poorly paid. There is little, if any, future in a consul's career. The State Department has difficulty in getting high class applicants for consulate jobs and one of the few privileges enjoyed by the consuls is the matter of the immigration quota. Lastly there are so many thousands of Jews who wish to enter the U.S., the Jewish Propaganda Committee watches the manner in which the consuls handle the quota arrangements. If a gentile is given preference over Jewish applicants, hell is raised."

Madame's highly-developed sense of *noblesse oblige* bristled on reading this, appreciating the work Phelan was doing on her behalf, but failing to recognize the skill and commitment of his approach. His tenacity was legendary, however, and he urged her not to give up hope, while secretly suspecting he had done everything possible, and not even one of his most influential contacts, the distinguished financier and confidant of presidents, Bernard

Baruch, was able to help. Further informal talks with colleagues, however, led Beale to suggest a new approach: the Puacz family could forget their original intention to come to the United States on immigrant visas and travel instead as visitors.

Walska agreed without protest or further comment and Beale's office proceeded to draw up two affidavits. The one for Leon gave the reason for the proposed visit to his sister:

"My sister desires that my wife Marysia and my daughter Hanka and me, come to the City of New York, State of New York, United States of America, on a visit not to exceed ninety (90) days, as soon as possible so that she may arrange her financial affairs to the end that during her life she may provide for the maintenance of my wife, daughter and self, and on her death provide a trust fund for us thereafter."

Walska's affidavit detailed her ability to look after them, including staying at her New York residence:

"I am a woman of means, being one of the largest individual stockholders in the International Harvester Corporation and own two substantial estates in Santa Barbara, California . . ."

Additional information mentioned ownership of ninety percent of the capital stock in the company controlling "the Champs Elysées Theatre" - without revealing that it was virtually worthless at this moment - ownership of a Paris town house, and the château at Galluis in France. Guaranteeing support and maintenance while the family stayed in the United States, Walska submitted under oath the amount of her net income for the past five years (totaling 1.5 million dollars) and tax paid to the government (one million dollars.) A patriotic footnote mentioned that Leon's eldest son, Wladyslaw Puacz, died in Warsaw during the war "fighting in the Polish army on the side of the United States and its Allies." The document was signed and sworn before a notary public, attached to Leon's draft, and sent to Dr. Adam Nagorski, an English-speaking lawyer in Warsaw.

Tensions surrounding these convoluted arrangements resulted in Walska's nervous over-eating resulting in putting on weight. Dr. Herbert Koteen suggested a diet which avoided sugar, jelly, jam, honey, candies, nuts or chocolate, pies, cakes, cookies, puddings, ice cream, pork, ham, bacon, sausage, duck, fish canned in oil, cereals, potatoes, grains, oil, dressing, cream, soft drinks, beer, wine and alcoholic drinks. Ganna never touched most of the items listed, and reported to him that she lost three pounds in the first

343

seven days; the only taboo she craved was honey to sweeten her coffee. Over the next few weeks, superfluous avoirdupois was shed to the point where Koteen had to caution his patient about losing too much too soon. Ganna's joy over the new sylphlike shape was only tempered by the inconvenience of having to employ a dressmaker to take in her clothes.

In addition to the Puacz family's visit, Phelan Beale was asked to find out what happened to some of Walska's jewelry and valuables left in France on fleeing the country in 1939. She had thought that nothing was lost during the Nazi occupation, then remembered several valuable pieces of jewelry and twenty-one gold dollar pieces left either in a safe deposit box at Morgan's Bank in Paris, or at Galluis. She told Beale that when the Germans seized the French bank, they may have compiled a list of her articles, and she wanted to see a copy, also demanding that other valuables still in the bank "or somewhere in France" be forwarded to her in New York. He passed on this "conglomeration of questions" to a French associate, together with instructions that her 570 shares in Société Immobilière du Théâtre des Champs-Elysées and 100 shares in Parisienne de Spectacles must not be discarded.

A year passed since Ganna was initially shocked - and then relieved - by Theos Bernard's cynical divorce action, and she had heard nothing from or about him, assuming he must have gone off to Tibet, as intended. This was confirmed when Count Walewski, the "fake" count of Ganna's anonymous correspondent and a friend of Bernard, received a newsy letter from Theos written in a small Himalayan village, and subsequently mailed to him from Thomas Cook's in Calcutta. Walewski sent Ganna a copy which revealed that for the past few months, her former husband had been touring India, from Darjeeling to Cape Cormorin, and Bombay to Calcutta, furthering his philosophical research and gathering material for a new book. His main impression was of an entirely different land from the one he'd experienced before the war, on the brink of gaining independence from Britain and he feared that the India of old had gone forever.

Walska learned that Theos had been able to meet the leading lights of the nation, giving an excellent insight into what he called "the mental state of present-day India." The letter was written on the Tibetan border, where it was possible to contact lamas coming down from Lhasa, and a good place to gather manuscripts. Bernard said he was wary about venturing into Tibet itself because he no longer fancied the idea of trekking across fourteen thousand-foot plateaus and crossing seventeen thousand-foot passes, deciding to go no further beyond his present location, unless absolutely necessary. It was uncertain how long he would remain in the region because he planned to visit China to gather more material, explaining that the Chinese had taken many important Sanskrit manuscripts from India in centuries past, "So what has been lost in India may be discovered in Chinese sources." Ganna was glad to hear that his travels were bearing fruit, whoever was paying for them now.

The labyrinthine procedures necessary to bring the Puacz family to the United States suddenly evaporated, and by mid-May, 1947 - barely a month after the affidavit guaranteeing sponsorship was signed in New York - the way was cleared for them to leave Poland. Dr. Nagorski had worked quickly and efficiently on Beale's instructions, assisting Ganna's brother to surmount the remaining barriers of communist bureaucracy, and arranged for American visitors' visas to be issued in Warsaw. On learning that she would soon be reunited in a routine way after such a long and worrying time, Ganna reflected on the possibility of Eastern bloc politics being not as bad as everyone told her they were.

Mary Placek's condition worsened, suffering a massive heart attack, and Dr. Koteen's prognosis was ominous as she lay in hospital, visited daily by Walska bringing bunches of exquisite flowers to the bedside. Her faithful Mary was in a weakened state, hardly able to talk, and the end was obviously close.

"Who will take care of Madame when I go?" she whispered to Koteen.

"I will, of course. It's the least I can do as her physician."

"I thought you'd say that, but Madame was very disappointed when your Christmas card arrived."

The doctor had to stop and think for a moment, wondering why Madame Walska should have been offended by an ordinary greetings card sent out to his widening circle of patients, many from the world of show business including the stage and screen actress June Havoc and her elder sister, Rose Louise Hovick, the former burlesque stripper now famous as Gypsy Rose Lee.

"Why did my card upset her?"

"Well, when it arrived with that picture of your lovely little boy, we realized that you were married. Madame assumed that you would respond to her charm and be the next."

"The next what?"

"She was devastated because she planned to marry you."

Flabbergasted by the suggestion, Koteen wanted to know what he had said or done to suggest he might be interested in marriage. Mary gave him a long, hard look before responding.

"Madame is a smart woman - and a mystic. She thinks she can influence events, particularly regarding men. You remember her gifts: the scales, the clock, the thermometer case . . ."

"Well, yes."

". . . dinner invitations, opera tickets, the use of her car and chauffeur?

"Uh, huh."

"Well, when she was determined to marry somebody, she married him."

Mary died the next morning, an hour before Ganna's daily visit and Koteen found it impossible to express his grief, stuttering over the words, though Madame seemed far from shattered by the passing of someone she had depended upon through thick and thin for many years.

"Doctor," she addressed him, "I remember telling you once that I never look back, I never talk about yesterday. Mary was yesterday. What are your plans for tomorrow?"

The Puaczs arrived in New York on June 16, 1947 on board the M/S "Batory" of the Polish merchant fleet, which had served as an Allied troop transport and hospital ship during the war, and immediately traveled on to California. Ganna had moved heaven and earth to bring them to the United States, and it was a particularly exciting moment for Hanka, aged thirteen, who'd spent six of her formative years under Nazi rule just outside Warsaw, while her father was interned in a labor camp. She was too young to remember much about visiting her aunt at the Château de Galluis in the late 1930s - though some happy snaps survived from the time - and only recently had discovered that Aunt Andzia, as Ganna was affectionately known *en famille*, was a powerful lady. After the atmosphere of distressed Eastern Europe, America was like attaining an impossible dream for the impressionable young teenager, and Lotusland its ultimate paradise. Hania Tallmadge, as she became, recalled: "I was looking for cowboys in Montecito - where were they? It was wonderful to experience such freedom after the terrible war years."

The thirty-seven acres of Lotusland seemed confusingly vast to her parents, with Hanka and father Leon exploring the gardens while mother Marysia lagged behind calling out for help when she became hopelessly lost on paths winding through the dense greenery. A new swimming pool was ready in time for their summer pleasure, but Hanka could neither swim nor speak English, and Ganna sent her off to camp for swimming lessons and a crash course in the language.

On returning to the estate, Hanka experienced the surprisingly formal Lotusland lunches, even when taken only by family members on a patio overlooking the broad sweep of the main lawn. Occasionally, they were joined by house guests - milliner Mr. John came quite often, as well as Madame's sister-in-law, Sandra - the sister of Arcadie d'Eingorn. She told colorful stories of life in Imperial Russia when, as a little girl, her brother brought his wife-to-be to her school. "Life at Lotusland," Hania Tallmadge remembered, "was formal, but only in a certain way. My aunt said she was living in the country, and it was certainly less rigid than Paris or New York, but she always observed the proper etiquette." Walska was now more relaxed with her family present and Hania recalled her reminiscing in Polish about some of her marriages, though never once referring to Theos Bernard or Grindell Matthews. "Perhaps she remembered Arcadie because his sister was visiting, but the husband mentioned more frequently was Harold. I think he was the one she loved the most."

In the eyes of the Puaczs, Ganna was the Queen of Lotusland, while remaining a curiosity to most outsiders, particularly her Montecito neighbors among whom the racy reputation as a femme fatale made her a colorful, but remote, addition to their rather staid society. She was not a permanent resident, being absent from California for many months each year, and invitations to the big events of Santa Barbara's busy social calendar were rare. Dr. Warren Austin, her friend and physician from the nearby Val Verde estate, thought people were a little afraid of her: "They all wanted her as a guest, but most didn't have nerve enough to ask. And she as a rule didn't go out to dinner."

Stories had circulated about the exclusive clubs Madame Walska considered joining - the Santa Barbara Club, the Town Club, the Valley Club among them – but some excluded Jews and blacks at the time and may have hesitated to welcome a multiple divorcée, especially one with a reputation as a marriage-breaker. Ganna must have resented being cold shouldered, though well- aware that it was the penalty for living in one of America's bastions of old money and atrophied attitudes.

Fortunately, there were cultural stirrings in Santa Barbara after the war and they were just what she needed to help her feel at home while in residence. At the time of her leaving for New York after spending the previous summer as the divorced wife of Theos Bernard, a public meeting heard a proposal from Isabel Morse Jones, a patron of the arts and a critic for the Los Angeles *Times*, to establish a music school that might balance, geographically, New York's famous Juilliard School, founded in 1905 with a mission to train American musicians at home, rather than having to go abroad for study. Mrs. Jones had spoken at a small gathering of music lovers and performers, including the German opera singer Lotte Lehmann and her equally famous compatriot, the conductor Otto Klemperer. They discussed the state of music training in the United States, and particularly in the West, from where few were able to gain entry to the Eastman School, Curtis Institute or Juilliard because of poor preparation.

For the visionary Mrs. Jones, musical education should be independent of university connections to avoid the politics of academe, and far enough from Los Angeles to be free of the coruscating influence of the movie studios. Hollywood was the largest single employer of professional musicians in the country, but regarded in refined Santa Barbaran circles as exploiting musical talent, rather than nurturing it. With speed that only a single-minded individual with the necessary funds and the right connections could achieve, Isabel Morse Jones had been able to announce at the start of 1947 that the celebrated pianist, Arthur Rubinstein agreed to play a benefit concert for the proposed academy, and Lotte Lehmann would give master classes. Mrs. Jones was appointed the director in early March, and by the middle of the month the first faculty members were announced. Their names read like a roll-call of the best in classical music: Swiss composer Ernst Bloch, Metropolitan Opera tenor Richard Bonelli, violinist Roman Totenberg, guest artist Lotte Lehmann, and the Griller String Quartet. A board of advisors was recruited including Yehudi Menuhin, Pierre Monteux, William Primrose, Artur Rodzinski, Arthur Rubinstein, Robert Shaw, Joseph Szigeti, Lawrence Tibbett and Helen Traubel. Some were welcome guests at Lotusland during the academy's first summer season which was based on the facilities at Cate's School in nearby Carpinteria.

Madame Walska became a supporter of the fledgling academy and was expected to play an active role in its teaching program. It was, after all, taking place virtually on her doorstep, and if the publicity was to be believed, would put Santa Barbara on the musical map of the United States. But she had presented a few private recitals at the beginning of her West Coast stay that ended up as fiascos and was wary of inflicting further disappointment on herself - or anybody else. A summer festival was held, and its first attraction was a sellout benefit recital by Lotte Lehmann, as the Santa Barbara *News-Press* reported: "Last night the Lobero Theater witnessed the epiphany of the Music Academy of the West, and certainly the event fell under the influence of a gracious and most fortunate star." Lehmann, much admired by the composer Richard Strauss, had been a star of the Metropolitan Opera since 1934, and led a colorful private life, with a string of lovers and a short-term husband. She alone was reason enough for Madame Ganna Walska not to be taken seriously for her art by the academy, leaving her to become a generous benefactor, and to form an uneasy relationship with one of the greatest singers of the century who'd decided to retire to Santa Barbara when her brilliant career ended. Lehmann became, in effect, Walska's nemesis because the place was not big enough for two prima donnas - real or imagined.

With the Puaczs ensconced in Green Cottage and Hanka enjoying the luxury of a brand-new pool once she learned to swim, summertime within the boundary walls of Lotusland was like living in a small city state with Polish as its *lingua franca*. Hania Tallmadge (Hanka) saw her aunt in those days as a strong, single-minded person, used to getting her own way, recalling, "She had a most beautiful laugh - a pretty laugh, and anyone who got to know her well would never forget it." Aunt Andzia's normal demeanor, however, was rather serious, telling her family about amusing incidents, but rarely cracking jokes; she led an austere life, neither smoking nor drinking - and took great pride in her abstinence. Hanka observed that most people from beyond the estate's perimeter - with all but family members and a few close friends regarded as outsiders - were extraordinarily deferential on meeting her aunt, as if she were royalty: "Bowing and scraping and practically walking backward in the presence of the great Ganna Walska, hardly knowing what to say when introduced." She continued singing practice every day in her studio - the converted stable not used by La Varnie as a laboratory - but never discussed it. As a believer in reincarnation, Ganna may have anticipated a head-start in the next life by continuing to practice singing as a form of strict personal discipline in the present one, but whatever the reason she remained silent on the subject.

Lotusland may have been a teenager's earthly paradise, but living there became difficult for her parents after the initial thrill of being reunited as a family. They understood very little English, complaining of being too old to make the effort required to become even mildly proficient in the language, with much of what went on around them lost in a fog of incomprehension. Leon and Marysia were happy to return to totalitarian Poland before their visitor's visas expired in mid-September, but decided to stay on for Hanka's sake, agreeing with Ganna that it would be advantageous for her to have an American education. But to remain longer in the United States, their visas would need to be renewed before expiry on January 28, 1948. It was another task for Phelan Beale, though he couldn't face any more immigration or passport business after his previous experiences, and handed over the voluminous files to one of his associates to handle.

Development of the Lotusland estate slowed almost to a standstill while the Puaczs were first in residence, with Walska's attention focused on their welfare. But work was done around the new swimming pool, whose beach-like landscaping remained to be completed and a low sandstone wall built to delineate the leisure area constructed by a Santa Barbara contractor named Oswald da Ros. He would become associated with many future projects, observing how "The Madame," as he called her, went about ruling her domain. He remembered that working there was never straightforward because Ganna would shout a lot when things failed to go her way, but coming from a volatile Italian background, regarded these episodes as a front behind which lay a big heart. "She rewarded her employees and my employees as a contractor generously, which she didn't need to do," he recalled. "She appreciated their interest in her garden in helping her create what she wanted."

Da Ros timed his supervisory visits to coincide with Walska's own tours of inspection to discuss countless questions about paths, walls and rocks, recalling that she put in a full working day that could start with telephoning him at six in the morning. He was not involved in planting - which was the gardeners' responsibility - but noticed that Madame had a tendency to want any shrubs that should have remained at the back of borders, brought forward so she could enjoy their flowers with her poor eyesight. He remembered, in particular, the camellias, normally massed at the back of beds, were planted next to the paths. "But you didn't fight the Madame on these issues," he emphasized. "It was her garden, and you went along with it."

The Ganna Walska approach to the art of horticulture - usually defined as garden cultivation or management – might best be described as eclectic. It included areas in which da Ros specialized, like searching for stone to provide dramatic effects in highlighting precious plants, and bringing in tufa (porous calcium carbonate rock) from dry beds out in the desert to decorate her fern gardens. Granite came from near Mount Palomar, and volcanic rock was trucked long distances for the estate's ornamental waterfalls, as well as to embellish the succulent garden. No challenge was too great, and when Madame wanted something, she was prepared to pay for results.

Her new neighbor, Dr. Warren Austin, visited Lotusland regularly, reminiscing: "I was supposed to go to lunch every day [after his wife's death] because she thought I didn't eat right." He enjoyed Marysia Puacz's excellent - but dangerously rich - Polish cooking, and saw how the estate gardeners were treated. "She'd tell one of them, 'Now you just stand there,' and then wander away, either forgetting about him or becoming too busy, leaving

351

the poor man probably to stay there all day." Some of the workers found Walska's aberrant behavior hard to accept, resulting in a constant turnover of staff until she gathered a loyal, more permanent group around her. Austin said that some of them, however, would get drunk on the job, "and my job was to get them out of jail. It happened all the time."

He became Ganna's regular companion for trips to Los Angeles, driving her there to shop or to attend concerts and the opera, soon learning about her aversion to anything involving sopranos: "She simply didn't want to see or hear them. I admired the 'Love-Death' music from *Tristan und Isolde* but had never seen the work, and when a production was staged in Los Angeles, I took Ganna down there. She had sixteen cars and a chauffeur at the time, but wanted me to drive her, so we took the open Rolls, with her traveling like Isadora Duncan, insisting on wearing the same sort of things as Isadora - which scared me to death. Her long silk scarf billowed out behind her, and it was a miracle that it didn't get caught up in the wheels and break her neck [as happened to Duncan at Nice in 1927]. Hollywood celebrities were everywhere at the theater and she asked me to wait with her until they'd all gone in before making her entrance. Finally, we settled down for the performance but after the Vorspiel she announced, 'We go now, there's nothing any good after this.' So I never got to see the whole of Wagner's great music drama until years later in Paris."

Leaving the Puaczs to look after themselves at Lotusland and returning to New York for the winter, Walska was surprised one day to see a photo of Theos Bernard in the pages of the *Times*. Its caption read: "U.S. Tibetan Scholar Is Missing In Punjab After A Tribal Attack." The accompanying story was headlined: "Theos Bernard, Author, Feared Dead by Wife Who Reports Incident in New Delhi."

"Theos dead?" Ganna asked herself out loud, stunned by what she read. "Wife? Who?"

The Associated Press dispatch quoted Mrs. Bernard saying that her husband had been missing since mid-September on a trip to a Tibetan monastery and was now feared dead. His new wife, who was not identified in the report, except as Helen, said shepherds had told of tribesmen attacking her husband's party in the Himalayan Mountains of northern India and killing his servants.

Theos was short of food and she feared that he may have lost his heavy clothing to the raiders. The only facts were that they set out on August 20 from remote Kulu Valley in the northern Punjab where rioting broke out six days later, and she fled more than 120 miles on foot, south to Simla. Walska prayed that Theos had survived the attack, and read the paper each day seeking further news.

She returned to New York for the opening of the Metropolitan Opera's sixty-third season, choosing a pink satin gown with built-up bust line, and displaying more jewelry than ever, including a diamond and emerald tiara, two chains of birds-egg-size emeralds and a diamond necklace above her much-photographed *décolletage*. The press estimated the combined value of these treasures at more than a million dollars. Mrs. Cornelius Vanderbilt, the grand old lady of a generation of opening nights, was conspicuously absent for the second consecutive season, though a popular young crooner named Frank Sinatra was there attending his first opening, modestly informing reporters he had no plans for a Met career. As usual, the performance on stage seemed secondary to the show put on by first-nighters, and long after the golden curtain rose on Verdi's *Un ballo in maschera* (*A Masked Ball*) at eight o'clock, bursts of applause continued to come from the balconies as diamond-encrusted dowagers arrived strategically late, while other first-nighters stayed in the bar to watch the high jinks of an ermine-clad matron parading with a highball in one hand and a cigar in the other, while a man in white tie and tails, who'd imbibed rather too freely and fast, was carried out by two bartenders.

By the first intermission, the buzz around the auditorium was about the glamorous Serbian soprano Daniza Ilitsch for her spirited singing in the role of Amelia, though Ganna would have liked her to shriek a little less in her higher register. There was polite praise for the two male leads, Jan Peerce and Leonard Warren, but Madame found it more difficult than usual to concentrate on the music of this engrossing work because of worrying about her brother's immigration affairs, with time running out. Her concern was eased next day when the Bouvier Beale law office sent two application forms received from the Polish consulate to extend the validity of Mr. and Mrs. Puacz's passports. An accompanying note

353

stressed urgency because their temporary stay in the United States expired in little more than a fortnight. Another six weeks would elapse, however, before Phelan Beale received the news that Leon and Marysia could stay longer; their daughter was too young to need a passport.

Walska told herself that perhaps she should spend Christmas in Montecito next year, on hearing this good news. She also learned of the death of her neighbor and former brother-in-law, Stanley Robert McCormick. The seventy-two-year-old passed away while still a prisoner of his demons (and the McCormick family) at Riven Rock estate, close to Lotusland. Stanley had been separated from society in the sixteen-room mansion for forty years, living the life of an incarcerated country squire while continuing to show unflagging interest in the outside world, particularly movies, literature, art and music. When he died from pneumonia, it signaled the end of a colorful era for the great Montecito estates because few owners could afford the rising costs of their staffing and maintenance. Stanley's personal wealth was estimated at fifty million dollars, providing him with an annual income of over three million dollars a year: more than enough to look after the beautiful ninety acres of woodland and lavish gardens. But Riven Rock would disappear - except as the name of a future gated community - its mansion torn down and the land sold off for development by his widow Katharine to pay inheritance taxes.

The funeral service was held at the Unitarian Church in Santa Barbara - no flowers by request - prior to interment in Chicago, and the real story of Stanley's incarceration went to the grave with him. The mystery of Theos Bernard's disappearance was never solved, either, in spite of Professor Don Brown trying his best to discover the facts, both for himself and his friend's father now living alone in the San Fernando Valley. At the end of 1947, Brown drove from Santa Barbara to see La Varnie, who knew only what he had read in the newspaper about his son's apparent demise, asking the professor to find out if he was still alive, because rumors persisted that, after the attack, Theos had made it to a remote Tibetan monastery where he was busy writing a book which would match the popular success of "Penthouse of the Gods."

When he reached India on sabbatical to gather material for a book

354

of his own, Brown contacted the United States Embassy in New Delhi and was offered the most likely explanation for the disappearance of Theos.

"Just before Theos Bernard started his pack-train up the Kulu Valley, Moslem rioters had raided and murdered many Hindus in the Valley (as was happening elsewhere.) The best packers were Mohammedans in that area and Bernard had hired them to go to Tibet with him. After the slaughter of the Hindus there was a cry for revenge and a band of Hindu men followed the pack-train and at a narrow place in a steep canyon ambushed Bernard's party. The Moslems were killed and in the melée Bernard was himself shot and his body rolled down the canyon side into the rushing torrent below."

These details were obtained by the embassy from locals who were told what happened by members of a raiding party during the brutal India-Pakistan partition riots. When they searched for the American's body, a cloudburst during a violent mountain storm erased all traces of the massacre, washing away any evidence far down the river.

After receiving this information in Brown's letter from India, Mr. Bernard Sr. petitioned the Superior Court in Los Angeles to have his son declared legally dead, allowing for the disposal of an estate estimated to be worth $25,000. That was the last word on Theos Bernard, except perhaps for an epitaph-like footnote provided by Don Brown in 1982, recalling that Lowell Thomas, the famous radio and film commentator, told him that it had been his lifelong ambition to go to Tibet, and he did so just before the Chinese invasion, resulting in a series of popular broadcasts. "On one he said he had talked with some of the lamas about the visit of Theos Bernard in 1936," Brown noted. "They told him that he used to get roaring drunk at times in Lhasa, telling them that when he got back to America he was going to wow the whole country with his stories and make his fame and fortune." As a close friend and fellow academic, Brown defended Bernard's reputation as a scholar: "He earned his Ph.D. at Columbia under a demanding Oriental scholar. He published a grammar of the Tibetan language and a clearly-written summary of Indian philosophy. He was a brilliant lecturer."

Several of Theos Bernard's textbooks remain in print, while his travel writing was soon forgotten, though a biographical archive was established at his alma mater, the University of Arizona, in parallel with a family repository at the Arizona Heritage Center in

Tucson. It was intended to be part of a major study of Bernard's life, documenting his achievements and reflecting his significance in the field of South Asian religious studies. But the White Lama still divides opinions. David L. Kamansky, former executive director and senior curator of the Pacific Asia Museum at Pasadena, an expert on Tibetan art, thought his reputation was tarnished:

"In my own view, and in the view of many of my fellow scholars, he was just an opportunist. He used a fascination with Buddhist philosophy to create a career for himself, whereas we all feel that Alexandra David-Néel was serious. She turned a rather remarkable trip into a career as well, but in fact became a serious scholar. Theos Bernard couldn't do that: he was a very pretentious fellow, always looking for the next rich widow in a life of the flesh rather than the hereafter."

Some writers and researchers have suggested that many of the experiences documented by the White Lama - particularly in "Penthouse of the Gods" and "Hatha Yoga" were fabricated by his father Glen, who had walked out on his family when Theos was still a baby and went to India to pursue yoga studies. But a renewed interest in the Bernard persona has seen others regarding him as an unsung hero, whose work was a vital contribution to Western knowledge of Eastern wisdom.

The identity of the last Mrs. Bernard was not made public beyond the name of Helen Park and her husband's demise brought the long saga of Ganna Walska's tumultuous marriages to an end, with only a distant echo to disturb her. In December, 1947 a letter sent care of her publisher Richard R. Smith from Doctor Blake Pritchard, Grindell Matthew's British physician, stated that in winding up her fifth husband's affairs, the solicitor had found an outstanding account for his medical services of one hundred and forty-two pounds, ten shillings, and funds available at the time had permitted a payment of only five pounds. He hoped that Madame Walska would now be able "to discharge my account personally."

All six husbands were gone, and whatever the intentions of the men who continued to court her, she was adamant there would be no seventh spouse. Of the polymorphous sextet who took her for a wife, two disappeared in uncertain circumstances - Arcadie in action during the Great War and Theos in the high Himalayas - and the other four got old, or sick, and simply faded away. It was just as well that Madame Walska was reunited with her family because, at sixty, she might have been alone, as she had claimed in her sworn affidavit to bring them to America. To them she continued to reign as the Queen of Lotusland; others suspected that she had become its prisoner, reminiscent of Stanley McCormick at nearby Riven Rock.

Family Matters
1948-1951

From the moment Ganna began the redevelopment of Tibetland, with Lockwood de Forest supervising the planting of a replacement orchard during 1941-42, she rescued a large, rambling estate from abandoning itself to nature - and perhaps the property developers as well. The cost in time, energy and money was considerable and she knew that Lotusland needed constant attention if her schemes were to be realized during her lifetime. As teenager Hanka Puacz understood from watching her on a daily basis, Aunt Andzia thought she would live forever, but now realized that time was running short. It was not simply a question of leaving Ralph Stevens to supervise her many projects, such as completing a beach around the new swimming pool to be strewn with giant southwest Pacific clam shells, or trucking in loads of cacti and mature trees as if they were props for a Hollywood movie set. Madame insisted on being part of every decision and operation, striving for dramatic effects but with no professional knowledge. They were a good partnership, however, with her respecting Stevens's talents, while he gave credit in return - as de Forest had done before him - to her sense of the spectacular: "She has an artist's feeling, using plants instead of paints for stage settings."

But what Walska was creating subconsciously lay beyond mere theatricality: an elaborate series of themed gardens influenced by her passion for Tibetan art, spirituality and culture. The influence went back to the time of the Great War when the celebrated operatic bass, Chaliapin, fired her with enthusiasm for things Tibetan he'd acquired during a concert tour of China, consolidated by reading about Alexandra David-Néel's adventures in Asia. Ganna's collection of Buddhist art originated with her third husband, Smith Cochran, developed through purchases from the Pasadena dealer Grace Nicholson, and, of course, the work of Theos Bernard. Whatever her residual feelings about him, Walska knew that she had been captivated and motivated by him.

Her Pasadena friend, David Kamansky, surmised:

"I'm sure she was lonely [when they first met] and he was a breath of fresh air. Theos Bernard was a handsome guy, interested in all the things she was."

He regarded Walska's gardens as - intentionally or otherwise - the culmination of her philosophy:

"It was a place of well-being that she could retreat to. She often used the word 'retreat' and that has overtones in a Buddhist sense as a place where you meditate, somewhere you go to regroup as a philosopher, and where you study."

Kamansky observed Ganna living as a recluse at Lotusland; she didn't open it constantly to the public like many of the other great estate owners; she didn't engage in rounds of dinner parties, which might have expected from a celebrity like her. He speculated:

"A lot of it was because of not being accepted by the locals and she probably found most of them quite boring because she was European, they were Americans, and probably quite provincial in her eyes. They didn't speak French; she was probably not comfortable in speaking English all the time. And she was constantly concerned about money. Her correspondence with dealer Grace Nicholson always mentions how much things cost. She was perceived as a very wealthy woman, but she was tight-fisted."

He concluded that Lotusland was intended to create, both in color and spirit, all the positive vibrations for Ganna's happiness, stability and safety. The estate would have been challenge enough for anyone bent on creating an earthly paradise, but Madame needed to juggle many overlapping concerns that filled her days with decision-making, and her secretary's office with mountains of correspondence. Organizing her life was like running a business in which she was the boss and made all the decisions. Spring and summer 1948 would see the construction of a grotto and a theater, in the spirit of those in the grounds at Galluis, and proceeded in parallel with her other interests: the second season of the Music Academy of the West, hosting the occasional private tour of the estate for specialist groups, and attending to the Puacz family's future in the United States.

Never far from friction, there was also some litigation thrown in for good measure when Walska brought a $10,000 suit against a spraying company for a tree allegedly damaged by them. It was no ordinary example, being the ancient Monterey Cypress dominating Lotusland's great lawn in the "main and pivotal point" of the garden, and the treatment was claimed to have resulted in "burning, poisoning, disfiguring, injuring and damaging said tree and well-nigh killing it." Fortunately, the noble cypress recovered from the chemical onslaught and the affair was settled out of court.

The Puaczs, having arrived on visitors' visas and obtaining extensions due to expire at the end of May, 1948, were flatly refused any further leeway, and Phelan Beale went to Washington once more to take up the matter with another of his friends in high places: Tom C. Clark, the Attorney-General in the Truman administration, and soon to become an Associate Justice of the Supreme Court of the United States. Beale was armed with an affidavit from the Santa Barbara physician, Hilmar O. Koefod, stating that Marysia Puacz suffered from a serious heart ailment requiring complete rest and treatment, with her life endangered if compelled to travel before the condition improved. It was sufficient for the Department of Justice to consider the claim and allow the family a further prolongation of their stay: until April 1, 1949.

Isabel Morse Jones could not have been more delighted with the first year results of the Music Academy of the West after the experimental summer session during 1947 had generated extraordinary enthusiasm from students and faculty members alike, attracting national attention. *Time* magazine praised the opening of this "musical finishing school" in its setting of private beaches and mountain scenery which established academies like Eastman, Curtis and Juilliard could only dream about. The article also mentioned the impressive list of teachers, advisers and sponsors "as long as an unwound French horn." The Californian journal *Music of the West* certified the academy's success, predicting it would thrive with the demand from students and the willingness of West Coasters to assist the cause of fine music: "The board of directors, in the beginning, had hoped to attract contributions for a dozen scholarships. They got twice that number - from millionaires, movie stars and magnates, concert artists, foundations and Chambers of Commerce, and the butcher and baker, launderer and service station operator."

This musical world had come to the very spot that Madame Walska chose to escape the horrors of war, and she showed her appreciation by writing a check for $5,000, prompting an editorial

360

in the Santa Barbara *News-Press* praising her generosity, seen to typify the civic-mindedness of Santa Barbarans. This laudatory piece, headed "A Generous Gift to a Worthy Cause," tended to perpetuate the myth of her musical stature, but enhanced her standing as one of the area's more charismatic identities:

"Mme. Walska, famous in musical and social circles in Chicago, New York, and the capitals of Europe, has been a resident, at least part-time, of Santa Barbara since the year 1941. She is no 'outlander,' living apart from the community of her choice, but a warm-hearted supporter of cultural activities, a generous hostess, to friends and acquaintances of the musical world, to garden tour visitors, and during the war to servicemen on leave. Now she appears also in the role of the largest single contributor to an institution which has become one of the prides of Santa Barbara."

Some Montecito residents commented that you couldn't buy that sort of kudos; cynics pointed out that she just had - by the stroke of a pen.

A new theater garden for Lotusland was to be located at the extremity of the great lawn stretching from the terrace of the main house, beyond the towering Monterey cypress planted by Kinton Stevens around the time Walska was born, into the middle-distance of the estate. His descendent, Ralph Stevens, designed a sunken area capable of seating a hundred people on tiers of sandstone benches surrounded by clipped hedges of dense cypress, all within an area bordered by olives on one side and coast live oaks on the other. Walska would never lower the tone of her creation by displaying common-or-garden gnomes like many a suburban villa, but her outdoor theater was just the place for some stone grotesques shipped over from Galluis.

They were part of a long tradition of decorating Europe's aristocratic gardens with dwarf-like figures that were probably the ancestors of mass-produced - and much-maligned - garden gnomes. Similar figures inhabited Walska's French country estate, perhaps as a delayed response to hearing lines from "Hermann and Dorothea" by Goethe, Dr. Fraenkel's favorite writer:

"Then amongst all the neighbors my garden was justly renowned, And every traveler stood and gaz'd thro' the rose-colored railings At the figures of stone and the color'd dwarfs I had plac'd there."

How such objects came to be displayed at Galluis - and they may have been there when she purchased the château – is not known, but Ganna wanted to have a whole family of stone figures as a

361

permanent captive audience for her new outdoor theater. Three were probably shipped from France to California, and, keen to purchase more in the United States, she alerted dealers in Los Angeles and New York to her requirements, and asked friends to look out for them on their travels. Meanwhile, the three already at Lotusland kept a rather lonely vigil in the grassy auditorium.

Madame also asked Stevens to design what she called a Silver Garden, adjacent to the theater featuring trees and plants with a silvery to blue-gray foliage, with Blue Atlas cedars standing above the ground cover of blue fescue and *Senecio mandraliscae*, with other shrubs, plants and trees in the same color-range to add accent, like Mexican blue palms. The paths through this new garden were bordered by chunks of green glass slag from a nearby bottling plant, obtained by Oswald da Ros from the Arrowhead Spring Water Company which sold him the material chipped out of their kilns. This unique ornamentation, looking like giant uncut emeralds, added an ethereal translucency to the original Silver Garden. "If it was something different," da Ros remembered, "and if she could find a use for it, the Madame would bring it in for added effect."

Friends collected unusual pieces on their travels, and she was thrilled to have a sizeable amethyst rock Warren Austin brought back from Brazil. On another occasion, Walska wanted some blue stone for a particular effect and the only acceptable hue came from North Africa; it was expensive and had to be negotiated through a dealer but, as da Ros said, "That's what she wanted and we brought it in for her." Walska's niece recalled that after the upmarket garden gnomes and furniture arrived from France, her Aunt Andzia seemed to acquire a new energy, bringing in decorators for extensive remodeling of the main house, hanging pictures, and renovating the estate cottages. "She had a passion for painted furniture," Hania Tallmadge said, "looking everywhere for good pieces to add to what came from France. She became very involved with the interiors, while the garden was kept tidy with five gardeners."

But one element of Ganna's complex character remained annoyingly constant: the tendency to turn her life into conflict by engaging in verbal combat with those who served her. She was, using the evocative Anglo-Australian colloquialism, a battler -

defined as someone who fights against the odds and does not give up easily. This idiosyncrasy had manifested itself in her dogged determination to be a successful opera singer, and when that failed, she continued vocal practice as if it were a combination of daily exercise and moral balm. Like a female Quixote, she tilted at bureaucracy on behalf of her family, argued with attorneys, attempted to regularize her own United States citizenship, and pressed for a regular passport - all the while spending many hours toiling under the Californian sun like a simple peasant in the field to develop her beloved estate.

"Mata Hari" passport photo

Phelan Beale, having tried and failed several times to obtain a new passport for her, was wary of a situation his client brought upon herself by having declared under oath in 1928 that she was a resident of France and had no intention of living in the United States. He reluctantly took up the cause again by writing to Mrs. Shipley in Washington, D.C.- by now well-acquainted with the bulging Walska dossier - asking about issuing a certificate of citizenship to allow his client to return without immigration problems from planned trips to Mexico and Canada. The response

363

was brief and to the point: the department would not issue a certificate for Mrs. Ganna Walska McCormick, though the emergency passport, issued to facilitate her flight from Europe in September, 1939, was returned with a note: "It is believed that this document will be sufficient to identify her as an American citizen when crossing the Canadian border." Madame's planned journeys never eventuated, and Beale used the fruit of his considerable efforts in taking Ganna to task, saying that the photograph in her returned emergency document made her look like Mata Hari; but worse, "is the way you have deceived the government about being born on June 26, 1891."

The Puacz family woke up each morning to peace and calm, surrounded by trees and lawns, rose gardens and birdsong, unaware that anything - or knowing that everything else - existed beyond the pink perimeter walls of the semi-fortified estate. Their fabulous retreat, Aunt Andzia's Montecito bailiwick, seemed to have the power to suspend time and space for its privileged occupants, affording them a private paradise, while presenting an air of impenetrable mystery to outsiders. Only a favored few were invited inside the gates and visitors were not encouraged. Everyone had heard of Lotusland and its reclusive owner, with the consequence that the estate's legendary reputation increased in direct proportion to its inaccessibility.

This did not mean that life within the walls was eternally austere. Madame loved to dress up and show off, and it was an opportunity with her family in residence to celebrate events that were dear to her heart, such as donning traditional Polish costume at Easter and sharing the great religious festival with family and close friends. Walska once declared that she was finished with extravagant parties at her Château de Galluis, but fifteen years later she used Lotusland as a perfect setting for socializing. To receive an invitation was a highlight for Santa Barbarans, and those who had been lucky enough to see the house before, found it much changed after Madame's furniture and furnishings arrived from France. She described its current ambience:

"I was collecting only Tibetan, and all my house was decorated in Tibetan style. But since last Spring I received my furniture from my Paris house, and as they are all mostly French 18th Century, Venetian 16th Century, etc., I was obliged to change everything, leaving only the library completely

in Tibetan style, and from time to time one or two banners on the stairs, etc., not having the place to put the remaining things."

With their visitors' visas about to expire, Phelan Beale reviewed the Puacz's immigration situation and decided that the only way to extend their stay and avoid deportation was on health grounds. He wrote to Dr. Koefod at the Santa Barbara Clinic:

"The Immigration officials are arbitrary and invariably ask for a second physician to give his diagnosis when application is made for further extension. Madame Walska hesitates to ask that another physician - naturally of your own selection - join you in certifying to Mrs. Puacz's condition and her inability to travel without endangering her life, as your Clinic is nationally known and your name and reputation are held in the highest esteem by the medical profession as well as by the public."

Beale was always a flatterer, as Ganna could attest from long experience, but before his letter was answered, it was decided that a better strategy was for the Puaczs to apply for a change of status: from visitors to legal permanent residents. That altered everything, with extra attorneys added to their case, including two New York experts: Alfred Rice, who already advised Walska on financial matters, and Joseph Abrams, a specialist in immigration law. Rice needed more information than he held on file, and peppered Walska with queries for the many forms to be filled-in. She consented for a while, but it was frustrating to compile Leon and Marysia's dates and places of birth, together with marriage details, and exact foreign addresses. Outside her window were verdant vistas of the estate crying out for attention, while its owner remained confined to her pavilion laboriously logging facts and figures she could not be expected to have in her head - and which Leon was unable to provide in the obligatory English. Ganna did her best in translating from the Polish, but became increasingly short-tempered:

Q. "Did any of them have alien registration cards? If so what are the numbers?"
A. "They have no registration cards because they are here on a visitor's visa. I don't understand the meaning of registration cards anyhow."

In the midst of these distractions, she found time to arrange one of the most attractive parties of Santa Barbara's Old Spanish Days Fiesta for a cosmopolitan group of friends in a setting designed by Ralph Stevens and Mariano Soyer. Guests arrived at the Lotusland main gate to find the long driveway festooned with banners and paper ribbons, and were greeted by Madame on her terrace wearing a gown made from a shawl of old Brussels lace with a huge bow of white taffeta ribbon in her hair. The buffet table was screened from the sun by a carousel canopy of lime green canvas held in place by steel standards painted the same color, and huge silver balls were scattered across the lawn to reflect the deep blue sky. Sunday luncheon was al fresco, with the guests entertained by Manuel Contreras and his Spanish Orchestra, and invited to request their favorite melodies as they ate in an atmosphere of non-stop gaiety. Nobody was aware of the immigration drama being played out behind the smiles of Lotusland's residents.

Alfred Rice needed many more details to support the Puacz claim, and as soon as Walska returned to New York for the winter of 1949-50, she found there were affidavits to be witnessed and signed, photographs taken of each family member, and copies made of the parents' passports. Feeling abandoned in a bureaucratic maze, she prayed for guidance to find her way out. In early January 1950, her attorney learned that the hearing could not be held for at least a month, and four weeks later a letter arrived from the Immigration and Naturalization Service dashing everyone's hopes: "Due to the large number of cases now pending at this office, it would be difficult to state the exact date that hearing would be held . . . "

To make sure there was no pressure to send her family back to Poland before the hearing - whenever it was - Warren Austin agreed to certify that he was their physician, having had Marysia under his care for more than a year. In his statement, he mentioned that she had just returned from hospital after undergoing several diagnostic procedures:

"Since then her condition has become much worse and at the present time is confined to bed. She has been in no condition to travel and now is not even able to be out of bed. It is my opinion, and that of several consulting physicians and surgeons that Mrs. Puacz's prognosis would be most grave if she does not remain very quiet for months to come."

It met Phelan Beale's request admirably for a doctor's certificate that was "more elaborate and persuasive" than usual.

In spite of the demands in organizing her family's future in America, Walska continued to be fascinated by great singing and outstanding performers, inviting one of her idols, the Wagnerian soprano, Kirsten Flagstad, to stay at Lotusland during her

366

American concert tour. It required her to "open the house and hire servants," as she told a New York friend in a letter, and "as soon as she left I went to Los Angeles to hear her sing there and as soon as I came back, I closed again the house, sent away the temporary servants and went to Arizona where I wanted to go for many years." Walska began a new diet "as in these past few months I put on five pounds and I want finally to get rid of them and, not having servants, the kitchen being in the big house that is still closed, it is much easier than when a cook is there."

Her rather mundane life at Lotusland during the summer of 1950, led mostly in her pavilion adjacent to the main house, was described in a letter Ganna sent to Marie Piscator, who was thinking of paying a visit from New York City. Written in a mixture of French and English, inexplicably it changes language in mid-sentence:

"As I told you I have no servants at all for many reasons that are too long to write about *et même la femme de ménage qu'on à présent par exemple, ne vient pas depuis deux semaines, son fils étant opéré. Aussi n'oubliez pas qu' ici n'est pas New York, que vous ne pouvez sortir et* **have lunch or dinner at the corner of your street and there is not even a grocer nearby - we are living in Montecito residential district and all shops are in Santa Barbara. We order everything by phone and the things are delivered; milkman comes every second day, but, but, but once you order, they bring it to you and you have to cook it for yourself..."**

The immigration hearing was finally scheduled for July 19, 1950, and Alfred Rice, who inherited the entire matter after Phelan Beale became too ill to serve Walska any longer, told her that it was essential for Mr. Abrams to be present at the meeting with the Immigration Service at Ventura, along the coast from Santa Barbara. Abrams suggested arriving on July 17 to discuss the case with her, her brother and his wife, with Rice advising: "You indicated to me that they do not speak English. It would be well if you could arrange to have someone in addition to yourself present, who understands Polish and English fluently." He asked for $500 to cover Abrams' expenses, which incensed Walska. She vehemently disagreed that his presence was necessary, refusing to pay for his air fare from New York for a routine hearing because a friend of hers - the Mexican consul in Santa Barbara - "would be much more useful than a stranger, together with a Polish friend who would act as an interpreter."

Rice's professional pride was wounded by Ganna's tendency to dismiss legal opinion as if it came from cretins. He said he was shocked because Abrams' absence might mean the difference between success and failure. He also found it difficult to accept her condemnation of his own expert opinion: "Though I respect the Mexican Consul in Santa Barbara's relationship with the immigration authorities in Ventura, I must emphatically disagree that this qualifies him to act in a matter of an immigration hearing to determine whether your brother and family are entitled to permanent residence, which can be granted only upon proof of complicated facts applying particularly to their case and on which your Mexican Consul could not possibly have had any experience."

Point made - and driven home forcefully - Walska cabled Rice on July 3: "Thanks for explicative letter. Mailed today traveling expenses. Please inform when Mr. Abrams arrives. Thanks. Ganna Walska." He reached Los Angeles on July 17, as scheduled, stayed overnight at the Beverly Hills Hotel, and met Madame and the Puaczs the following day accompanied by Alfred Rice, who was also on the Coast negotiating the sale of motion picture rights to a new book by Ernest Hemingway.

The immigration proceedings proved to be routine, and the officer in charge, Mr. Harrison, agreed that the application for United States residence could proceed to the next stage after examining proof of Leon's financial resources and receiving the medical certificates. Walska assumed this meant the end of her involvement in the affair, allowing her to make up for lost time in the garden., and it happened for a while, with her writing to Rice at the end of July, "Here nothing new - work, work and more work; days too short to do all the things I want to." Ganna sought his advice about what to do with her New York house now she was thinking of moving permanently to California, and also ways of augmenting her income: "or rather diminish the horrible paying of income tax which since you left went again higher up."

Anxious to strike a better deal over her financial affairs, Ganna nevertheless refused to entertain any suggestion of her dying, and was suspicious of loans because she never needed them. Rice demonstrated that if she left an estate worth ten million dollars on her death, the tax demands would be at least six millions; on the other hand, if the value were reduced to eight million dollars, the tax burden would fall to about four millions. He apologized for introducing a mortality factor, emphasizing that by using loan money of – say - two million dollars, her beneficiaries would receive the same amount in both examples quoted, but, "in the first case, the Government takes the two million dollars in taxes, whereas, in the second case, you have spent in your lifetime the two million dollars free of tax which otherwise would have to be paid to the Government after your death." It made sense for her circumstances, but was dismissed out of hand.

In the fall of 1950, Madame took a trip south, "towards Mexico," as described in a letter to her New York friend, Alma Frank. Apart from that, the routines of the estate kept Ganna busy:

"My last weeks working in the garden. Fortunately, even in California, you cannot plant and transplant in winter time. Also night starts much earlier, especially now since winter clock is reestablished - so from five o'clock I can be already in my room, working yes, but not rushing from one end of the garden to another, discussing technical things with electricians, plumbers etc."

Walska told Frank that she did not expect to be in New York again soon: "I never make plans and never think when plans are ready - they speak for themselves so loudly that I know what to do . . . I never live in the past or future but only in today's day."

She spent her first Christmas in California, foregoing the opera season at the Met for the first time in many years, to share the festive season with her family, still waiting for the outcome of their immigration case. Joseph Abrams proved his worth, and earned his fee, by going to Washington, D.C. during Christmas week where he was able to verify that the Los Angeles office recommended changing the status of the Puaczs from visitors to legal permanent residents. Now they must wait for the Immigration and Naturalization Service of the United States Department of Justice to make the next move. Wishing Walska the season's greetings, Alfred Rice was able to give her the good tidings that alien registration numbers had now been assigned to them; the bad news was that hundreds of such cases were pending - some for over a year - though by pulling a few strings in high places, he was confident that the Puaczs' case would be examined shortly and sent to Congress."

He was right, and proceedings for adjustment of immigration

status took place on January 3, 1951. The Puacz dossier acknowledged that all three applicants were citizens of Poland, had arrived at the Port of New York on June 16, 1947, and their testimony led to the conclusion that they were bona fide nonimmigrants at the time of entry:

"The male applicant testified that after the occupation of Poland by the German Armed Forces during World War II he was placed in a labor camp and that he remained so confined until being liberated after the overthrow of the German Forces in 1945. It does not appear from the record that either of the female applicants was confined by the Germans during World War II . . ."

A review of the original Ventura testimony continued, paragraph by paragraph, page by page, in rigid offialese, obscuring the fact that their case, along with many thousands of others, was the human drama of a family caught up in circumstances that changed their lives forever.

It took four years and seven months from when they first arrived before Alfred Rice forwarded an official letter declaring that the family became permanent legal residents as of their original arrival date in 1947. He presumed they would now like to apply for their citizenship papers and offered to prepare them - if Walska would supply the required additional information, such as "the weight in pounds of Leon, Marysia and Hanka." She promptly popped each one of them on her Lotusland scales, combined the individual readings, and answered "450 pounds." When paying Rice his fee of $2,101.35, Ganna added a personal note:

"I don't know how to say it, but you can understand how it has made me happy that family have those papers, and now hope that soon they will become American citizens, and then all question of property, legacy, legality, will be easy to straighten out, and I could ease my responsibility, knowing that they are taken care of no matter what happen."

During 1951, while battling bureaucracy on behalf of her family, the Music Academy of the West acquired a permanent home through the generous gift from one of its most enthusiastic supporters, Helen Marso, the longtime secretary and devoted friend of the Jefferson family, who owned one of Montecito's finest estates bearing the sweetly harmonious name of Miraflores. Miss Marso bought the property from the Jeffersons' niece, who inherited it when Mrs. Jefferson died in 1950, and a year later donated eighteen of its twenty-three acres to the academy. She

370

specified that her gift must be used exclusively for a conservatory of music, with Miraflores a permanent memorial to her former employers. The house, dating from 1909, was designed in the popular Spanish Revival style on the site of the original Santa Barbara Country Club, set close to the sea in formal gardens. Acquiring these splendid premises was a huge boost for the young academy, though the financial burden of conversion costs was daunting and could only be achieved in an affluent community where philanthropy was a way of life.

Lauritz Melchior, Judith Anderson, G.W. and Gregor Piatigorsky

Miraflores was not ready for full operation during the 1951 season, and another year passed before Madame Walska began to involve herself more fully in the social life of the academy by playing hostess to the celebrated operatic baritone Lauritz Melchior and his wife at Lotusland, arranging an alfresco luncheon for the star performer of the 1952 summer festival. Others included the virtuoso cellist, Gregor Piatigorsky, and Ganna's friend, the Australian-born stage and Oscar-nominated actress, Judith Anderson, famous for her *Medea* in the theater and a chilling portrayal of Mrs. Danvers in Alfred Hitchcock's 1940 movie *Rebecca*. The summertime delights offered by the Music Academy of the West, combined with the gradual development of Lotusland, together with rescuing her family from the clutches of communism, made Madame Walska one of Santa Barbara's most talked-about personalities.

Queen of Lotusland
1952-1958

Ganna told a friend that she regarded Lotusland as "Out of this world!" describing how she had kept working all summer long in spite of many interruptions, and that her gardens now contained "the most valuable and rare collection of cacti, palms, agaves etc." Most striking were Lockwood de Forest's contributions now maturing from a decade before, and Ralph Stevens' more recent improvements coming on stream They reflected her love of desert plants and a predilection for mass planting, evident along the main drive of the estate with a host of New World cacti on one side and Old World desert Euphorbia on the other. Massed agaves flanked the curving roadway for nearly four hundred feet, forming a spiky green wall, backed by tree aloes. The crowded beds also revealed sparkling glimpses of colored stones - amethyst quartz, mariposite and rose quartz. Succulents gave way to surreal clusters of sun-worshiping golden barrel cacti at the corner of the main house, near the swimming pool, where Madame took to the water regularly, splashing and paddling with the determination to keep a trim figure after recent dieting.

She took long, proprietorial walks through the 1920s parterre - a series of formal planting beds and brick walkways divided by hedges, and incorporating a rose garden, water features and the Neptune fountain - crossing the wide lawn toward her open-air theater and adjacent blue garden, Ganna quietly admired what was already achieved, but wanted to get more things done: faster. She discussed with Stevens the installation of a large horticultural clock on the lawn beyond the parterre and there was also a scheme to install a topiary "zoo" once the landscaping surrounding the clock was completed. The water garden was developing nicely on the site of the original swimming pool, full of estate-defining lotuses, and there were constant requests for visits from horticultural groups.

Madame, however, was more at ease when showing off her

domain informally, asking Ralph Stevens to accompany her when Verne Linderman was given a private tour in December 1951.

"Most people who collect plants," Stevens told the local journalist, "have an interest in the individual quality, - the history and so forth - of each plant. But not Madame Walska: she won't even learn the botanical names!" Ganna protested vigorously at such a disgraceful suggestion, her hair drawn up in a ponytail, and dressed in a cashmere sweater over gray slacks, with red sandals on bare feet, as good-natured banter bounced between them.

"It's typical of Madame's feeling - her sense of the theatrical and spectacular, rather than an intimate interest in the plants themselves," Stevens told Linderman. "In order to obtain the strong effect she's after, she masses plants of the same kind - not one or three, but five hundred if she can get them."

A local tradition going back to the 1920s saw many estate owners opening their gates to the public as part of National Garden Week, and soon after taking up residence for the first time, Walska had been approached by Pearl Chase of the Santa Barbara Plans and Planting Committee to include Tibetland in the annual garden tour - as it was during the Gavit era when called Cuesta Linda. These benefit inspections recommenced during 1943, augmented by occasional visits from the American Women's Voluntary Services, wounded servicemen at the local military hospital, benefits for Our Lady of Mount Carmel church in Montecito, and continued more recently with members of the Cactus and Succulent Society and the Music Academy of the West.

Hania Tallmadge remembered an imminent visit from the Begonia Society when her aunt panicked. "I don't have enough begonias!" she cried, as if it were the end of the world, and promptly drove to a local nursery in the Rolls to buy many dozens more - red, pink and rare - to cover her patio in a blaze of color. On another occasion, when the Palm Society was meeting in Santa Barbara, she decided there were insufficient palm trees on the estate. Nurseries in the area were alerted and the order went out for everything they had in stock to be delivered to Lotusland.

The gardens were fine for entertaining, but Ganna was nervous about having strangers inside her house, though she relented in May, 1953, on agreeing to host a fund-raiser for the Music Academy of the West, with hundreds of tickets sold in advance with people taking advantage of a rare opportunity to see how Madame Walska lived. Whatever conclusions drawn would, of necessity, have a mythical tinge like so much of her life - because her private quarters in the adjacent pavilion were strictly out of bounds, and what the general public saw in the main house was a gallimaufry of art work, furniture, fittings and possessions accumulated in France and locally over the past thirty-five years.

Ganna compounded the illusion by posing in what press publicity photos captioned "an authentic Tibetan princess gown," and on the big day wore a shocking pink felt skirt and pale blue hand-dyed silk blouse, with a lotus flower pinned to her hair. She smiled and smiled, ever the gracious hostess, while volunteer guides took visitors through the principal rooms to discover brooding bronze Buddhas, still, silent and withdrawn, adding their own blessing to this worthy occasion. The gold-ceilinged, blue-walled library, crammed with Tibetan and Buddhist objects from floor to ceiling, attracted the most attention, particularly some ancient skulls transformed into teapots, and a collection of ceremonial drums reportedly made from human skin.

Walska told a group of wide-eyed visitors that what she called Tibetan collection was gathered long before the Orient became fashionable, and contained some objects - such as temple gods and pieces incorporating human remains - which really shouldn't be used for decoration. The staid burghers of Santa Barbara probably agreed with her when they encountered erotic images of fierce gods with erect penises, and other deities *in flagrante delicto*. To Madame they were central to Buddhist thought about duality and the completeness of life, though she left that unexplained.

The milling crowds were more comfortable with less-challenging Western cultural traditions of Boucher and Beauvais tapestries in the drawing room, a delicate Pleyel harpsichord bearing a "Do Not Touch" sign, her gloomy Rembrandt etching contrasting with a colorful Chagall painting, a Christophe Huet panel next to a Joseph Vernet pencil sketch, and youthful portraits of Madame herself from Imperial Russia. A sculpted marble bust of the chatelaine was also prominently displayed, similar in style to those that divas like Melba and Patti commissioned for their immortality.

In the morning room, floor-to-ceiling cabinets were stuffed with Sèvres, Dresden and Meissen china, the coffered dining room ceiling was decorated with *Porcelaine de Marseille* platters, and the huge dining table set with blue-and-white ceramic-handled cutlery. Walska was proud of her porcelain, telling visitors that she owned hundreds of complete sets, and pointing out that the champagne glasses on display were all very old - some with a royal provenance.

"In France," she reminisced, "they have no gardenias, so I always had some flown in from London for my dinner parties and they looked so lovely in those blue *dechine* bowls over there!"

Ganna was in her element during the three-hour tour, tirelessly showing-off her favorite possessions, including a huge decorative birdcage in the courtyard separating the main house from her pavilion, the home of an Australian dwarf cockatoo named Maly. This outrageous cage, she said, said had been featured in a well-known Hollywood movie and acquired from her friend, Christian Rub. Now a local antique dealer, he was formerly a character actor in dozens of movies including *Heidi* (1937), *You Can't Take It with You* (1938), and was the voice of the woodcarver Geppetto in Walt Disney's *Pinocchio* (1940.) He may also have been recognized by keen movie buffs as the genial carriage driver who endured the high-pitched coloratura warbling of the voluptuous soprano, Meliza Korjus, in MGM's *The Great Waltz* - or "The Great Schmaltz" as cruel critics called the sugary 1938 screen biography of Johann Strauss - the claimed provenance of Ganna's big birdcage.

The tour raised much-needed funds for the academy and helped finance the music academy's pre-season event in June, 1953 of a symposium under the chairmanship of Darius Milhaud, which attracted a galaxy of fellow composers, including Virgil Thomson, George Antheil, Roger Sessions, Mario Castelnuovo-Tedesco, Franz Waxman and Bernard Herrmann. Walska reveled in cultural and academic socializing, with the Santa Barbara and Los Angeles press devoting considerable space during the Old Spanish Days Fiesta in August, 1953 to the afternoon party she threw at Lotusland - described as "a large tea" - for Kurt Schuschnigg. He was a visiting professor at the University of St. Louis, having been Chancellor of an independent Austria before being arrested by the Nazis and forced to languish in a concentration camp for much of the war. The professor turned up in an elegant white summer suit with matching shoes, to be greeted by the hostess wearing a bobbled and embroidered dirndl-inspired skirt and Tyrolean blouse, no doubt to make him feel nostalgic for his war-torn, and still-occupied by the Allies, country.

Those carefree occasions gave the impression that Madame was one of the luckiest people in the world, doing precisely what she wanted, when she wished. But behind the façade of sophistication and glamor, there were always problems simmering at Lotusland, as if to remind her that the profusion of roses blooming in her parterre beds grew on stems studded with threatening thorns. Ganna became increasingly anxious about the properties she had abandoned in France, the state of her New York house, which needed repairs that never seemed to be carried out, and the continuing delays in her family's citizenship process. Their naturalization hearing was yet to be set, and she feared that her brother and sister-in-law might fail it.

Walska sought Alfred Rice's advice, after explaining to him that Leon could not speak English: "He rarely opens his mouth to speak in Polish even. Naturally he knows and can learn more about the history of America and speak through the translator, but he has no talent at all for languages." Her attorney's response was brusque, but lucid: "Your brother's failure to speak English will be a serious obstacle for his obtaining citizenship. We may be able to teach him enough English to get by. If not, he will be in the class of many thousands of legal resident aliens who never become citizens of the United States but always can legally remain here."

A new linguistic régime was introduced at Lotusland which, Madame admitted, "Is hard work for everybody." She wondered if the test would be held by a local judge, knowing she might be able to charm him in treating her brother gently. Rice advised that it was likely to be a long time before the family was called, and, frustrating as she found delays, Ganna welcomed it because with less work in the garden during winter, she could make sure that the Puaczs concentrated on practicing what little English they had.

Months passed without further news, and Ganna became edgy again, though retaining her sense of humor by recognizing the ridiculousness of the situation.

"We already toward the end of March," she wrote Rice in English uncorrected by her secretary, "and at least once a month here in Santa

Barbara some foreigners are naturalized. Brother study so hard, even though he never speak, that soon I am afraid he will know so much that judge wouldn't accept him as he will know more than the judge himself and his vanity will not allow him to accept the situation!!!"

Then it was Madame's turn to be challenged by bureaucracy: in trying to obtain an official document stating definitively that she was an American citizen, in order to settle her business interests in Paris and to ensure that the Puaczs inherited Lotusland without complications. Few reaching the age of sixty-seven found themselves in this situation, and she complained to Rice in a letter, "Again and again and again SOS, SOS, SOS. Oh possessions, possessions! Soon as I am finish and make it easy with one thing, then come another and another and each day its worse and worse."

This tragicomic *cri de coeur* came from hearing that the French government would offer compensation for the gold pieces confiscated by the Nazis during the war if she gave power of attorney to the bank or to the American consulate to collect the proceeds. But proof of nationality was obligatory, and she had none. Losing the value of a handful of gold pieces was a mere trifle, but the French government had also agreed to pay reparations for damage to the Champs-Elysées theater, though only on proof that she, as the majority shareholder, was an American citizen.

Walska tried her hardest to answer every question on the naturalization papers, but few made sense, and Rice was not familiar enough with his client's past to insert everything himself. She asked him in a letter:

"You put my last permanent foreign residence as Poland. What do you call permanent? I came to the United States, when I came the first time, from Paris where I was living not less than one year, so I don't know what is right to put. Perhaps it is better to put France, as Poland they mix with Poland of today - Red Poland."

There was a standard query about where the applicant boarded the ship or train to the United States, which caused further consternation:

"I don't know if they meant the first time. If so first time I took the boat "Arabic" from Liverpool, England, during the first war in Europe. All subsequent trips by ship were made always from France and to France, excepting the last time during the 2nd war evacuation that I left by plane for America from Lisbon."

Ganna tried hard to stir the shards of her memory, wanting to come up with answers, but for someone who preferred to discard the past, it became a near- impossible task.

In September, 1954 she faced more pressure after receiving a letter from the board of the Théâtre des Champs-Elysées informing her they could wait no longer for proof of citizenship and asking for a notary-witnessed paper instead stating her nationality. When they received it, proceedings to reduce taxes could start, but by waiting any longer, a whole year's benefit would be lost. It meant another letter to the attorney: "So, dear Mr. Rice, again S.O.S., S.O.S.! Save the situation and send me such paper signed by the notary, but if in my absence the notary cannot sign, then send me the paper and I will sign it here with a notary." He forwarded a document authenticating the copy of a State Department letter confirming that citizenship would be granted when all evidence was received, and this was sent off to Paris, but returned as inadmissible. Madame had to search through countless boxes of letters, personal files and unsorted memorabilia scattered throughout the house for her marriage certificates with Cochran, McCormick and Bernard, evidence of termination of those marriages - either divorce decrees or death certificates - and details of United States citizenship as shown on the birth certificates of Cochran and McCormick. Alfred Rice himself researched documentation on the Walska-Fraenkel marriage and sought the testimony of someone who had known the couple to swear under oath that she was the person who, forty years before, married Dr. Joseph Fraenkel.

Ganna's visits to the East Coast had become infrequent, and it would have made her attorney's sleuthing much easier if he could discuss these matters face-to-face. But the thought of flying back and forth across America was anathema to her, though being in New York during the winter season still seemed attractive as a cultural concept. "I am sorry I will not be there for the freezing weather because I love it," she wrote Rice. Searching for details of her marriage to Theos Bernard, Ganna came across a copy of Dr. Fraenkel's own naturalization papers and a press clipping about William F. Cochran, her former husband's brother-in-law, indicating that the family originated at West Farms in the Bronx, New York City. They were small crumbs of comfort for the attorney, who pressed on, methodically, piecing together the minutiae, knowing that had she had been the wretched spouse of a dirt-poor Mexican laborer who crossed the border illegally to find work in California, Madame's application probably would have been approved years before. Such was the quirk of fate that condemned Madame Ganna Walska, multi-millionairess, owner of one of Montecito's great estates, recipient of the Légion d'honneur, and former wife of four prominent American citizens, to this purgatory.

Then a completely unexpected query came from Alfred Rice: "Who is Anna Grindell?" Walska attempted to explain "this new name on the horizon" by castigating him for not using her "Always Room at the Top" for background information. Had he done so, she insisted, "you would not be so surprised in hearing the name," adding: "By the way, if you do not have the book I shall be glad to send it to you." He learned the fact - which must have sounded like science fiction - that Walska acquired the Grindell name when she married "the Englishman who died before I married Mr. B. and as they always ask the maiden name, and as I was christened Anna and not Ganna, that explains the two names." Displaying impatience, Walska asked Rice, more in sorrow than anger: "When will our correspondence entitled Citizenship be finished?"

Finally, her mood swung from despair to triumph when able to inform him: "Just two words to tell you that finally I got this certificate!" Morgan's Bank and the Champs-Elysées theater in Paris were both waiting for this hard-won document, but he had to infirm her that American law did not allow a copy to be made.

Visitors to Lotusland during the summer of 1955 could hardly miss Ralph Stevens' latest creation dominating the grassy area beyond the parterre: a huge horticultural clock, twenty-five feet in diameter with Roman numerals. The moving hands were planted with small cacti, and the domed face edged by concentric circles of other succulents representing the twelve Zodiac Signs. It may have looked like an abandoned flying saucer - UFO sightings were popular at the time - but Walska was more than delighted with the result, particularly when somebody told her it might be the largest floral clock in the world.

The surrounding landscaping could now be completed after a group of topiary animals was installed to tread the narrowest path between good taste and vulgarity - in other words, pure Ganna.

The journal of the Cactus and Succulent Society of America gave a detailed account of how Lotusland looked during the late 'fifties in "a picture travelogue to convey what words fail to do." A black-and-white photograph shows the broad sweep of the main driveway planted with massed *Agave attenuata* - "as many as 2000 plants were used" - and in the background are well-developed tree aloes standing out dramatically against a wall of foliage. "Madame Walska," the authors wrote, "keeps in mind a massed effect, not a straggling plant here and there, but the largest and most mature plants she can obtain are arranged in one of the finest landscaped estates in the country." The planting of specimen cacti around the main house by Lockwood de Forest, had climbed to roof height by now - forty feet - and a host of flowering golden barrel cactus (*Echinocactus grusonii*) flourished at ground level, looking like a colony of alien life forms - a botanical version perhaps of little green men who'd decamped from the 'flying saucer' of a floral clock nearby. The journal noted that planting of this kind required an understanding of their needs: "Some like the heat and warmth projected from the stucco walls of the house. Others need the protection by partial shade while some thrive in heavy shade with ferns and rain forest plants."

With a network of advisers and suppliers, the Lotusland estate increasingly mirrored Madame's singular personality. But after the floral clock and supervising some further landscaping, Ralph Stevens retired, leaving her to search for a replacement, which proved to be another problem. Many were called, some hired for brief periods, but her reputation as a demanding employer meant that nobody stayed for long, either quitting or being fired. Ganna despaired of ever finishing the gardens, forced to assume the role of head gardener herself, ably assisted by a devoted staff which somehow developed a fragile coexistence with the boss. Once again, she had to face the fragility of life on hearing that her long-serving friend, confidant and attorney, Phelan Beale, had died at the age of seventy-five after a long illness.

The Santa Barbara press quoted her in June, 1957 saying "I am doing this because I am weak and stupid," and she wasn't referring to toiling under the hot sun for hours every day, but treading the boards again in a local production of the Moss Hart and George F. Kaufman comedy *You Can't Take It with You*. Ganna's cameo appearance of a Russian grand duchess came during the third act, which allowed her to leave home at 9.30 p.m. - three hours after her normal retiring time - ready-dressed for the role in tiered ruffles, a purple and lavender feather boa, and a Mr. John hat featuring ostrich tips. She had arrived at the Lobero Theater's green room for the dress rehearsal followed by Walter, her chauffeur, carrying a huge tray of blinis and fake caviar to be used as props in the production, complaining that it was barely ten days before her niece's wedding and she was preoccupied with endless weeding to make the estate look perfect for the reception.

While waiting for her cue, Walska fidgeted with the feather boa, wondering whether director Frank Fowler would prefer it, or perhaps the beige-and-white, or the black-and-white versions brought along as replacements. She'd been persuaded to give up her valuable time at this significant family moment because of being required simply to look suitably aristocratic and speak a few lines in a thick Russian accent, which was not acting at all because she'd never forgotten the Russian learned at school. "To this day," she revealed, "when I want to count quickly, I do it in Russian." Taking her cue on first night, Ganna cast aside the boa altogether, hitched up her gown, donned an apron and pretended to cook her blinis on stage, according to the script. She loved being in the spotlight again, and audiences adored her all-too-brief celebrity appearance.

A casual visitor to the estate would never have recognized the old woman in peasant garb working in the garden from dawn to dusk as Madame Ganna Walska, the chatelaine of Lotusland, currently starring at the Lobero Theater. But nothing pleased her more than providing an unrivalled setting for the celebration of her niece's wedding to Mark Addison Bacon of Pasadena. Initial plans involved hundreds of guests at teas, dinner dance showers and the customary formal dinner following a church rehearsal. There had remained the question of invitations to the ceremony itself because Montecito's Our Lady of Mount Carmel church could accommodate only 250 people, and who they were, and how many were invited to the Lotusland reception became a family issue. That settled, on the Saturday afternoon of June 22, Lotusland's big moment arrived with pink blooms floating on the lotus pond, matching the hues of the pink rock driveway and the pink two-storied main house, framed by its impressive display of towering cacti. When the great iron gates swung open for the reception, all was sweetness and light as Montecito became a Mecca for guests from all over the world to celebrate the happy occasion.

Walska had wanted her new zoomorphic topiaries from the Osaki Plant Zoo in Los Angeles to be in the ground for the wedding, but the landscaping had not been completed and, still in their delivery tubs, the shrubby creatures in the shapes of elephants, horses and bears were stationed around the horticultural clock, becoming a talking point for guests. After her good time in *You Can't Take It with You*, Ganna further committed herself to the Santa Barbara arts scene by sending a check for $3,840 to complete the amount needed for a new electric switchboard at the Lobero Theater, replacing the original one that had done sterling service since 1924.

GW full bloom

The late 1950s saw Madame enjoying the undoubted pleasures of living in leafy Montecito, though life rarely remained settled for long because there was always much unfinished business. A pressing matter was her New York house, now in such a poor state of repair that neighbors threatened legal action. One of them was

Louis Pierre Ledoux, living at 1205 Park Avenue, who'd informed Alfred Rice by letter at the end of 1957 that the front door of Madame's property was ajar and a grill over the cellar window broken, allowing anyone to enter. She instructed the attorney to look into the matter which, presumably, he failed to do because Ledoux wrote again in March, 1958, after gangs of kids had been seen coming out of the property, after leaving the floors strewn with paper and presenting a serious fire hazard if anyone smoked in there. "It is an invitation to vagrants, or criminals who are looking for someplace to hide," Ledoux wrote. Ganna had no intention of living again at 101 East 94th Street, corner of Park Avenue, or wanting to see what had survived the break-ins, instructing Rice to make arrangements for its sale. An offer of $116,000 was accepted in March, 1959 and the transaction was closed four months later with a developer intending to demolish Dr. Fraenkel's once-fine town residence and erect nondescript apartments in its place.

Links with Ganna's past were gradually disappearing, and none was sadder than the death of her brother Leon on June 2, 1959 at the age of sixty-eight. His closest relatives - wife Marysia, daughter Hania and son Tadeusz in Warsaw - suffered intense private grief, though Ganna showed little outward emotion, having made it perfectly clear that she lived for the present, and her present was the future. But when a precious part of her life was lost, like dear Leon, it was replaced by something new at Lotusland, as if balanced by the natural order of things.

- 29 -
Cactus and Codicils
1959-1965

For the first time in more than forty years Ganna Walska was left without a home of her own in New York City, though she kept an apartment at the Hotel Dorset on West 54th Street during the late 1950s for occasional visits to the opera, meeting friends, attending to financial business - and affairs of the heart. One romance was with Richard Gentry of Delaplane, Virginia, who also used the Dorset as his New York base, spending time in her company, and squiring Ganna to concerts and Broadway shows, like the smash hit *The Sound of Music*. She refrained from commenting about his taste, though "Climb Every Mountain" might have struck a chord or two with her if she listened carefully to Oscar Hammerstein II's uplifting lyrics in the musical. When they were apart, Madame communicated with Gentry through rather formal cables, as she tended to do with admirers:

"I Must Thank You Again For Your Kindness During My New York Visit. Kindness Of The Heart That I Appreciate Above Other Human Qualities. May All Blessings Be Yours."

He, on the other hand, produced handwritten notes full of passion addressed to "My dear, beautiful Lady" or "My very dearest," suggesting theirs was a rather one-sided attraction:

"I have just laid aside the books you entrusted to me for reading. If you were here now, I would take you in my arms. I realize now that I must tell you that I love you. You must know that, surely, or you would not have shared a part of your heart with me . . . When next I speak to you and say, Good Morning or Good Night, I will be saying I love you - I love you."

When it was time for Ganna to return to California he wrote:

"You've been busy packing and I have become panicky about the favor I requested. So today I acted on a pretext and had a maid bring me your drinking glass. She was going to put one in its place, however, but I wanted you to know that your 'stem ware' is in my hands – my lips placed where your lips had been – and my thoughts with you."

At the age of seventy-three, the old chemistry still worked for Ganna with bewildering ease. In March, 1960, however, the manager of the Dorset announced that her preferred apartment - number1605 - had been leased on an indefinite basis, and invited

Madame to select another suite for her occasional visits. This led to severance of all New York ties, which were becoming increasingly expensive and time-consuming, hindering her work at Lotusland and she retired to Montecito, a long inning as a femme fatale almost over, after receiving a birthday telegram from "RG " (Richard Gentry) offering,

"Tenderest Wishes For You Today And Every Day And My Love Always."

Ganna would now concentrate all her energies on the estate, and settle the remaining business affairs in France.

Following the horticultural clock and its attendant topiary, the next big projects at Lotusland were to establish a crescent-shaped aloe garden and the renovation of an old kidney-shaped pond dating from the 1920s to become an outrageously theatrical pool. Aloes are succulents native to Africa and Madagascar which bloom in California during the winter months and she liked the idea of a splash of color during the drabbest time of the year; the pond, however, was something different. It would incorporate little islands formed from tufa stone to look as if they were floating on the milky-white surface, while fountains were to be fashioned from giant South Pacific clam shells, adding the sound of splashing water to a fairyland scene. Reliable Oswald da Ros was the mason-contractor for the job, and a keen observer of Walska's work methods which others regarded with suspicion. "One of the reasons we got along well," he remembered, "was that I was not very 'Yes, Ma'am.'" The Madame, as he continued to call her, demanded unreasonably fast progress, impatiently supervising the work wearing the same old smock with pocketed apron and a threadbare sweater. Da Ros was fully aware that his employer's bubbling self-confidence resulted from seeking answers to garden problems from several sources: all needing to match before she would proceed on a project. A gentle and patient man as well as a skilled organizer, he also recognized there was always a way to get a job done, even when something seemed technically impossible at first. "We're building the roof before we have the foundations," he sometimes had to tell his employer. "What do you mean by that?" she would respond, pretending not to understand. Both understood that explanations were unnecessary.

The outrageous shell pool proved to be one of Da Ros's most difficult challenges because Walska was adamant that it be constructed within the existing paths of the esstate, and its color was to be white. Then she preferred green, before reverting to the original choice. "Fortunately," he explained, "on my advice she brought in Joe Knowles to help her and arrange how we were going to set the abalone shells together as groups and designs, using the large clam shells as the waterfall." These were already at Lotusland, but da Ros had to collect the others, which was not too difficult in Santa Barbara with its abalone fishing industry. Confirmation of Walska's satisfaction with the result was having her driver clean the pool every day so that its chlorinated water sparkled with dazzling brilliance, as if illuminated from below.

Gardener Bruce Van Dyke worked at Lotusland for many years, often bearing the brunt of Madame's insistence on speed and unconventional planting. "Every plant had to be positioned correctly," he recalled, "everything had to be interesting." He accepted that she liked height because of poor eyesight, "which horticulturally is the best thing you can do, especially if you have a fungus situation from too much watering. But she never considered that; it was just one of those circumstances that happened to work in her favor." Van Dyke remembered the time when he inadvertently damaged a precious plant and dumped it on a distant part of the estate known by his colleagues, for obvious reasons, as Siberia: "Two weeks later she came up to me, like a dog with a bone. She'd found it. There was no hiding place at Lotusland with her in the garden all the time!"

However much she wanted to concentrate on her creativity, Ganna's attention was frequently deflected from the job in hand. After protracted negotiations, a buyer was found for her Penthouse of the Gods property - fifteen years after Bernard's departure - and attorney Rice was asked to deal with yet another matter, though he thought it frivolous. He made the mistake of overlooking Madame's pride in her acquired name, which she insisted being defended when used for a popular cartoon strip, George Wunder's "Terry and the Pirates" which was syndicated nationally from New York, and she saw in the *Los Angeles Times* delivered daily to Lotusland.

Rice's stern, but not altogether convincing letter to News Syndicate Company Inc. drew attention to the character named Madame Walska "of which my client could not be proud." He explained that she was at one time married to Harold McCormick of the International Harvester Company and was known as Ganna Walska McCormick, but after his death and to the present time preferred to use only the name of Ganna Walska. Like a naughty terrier snapping at her attorney's heels, she refused to ignore the cartoon strip, complaining that he had failed to stress that Ganna Walska was her professional name:

"McCormick or any other has nothing to do with that. I was Ganna Walska when I arrived here and am still, no matter which name had husband. There is only one Madame Walska, therefore what they say, good things or bad things, it is about me."

Fortunately, the fictional Russian ballerina bearing her stage name soon disappeared from the strip, and Rice returned to more pressing matters, such as his client's state and federal taxes, and looking into an odd request to find out if she was eligible to receive old age benefits. His advice was that the State of California only paid if a person was in need, defining the needy as worth less than $1,200. As far as social security was concerned, Madame did not qualify because she was neither employed nor had made any contribution to the social security plan. Somehow, she would have to muddle along on the income from her invested millions.

Walska was never mean with money if she thought it was for a good cause, however, and one was contributing to a fund for new additions to Our Lady of Mount Carmel church in memory of her late brother. The pastor, the Rev. O.B. Cook, wanted to raise $90,000, suggesting that an appropriate memorial to Leon's memory might be pews, chandeliers, a pipe organ, "or some other necessary furnishing." Ganna asked her head gardener, Gunnar Thielst, to find out about pipe organs and discovered that the H.T. Bennett Music Company of Santa Barbara (advertising slogan: "We Sell Happiness") had a Hammond organ and associated amplification equipment in stock which could be purchased and installed in the church, with walnut cabinets, for $2,768.46. Ganna confirmed her donation within two days to the minister's delight, who told her that Father Patrick Maloney, on sabbatical leave from Notre Dame University to study voice at the Music Academy of the West, would give professional and technical assistance for the new instrument.

A less altruistic gesture, however, concerned Madame's Marc

Chagall painting acquired when living in Paris, whose value had grown over the years with the artist's soaring reputation and auction prices. She had never really liked Chagall's work, with its fantasy memories of Jewish life and folklore in his native Russia, and decided to donate the painting to the Santa Barbara Museum of Art and claim the appropriate tax concession. Alfred Rice obtained valuations from several experts ranging from $55,000 to $60,000, proposing a median figure as the basis for the gift, which would result in a saving of about $36,000 on the next three-quarterly federal tax payment. The picture, in vertical format, 35 inches by 19, was thought to have been painted around 1914 and showed a young girl in profile - perhaps with a disability - clutching a walking cane and seemingly transported, her long hair inset with another, much smaller figure bearing a bouquet of flowers, as if representing the main subject's dream of normality. Titled "Young Girl in Pursuit," it joined other recent acquisitions by the museum on display in July, 1963, placed alongside an early Piet Mondrian and a large Georges Roualt watercolor.

Contrasting with the straightforward negotiations over the Chagall, Walska was no nearer to settling her French properties almost twenty years after the end of the war in Europe. They languished unsold in the hands of the Paris lawyers Coudert Frères who, through lethargy or *laissez-faire*, had achieved little during that time. This weighed heavily on her mind, instructing Rice to terminate their retainer and seek better service from a more committed firm. That was achieved in April, 1964 when Cleary, Gottlieb, Steen & Hamilton rather reluctantly agreed to represent Madame, and the rue de Lubeck property was leased for $7,000 a year as office space for the Citroen company, declining an offer to purchase at the appraised valuation of $300,000.

The once-immaculate Château de Galluis, now almost derelict, was worth little or nothing as a building, though the land value had been estimated at $185,000. An offer was made for $140,000 and Rice thought that his client would consent to a sale if something a little closer to the asking price could be obtained.

The Théâtre des Champs-Elysées was even more of a problem, being owned by a French corporation, with the majority non-voting and voting rights held by Ganna Walska, who wanted the French Ministry of Culture to acquire her shares to ensure that it continued to be used for cultural purposes.

When Rice phoned to tell Madame about the lack of positive moves in Paris she saw red. Never noted for her forbearance, she was convinced of cruel manipulation by the lawyers on both sides of the Atlantic, accusing him of incompetence and collusion with his French colleagues. He found it difficult to explain his actions in a long-distance call, and waited for Ganna's mood to settle before writing a personal note regretting that it should be necessary to justify himself. A further delay in the tortuous negotiations gave her the opportunity to reprehend Rice for a second time, saying how devastated she was that he seemed incapable of separating friendship from business, proceeding to censure him for neglecting her interests and misleading her about prices. This led to an acrimonious long-distance shouting match, followed by the attorney's lengthy letter apologizing for his immature behavior over the phone and insisting that he had never committed any misrepresentation. "Most important," he declared, "the strength of my efforts for you is my fondness, affection and love for you" - a sentiment that so many men had been led to express in the past, and which she graciously accepted.

Walska turned out prodigious amounts of correspondence, much of it couched in her idiosyncratic speech left uncorrected by the French secretary, Suzanne de Marquette, complaining that she constantly had to "write, write, write, to explain, explain, explain." Now, with a pressing need to settle the future of her French properties, as well as attending to the eventual fate of the Lotusland estate, Ganna needed someone who could better manage her chaotic affairs and present them in plain English. A small advertisement was placed in the Santa Barbara press: "Private Secretary for Estate in Montecito, Mondays, Wednesdays and Fridays. Only Those Highly Qualified Need Apply." An Englishwoman with a Polish name - Patricia Tarkowska - responded to the box number.

Patricia had studied ballet, but was forced to abandon a dancing career after contracting a mild form of polio at the age of twelve, working later in public relations for the Royal Ballet School in London and becoming a personal assistant to prima ballerina, Dame Margot Fonteyn. After the failure of her marriage to a Pole, a friend in Montecito helped her obtain a green card to live in the

United States, working for an antique dealer in Santa Barbara and after developing a chronic bronchial condition, she sought something else - perhaps a part-time secretarial job. She met Walska's niece, Hania Tallmadge (a surname from her second marriage, following the death of her first husband) who mentioned that her aunt might be looking for a new secretary. Hania had hesitated recommending anyone for the job, explaining "She is a very difficult woman, always changing staff because she's so demanding." With some trepidation, Patricia went to Lotusland for an interview.

The housekeeper greeted Mrs. Tarkowska at the kitchen door (only guests were allowed to use the formal front entrance) and her first impression was "What a horrible house! So gloomy." She was ushered into a chaotic office and Madame appeared, all bustling and businesslike, carrying a large checkbook.

"You may sit down and start work."

Patricia was struck speechless by the absence of any preliminary discussions about her experience, what duties she was expected to perform, and the remuneration offered.

"Please sit down. I don't require any references because you come highly recommended by my family."

Completely taken aback, she found herself writing checks for the estate gardeners, whose salaries were weeks in arrears. Too much in awe of Madame to complain, she remembered: "There was no 'Do you want the job?' and I was already thinking I must walk away from this crazy situation.

"Normally I would not expect you to come tomorrow," Madame told her, "but as Friday is a holiday and there are more checks to write, I will expect you here."

Next day, there were many more overdue payments to be made, and then Patricia was asked to take dictation in Madame's broken English: "all back to front and inside-out," as she described it. There was a complicated will to compose, and a letter to the French minister for culture, André Malraux, about disposing shares in the holding company of her Paris theater. To complicate matters, the Lotusland typewriter was a museum piece, its keys constantly jamming because the mechanism had obviously never been oiled. Patricia decided to make a stand.

"Madame, if we are going to work together, I must tell you that it is impossible for me to use this old typewriter."

"What's wrong with it? My secretaries never complained before."

"It's just terrible. I'm sorry, but that's how I feel about my work." There was a hostile pause.

"Very well then, you can spend the time before you return next week looking for a new machine."

The result was an IBM Selectric, and like the manual predecessor, would remain in use long after its planned obsolescence. "The cost was $195, which was a huge amount in 1965, but Madame didn't complain," Patricia recalled.

1960s

Attempting to bring a semblance of order to Lotusland's affairs, whose filing system was stacks of correspondence piled on every available surface - including the floor - Patricia was able to observe her seventy-eight-year-old employer at close quarters: "She was very temperamental, always throwing tantrums. I would arrive at the house in the morning and she'd comment 'Well, we have a very pleasant day - but *I* don't have.' There was always a problem with the garden: something that was not responding to her preconceived ideas." But in spite of advancing years, Madame

393

seemed ageless to the new secretary: "She was such a lively and vigorous person, so much in command of everything, including the poor little Italian housekeeper who was scared to death of her and frequently in tears.

Her new secretary's efficiency was appreciated, and knowledge of the way Polish people thought and acted - having been married to one of them - led to employee and employer finding themselves on more-or-less equal terms. Mrs. Tarkowska sensed that Madame had found peace and harmony with Lotusland: "The garden was her creation and would be her memorial; there was no doubt that she was building it as a monument to herself, although she already felt that time was running out and so much remained be to done."

Walska complained constantly of feeling ill and Patricia suspected that diet was partly to blame - too much butter for one thing - and her widowed sister-in-law Marysia, still living in Green Cottage, prepared mainly Polish-style meals, resulting in rich, heavy food. Madame was hopeless in the kitchen, a legacy of her closeted upbringing and early marriage into the Russian aristocracy, which provided servants to attend to all matters domestic, so that even simple tasks like boiling an egg or making toast were almost beyond her capabilities. Nevertheless, she found it difficult to delegate duties, including household ones, resulting in a rapid turnover of domestic staff. One cook prepared a revealing report about her difficulties at Lotusland to support a claim for wrongful dismissal:

"I know she is old, in pain, bitter, overtaxed and overburdened. And that's why I again and again tried not to take her insults personally but I am afraid that I might really lose my memory if I keep trying to comply with her continuously changing, contradictory, inconsistent, illogical and random orders . . . Once I suggested a toasted cheese sandwich. She was seriously insulted and said: 'I never eat bread.' One day after that she ordered a toasted cheese sandwich and has ordered six since. The same with chicken - 'I never eat chicken,' when I suggested it, then two days later: "Cook a chicken . . ."

The rest of the household followed the kitchen chaos, as museum director David Kamansky noted during an inspection of Madame's Tibetan collection:

"I remember the first time I saw her house it was so remarkably gloomy with about eight hundred objects crowded through it. There were huge banners, large tankas, bronzes and all kinds of interesting things everywhere, but all covered in dust and not well maintained. She didn't

want the housekeeping staff to clean them or touch them. Quite frankly, I think they must have been frightened to death with them because Buddhist art is often full of fierce-looking figures with fangs and teeth and long nails - and sometimes mythological animals that also look fierce, called protector deities. Madame Walska knew that, and so the house was full of these images which were supposed to ensure protection against evil spirits."

He was sure that her main interest in the collection related to the Buddhist concept of nirvana - the supreme enlightenment that came through the right vibrations from displaying these objects.

Put the House in Order
1966-1972

Madame Walska wanted the Lotusland estate to remain intact after she was gone. Her first inclination had been for the family to take control, suggesting that her niece accept the responsibility. "My aunt was always changing her mind," Hania recalled. "At one early stage she left the whole thing to me, and then to my father. The reason she withdrew it from him was presumably because he did something to annoy her." Hania later declined because of family commitments, and the fact that Aunt Andzia's scheme required her to reside at Lotusland. "I guess I was too young to devote myself to the estate," she said. "But she was furious." That left as family, sister-in-law Marysia and half-brother Edward in Chicago. He was keen to take control, though Walska was not entirely comfortable about him. A stopgap solution was to follow Alfred Rice's proposal for a foundation, and that had been formalized in 1958.

In April, 1959, Ganna dictated and signed a will appointing Rice as one of the executors and trustees. It included several generous bequests to close friends and associates, together with the specific instruction that her body should be concealed from view after death, taken immediately to a specified mortuary and cremated: "The ashes placed in an urn in my bedroom at Lotusland." No one would be permitted to view her remains and there was to be no funeral service. The executors were also instructed to publish Walska's manuscript "My Life with Yogi" to help others better understand Eastern teachings. Her stated wish for the estate was:

"Lotusland shall continue to exist and be maintained for the extension of intelligence and knowledge concerning the growing of specimens of cacti, trees, shrubs, flowers and succulent plants as presently done by me in Lotusland, and to make the gardens available to universities, colleges, botanical societies and study groups, and all persons interested in horticulture, all without profit."

Ganna had worried about the foundation's status over the years, and during one of Rice's regular visits to Santa Barbara asked him to arrange the appointment of an executive committee to ensure a seamless transition after her passing. He thought it unnecessary, and while trying to resolve complications with the French properties, nothing further was done, prompting Madame's tetchy rebuke: "Evidently the day you were here your memory was left in New York!" Then, in November, 1967 on another of her bad days, Walska's patience snapped and she dictated a short, sharp telegram to "Alfred Rice, Esquire." In New York:

"For Two Years You Are Unwilling Follow My Instructions About Foundation Or Sending Knowingly Unlawful Papers. Cannot Tolerate Any Longer Such Mismanagement. Bid You To Send Immediately All Foundation Papers That I May Direct It In Accord With My Wishes. Ganna Walska."

This tested their long relationship to the limit. Rice relinquished all responsibility for the foundation, including the preparation and filing of its annual return for income tax exemption, and attached a personal note couched in rather glacial terms: "I am sorry that you have reached a point at which you knowingly and purposely accuse me, unjustly and ruthlessly, of a most serious charge against a lawyer - that of preparing 'knowingly unlawful papers.'" He pointed out that he never sought to influence the foundation's direction because, as constituted, there was nothing to manage since it was attributable entirely to Madame herself. Rice added some words of warning: "I should also like to point out to you that to falsely accuse a lawyer of doing an unlawful act is a libel and I would thank you not to repeat it."

The matter was let rest for a week before Ganna repeated her claim of maladministration: "If there is any other word for such acts than mismanagement I don't know it being a foreigner." She played upon Rice's sympathies by adding: "Being near eighty years old [that milestone was passed five months previously] and being not well at all, it is my duty in order for my successor and not at all for doing it, as you say, purposefully to accuse you . . . I could write much more about this subject . . . but if description of those facts are not satisfactory enough to you I may amplify and stress my only desire is to leave Lotusland Foundation in as perfect order as possible."

Reason prevailed after a truce was called, and it was business-as-usual for attorney and client as Walska, accepting that time was getting ever shorter, knew she must press ahead in the garden. The need for urgency was jogged by news of the death of Katharine Dexter McCormick at her Boston mansion in December, 1967 at the age of ninety-two. She was the widow of Harold's manic brother Stanley, and the last direct link with the longest and most compatible of Ganna's six marriages, as well as the end of an era for the McCormick clan. Katharine had lived in Santa Barbara since her husband's death in 1947, supporting the Museum of Art, the Museum of Natural History, the Cottage Hospital and the Unitarian Church, all benefiting from her estate valued at more than eleven million dollars. The paths of these two remarkable women rarely crossed, however, though Madame, in the throes of planning the future distribution of her own assets, was interested to note that the Planned Parenthood Federation of America received half a million dollars from Katharine's will, and the bulk of the money - with no children or close relatives - went to Katharine's alma mater, MIT. There were lessons to be learned here, and Ganna was spurred into speedier progress at Lotusland before it was too late.

She supervised the planting of a "forest" of Australian tree ferns on the western side of the swimming pool, and during 1967 hired William Paylen to create a fern or shade garden around the area to welcome visitors entering from a parking area on the edge of the estate. Paylen, a Dutchman born and raised in the East Indies on a plantation managed by his father, developed an early interest in horticulture, not with the native tropical plants of Java, but imported exotics like zinnias, gladioli and tulips. He was sent to Holland to finish his education with the intention of becoming a plantation manager himself, gaining a degree in agricultural engineering just before the war started, but after becoming cut-off from his family, decided to try his luck in California, which led to a successful career in landscape design in and around Los Angeles. Walska read about his method of planting ferns and invited him to a Lotusland event for the International Palm Society. She mentioned to Paylen that a bright young man from Kew Gardens in England was appointed as her estate manager, but had proved to be unsuitable and left. He protested that someone with that sort of background must be worth a longer trial.

"No, I always like grey-haired men with experience."

"But Kew Gardens, Madame, they're the best."

"Oh, no, he lasted three months."

Paylen agreed to consider developing her fern garden, but after inspecting the site found it disappointing with only a group of tree ferns adjacent to a dump. He told her he would think about it.

"You're not going to leave," Ganna insisted.

"Well, Madame, I don't have pencil and paper with me."

"I have everything ready for you in the house."

He recalled, "She gave me five minutes to draw up a kind of quick design, approved it, and I could start."

But soon there were difficulties. When excavating the new swimming pool in 1947, much of the waste was piled up around the existing trees, including large oaks, with no concern for the effect on their root systems. In addition, pittosporum and acacia grew throughout the area and needed clearing before Paylen's plan could be realized, included a network of meandering paths to be covered with pink aggregate and edged with decorative tufa rocks from Lake Mono. When they were delivered, Walska phoned to say she hated them. Most professionals would have found it impossible to accept these restrictions, including a demand that nothing be removed from the site. But with inherent good humor, gentle tolerance, and knowing that his client knew little about the rudiments of planting, William Paylen waited until Madame retired for lunch and then instructed the nursery workers to get chain saws and cut down any obstructions to make way for planting delicate begonias, patience and ferns.

On one occasion, Madame Walska asked him to accompany her to a local fern show where she saw several that she coveted.

"Mr. Paylen, try to buy this for me, and I also want that one over there," she ordered.

"Madame I couldn't do that. They're the owners' favorites; the last thing they would want to do is part with them."

To prove she was serious and prepared to go to any lengths for something she wanted, Walska pointed to the purse she was carrying, which was stuffed with hundred dollar bills.

Making conversation, Paylen asked how far Madame thought she walked around the estate, and she replied, quick as a flash, "Eighteen miles a week," pulling out a pedometer to show him. After completing the fern garden - which she loved, in spite of the rocks - there were discussions about constructing a large conservatory and starting a bonsai collection, but neither eventuated and William Paylen was left with tender memories of her working away in her garden wearing a "kangaroo pouch" apron containing small gardening tools, and sporting an old straw hat that started life as a Mr. John creation for Hania's wedding and proceeded to disintegrate so that, while working, he thought Madame looked like a witch.

Another project was a pebble mosaic for the parterre, with Walska asking Oswald da Ros for a flame motif.

"I don't know about that," he responded, not being a designer himself, "But you already have a man on your staff who can do it."

"And who would that be?"

"Jim Minah, who waters the geraniums. He's an art major."

Da Ros recalled: "So Minah designed them and I had to find pebbles in all the required colors, but some were unavailable and I devised a way of making my own by coloring them and tumbling the stones in a cement mixer; I'd never done that before. The Madame asked for a price and I took a figure out of the air, but when the job was done it came out double what I'd estimated." Walska was usually a prompt payer, but two weeks went by and no check appeared in the mail.

"Madame, can I be paid for the pebble work?" he asked when next they met.

"I'd been waiting for you to ask," she responded, handing over the check immediately, and commenting with a twinkle in her eyes, "We all make mistakes, don't we?" Ganna had been carrying it in her gardening smock all the time."

After sporadic progress earlier in the decade, the 1960s ended in a flurry of activity with the largest and most expensive project of them all to date: the Japanese garden. It involved a big earthmoving operation: another job for Oswald da Ros. When Madame asked him to discuss her latest scheme he found that she had plans from three different designers unrolled on her table, admitting that they meant nothing to her.

"How are we going to build this Japanese garden I want?" she asked him in despair

"You've got the expertise right here on your staff: Frank Fujii." He looked after her topiaries at the time.

"Frank can do this?"

"I'm sure he can. His father was a Japanese landscape architect. In fact, I worked with him on several gardens at Ojai."

Kintsuchi Fujii arrived in America in 1904 and helped to create the Japanese garden in San Francisco's Golden Gate Park at San Francisco. Da Ros recalled: "So between Frank, the Madame and myself the project at Lotusland evolved more or less as she wanted it, and whether rightly or wrongly, you did not argue with the Madame."

It was inevitable that the scale and complexity of this new venture would produce problems, even with experts on the job. Da Ros remembered: "We were constructing the waterfalls and appropriately, considering the Madame's connection with the company, we had an International truck with a boom on it, but it always seemed to be in the way, preventing her from checking on us. One day she came up to Frank and me, pleading, 'I don't give a blankety-blank if it is an International. Move it so I can see what you're doing!'"

The site began to look more like Nagasaki after the atom bomb than a haven of Oriental tranquility, and according to Frank Fujii there was no specific plan, "We just started from one location and worked our way through, depending a lot on what Madame liked." He recollected that the area was mostly filled with palm trees, devoid of any planting, with a muddy pond sitting in the middle. After Jim Minah's success with designing the parterre mosaics and a pelargonium terrace behind the main house, his talents were employed to create an island for the center of the proposed lake. All the stones and boulders for the landscaping were brought in, many coming from near the wine-growing and tourist city of Temecula in southwestern Riverside County, from where they were transported 180 miles to Lotusland. Fujii estimated they carried about 850 pieces, some weighing two to three tons, "In fact, one was so huge that it took two days to bring it through, because we couldn't move that stone through these little towns along the way without a permit."

Ozzie da Ros had to devise strategies as they progressed, facing constant compromises. Everything needed to be dragged in by tractor to the center of the estate, and a raft was constructed to float the crane truck on the pond where the island was to be formed. By his own description, it looked like a battlefield, and Lotusland's

401

owner was not amused, though unfailingly friendly with the workers on his team. Frank Fujii regarded Madame Walska as a gracious lady, but with his formal Japanese background, found her refusal to accept any kind of normal courtesy, such as opening the car door or stepping aside to let her pass, hard to understand.

Da Ros refused to carry out Madame's wishes only rarely, but when the stone torii gate leading into the Japanese garden, salvaged from another Montecito estate, was placed on a platform rock projecting into the driveway, she insisted that it be cut to align with the curb.

"I just won't do it; this is the way it's meant to be set," the contractor insisted.

"I'm glad you didn't cut that stone," she admitted to him two weeks later.

On another occasion, when Walska thought that a single, flat stone bridging the stream running from the waterfall into the pond was too small, Ganna ordered a larger replacement, though it had to be trucked all the way from San Diego County.

In time, the garden would become dense with massed rhododendrons, camellias and azaleas, with its pond attracting a variety of wildlife, including turtles and frogs, green and great blue herons, wood ducks and belted kingfishers. Its site in a hollow, insulated from traffic noise, acquired a simple serenity suggesting a place for meditation, and became a focal point for Ganna's daily walks around her domain. She was delighted with the work, even if the garden was obviously more Japanese in spirit than appearance. William Paylen thought it was because few were prepared to contradict her: "She wanted to have incorporated a lot of plants which didn't belong there. So it was not true Japanese."

"Why didn't anybody correct me?" she asked him when told this.

"Madame, they were afraid of you."

Da Ros admitted: "We did let her have a lot of her own way in the Japanese garden - not so much with the stones, but with plants. If a camellia came into bloom, it had to be put right where she could see it; it should have been in the background, but she wanted it put next to the path. The Madame would scream out: 'I want to see it! I want to see it!'"

Walska's half-brother, Edward, from her father's second marriage, ran a business based on herbal remedies in Chicago, and kept in touch with her by mail over the many years since he'd failed to make contact when a penniless student in Paris. They became closer after paying a visit to Lotusland in late 1969, when he was able to see for himself the extent of his half-sister's affluence. Edward's own life was fragmented and financially difficult, but he retained Polish connections and kept Marysia and Andzia informed about their obscure family members. His communications tended to be inconsequential, however, like telling Ganna of his intention to buy a television with the Christmas check she'd sent him, or complaining about the bitterly cold weather in Illinois and dreaming of living somewhere warmer, such as California. In one letter, he said he had managed "to take care of the loose ends" among his affairs by buying a building on North Milwaukee Drive; it had a shop front downstairs and a four-room apartment in the rear for him. Above were two more floors, each with a six-room apartment, which he intended to rent.

During one of her lawyer's regular visits to Santa Barbara, Walska said she would like to help Edward with his new property and asked Alfred Rice to obtain details of the mortgage. His letter to Edward reminded him that "Madame never discloses her affairs to the family, and would you, therefore, respect her wish." Edward was "deeply moved" by the offer, enclosing a copy of his $18,000 mortgage, which she promptly paid-off. Ganna's action demonstrated a quirky aspect of Polish personality: abhorring thanks or praise for generosity extended, emphasized by Rice's stern instructions to her half-brother that "you should not contact either by letter or by phone Madame Walska about this. She wishes to speak to you on the phone about a family matter in Poland, but will not call you unless she can be certain that there is no discussion or talk with her about the mortgage."

It took until now for her long association with the Théâtre des Champs-Elysées to be concluded, after being the controlling company's major stockholder since 1923. She could have waited a little longer and probably sold the shares for a reasonable profit, but in a spirit of benefaction agreed, after lengthy negotiations handled by Walther Straram's son Enric, to hand them over to the French government for a token $14,000, clearing the way for a permanent home for the Orchestre de Paris. Ganna would have loved to be at the opening concert of their 1970-71 season under the baton of Herbert von Karajan. It began with Symphony No.2 for strings with trumpet obbligato by Arthur Honegger, a composer who'd been one of the circle of artists and musicians who frequented her Paris salons in the 1920s and 30s. The world's most famous conductor drew sumptuous tone from France's finest orchestra, as the theater she owned for nearly half a century took its place again at the forefront of European cultural life.

When work on the Japanese garden extended into the 1970's Walska became increasingly pessimistic about the value of her International Harvester stock. It served her well for nearly half a century, but had fallen alarmingly, leading to worries about her being able to afford further development of the estate. One solution was to sell some of her fine jewelry for which she had little use now because of rarely dressing up and going out. A sale was arranged at Parke-Bernet in New York, a glossy catalog printed, and 146 lots went on display from March 27, 1971, generating wide interest because of some outstanding pieces offered, even if the buyers had never heard of the owner, who was described as "the Polish opera singer."

The auction took place on Thursday, April 1, with brisk bidding bringing prices above estimate. Walska's famous "Mogul" emerald and diamond pendant, comprising a circular carved emerald weighing about two hundred carats and set with a large rose diamond, went for $54,000. It was chipped, but far exceeded the estimate of $10,000 - $15,000. Her sapphire and diamond necklace set in platinum, with sapphire beads spaced by 477 diamond divides around a rectangular-shaped stone, brought $17,500 - double the expectation. A stunningly simple sapphire, diamond and emerald pendant, incorporating three pear-shaped sapphires weighing 135 carats, sold for $40,000, following its estimate of $30,000 to $35,000.

Now she had ready cash to realize some more ambitious plans in the further reaches of Lotusland, if only Madame could find somebody she trusted to take charge. She was increasingly burdened by arthritis - "aggravated by much too hard work and lack of restful vacation for over ten years" - which affected her ability to "attend and direct my financial affairs, so to speak, through the long distance telephone."

These sentiments in a letter to her long-suffering lawyer revealed that she had appointed a new financial adviser who lived locally. Reginald Faletti was authorized to seek any information he needed about her affairs from Alfred Rice, who accepted the change as a *fait accompli*, though admitting it came as a complete surprise. "I understand your need to simplify your daily existence," Rice responded stiffly on being informed. "You may assume that to any extent that it is possible, I will fully cooperate with Mr. Faletti so as to save your health, your spirit and your energy for the most important work that you are required to do."

"Reggie" Faletti was the senior partner in the Santa Barbara accounting firm of Faletti, Roberts and Price. Formerly a keen tennis player, he had acted in dozens of local theater productions, entertained the troops at nearby Camp Cook during the war, and became a patron of the arts through strong links with the Music Academy of the West, the Lobero Theater Foundation and the Santa Barbara Museum of Art. A love of music and poetry, together with an interest in gardens and horticulture, made him Ganna Walska's natural ally, and, in spite of her New York lawyer's deep suspicions, well-equipped to look after her financial affairs.

A problem shared by all who dealt with her, was that Madame tended to swing wildly between generosity and stinginess: all too ready to aid causes while withholding payments to those who worked hard for her professionally or domestically. Attorneys and housekeeper alike were victims of her mean streak, while less worthy recipients often benefited from Ganna's munificence. Her latest philanthropic gesture was a gift of $10,000 that Edward Puacz persuaded his half-sister to donate to the Royal Castle in Warsaw, which had been bombed in 1939 on Hitler's orders for symbolizing an independent Polish nation. As president of the Polish-American Council of Retired Persons in Chicago, he convinced Andzia that the restoration of this historical monument, once the official residence of Polish monarchs, was a national duty.

This was only the latest in a tally of Ganna's big-heartedness since living in the United States. Other examples went back to 1946 when Albert Einstein, as chairman of the Emergency Committee of Atomic Scientists, wrote her personally, urging assistance in their program of public education "to awaken America to the realization that the whole future of mankind is now at stake." She had responded with a sizeable donation, and to a further appeal in 1948 for funds to press for an agreement on the international control of atomic energy. With Linus Pauling and Einstein on a committee concerned about the fate of civilization itself, Madame felt she could hardly resist doing her bit to help save the planet, and was happy to send off a generous check.

Maria Piscator was another beneficiary. With her husband, Erwin, she founded the Dramatic Workshop of the New School for Social Research in New York, aiming to provide American drama with a new generation of actors, directors and producers through their teaching methods. Benevolence like that covered a wide range of activities and subjects over the years. In 1959, $10,000 went to the Constructive Research Foundation, with offices on Fifth Avenue in New York, described as a nonprofit medical research organization, with Cecil B. De Mille on the board of directors. The Music Academy of the West's 1960 opera production was *Arabella* by Richard Strauss, in which Madame's longtime admirer (and sometime lover) the distinguished Austrian bass-baritone Alfred Jerger had created the role of Mandryka at the 1933 world premiere in Dresden. He came to produce the Academy's performance, and Walska's check for $1,000 helped to defray the costs. She bought a house in Warsaw in 1968 for her nephew, Tadeusz Puacz - categorized as "a one-family, type AC" dwelling - with a down payment of $2,500 and second remittance of $9,250, and the largesse continued by sponsoring a visit to Santa Barbara of the superb Polish National Radio Symphony Orchestra. By the start of the 1970s she decided, however, that her fortune must be spent exclusively on her beloved garden.

New Direction
1972-1976

Ganna Walska's significant contribution to French life through the Théâtre des Champs-Elysées was recognized by the government in 1972 with the award of the prestigious Ordre des Arts et des Lettres. Together with her Légion d'honneur from 1934, it brought to an end to fifty years of propagating European culture. Now, at the age of eighty-five she knew she had to proceed as fast as possible to complete her New World passion, which depended on finding a director for Lotusland.

Ganna could no longer run the estate by herself, but William Paylen turned down the job preferring his independence in Santa Barbara, the young man from the Royal Botanic Gardens at Kew had been sent packing, and his successor who thought he could run the Lotusland herbarium from a comfortable office in the main house and objected to reporting to Madame every morning at 8.30 like a schoolboy, lasted little longer. She was in a quandary of thwarted ambitions until reading the *Cactus and Succulent Journal* with an account of Lotusland by its editors, the cactophiles Charles Glass and Bob Foster. Two sentences fired Ganna's imagination: **"One does not eat lotuses at Lotusland, but one does experience the lotus-eater's dreamy forgetfulness of the outside world. Lotusland is meant to be experienced, not to be documented."**
These were the people for the job.

The thirty-eight-year-old Glass had impressive qualifications, both botanic and artistic. Born in New York City and raised in coastal New Jersey, he came from a musical family whose father, Beaumont, had been first violinist in the Philadelphia Orchestra under Stokowski, and his mother, Lillian, was an accomplished opera singer who performed as a soloist in radio broadcasts. Charles's sister, Virginia, sculpted, and other members of the family had professional opera connections in Europe. Madame Walska would have found that background alone most attractive, but there was the additional bonus of a childhood steeped in the love of gardening and an education that included studying French at the Sorbonne, a year at Yale, a language degree from Columbia University and repertory acting in summer stock. There was even a peripheral connection with her own estate because Glass had come to Santa Barbara in 1958 for his brother's wedding and stayed to watch master classes at the Music Academy of the West given by Lotte Lehmann. He visited Lotusland on a garden tour with his mother that summer, which was his introduction to cacti and succulents en masse.

Walska phoned him soon after reading the article, begging Glass and his business partner Robert Foster to come and work for her, insisting that only they seemed to understand what she was trying to achieve. They were also proprietors of the flourishing Abbey Cactus Gardens - one of the largest and most respected specialist nurseries in the country - together with Abbey Garden Press, established in 1929 and the oldest publishing house specializing in books and magazines about cacti and other succulents. But the thought of giving up their satisfying life to work for the temperamental legend of Lotusland did not appeal. "I well knew her frightful reputation," Charles Glass recalled, "and made excuses why we couldn't come to work for her: among them being the fact that we were totally happy doing exactly what we wanted to do."

Never one to take no for an answer, persuading Charlie Glass and Bob Foster to look after Lotusland became a matter of head-hunting honor for Madame. She strategically bought plants from their nursery and had them supervise their installation, which gave the opportunity to press for a favorable response face-to-face. On one occasion when they delivered clusters of Pincushion Cactus with their white spines and fluffy white wool, she admitted trying to copy the effect at the Huntington Botanical Gardens, established by the railroad and real-estate magnate, Henry E. Huntington, at San Marino.

"Monkey sees, monkey does!" Ganna commented shrewdly.

During another of the partners' visits Glass complimented her on the estate.

"What are you? Hypocrite?" she responded sarcastically. "You tell me it's beautiful, and yet I am trying to give it to you and you say No!"

408

1970s

This set him thinking about the future - or perhaps future failure - of Lotusland, which might rest with him and Bob Foster. If they took over its management, the estate could become a significant botanical institution; if not, they would never know if they had contributed to its fate after Madame Walska's death, when the place might be broken up and sold to a developer. In tediously long phone conversations Ganna explained that an endowment of thirty to thirty-five million dollars would be provided if she could find someone she trusted to take over as director.

Charles Glass admitted that he loved Lotusland for what it was: a visually ravishing, unique private garden, but remained opposed to the idea of becoming Madame's director.

"Our interest in plants," he explained to her, "is totally different and enumerates our dreams and goals: our field expeditions in search of new plant material, the introduction and propagation of new and rare documented material of cacti and succulents, the maintenance of a reference collection . . ."

Hearing this only made Madame more determined to have him run her estate.

"That's exactly what I've been wanting to do," she responded

409

enthusiastically, "but I'm old now and will die soon, and I can't find anybody who understands and can help me achieve these goals. We could combine our collections and accomplish great things together!"

The partners continued to demur because their friend Paul Hutchinson, who had been director of the Botanical Garden at the University of California at Berkeley, had told them that he was going to work for Madame Walska. They asked her casually how things had worked out.

"I don't know! I never see him!" she told them. "Everywhere I go he's been there moments before and just leaves me notes!"

Hutchinson may have been tactless with Madame in telling her that all the plants at Lotusland were worthless because they were not documented, and since there were no pedigrees, should be thrown out and the collection started again from scratch. That radical approach was not well-received, and Hutchinson left.

The same problem would confront Glass and Foster if they accepted Madame Walska's invitation, but after many discussions they decided to take the risk, agreeing it would be better to try and maybe lose, than not to try at all. They planned to commute daily from Reseda on the western fringes of Los Angeles to Montecito, but that proved too onerous and in late 1973 their properties were sold and they moved to Santa Barbara, beginning work in January, 1974. There was a great deal to be done.

Life at Lotusland continued very much as before: alternating between periods of calm and stress, depending on Madame's moods. As gardener Frank Fujii had seen at close quarters, she loathed being helped in spite of increasing immobility, and Glass soon discovered that he had to be surreptitious about it. "I'd piled up a mass of weeds, cuttings and debris on a path," he recalled, "and, seeing her coming in the distance, subtly tried to move the trash out of the way so that she could get by easily - as if it were something I was doing anyway. She saw me and immediately began to berate me for treating her like 'the Queen of England,' and not just another gardener."

"Madame Walska," he insisted, "I would do the same for Mario!' - the little old Italian gardener, Mario Franceschini.

"Mario doesn't have to worry that he's a feeble old lady!" she shouted back.

In similar vein, the Lotusland chauffeur, Walter, was forbidden to be seen giving any assistance to his employer in public. He had been rather proud of her stoic independence when driving Madame to some smart event where the other drivers actively helped their aged charges out of the vehicles. Walter would watch them, standing by smugly with his arms folded across the chest, while Walska struggled to open the door and get out by herself. "I don't work for no cripples or invalids!" he once turned to his colleagues and announced proudly. But now, with Ganna involved almost totally with her estate, and rarely venturing out beyond its main gates, his main job was to clean the swimming pool and aloe fountain every day - rain or shine.

The main house, standing isolated at the center of Lotusland's sprawling acres, was becoming ruled by anxiety and termites: the fear of break-ins by vandals, robbers or attackers, together with a threat from the voracious little pests to Walska's valuable antique furniture. An eradication company worked for months to rid the infestation, filling the rooms cluttered with magazines, books, accounts and correspondence with breathtaking fumes.

Ganna devised a complicated security system, haunted by the fear that staff who'd been fired might return to ravage the garden. Her housekeeper lived in a dormitory attached to the back of the kitchen and was locked out of the main house by late afternoon when the gardeners left for the day. Margarita had her own small kitchen, taking any food she wanted for the night, and in the morning had to phone her mistress to be let back into the house. Patricia Tarkowska remembered: "Madame was like a jailer with a huge bunch of keys, making sure that everything was locked overnight. It was extremely dangerous if there'd been a fire." Only an old maintenance man who lived in Red Cottage far away on the edge of the estate could help in an emergency, and when Walska mislaid her keys, or fell and was not able to reach them, he had to be called to come and break in.

In the strict privacy of her own quarters, where she "got up with the birds and went to sleep with the birds," Ganna was an avid reader, mostly of horticultural journals and interest group magazines. The *Los Angeles Times* kept her informed of social and cultural events, and there was also television which she found hard to watch with poor eyesight, and a radio was kept tuned

411

continuously to news station KNXT. Before Patricia met her employer she had been told about her great beauty, but had found Walska "incredibly plain," overweight with a puffy face, most probably due to an unsuitable diet. After the arrival of Glass and Foster, knowing that the garden was in good hands, Madame's former looks began to return, though Louise, the wife of head gardener Gunnar Thielst recalled that Madame only bothered about her appearance for visitors: "Her dress at home, for as long as I knew her, was the same pair of pants in red corduroy and a hat with just a rim." Having had a Polish husband, Patricia Tarkowska knew something about the national temperament, and watched Madame "storming through life, never seeing any limitations."

Regular visitors to Lotusland - Warren Austin and his companion, the Peruvian portrait painter Mariano Soyer de la Puente, accountant Reggie Falletti, and a few women friends - were given royal treatment, though Walska tended to regard people by their class and Patricia remembered she had a derogatory term for the household staff: "scrub women." Madame was also secretive to the point that nobody outside the inner circle knew her telephone number, and there was no line into the office, which meant having to use the instrument installed in a little alcove with its extension to her pavilion. The house was run on a shoestring, as if its owner were poverty-stricken, with Margarita afraid to buy expensive food to cook, and having to keep account of every cent spent.

Those regarded as necessary intruders were classed somewhere between the extremes of good friends and lowly scrub women. One was a young lawyer named Arthur Gaudi who worked for the old-established Santa Barbara law firm of Price, Postel & Parma. He was asked by Reginald Falletti to visit Madame for discussions about changes to her will, and, aware of her fearsome reputation, was determined to keep their relationship strictly professional by following the honorable and ancient profession of the scrivener: simply recording a client's instructions rather than taking a counselling role. "I carefully stayed out of other matters," he admitted. "Falletti looked after those because they were a sort of quagmire. She was very, very secretive; I don't know that she confided in anyone - except maybe Patricia."

Ganna signed a contract with Glass and Foster guaranteeing job security for at least two years, agreeing that their collection of ten thousand cacti and succulents could be housed and cared for at Lotusland. Having disposed of their businesses in Reseda, Foster sold his family home, and was looking for a property in considerably more expensive Santa Barbara, when Reginald Faletti called them into his office to say that Madame Walska had changed her mind and decided not be constrained by any contract. If they wished to continue being employed by the estate, they would have to tear it up "and work together under mutual trust, or not at all."

Madame was once the joke of opera, and now became dangerously close to being the laughing stock of local horticulture by paying outrageous prices for plants and then, through idiosyncratic planting, killing off a large percentage of them. Charles Glass noted: "She wanted to get just the right angle from just the right viewing position, and to achieve this she would have the gardeners twist, pivot or move a plant so many times that usually its root ball would collapse." A replacement was ordered, delivered and placed where she wanted - or thought she wanted it. After much moving and shuffling, with bemused gardeners standing around watching, Ganna finally gave instructions to dig the hole while she retired to her pavilion. With that job done, she was summoned to supervise the precise position she wanted, but the effect was often ruined because the height was not right, and to her way of thinking less impressive. One time, Glass suggested they raise the soil level.

"Don't raise the soil. Just raise the hole!" Madame ordered him.

Money poured into garden projects, though the new director thought Madame's "safe" ideas of landscaping conflicted with the estate's unique potential because of her penchant for geometric formality, more appropriate to a European garden. Her rigid principles meant that plants progressed from smaller to bigger, short to tall: "smaller at the front and at one or both ends, and taller in the back . . . She also liked borders, and felt they, too, were 'safe,' that is pure, typical, unadulterated Lotusland!" These techniques were most in evidence along the curving drive from the front gates, lined with towering eucalypts. Beneath stood rows of arborescent aloes, and in front, ranks of massed Agave *attenuata*, shorter than the aloes. At the edge sat a border of ground-hugging sedum. In Montecito's benign climate everything flourished, progressively narrowing the drive itself until two wheelbarrows had difficulty in passing, and vehicles had no room to manoeuver. Glass admitted that it looked quite impressive but could see that some plants were suffering: some from poor irrigation, others from nematodes and oak-root fungus. He suggested building a berm (raised terrace) of looser, more porous soil for the Agave *attenuata* to avoid their roots rotting. It meant removing every single plant, trimming the roots, taking fresh cuttings and replacing them in new soil. Walska viewed this work with intense suspicion, and advantage had to be taken of her lunchtime absences to widen the drive surreptitiously. She suspected that something had happened, but liked whatever it was, apparently oblivious to the fact that the driveway had reverted to its original state: twice as wide as before.

While all this activity was going on, Alfred Rice wrote "with love" to her with the news that a long-standing tax case for the years 1964, 1965 and 1967 had been settled in her favor. Instead of having to pay the federal government $101,584.55, with perhaps another $60,000 interest, Ganna need send them only $42,070.98, with interest of approximately $20,000. The unexpected windfall of around $100,000 would help defray estate expenses, especially when Glass was appalled to learn that Madame Walska was prepared to pay $10,000 for a rare cycad she coveted which he could obtain from his contracts for a fifth of that price.

Rice made up their previous differences with a telephone call, saying it was a rewarding experience to be talking to Madame again, and he imagined that the result of his lengthy negotiations with the tax authorities would be warmly received, suggested that his fee of $10,000 was not unreasonable in the circumstances, and requesting payment. Walska let the matter lapse for a couple of months before replying, completely ignoring the substantial saving and accusing him of leaving unfinished business. She refused to send a check, returning his typewritten reminder note scrawled with the comment: "Don't be afraid I am still alive but miserable - that my destiny."

Incidents like that kept everyone on edge and off-balance, generating tensions in what could have been an earthly paradise. Glass recalled, "We had arguments and then we had real fights. The fights were emotionally devastating to both of us. It could take

414

me days to recover from the effects of a few moments of her screaming. I would usually argue when her decision endangered the health of a plant, and usually she would give in after days of refusing to talk to me." He accepted, however, that one of the most dramatic aspects of Lotusland was its bold planting scheme, and was moved when Ganna described her goal as "making a beautiful frame" in which the rarest, most exotic, most beautiful plants from around the world might be displayed.

The main horticultural considerations for the director were the debatable question of aesthetics and the undeniable problem of irrigation: how to let water penetrate the soil effectively instead of running off the steep slopes. Both concerns affected Madame's collection of about five hundred Golden Barrel cacti displayed to wonderful effect outside the main house. As Charles Glass saw it, the aesthetic challenge in re-landscaping the garden was how to use many examples of one plant "and not end up with them looking like a field of corn." A solution was to separate them into clusters between rocks, allowing water to penetrate the hard ground more effectively. He devised a ground cover in the succulent areas of mixed red and purple volcanic gravel which contrasted dramatically with the golden yellow of the Barrels.

Walska was almost beside herself during this lengthy procedure, having to accept that he and Foster, as recognized cactus experts, must know what they were doing because it involved leaving hundreds of Golden Barrels lying upside down, scattered across the courtyard in front of the house, their roots in the air and covered with burlap sacks to prevent sunburn. Madame refused to believe that any plant could survive such treatment.

A major obstruction, however, was her refusal to allow large boulders to be incorporated in the new landscaping until everything had been replaced. Some were sandstone slabs six feet in diameter which needed to be partly buried in the ground for the best effect, which meant using cranes and A-frames instead of trucks and forklifts. While discussing the situation, Ganna came up with an unexpectedly lyrical description: she said she liked a rock "with time on it," meaning a patina of moss or lichens acquired through long exposure to the elements. But she remained wary of the proposed ornamentation because she imagined people saying, "Crazy woman! Garden of rocks, not plants."

415

Discord became the way of life, not only between Walska and her employees, but also among the staff members themselves. Patricia Tarkowska found herself spending much more time at the estate than the originally agreed three days a week, and, after Charles Glass arrived as director, gained the impression that he was running the place instead of Madame. As she said, "Madame always referred to 'her' gardeners . . . then when we got this director, who wanted three gardeners to her one, she referred to them as 'Charlie's gardeners' and there certainly was a difference." It resulted, in a kind of turmoil where most remained compliant - summed-up by one employee who admitted that working at Lotusland was a nice job where "you never had to break your ass," while newcomers would, in the words of the director, want to "get their hands in the dirt" for the sheer joy of gardening.

Patricia thought she understood Walska better than anyone else - certainly better than the new director. What she didn't realize at the time was that, when growing up, his cook and nursemaid, named Anna, happened to be Polish. In addition, his mother had been an opera singer, his brother's professional life was in music, which allowed him to understand and sympathize with at least some of Madame's complex persona. He recalled, "Anna, for instance, could never apologize, never say she was sorry, but if you asked her to do a favor, this was her form of an apology. It was as if accepting a favor was allowing you to be placed in debt to that person, and, as such, it was a very special gift. Madame Walska was a bit like that."

In April, 1975, Marysia Puacz, virtually bedridden and confined to Green Cottage, was taken to hospital and would never return to the estate. Her death cast a pall over Lotusland, making Walska, suffering from arthritis, keenly aware of her own mortality, increasingly worried about getting around with her eyesight failing. When Alfred Rice heard of this, he sent her a pair of reading glasses from New York, and, after refusing to accept them, Walska asked if he wanted them back. "No, just throw them away," he replied rather too flippantly, upsetting her for days. But he continued to be concerned about Lotusland, whose future was by no means assured in spite of its foundation status, and visited Santa Barbara to discuss this and other matters with his client.

When they were together, tensions between them melted;

becoming like lifelong friends meeting again after a lengthy separation. He managed to convince Walska that no one except she could decide on her estate's future, suggesting abandoning the foundation to consider bequeathing the property either to the Santa Barbara Botanical Gardens - with or without the necessary funds to provide income - or will the plants to them, to be removed from Lotusland, and allow the empty property and its buildings to be disposed of by her executors in the usual way. She mulled over the options and came up with another possibility: bequeathing the estate to the University of California, Santa Barbara.

Glass and Foster spent much of the summer of 1975 renovating the Aloe Garden. Almost everything was taken out of the ground, fresh soil introduced and then newly landscaped with many tons of sand, gravel, topsoil, planter mix and several hundred large black volcanic rocks. The work was done by hand to avoid disrupting the neighboring areas, which pleased Walska immensely. In some places, the ground level was raised by as much as seven feet and the spectacular results, incorporating a hundred different species, created a primordial atmosphere in which it would not have been surprising to come across a grazing Brachiosaurus.

Bob Foster took leave of absence to look after the *Cactus and Succulent Journal*, still owned by the partners but having run up $8,000 worth of printing bills, with a threat of closure. After escaping the hothouse atmosphere at Lotusland, Foster realized that nothing would induce him to return - except occasionally to help his partner - because he had a family to look after and valued them, more than the loss of his sanity. By now, they both had a deep insight into Madame Walska's way of ruling her Montecito fiefdom, and Glass started wearing a suit and tie at work. She pretended not to be aware of his motives, half-teasing that he must have another girlfriend - other than her was the flirtatious implication - to explain his sartorial metamorphosis. Ganna knew about power dressing, however, aware that her director's sharper appearance was to gain a more equal footing in their discussions and arguments. "In the future she tended to give me hell," Glass admitted, "but in slightly more respectful terms."

This may have helped during the fall of 1975 when he proposed a brand-new garden at Lotusland for a neglected stretch of the estate that had been a grain field back in the Gavit era. Walska had collected rare cycads for a number of years, and a Cycad Garden would bring them together in an area of broad sweeping lawns, with a koi pond as the focal point. She agreed, and the first paths were laid out, with the work expecting to take three or four years, when it was hoped to be one of the finest and most comprehensive collections of these rare plants anywhere.

Cycads are a type of slow-growing palm with cones instead of flowers - one of the more popular varieties is known as Sago Palm. Sometimes they're called "living fossils," because of belonging to an ancient group dating from before the appearance of flowering plants on the planet millions of years ago. The large and expensive project at Lotusland - some estimated it would cost as much as two million dollars - would prove to be the most harmonious of their collaborations, once problems with the estate workers were overcome, because dissent had become rife among the gardeners.

Glass explained: "Madame was afraid of their jealousy of each other and it is true that everyone around Mme. Walska was always scrambling to get as close to her good side as possible." To combat the situation, she tried to treat them equally, and, with a couple of exceptions, all received the same pay and bonuses. The rule was relaxed only to reward a particularly slack worker with a bonus as a sort of bribe to mend his ways, which was anathema to the director. "I tried telling her that this was having a very bad effect on morale, for there was no incentive to do better than the others." It was not until one of the men claimed that his doctor had ordered him to take time off because he was too sick to work, that things changed. Walska herself phoned his home to find out how he was but there was no answer and she had Glass call his doctor, who said he hadn't seen him recently. This was going too far, and when the worker failed to turn up again after a warning, he was fired. "Morale rose considerably among the remaining gardeners!" the director noted.

The generous side of Walska's nature revealed itself in the wages she paid, with most of the estate employees receiving $472.20 bimonthly, with a couple of the seniors making $494.20; Gunnar Thielst, as chief gardener, received more than $500, and Charles Glass had a salary of about $1,100. There were additional tax-free additions throughout the year: Easter checks of $500, a "Fiesta" bonus in August, $500, Labor Day checks and a Christmas payment of $1,000, as well as the usual additions for vacations. One year, Glass's bonuses totaled $14,000, and yet Madame had baulked at paying Alfred Rice's legal bill of $10,000 for the responsibility of looking after her myriad affairs on two continents - and saving her a whopping $100,000 in taxes.

A more pressing consideration, now she was in a mood to settle her affairs, was what to do with all the artifacts in the Tibetan collection, though a large proportion of the pieces probably had their provenance elsewhere. Experts like David Kamansky would conclude that most were Sino-Tibetan - objects made in the Tibetan style, but coming from China, with many dating from the Ch'ing Dynasty, China's last. He identified the main part of Madame Walska's collection as coming from the old summer capital of the Ch'ing, originally tribal people from Manchuria, but Buddhists in the Tibetan manner. "She would have been horrified to realize this," he said, "because she was so interested in Tibetan philosophy."

When Ganna first considered her collection's future she had wanted to build a museum on an undeveloped part of the estate, but it soon became obvious that planning permission would never be granted in super-exclusive Montecito. She had direct connection with the local art museum through her accountant, Reginald Faletti, who was president of its board of trustees, and convinced herself in an early version of her will that the collection "should be visible to the great public and not hidden in private dark rooms. When I am gone, this wonderful assemblance will be seen at the Santa Barbara Museum of Art." The director, Paul Mills, had different ideas, happy to put her Chagall painting on permanent display and anxious to acquire the best Oriental examples, but had insufficient space to show everything. Hundreds of pieces filled almost every square inch of wall space downstairs in Lotusland's main house, but they did not amount to a uniform collection of Buddhist art, perhaps no more than an interesting group that might be retained in storage by a museum for study purposes.

The question of what to do remained unanswered until a chance meeting in 1976 with one of the workers in Walska's garden. Griffin's Nursery had crews at the estate for about six months of the year for the apparently routine task of lopping tree branches. Arboreal trimming at Lotusland, however, needed the finesse of a surgical operation to avoid damaging or destroying the precious plants massed beneath because Madame insisted on a light once-over, and if another was needed next month, Griffin's experts were called to do it.

A young man named Michael Monteabaro, a member of one of the teams, had recently returned from Nepal and India where, attracted to Buddhism, he collected some art works which were shown at a small exhibition in Chicago. Monteabaro liked working at Lotusland and applied for a permanent job as a gardener, mentioning on his résumé the Chicago show and his Asian travels. To his surprise, Madame Walska wanted to interview him personally. He recalled, "She invited me in and I saw her Buddhist art filling the rooms wall-to-wall and I could tell immediately that they were the real thing. She invited me to wander through the house; I asked if I could return at some time to take photographs, and she agreed."

When he came back with a camera, Walska was interested in his suggestion that the collection be kept intact for use in a psycho-spiritual way, not broken up to be widely scattered. Monteabaro was unable to tell if she knew the importance of some of her individual pieces, but was eager to guide their destiny, particularly when she asked him to categorize them and "do whatever I wanted to do with them." He felt that the collection should find its home in a spiritual place. "It was an amazing situation, completely unexpected," he recalled, suggesting she meet Vidyadhara Chogyam Trungpa Rinpoche, an incarnate who fled Tibet in 1959 and taught at the Dalai Lama's Young Lamas' School in India and later studying at Oxford University before moving to the United States in 1970, establishing a foundation in Colorado. "I mentioned him and she thought it may be nice to bequeath the collection to his foundation. I set up the meeting and it was kind of a done deal." Ganna, however, made no decision about the future of her Buddhist collection.

One chilly morning at the estate, Charles Glass teased her by asking what she thought of the "Polish weather."

"We never say 'Polish,' we say 'Russian weather,'" she retorted. Anything bad we say Russian."

This triggered her memory to talk about her pride in having been Mrs. McCormick because the people in Poland had never heard of the Rockefellers, but knew Harold's name thanks to International Harvester. It explained why she insisted on keeping Lotusland's old International truck in service long after it became a liability. "It was very old and battered," Glass remembered. "We had to have a certain number of repairs done on the premises before getting a license to take it out on the road just to drive it to the shop for fixing a broken axle. When apologizing for the rundown state of the vehicle to visitors, Madame would say she kept it as a promotion for International Harvester to show how long their products lasted!"

An unexpected setback to challenge Lotusland's identity occurred when the aquatic plants that gave the estate its attractive name began dying. Where they had once filled the ponds in high summer with their ravishing blooms, completely hiding the water, the display was now reduced to a few straggly stems struggling to survive. The villains were freshwater crayfish - or "crawdads" as some called them - introduced by Gunnar Thielst several years before. He enjoyed eating eat them, and Madame herself liked to feed breadcrumbs to her "little red crabs."

When the crayfish population reached unmanageable numbers, the lotus blooms were reduced to a miserable token appearance during springtime, and eventually there were none at all. This was a crisis situation that needed some urgent detective work to guard the very name of the estate. "Not only was Lotusland without a lotus," Glass noted, "the rotting roots and stems started to pollute the pond and turn its water into putrefying muck." The problem was referred to Griffin's Nursery who discovered that the lotus was a favorite food of crawdads, and war must be declared on the crustaceans.

At first, the enemy outsmarted all attempts at eradication, in spite of fast-dissipating poison being used, which killed many dozens of goldfish instead, their bloated bodies floating to the surface to cause worse pollution. The smart crayfish simply crawled out of the water and waited on the grassy banks for it to become habitable again. Catfish were introduced to attack the offenders, but the infestation was too large for even the most ravenous fish failed to eliminate them. Charles Glass came up with a scheme for catching them with string, lead weights and fish heads, like his crabbing expeditions when growing up in New

Jersey. "I removed crayfish by the bucket loads, by the hundreds! I'd take them home and boil them for many feasts of crawdads, until my friends and I couldn't stand their slightly sweet and somewhat mushy taste anymore!" This rudimentary method depleted numbers sufficiently for the catfish to keep survivors in check, and, finally, lotus plants were reintroduced to bloom again in profusion.

Marauding crawdads were an unexpected hazard, but the estate remained a constant attraction for hippies and flower children, as well as students from nearby Westmont College - and just about every youngster growing up in Montecito looking for excitement or romantic privacy on moonlit nights. Most trespassers only wanted to see the gardens and boast about being there; some indulged in a little vandalism and theft, though it was rare for valuable plants to be stolen or damaged. Little animal ornaments cast from bronze had been placed on the spigots of the watering system, adding a nice decorative touch to otherwise utilitarian faucets, and they were constantly missing after being 'souvenired,' sometimes as many as nine a night. But there was one spiritual benefit from these nocturnal intrusions when somebody picked a camellia blossom in the Japanese Garden and left it in the lap of the Buddha statue; Walska noticed it while making her rounds the next day and was so taken with the effect that she instructed Frank Fujii to place a fresh flower there each day.

These incursions made Madame fear for her own safety because of spending the nights alone, except for one full-time servant who slept in the tiny bedroom next the kitchen of the main house. Charles Glass suggested raising the perimeter wall of the estate - constructed in the 1920s from cement blocks and plaster - for added security, but Ganna rejected this, claiming it would feel like living in a prison. She did agree to a black chain-link barrier inside the wall to be less visible, but at almost five dollars a foot it proved to be an expensive and largely ineffective way of keeping intruders at bay: the more determined simply climbed over, under, or cut their way through, after scaling the wall.

Patricia Tarkowska's role in the household changed from part-time secretary to full-time personal assistant, with a salary increase and annual flights home to Britain to visit her daughter. It was a mixed blessing, however, as she explained: "I'd barely arrive in

England and she was on the phone - 'Do you remember where that letter is? Did you pay that bill?'" Patricia took over the responsibility for running the house and found herself enmeshed in an endless cycle of hiring and firing housekeepers. "Madame would call me at five in the morning and demand, 'Get rid of this one. Get rid of that one!' The money offered was good, but it was confining, and she didn't want alternate people - just one to do all the cooking and everything else. And she didn't want them to have any time off, so I couldn't find the right person for her."

Walska wanted Patricia to move into Green Cottage, which had remained unoccupied since Marysia Puacz died, but she baulked at 24-hours-a-day supervision. Secretarial duties occupied only part of her time now; there was also planning Madame's diet, "taking control of what she was eating, making sure it wasn't fried and fried again and that the vegetables were freshly brought in and freshly prepared, instead of having them sitting in the refrigerator because the cook complained that Madame always wanted to eat in such a hurry." A steamer was bought for the kitchen and arrangements made with one of the estate gardeners to supply vegetables, with the result that Madame lost weight and looked better. But there lurked a suspicion that people were trying to poison her and sometimes when the paranoia became rampant, Ganna would insist on having food taken away by her doctor and tested, perhaps remembering her long-ago experience of dining with the Baron Fassini in Mussolini's Rome.

In a lifestyle restrained by phobias and ruled by lawyers and accountants, the garden, at least, provided an oasis of calm where much was still to be achieved, in spite of Madame's increasing frailty. In May, 1977, nearing ninety, she fell after walking into a glass door inside her pavilion apartment early one morning and was unable to get up. Gunnar Thielst found her lying on the floor two hours later, having to break the lock to get in and was rewarded for his rescue efforts by being bawled out for the damage caused. Ganna remained in bed for ten disoriented days recovering from what may have been a mild stroke, and then began walking all over the grounds again as if nothing had happened, complaining that the Livistona palms in the new cycad area were in a hole." In Walska-speak that meant they were not prominent enough.

The director had made the mistake of telling her that he planned them as background foliage, knowing that because of being downhill from the path, they could not be the way she liked to look at palms. He was determined to avoid replanting them on "volcanos," as he termed the ugly mounds that were often the only solution to Ganna's demands for more height: "She insisted on this occasion, however, so I went down, lowered the basins around the palms and wired up the leaves a little bit to make them appear higher. She came by later and was delighted to see how much better they looked, assuming, I guess, that in those few hours we had raised these palms that weighed several hundred pounds each and replanted them!"

Glass accepted that Madame rarely planted for tomorrow; unsure of still being around for much longer, she demanded almost instant effects. On coming across a gap in the landscape, she would want to place a tree or bush there to fill the space, overlooking the certainty of subsequent growth, and the need for it to be cut back or moved later. This happened in the Japanese Garden where an uncooperative magnolia produced a magnificent bloom on the wrong side. Ganna had the gardeners bag and ball the offender and turn it around 180 degrees until the flower faced her on the path.

The need to stage elaborate charades became hard to take for a committed professional like Charles Glass, particularly when Walska complained about everyone. The closer the person was to her, the more denigrating she became.

"My secretary is so dumb! She doesn't even remind me about the gardeners' checks." And when she forgot things, it was invariably someone else's fault for not having reminded her. Patricia was overheard at a tense moment to remark: "She's much better today, she's only mean and cranky!"

Somebody persuaded Madame that Lotusland, as a proper botanical garden, should display plant labels, and she ordered some imitation wood-grain panels like the ones used as name plates on office doors, which quickly deteriorated outdoors, becoming faded, brittle, cracked and broken. A lot of money was paid for what she considered unnecessary, refusing to accept that if there were to be labeling at all, it should be done properly. Her response was a petulant, "I don't want to do things right!" but eventually gave-in when her director found an aesthetically acceptable, and more durable, brown plastic. He received grudging approval for his informative labels, with added catalog or plant acquisition numbers, and country of origin, well-aware that Madame thought it a gross waste of his time and her money.

When Glass took leave of absence for a few weeks, intending to think seriously about his future, Bob Foster returned to Lotusland to fill-in as director at a time when Walska decided to have the front entrance to the estate repainted by Oswald da Ros and his men. It was not the mason-contractor's usual line of work, but she preferred to have people around she knew and trusted. Ganna made her way along to the gate accompanied by Foster to see how things were progressing just as the men finished painting it a vivid pink. Wary of showing any reaction for fear of being wrong, she leaned on her two canes and asked da Ros how he liked the effect.

"Oh! It's beautiful, Madame," he lied dutifully.

The workers nodded in mock agreement, and she turned to hear Foster's opinion.

"It looks like a French whorehouse."

Madame became rigid, pushing herself bolt upright on her canes.

"Repaint it!"

June 24, 1977 should have been a time of celebration for one of
Montecito's most famous resident's ninetieth birthday. But there
were no congratulatory telegrams, no cards, and no telephone calls;
it was just another beautiful sunny day at Lotusland with people
performing their habitual tasks. The reason was that nobody knew
for certain Madame Walska's age - including the lady herself -
who had admitted recently to Ozzie da Ros that she really didn't
know within a few years. She explained to him during a rare
moment of retrospection - and misconception - that when she
married her first husband, Arcadie, the son of the Tsar of Russia's
doctor, he had falsified her birth certificate because she was only
sixteen. Ganna assumed it had been rectified after coming to
America, but couldn't be sure, and she must now be somewhere
between ninety-six and a hundred. Perhaps she only felt that old,
because previously she had usually given her age as several years
younger.

Lotusland was closed to organized visits for much of the 1970s
because of the disruptive renovations, renewals and innovations,
but when the estate became presentable again, negotiations began
with Santa Barbara Beautiful for the first big benefit tour in a
decade, and no opera performance ever produced such stage fright
for Ganna Walska. The director compiled a brief guide for the
occasion, showing it to her for approval. She called Charles Glass
to the door of her quarters and stared at him through the insect
screen for a long moment, waiting for her tired old eyes to focus on
his face.

"I feel sorry for you!"

"Why?"

Because you have to do things like this when you could be
writing something beautiful: books, everything, all the time."
Ganna refused to accept his guide because the action of having it
printed struck her as far too commercial.

"We are not a business!"

Maybe not, but every ticket was sold well ahead of the event, and a sense of show business excitement pervaded the flower-scented air of the estate, with the general public clamoring to see what had been happening out of sight for so long behind its pink stucco walls. There was equal curiosity about the owner, who rarely ventured out these days, except by ambulance to the hospital following one of her falls. Madame Walska had been regarded as a recluse for many years, with people driving past the estate's grassy verges planted with cacti calling her the Cactus Lady."

It was like old times - "*Comme avant*," as she expressed it - choosing an enormous pink hat for her comeback.

"It's the biggest I could find to hide my face," Ganna explained self-effacingly at the unnerving experience of people milling around trying to catch a glimpse of her, as if she were a movie legend. Many were eager to take pictures.

"Do you like plants?" she asked one woman pointing a lens at her face.

The visitor nodded.

"Then why photograph me?"

Ganna welcomed another legendary figure, the redoubtable Pearl Chase, longtime civic activist, who was taking the tour in a wheelchair. She had never forgiven Pearl for complaining publicly about the destruction of birds' nests in the palms lining Cabrillo Boulevard along Santa Barbara's East Beach, after Ganna donated $10,000 to the city in 1972 to tidy up their scruffy appearance by clearing a forty-year accumulation of dead fronds. After graciously greeting her former arch-rival, she whispered to Charles Glass, "I wouldn't have recognized her. She must be at least two hundred!"

Leading the tour proved to be a demanding day, and after the last stragglers departed, the gates were locked and the gardens returned to their normal calm. Walska retired exhausted to her pavilion and Glass and Foster called by her door to say goodnight.

"So, were you satisfied?" she asked them.

It sounded like one of her loaded questions.

"Yes, I felt everything went very well," the director answered guardedly. But there were no overtones this time.

"Me too," she responded with a sigh of satisfaction, and shuffled off to bed, remembering an incident half a century before, when she performed *Madama Butterfly* at Wagner's shrine, the Festspielhaus at Bayreuth. While enjoying a simple, open-air *wurstchen und bier* lunch with the composer's son Siegfried and his English wife Winifred, the people around them suddenly rose as one, removed their hats reverentially and waited in silence with transfigured expressions for something that was about to happen. A sudden burst of applause erupted accompanied by cries of "Hurrah!" as Walska saw an old-fashioned carriage trundling toward them carrying Cosima Wagner, dressed all in black and holding open a lace parasol. Amid thunderous shouts of *"Hoch!"* the horse and carriage made a leisurely circuit of the Festival Theater and then disappeared out of sight.

The wonderful old lady, widow of the monumental *Ring* cycle's composer and inspiration for his sublime symphonic poem the "Siegfried Idyll" - a birthday present for Cosima after the birth of their son in 1869 - was too old and too weak to go to performances any more. "But until her death, by thus appearing in her carriage," Ganna noted in her diary, "this glorious daughter of a glorious father [Franz Liszt] helped keep the audience from all over the world in that elevated, ecstatic state which accompanied Wagner's creations during his life and after his passing to immortality."

Madame's own celebrity appearance, at the Santa Barbara Beautiful tour of Lotusland, had some of the mystical quality that Cosima Wagner displayed held that day ago in northern Bavaria. Once it was over, however, her remaining energy was needed to supervise the completion of the new Cycad Garden. Dozens of trees were removed from the site, loads of topsoil brought in, and tractors contoured the terrain. The rocks that Charles Glass, as the designer, considered necessary for its topography would come next, and he gave Walska a note requesting approval for purchasing fifty rough sandstone blocks from Oswald da Ros. She agreed, but after having second thoughts, perversely decided to accept the load but not use it. The rocks were duly delivered, along with a bill for $4,685.

"Couldn't you have brought bigger?" Madame asked the stone mason Sam sarcastically as they were being unloaded from the truck.

"You want bigger?" he wanted to know, in all innocence.

"I don't want any!"

428

Ganna was horrified when the total cost of that exercise was revealed as $13,000 for purchase and installation but settled the account, muttering: "Too many rocks at Lotusland!" Her mood improved when about five hundred precious cycads were moved in, to be grouped by their areas of origin: Asia, Australia, Africa and Mexico. Once in the ground, Charles Glass could bask in what he called "the unadulterated pleasure" of having had the chance to landscape on such a scale with a wonderful collection of rare, virtually irreplaceable plants, making this one of the finest gardens of its type anywhere."

Moving into her nineties without any fanfare, Madame's interest barely slowed despite her greatly reduced mobility, and when the day-to-day business of the estate was not monopolizing her attention, its future filled her thoughts. Whenever she called for her Santa Barbara attorney, Arthur Gaudi, he would drive out to Lotusland, and, forsaking front door formalities, present himself to Madame at the pavilion. Conditions in her large bedroom had become rather squalid, with a desk in one of the bay windows overflowing with papers, and he saw that the place was "frankly not clean." During their meetings, documents were scattered across the unmade bed: "Papers involving me, papers involving the garden, because she was very careful about what was done. She was not one to delegate much authority."

When Gaudi attended to Walska's will, he explained that it was his practice, for the sake of security, to place the originals in his law office safe, but she wouldn't hear of it, insisting on stuffing them into a wooden cabinet at Lotusland. Furthermore, she constantly changed her mind about beneficiaries and how much they would receive, leading to codicils reflecting her financial position, together with the ebb and flow of personal relationships.

In a twelve-page Last Will and Testament, drawn up in August, 1979 and witnessed by Gaudi, there were twenty-seven bequests to individuals, including family members: Mrs. Tallmadge (niece Hania), Edward Puacz (half-brother), Tadeusz Puacz (nephew, living in Poland) and Stefan Puacz (Edward's brother in Poland). They were to receive a total of $675,000 between them. Members of Walska's household and garden staff - past and present - together with a few friends, would share $325,000, in amounts ranging from $3,000 (Miss Pauline M. Finley, former secretary) to

$50,000 (Margarita Zucconi, housekeeper.) There were additional bequests of between $10,000 and $15,000 to four Santa Barbara organizations with strong Walska connections: St. Francis Hospital, the Lobero Theater, Santa Barbara Horticultural Society and the Music Academy of the West. These cash payments, totaling $1,045,000, left the residue of the estate - apart from her Buddhist collection and personal effects for family members - to go to the Ganna Walska Lotusland Foundation, whose executors were named as Edward Puacz, Reginald Faletti and the Security Pacific National Bank. In drawing up this detailed document Arthur Gaudi was surprised at Walska's insistence that fellow lawyer Alfred Rice, who had served her faithfully for many years, would receive nothing – with no mention of two valuable antique chests from her bedroom she had promised him.

Edward Puacz became a regular visitor to Lotusland after fulfilling his dream of escaping Chicago's bitter winters to live with his wife at nearby Goleta in Santa Barbara County, then the largest unincorporated area of population in the United States. Charles Glass suspected that Edward had his own agenda for Lotusland after Ganna's passing: "He would try to catch me and ask questions about the work being done in the gardens, and it seemed to match certain subtle hints about him made by Madame Walska herself. Once when talking to me about Leon Puacz, she said 'Leon, my beloved brother - I call him that to distinguish him from the other one.' On another occasion, she explained that Edward 'is only my half-brother, no - less than that - he's my quarter-brother.' It was perhaps biologically impossible, but emotionally sound, and probably reflected what she really thought of him." Rumors were rife about the man who was seen walking the grounds as if he owned the place, and then spent hours talking to Madame in the privacy of her pavilion. Gunnar Thiele joked with Patricia that he and Edward were "in cahoots" to take over the estate and have Madame committed.

"You'll see a lot of people moving out then!" he added darkly.

"Yes, including me, Thiele!" was her crisp riposte.

Glass predicted that the Cycad Garden would be "one of the greatest achievements of our lives," because anything that followed would be an anticlimax. "Madame would be too tired to embark on any further major developments like that," he noted.

430

"She decided to concentrate instead on 'areas we've neglected to make everything even,' which meant in her language changing things she had grown to dislike over the years, such as the topiaries and the horticultural clock situated off the main lawn."

Those topiaries were installed during the 1950s when there was a renewed interest in the ancient garden art, but Ganna's were a kind of "instant topiary," in which bushes were grown in wire cages of animal shapes or geometric forms, with the shrubs trimmed from the outside. The genuine article could be developed only after a long growing period and required specialized care and artistic pruning. The result was that most of her expensive acquisitions from 1957 died, leaving only their rusting wire forms looking like avant-garde sculptures.

There were also problems with the giant floral clock whose quarter-hours were once sounded by amplified chimes from a carillon installed in a small room of the main house. The gears of the motor were constantly being stripped by young intruders riding the huge hands like a merry-go-round in slow motion, and Walska gave up her battle to keep it working, allowing time to stand still on the estate. The associated Zodiac calendar, formed of colored gravel with movable forms representing days, months and years - like "cookie-cutter molds" as Glass dismissed them – had been one of her showpieces, but in time Ganna came to regarded them as tacky: "Fine for children or at a circus,"

Her will of August, 1979, would change direction as frequently as the wind, with the addition of fourteen codicils. By the time the fifth was signed in June, 1980, Edward Puacz, having been dropped as an executor earlier, was reinstated and joined by "Mrs. Edward Puacz" six weeks later. The ninth variation of November, 1980 had Madame formally gifting her Buddhist art to the Vajradhatu Foundation in Boulder, Colorado, together with $20,000 for transportation costs. She seemed bent on erasing many traces of past when, in the eleventh revision of March, 1981, she left specific instructions for Edward and his wife ". . . [to] come immediately to my house after my death. They must have a key. I request that they take care of Necessary things at my house at that time. I have many important papers at Lotusland. I request that my brother examine my papers and that he destroy my private and personal papers."

Walska specified that business documents were not to be touched

431

and that her clothes and "feminine things" be removed from the house as soon as possible and divided between Edward's wife and Hania. Her niece would also receive one of the two Lotusland pianos, the other to remain in the house together with "the furniture and furnishings in the dining room and parlor and the two cabinets and clock and mirror in the bedroom." She gave the Edward Puaczs and Hania the power to choose the items they wanted, and "if there is a dispute over the choices, my brother shall decide." The three of them also had the right to take away any photographs and portraits, "except the portrait of me which is opposite the entrance to the parlor. That portrait is to remain *with the house.*"

Madame signified her intention of giving $30,000 to Charles Glass in the will, "in appreciation of his work at Lotusland," telling him personally that after she was gone, he must move into the main house. This was incorporated in the twelfth codicil:

"For many years I have been in complete charge of Lotusland. I have managed it and made all decisions concerning it. After my death, it will be necessary for Mr. Charles Glass, the Director of Lotusland, to devote more time to the care and preservation of Lotusland than he does now. It will assist him in his work to live at Lotusland. It is my wish that Mr. Glass live at Lotusland during the time he is employed . . . He may have one person to live in the house with him."

Other details included the right to live rent-free, paying no maintenance expenses, insurance or property taxes - only the utility charges.

But the director was now seen as something of a closet quitter after threats to resign on several occasions, and the prospect of moving into Lotusland to keep his job following Madame's death weighed heavily on his mind. He knew the house needed extensive renovations before anyone could live there in reasonable comfort because Madame had used its rooms for years as a Xanadu-like repository for her vast acquisitions. People passing by on garden tours were shocked to see torn curtains at the windows, and a general air of seediness permeated the place. "Mme. Walska cared nothing whatsoever about the appearance of the house," he remembered. "She did not consider it part of Lotusland."

Inside, the dusty parquet floor of the library was piled high with stacks of old newspapers, magazines and scrapbooks, and the bookcases were stuffed with Tibetan-style artifacts. The faded salon had become a storage area for unused garden decorations and abandoned name plates for plants, watched over by silent portraits of Ganna as a *fin-de-siècle* beauty. The hallway was cluttered with her stone grotesques, kept there to avoid being vandalized by kids in the theater garden, and the dining room with its peeling paint contained all kinds of junk that she refused to discard, including a space-consuming collection of carousel animals. The thought of living there, even if fixed-up, made Glass shudder.

What would be a final codicil - the fourteenth - signed with almost illegible scrawl in November, 1981 suggests that Walska finally lost patience with her half-brother, because she canceled his nomination as an executor. Patricia noticed that his frequent visits left Madame in an agitated state, and decided to listen-in to their conversation one day. What she overheard, confirmed her suspicions when hearing Edward give his instructions in Polish about the estate's future. That evening, she plucked up the courage to telephone him in Goleta.

"Mr. Puacz, after your visits, Madame is always so terribly upset that I'm getting the idea you're trying to persuade her to do something she doesn't want to do."

"What do you mean?"

"You see, I know a little Polish and have the impression you're trying to get her to change her will."

"Well, it has to be changed. We must get her to cancel the foundation."

"Why?"

"Well, there's a large family in Poland; they need to be helped: they need to be brought out. They could live at Lotusland very comfortably."

"Mr. Puacz, I'm sorry to hear this. I hope that Madame Walska will not be persuaded. And I have to tell you that I'm going to inform the attorney what you're up to." Patricia did that, and the fourteenth codicil deleting Edward as an executor was probably the result.

Increasingly frail, Ganna fell victim to more tumbles which caused her to be bedridden much of the time, which led to atrophied muscles through stubbornly refusing to accept physiotherapy. For months she had been too proud to be seen using a wheelchair, though admiring the spirit of those women who could only take garden tours that way because of disabilities. A strong-willed Italian named Rosetta Bortolazzo working at Lotusland for a couple of days a week, finally took pity on her, determined to get Madame outside for some fresh air. She proceeded to lift her, weakly kicking and screaming, into a wheelchair and push her around the grounds to enjoy them for a little while longer, and the sight of Rosetta guiding Madame Walska across the lawn and along shady gravel paths brought a new spirit of purpose to the estate. She reported that Madame especially liked seeing the "Psychiatrical Garden" (Cycad Garden) and the gardeners seemed freshly motivated by Madame's reappearance and beaming smile.

The happiness was short-lived, however, because Rosetta was involved in an automobile accident, and, after making only a partial recovery, was ordered by her doctor to avoid exerting herself in the future. Patricia Tarkowska and Gunnar Thielst attempted to take her place, but their efforts of helping Ganna into the wheelchair turned to near farce, as Charles Glass observed one day: "Mme. Walska screamed at them, waving her cane in the air as they awkwardly and ultimately unsuccessfully tried to get her uncooperative body in the chair. Finally in despair, or simply too weak to support herself upright, Mme. Walska just slowly and limply slithered down toward the ground and the attempt had to be abandoned." It was the last time she went out into her beloved garden.

The public continued to clamor for visits to Lotusland, and in July, 1982 another big benefit tour was sponsored by Santa Barbara Beautiful. Former executor, Edward Puacz, whose wife had been removed from that position in the twelfth codicil to Madame's will, had by now adopted a blatantly proprietorial air when visiting the estate.

"Is it true my sister doesn't know anything about this tour?" he asked Rosetta Bortolazzo.

It was naive to assume that something of this magnitude and expense would happen without Ganna's knowledge, whether or not she remained bedridden, and Rosetta replied in no uncertain terms, telling him that Mr. Glass would never allow such a visit without Madame's approval.

"I know because I sometime read his notes," she added.

Edward decided to boycott the occasion and arranged his own

tour beforehand, which meant that the gardeners had to go around after him to rake paths and drives before the official function started. Two thousand visitors enjoyed seeing Lotusland hat day, and Santa Barbara Beautiful benefitted by $25,000. It was "an impressive enough sum," Glass admitted, "but, as was always the case, the preparations cost Mme. Walska far more than would ever be taken in.

Hania visited her aunt frequently but there was little she could do, except to make sure she was as comfortable as possible, urging her aunt not to worry about anything. "She was agitated about what might happen and her wish was to keep Lotusland as an entity," she recalled. "She couldn't talk, but sometimes her eyes looked frightened, so I told her that everything was going to be fine. It was a long, lingering departure and extraordinarily hard for her not to talk, but if you knew her well you could tell if she was cross or if she was bothered."

Patricia spent more time at Madame's bedside, shielding her from the demands of running the estate. "The house was like the setting for a Victorian melodrama," she remembered. "It was so creepy, so dark, and sometimes if the nurse had a cold, I would stay in the pavilion overnight and absolutely hated it. Occasionally, Madame would need something and there were no lights outside at all; I would say to myself, 'Patricia, what is happening? You don't have to be doing this.'"

Her words reflected a general mood of despondency at Lotusland, with Madame confined to her quarters unable to cope with anything but the simplest matters, and the director with no authority to initiate anything without her approval. Inevitably, more sparks flew between Tarkowska and Glass. With genuine concern for shielding her charge from unnecessary worry, Patricia asked him not to bother Madame with garden matters, but he insisted they were keeping her alive. On one of the rare occasions he managed to see her, Ganna indicated by sign language that she made the decisions: not Faletti, Gaudi, Edward, or Patricia. The director needed to clarify his role with the financial adviser and executor. "I went to Mr. Faletti's office and he patiently listened to me as I recounted my one-sided conversation with Mme. Walska and described her apparent concerns. He told me that without her written instructions he could discuss nothing with me."

As a result of the meeting, Charles Glass returned to the estate and composed a short note: "I hereby authorize you to discuss any and all matters relating to Lotusland and the Foundation with Mr. Glass," reading it over to Walska, who nodded agreement and added an illegible signature with the utmost difficulty. There was no response from Faletti after the document was sent, and the director would see Madame only once again. "She had aged incredibly, her face was distorted, both bloated and shrunken at the same time," he remembered. "Completely laid back in bed, she could hardly hear, no longer tried to talk, could barely nod. She just squeezed my hand touchingly."

Glass wrote to Arthur Gaudi, saying that he wanted it put on record that he was impotent to act in the face of Patricia controlling access to Madame, now that the regular maid, housekeeper and night nurse had departed. There was no reply to this, either; it was not Gaudi's direct responsibility because, as he'd indicated previously, his legal role at Lotusland was as scrivener rather than counselor, and little had changed over the years. Increasingly frustrated, the director made what he admitted was the "enormous mistake of suggesting that Patricia might possibly need psychiatric counseling," departing for the peace of the Aegean island of Samos on his annual vacation in September, 1983. He left, wondering how he could possibly return to what had become something of a Greek tragedy at Montecito - and without knowing the contents of a letter from Reginald Faletti which Bob Foster had kept from him because he didn't want his colleague's holiday ruined. It stated that Madame Walska could no longer afford the services of a director.

Reading this on his return, he could not believe it was a genuine expression of her desire, and told Faletti that under the circumstances he was prepared to continue working for a dollar a day. The response - by letter - stated bluntly that Madame did not wish to reconsider her decision, and Glass reacted skeptically: "I thought this sounded remarkably lucid for someone who could hardly speak, someone who could hardly see, someone who could hardly hear, someone who could hardly move!"

For most of 1983 and into the early months of 1984, Madame languished in bed with advancing osteoporosis, able to make only tentative eye contact. She indicated, however, by pitifully weak gestures, that she didn't want Patricia just sitting there in the bedroom, as if trying to say to her: "Go into the garden, talk with them, see what they're doing and don't just come back and tell me 'Yes, it looks all right,' or 'It's beautiful.' She wanted to know what they were doing." Patricia promised that Madame would not have to go to hospital again, but when she developed serious bed sores the visiting nurse was horrified by her condition and Patricia telephoned Hania.

"Do you agree to let us put Aunty into hospital because there's really no alternative? We will lose her if she stays here."

Hania concurred, and Ganna, at the age of ninety-six, entered Santa Barbara's Cottage Hospital at the end of February, 1984. After three or four days' treatment the sores began to heal, but one was so deep that it required a skin graft and she needed to stay there. Warren Austin rushed to visit his neighbor on returning from a European trip and saw immediately that her life was ebbing away. Patricia spent the night with Ganna, waiting until six in the morning to talk to the hospital doctor.

"There's no hope for her, is there?" she asked him.

"No, there really isn't."

"Well, I'll tell Hania."

She agreed that her aunt should go home to Lotusland, where a hospital bed had been installed and an oxygen bottle stood waiting.

Edward Puacz also happened to arrive at the estate on that morning of Friday, March 2, 1984, determined to see his sister, and Patricia was forced to hurriedly draw the heavy drapes in Madame's room, telling the nurse to inform Mr. Puacz that Madame was too ill to receive visitors.

"Then tell her I'm remaining in the garden until I *can* see her," was his blunt response. Back in the bedroom, Patricia sat gently brushing Walska's hair: "I was saying to her, 'Madame, you're home. You're at Lotusland.' There was a flicker of response in her eyes, and then she was gone."

The will made it clear that nobody was to see Ganna Walska's corpse after she died, yet her half-brother was prowling around outside. The other instruction was for the Haider Mortuary to be notified immediately to take the body away for cremation. Accordingly, Patricia telephoned the mortuary staff, who arrived quickly at the front of the main house and Walska's body was secreted out of her pavilion, carried across the linking courtyard to the mortuary's vehicle and driven to the crematorium before Edward knew what was happening. Leaving it as long as she could, Patricia then went outside to find their visitor.

"I have to tell you Mr. Puacz that your sister has passed away," she informed him.

"Where's her body?"

"At the mortuary."

He rushed off to the funeral directors, only to discover that his half-sister was already being prepared for cremation. He was furious," Patricia recalled. "First, he threatened to file suit against me for wrongful death, then another one for making arrangements for an immediate cremation. He said he had wanted to take Ganna back to Poland for burial, but once he knew he could achieve nothing more, he left and never came back."

A pink marble casket was chosen for Walska's ashes, with Hania and Patricia walking around the estate to decide where it should be placed, honoring Madame's unambiguous wishes in her will:

"My body is to be cremated and my ashes shall be placed in an urn. The urn shall be placed at Lotusland."

There had been discussion some time ago about it being housed in her pavilion, but Hania preferred somewhere in the Japanese Garden, which seemed to fit well with Aunt Andzia's concept of nirvana. They climbed to the top of the rise together and looked down to where two Australian swans with black plumage and red bills glided across the ornamental lake, agreeing that this was the perfect location. A simple ceremony of remembrance was performed, and the casket buried beneath pink and green ground cover.

Madame's final resting place on earth remained a secret: never to become part of a garden tour. But her indomitable spirit continued to permeate this extraordinary place, with Hanna Puacz's stage name taking top billing as her foundation prepared to take over stewardship of what would be known henceforth as Ganna Walska Lotusland. No prima donna could have asked for more.

438

Postlude

Lotusland's transition from private estate to not-for-profit foundation was never going to be easy. There was so much needing attention after Madame Ganna Walska had ruled her domain like the benevolent dictatress of a small city-state for more than forty years. A prime matter for attention was how ambiguities in her will should be interpreted, such as: "I hopefully dreamt that if given all the opportunities, having considerable finances at my disposal, I might fulfill my work to develop Lotusland to its maximum capacity into the most outstanding center of horticultural significance and of educational use." Putting that into meaningful practice was a challenge for the five trustees because the foundation, incorporated in May 1958, would be without funds until probate.

The beneficiaries were either delighted or disconcerted on finally receiving their checks: $20,000 for each of Madame's favorite gardeners, a token $5,000 for Warren Austin, owner of the adjacent Val Verde estate, who didn't need the money, and a miserly $10,000 for Patricia Tarkowska, who did. Thirty thousand dollars went to Charles Glass, after leaving Lotusland under a cloud before Walska died, taking with him a notebook and stacks of file cards containing information about Lotusland's plants compiled during his tenure as director. They were the sole botanical records, never sanctioned by Madame Walska in spite of her stated desire for "horticultural significance," and refusing to pay for the stationery, with Glass using his own typewriter for the job. Knowing that his action was petty and spiteful, he'd already decided to give back the material, but on return from a business trip to the Philippines a letter from Reginald Faletti awaited him threatening legal action unless he provided "certain papers owned by Lotusland." His immediate reaction was not to let anyone else have the documentation, but when confronted with a law suit mentioning a penalty of $35,000, accepted that "the farce" had gone on long enough and handed over the records.

Patricia Tarkowska had realized sooner than her employer how desperately the old lady needed her: "I was kind of her watchdog in the years when she was not able to go out into the garden, and then at the time the estate was in probate before the opening of the foundation, it needed someone there to give advice." Madame was often generous to her secretary, covering her house mortgage for a time and offering to write checks as gifts which, with Patricia's British reserve, including an inherent reluctance to discuss money - she did not accept. She had let attorney Gaudi know about the offers, assuming they would show up eventually in Madame's will. Hania, who inherited $300,000 (the same as Edward Puacz) was concerned that Patricia received so little, but the former secretary-turned-carer-woman, who was never one to walk away from awkward situations, simply shrugged her slender shoulders and continued to be employed at Lotusland to share her knowledge of its topsy-turvy world with those guiding its future.

A renovation program was initiated for upgrading all buildings on the estate, including fumigation against termites, painting and carpentry work, together with a complete overhaul of the plumbing and electricity. A fire alarm system was necessary for insurance cover, and structural strengthening of the main house essential to comply with the latest earthquake regulations. Ten gardeners -

three part-time - continued to tend the grounds, and their routines provided a continuity of purpose after Ganna's passing. Upstairs was cleared of her memorabilia, including opera costumes stored in a large cedar closet in the Venetian Room which remained in surprisingly good condition, considering their age. Many of Erté's best creations went for restoration and eventual display at the Los Angeles County Museum, together with her collection of André Perugia shoes, though other moth eaten clothes and hats fell to pieces when handled. Fortunately, much of Madame's mountain of personal correspondence in half-a-dozen languages, press cuttings, theater programs and scrapbooks, noted for destruction in her will, survived, together with many of her business papers. They would form the basis of a future archive documenting her singular life.

Ganna donated 1,700 volumes of her valuable book collection to the Santa Barbara Public Library years before (in 1968) and the rest were sold-off for next-to-nothing, including several volumes that might have been useful in tracing the origins of her interests in horticulture, the occult, fringe religions, and particularly Buddhism. David Kamansky was able to acquire signed books by Alexandra David-Néel for his own collection, together with a Tibetan philosophy by a Polish author from 1921, indicating that Madame Walska was already seeking such knowledge, although it was inscribed with scathing comments about how she thought the writer, in Kamansky's words, "was a total jerk."

The main house downstairs, cleared of its artifacts and junk, served as the foundation's offices where manager Fritz Amacher, a retired trust officer from the Crocker Bank with a passion for orchids, supervised the day-to-day running of the estate: everything from security to employment, planting policy to payroll control. The only buildings to remain unoccupied were Green Cottage, Madame's singing studio, and her private pavilion. Lotusland as the gem of a display garden remained intact, though Walska's private quarters for the past forty-two years soon lost all sense of her presence when almost everything was removed or sold in a series of auctions. Her estranged attorney, Alfred Rice, somehow managed to gain possession of the pair of Russian ivory-inlaid closets she had promised him and then tried, unsuccessfully, to stop the gift. They proved to be exceptionally rare and desirable Russian 17th century cupboards and were auctioned later in New

York fetching hundreds of thousands of dollars. There were many other treasures in the house that would be disposed of at auctions in Santa Barbara and New York during 1986 and 1987, including antique ceramic tiles, rare Venetian gilded silver, and a collection of coral objects. Some added to the Walska enigma, like a small coral figure of Jesus Christ she kept at her bedside. Although a declared Buddhist, she may have been hedging her bets on the nature of her afterlife.

Only now, were the origins of her Buddhist collection able to be assessed. During the thirties, forties and fifties, Americans rarely hung tankas (Tibetan religious scroll paintings on woven material) for display in their sitting rooms, perhaps because there were no familiar artists' names attached. European art looked right on the walls of their houses, but Tibetan temple banners never worked. Nobody had got around to cataloging Madame's unusual collection of these and other objects begun when married to Smith Cochran in the early 1920s. He had acquired a large number of Nepalese and Sino-Tibetan pieces through his polo-playing association with the ruler of Nepal, whose landlocked kingdom shared its northern border with Tibet. A metal plaque was discovered in Walska's collection reading "A gift to Alexander Smith Cochran from His Majesty Mahendra, Maharaja of Nepal." Although furious with Walska at the time of their divorce, he must have allowed her to keep these objects in the Paris and New York residences.

Grace Nicholson, the Pasadena collector and dealer in Southwestern Indian handiwork and Asian art, who set up business in 1924, reported seeing a large number of what she called Tibetan pieces at Lotusland which were purchased in Chicago when Walska was married to Harold McCormick. Ganna later bought a hundred or so objects from Miss Nicholson, though the bulk of the huge collection came from Cochran, McCormick and whatever Theos Bernard failed to whisk away before their divorce. Walska sent many objects from Tibetland up to Penthouse of the Gods to provide the appropriate vibrations while Theos worked (and partied) there, and no record was made of what came back when the property was sold. David Kamansky suspected "he might just have carted off a lot of things at the time because, much later, some turned up at a nephew's place in Bakersfield, California."

The Buddhist organization where most of the collection was

headed under the terms of Walska's will, engaged Kamansky to assess the state of the works, and he was approached about exhibiting some of the best pieces at the Pacific Asia Museum in Pasadena, where he was director, before they were sent to Colorado. He lodged uncomfortably in the oppressive pavilion at Lotusland while making his selection; it was there that Walska had kept most of her important things, but, as he observed, "Madame wouldn't spend a nickel on having anything cleaned because she was too penurious." About 150 pieces were chosen for display: "We cleaned them because they were in a bad state. They were filthy, and the sea air in Santa Barbara had caused considerable corrosion; there was terrible dust and dirt on the tankas, many of which were not framed."

Everything was made ready, but after expending considerable time, money and effort, one of the monks at the Buddhist complex told him, "We've changed our minds. We feel that many of these pieces are not pertinent to our order; we don't want to attach our name to them." Kamansky was familiar with rivalries between various orders of Buddhism based on philosophical differences, such as certain deities worshiped or admired by one subgroup but not recognized by others. "In fact," he said, "some may have been considered to be almost negative in their worship, so they wanted to remove all their pieces." He understood the point of view, but thought it unfair not to allow an exhibition because it was Madame Walska's unique collection he wanted to show, not "to present a survey of controversial Buddhist art."

In fact, Kamansky discovered only two outstanding genuinely Tibetan objects among hundreds of pieces: one was an eighth century box which he considered unique in America: "I'm sure that Madame Walska never dreamed she had one of the most important pieces ever to come out of Tibet: this reliquary of gilded bronze with an interesting engraved frieze, made to hold something very special - perhaps even the bones of Buddha." The show would have given the opportunity to compile a catalog, but everything was trucked off to Colorado under the terms of Madame's bequest and never seen in public. Kamansky lost track of it, only to hear several years later that the Buddhists were moving to Canada because of tax problems in the United States. "Perhaps they were not the pure Buddhist individuals that Madame Walska was led to believe," he commented, referring to their decision to raise funds by putting her collection on the market. "I'm sure Madame was twisting in her grave when that happened."

Placing the Lotusland foundation on a firm financial footing was a priority for executor Reginald Faletti and his colleagues at Security Pacific National Bank, though it soon became apparent that the endowment was considerably less than Madame had indicated when telling Charles Glass, as an inducement to become her director in the early 1970s, that there would be up to thirty-five million dollars available. In the eleven years since then her assets declined rapidly as the cost of running and developing the estate accelerated and the value of her stock holdings dropped markedly. After Walska's death, the foundation received $9,662,000 in cash, together with the remaining French properties. The Montecito estate itself was valued at $4,700,000. Lotusland was not about to fall on hard times, but the financial and social obligations of its new status inhibited the seamless transition to a bright new future.

At first, everything seemed to be under control, with a master plan drawn up for public access, while small groups of visitors with an interest in botany, including students affiliated to the horticultural program of the Santa Barbara College, continued to be taken on tours by estate employees. Signs of trouble ahead emerged, however, after some nearby residents learned about a proposed on-site car park for visitors, and Lotusland's change from private estate to public entity rang alarm bells throughout the neighborhood. Fears were expressed that this could shatter the area's verdant calm, with increased traffic on the narrow, serpentine roads, endangering children at the local school and generally upsetting the reclusive, semi-rural character of this prime area of affluent Montecito. It was also implied - though not yet articulated - that hordes of tourists descending on the gardens would threaten property values.

In August, 1986, nearly two-and-a-half years after Walska died, Arthur Gaudi, as secretary-treasurer of the foundation, estimated that plans would be completed within four to six months, when the estate could apply for a conditional use permit from the County Planning Commission. But then a local resident, Jonathan Bassan, expressed disquiet to a meeting of about sixty invited neighbors at Lotusland: "It's a sensational place. It's a unique jewel," he admitted. "We're glad it will be open. At the same time we have a certain level of concern and anxiety that it stays as Ganna Walska had in mind - that it stays open to a limited number of people in limited groups." She never expressed this, and the foundation had an obligation to honor the terms of its federal tax-free status by opening the estate to the general public.

Gaudi thought there might be one busload of twenty visitors in the morning and a similar number in the afternoon, three days a week, and the neighbors would notice little difference. It was anticipated that tours would be guided, with visitors admitted only after reserving by telephone well in advance, and, in an attempt to calm local concerns, he added (with fellow foundation member Carol Valentine supporting him) that there was no intention of turning Lotusland into "another Disneyland." That throwaway phrase unwittingly raised the question of Lotusland's precise function, with some people expecting a theme park.

Charles Glass's acrimonious departure had caused a lull in horticultural activity until a new director appeared on the scene in 1987, and the appointee, Dr. Steven Timbrook, soon discovered that he needed to combine his extensive professional knowledge with the tenacity of an expert negotiator and the discipline of a seasoned diplomat to cope with growing hostility from Montecito residents. Before his arrival, he had regarded Lotusland as simply a botanical display garden, but realized on taking up the job that it embraced distinct personalities: "as an historical estate, unique landscaping - which I would consider as the display component - and the botanical aspect depending on the collection." It was similar to the famous Huntington Botanical Gardens, Walska's admitted inspiration for much of her work, which had already passed through the phase that Lotusland was facing. Timbrook wanted to avoid the institutionalization of a garden that had started out as a private estate and ended up run by a public entity, because, on taking over he regarded the interim management "more concerned with nickels and dimes than the big picture." This led, in his opinion, to so-called improvements being done on the cheap.

No garden, of whatever type or ambition, can remain inert, and vigorous growth - especially in Santa Barbara's climate zone - is endemic. The new director saw that growth patterns since Walska's stewardship of the estate had changed the character of individual areas like the striking Blue Garden, and needed urgent attention. When designed by Ralph Stevens during the 1940s, it was intended as a color statement, but nearly forty years later, the surrounding trees had grown to such heights that they shaded what was planned as a display that would look best in strong light. Timbrook was reluctant to cut them down, accepting that here, as elsewhere, compromises had to be adopted to adapt the estate while maintaining the spirit of Madame Walska's original concepts and fantasies.

A similar approach applied to the Japanese Garden, with its massed red maples, heavenly bamboo, black pines, azaleas, rhododendrons and camellias growing among the rocks, stone lanterns and pagodas. Everything looked serenely beautiful, but changes were necessary because the irrigation was inefficient and labor-intensive, relying on overhead watering, and the paths needed widening to accommodate an expected increase in visitor numbers. The challenges were the same everywhere: to make changes that did not appear to be too institutional and destroy Ganna Walska's unique vision.

Difficult decisions had to be taken about aesthetics as Steve Timbrook was assailed by shrill neighborhood voices opposing what they feared would become a popular attraction for the masses. Rumors circulated in Montecito that Lotusland was a future tourist site, likely to embrace the Disneyland horrors previously mentioned, but now joined by other threats, such as the random spraying of pesticides and excessive demands on the community's precious water supply. Local gossip spread virally, hinting at a conspiracy between developers and realtors to subdivide Madame Walska's thirty-seven-acre property for condos. It was a depressing time for those who believed in perpetuating her unique vision, and led to gloomy speculation about what might happen if the foundation failed to be granted a conditional use permit.

In the meantime, one asset remained to be realized after new zoning laws in France made the Château de Galluis virtually worthless. Madame's fashionable Paris town house remained tenanted and income-producing, but if anyone thought that dealing with the recalcitrant residents of Montecito was trying, attempts to sell this property was infinitely more frustrating. The French notaries were concerned that a Walska heir might be discovered at any moment, knowing that Madame had been married six times, and it was conceivable that somebody would come forward claiming a blood relationship and demand ownership under the strict laws of inheritance. An affidavit issued in California, stating that Madame Walska had remained childless, was little help because the intricacies of the Napoleonic Code made it possible for the most distant relatives to inherit, and there were, for a start, a niece in America and a nephew in Poland. Eventually, Arthur Gaudi went to Paris, and managed with consummate diplomatic and legal skill to strike a deal on the sale of number 14 rue de Lubeck in January, 1988 when the final tranche of Madame Walska's fortune entered the foundation's coffers.

In the face of community hostility, Lotusland had the local press on its side. The Santa Barbara *News-Press*, under its bold banner, "Without fear or favor or friend or foe," published an editorial on November 21, 1988, headlined, "Yes, Open Lotusland," urging the gardens to be shared by the public. But it had little effect, and a full year later when Anne Dewey, Steve Timbrook's assistant director, began working at the estate, the future remained clouded. "It was a difficult time," she recalled, "because we thought that all the things we were doing could be for nothing." There were endless discussions about what would happen if permission for public access was not granted, and some of the trustees were so upset about the local ill-will that they suggested selling the estate. Mrs. Dewey remembered them asking: "Do we even want to do business in a community that does not want us?"

Under the rules of the foundation, plants could be taken from the ground and sold separately, followed by placing the property on the market for sale. Real estate advice suggested that the estate could be subdivided into twenty-three prestige building lots and the proceeds used for grants to horticultural students. "No one wanted to do that," Dewey said, "but we were becoming so frustrated." Small-scale garden tours for groups with botanical or horticultural affiliations were allowed to continue, however, and such was the demand to see Lotusland - now in the public eye through extensive newspaper coverage - that some people invented garden clubs to gain entrance. By genuine and sometimes subversive means, about 1,800 a year visited the estate.

A peak of disgruntlement was reached when the foundation took its case direct to the general public by placing a prominent advertisement in the local newspaper the day before the County Planning Commission's crucial hearing. The *News-Press* appeared with a picture of the main entrance and a headline: "Will the gates to Lotusland be closed to the community forever?" The story explained that Ganna Walska's dream was threatened because "a few of our neighbors don't want any access to Lotusland, or only such limited access that residents of the community would find it very difficult to visit. If this happens, the nonprofit educational Lotusland Foundation could not operate the estate in keeping with Madame Walska's wishes, and the estate would be closed."

The packed meeting began at the County Administration Building in downtown Santa Barbara with a group of Montecito residents demanding the scaling-down of the numbers allowed to enter the garden at any one time, a demand that visitors be shuttled to the estate from off-site parking, objections to the construction of any new buildings, and the request for a representative of the Montecito Association Land Use Committee to be represented on the board of Lotusland.

Supporters and opponents spent the day in verbal jousting, with Irving Lebow claiming "our area is being raped," by zoning restrictions "being amended away." This was countered by Simon Droan, insisting that the properties immediately surrounding Lotusland did not constitute a neighborhood. He questioned the motives of the "poor, whining homeowners," portraying them as "a small, vocal minority" who should have been warned about the estate's possible development by the realtors who sold them their homes. Countering this, somebody claimed that street signs directing visitors to Lotusland would be an intrusion. "Sure, we'll put up a sign," one Montecito Association stalwart quipped, "it will say 'There's nothing of any interest up this way.'"

The daylong hearing raised more questions than it answered, with the planning commissioners seeking additional information about traffic flow and how much water an expanded Lotusland would use. Everybody - commissioners, supporters and protesters alike - agreed that the gardens as they stood, were beneficial to the community, with about half the sixty speakers backing the development proposal. This led to the withholding of judgment

448

until county planning staff advised on a list of possible options, estimated to take another three months, though a so-called second expansion hearing was called earlier - for Wednesday, February 13, 1991. After hours of polarized public testimony, the Santa Barbara planning commissioners voted three-to-one to allow the estate to charge admission for a limited number of individuals, school classes, and group visits each year. Their motion also permitted fund-raising events with the number of guests limited to three hundred each time; there were approvals for the building of a parking lot to accommodate a maximum of forty vehicles; a scheme to bus visitors into the area from outside the county; and the additional planting of five acres of the property when the Montecito Water District declared the current drought over.

These decisions were a welcome step forward, though the vital question of how many people could visit Lotusland remained unresolved, and the prized conditional use permit still awaited approval. Having won the battle, but not yet the war, the trustees took the initiative by seeking permission for 12,800 visitors per year, less than half the total in their original 1987 submission. During another long day of claim and counter-claim, many of the original arguments surfaced again. There was repeated concern that Lotusland would become a tourist attraction "like Disneyland, Knotts Berry Farm or the Wax Museum." Others worried about the fire potential and noise from amplified sound at fund-raising events. Trustee Anne Jones made the point that most of Santa Barbara's historic large gardens had been lost through subdivision and development, emphasizing that the foundation sought to keep intact their own property. A home owner whose house bordered the estate, David Brilliant, admitted that he had never complained about Lotusland's visitors during the past six years, but was against opening a private tourist attraction in the county because it would set a dangerous precedent.

Patience wore thin on both sides of the argument, until it was announced that county supervisors were expected to give final approval to an agreement to settle the Lotusland question on July 16, with the board having conceptually approved the application for the prized permit after extended mediation. The estate would be allowed up to 5,000 visitors during its first year of operation,

449

increasing to a top of 9,000 by the third year. The local press covered the neighborhood protest meetings which continued to be held, and was generally supportive of Lotusland's claims through reportage and editorials. Then in May, 1991, a minor revolution in the ranks of the opponents was revealed with the claim that some members of the Montecito Association - one of the primary advisers to the county on planning matters - did not live in the immediate vicinity of Lotusland, and that many neighborhood families had broken away to form separate protest groups.

One of the splinter pressure groups, the Northwest Montecito Homeowners Association, filed suit on August 19, 1991, alleging that in allowing Lotusland to be opened to visitors as a tourist attraction, it would detract from the semi-rural nature of the neighborhood, and that the environmental review had not fully considered the fire hazard, the impact of additional traffic, and the effect the garden might have on a nearby creek. This was in spite of proof that visitors would generate less than one percent of local traffic, the fact that the fire department was located right across the road from Lotusland's main gates to deal promptly with any conflagration, and anybody could see that construction was rampant around the estate's perimeter in remodeling already expensive homes and gardens to make them ever more desirable.

These delaying tactics pressured the usually mild-mannered director to comment publicly that he had every confidence in the county's environmental review and the suit from the homeowners association had absolutely no merit. "I think they are very intransigent people who are never going to be happy," Steve Timbrook added. They were also careless, because it was revealed when the action came to court that Lotusland was neither officially notified of the complaint, nor served with a summons. And when the nominated plaintiff, Gary Wayne, failed to show up at the proceedings on December 24, the action collapsed with his association liable to pay Lotusland's costs. This removed the last major obstacle in the foundation's long and often bitter struggle to open the gardens to the general public under the terms of their foundation status. But four years of community protest led to some daunting restrictions, including some of the most stringent conditions ever imposed by the county for a conditional use permit to operate as a commercial enterprise in a residential zone.

Unseen behind its pink-washed walls, the estate was able to develop by constructing a car park and a new visitor center modeled on George Washington Smith's 1920s bath house adjacent to the water garden. Its surrounds were transformed from the rather nondescript eucalyptus grove into a striking Australian Garden in the spirit of Walska's concept of mass planting. The first paying customers allowed under the county permit arrived in September, 1993, and Steve Timbrook observed: "When it became more available to the public, people really appreciated what an unusual garden it was - not because they'd never seen it, but because once seen, you know it's still unusual." The board's philosophy was to keep the experience of visiting Lotusland like being privileged to see the very special private garden it had always been.

This raised some new questions when the numbers increased after 1993 and nobody knew how much wear and tear the fragile surfaces could tolerate. An editorial in the *News-Press*, headed "Lotusland success," pointed out that since the permit was granted, the property had conducted its business professionally and quietly: "In fact, if you drive along Sycamore Canyon Road and pass the front of the Lotusland estate, it is difficult to tell there is any activity there at all. But there is. The proof is that most of the tours are booked months in advance." The paper quoted one Montecitan who joked that it would be simpler to arrange a meeting with the President of the United States than to get a peek at the lush gardens within the Lotusland compound.

Over the next few years, admissions and bequests increased, in spite of continuing local opposition. There was no doubting its success with the public, with growing national and international recognition in press, magazine and television coverage, but fuzzy details in Ganna Walska's will continued to cause confusion about the estate's future character. There was also a divergence of opinion about the extent to which Madame's personality should be reflected, which tended to divide trustees and staff: the former inclined to play down the personal connection, the latter keen to nurture it.

Trustee Arthur Gaudi stated: "One thing that has troubled me about the foundation is that I believe there's been too much attention paid to the husbands and to her life prior to Lotusland. I

451

have always thought we should not have emphasized that at all, but the public is inquisitive." A contrary opinion from the staff insisted that it was essential to perpetuate the founder's nonconformist character: "Even if you try to downplay her connection, there is constant curiosity about Madame Walska herself. Ask any volunteer guide. This was her great creative endeavor: her Last Hurrah - a forty-year Hurrah - but to say that only this is important and everything that went on beforehand - her social and artistic life, jewels, clothes, travel, fame - was unimportant, is unthinkable."

According to its mission statement, the aim of the Ganna Walska Lotusland Foundation is "To preserve and enhance the spectacular collections of exotic plants of the Montecito estate of the late Madame Ganna Walska, and through interpretation of these collections to foster increased knowledge and appreciation of the importance of plants and the need for their conservation." She spent considerably less than half of a long life at Tanglewood-Cuesta Linda-Tibetland-Lotusland. Before that, she achieved an enviable position in the cultural milieu of between-the-wars Paris by being honored for her services to music with the Légion d'honneur and receiving later the Ordre des Arts et des Lettres for her contribution to and propagation of French culture. After buying her Santa Barbara estate, the local community benefited from those European experiences through her generous gifts to civic and cultural causes; she also introduced expanded horizons and offbeat attitudes that allowed her to become respected - even accepted - as a passionate enemy of the average in a former rather stuffy society

Lotusland as an exceptional display garden was indeed Ganna's Last Hurrah, but the rich pageant of her previous experiences helps to explain the estate's radically distinctive personality which is defined by the fusion - rather than division - of the myriad facets of a remarkable life. The place is as much about extravagant Russian portraits and stunning Erté gowns, phonograph recordings and screen tests, glamorous photographs, Mr. John hats and exceptional jewelry - the memories and memorabilia of a lifetime - as it is about massed plants, trees and shrubs. It was once called Tibetland, and became the center of Madame's mandala, with its surrounding garden creating, both in color and in spirit, the positive vibrations for her happiness, stability and safety. As David

452

Kamansky said, "I think she built the garden because of her interest in Tibetan art, philosophy and culture." In other words, Lotusland became her sanctuary, her realm, her own Tibet.

The nature of Nature is to grow, and growth fosters change. Trees reach for the sky shading the flower beds below, and, all too soon, what was intended as an ultimate horticultural statement, assumes an entirely different character. The estate bears little resemblance to the Cuesta Linda that Ganna Walska acquired in 1941 because of the developments she introduced, together with some exciting schemes initiated after her death, and if such a foundation were proposed now, today's social, civic, political and financial pressures would probably block it. Madame's dear friend and neighbor, Warren Austin, spent many frustrating years trying to ensure the future of his magnificent Val Verde estate – yearning to convert it to similar status as hers for the enjoyment of everyone. But he failed. With major funding derived from bequests and public donations, Val Verde was re-classified as a public charity by the IRS in 2009.

Ganna Walska Lotusland has one magic advantage over other display gardens: it remains imbued with the maverick spirit of the woman who created a permanent smash hit - something she never achieved in all her singing years, except when buying fleeting fame. She paid a great deal more for a very different kind of immortality, and few would deny that it was money well-spent.

Acknowledgements

Ganna Walska belongs to the "clean slate" brand of biography: a former celebrity, now forgotten, whose life story requires almost total reconstruction. A few who were close to her during the Lotusland era shared their memories with me, and I was fortunate to find a couple of people who could relate personal experiences of when she owned the Château de Galluis in France. Nobody was left to provide first-hand accounts of Walska's childhood, performing career, and influential presence in Paris. In addition, most of the men in Madame's life tended to shy away from the limelight that she so blatantly craved.

But I had fallen under Madame's spell, and, like so many of her admirers, my labor of love had no fences, no boundaries, and few limits. I embarked on the task of writing her biography, impressed by the breadth of the (uncatalogued) material in the Lotusland filing cabinets, and encouraged by the generous support from those I met during several visits to Montecito. My thanks go principally to them.

Top of the list is Anne Jones, the trustee-host mentioned in the Preface, who kindled my initial interest and, with her husband, Bob, offered warm hospitality and sage advice on what I was letting myself in for. The Ganna Walska Lotusland staff gave me unfailing assistance, headed by then director Steve Timbrook, his assistant director Anne Dewey and archivist Deirdre Cantrell; trustees Carol Valentine and Arthur Gaudi were constantly supportive. Interviews with those who had been close to my subject allowed me to flesh out the Walska story: Hania Tallmadge, Dr. Warren Austin, Patricia Tarkowska, Jerome Dalseme, Bruce Van Dyke, Frank Fujii, Michael Monteabaro, Dr. Herbert Koteen, William Paylen, Oswald da Ros.

Dalseme recounted first-hand details of life at the Château de Galluis during the 1930s and his French connection brought valuable material about the same period from Mme. Léa Martin-Daszkiewicz, whose parents were Ganna Walska's housekeepers at the château. David Kamansky Director Emeritus of the Pacific Asia Museum, Pasadena, California, offered his expert opinion about Ganna Walska's passion for Buddhist art and philosophy, and the Santa Barbara Historical Society (Michael Redmon) allowed access to their oral history material. Much of the detail and chronology of Madame's long adult life comes from newspaper and magazine files in the United States, Britain and France, and I would like to thank Richard Johnston's tenacious sleuthing on my behalf at the New York Public Library. Carol Warner at Santa Barbara *News-Press* introduced me to the extensive coverage of Walska's activities during the more than forty years she lived locally, and other vital material came from the Westminster Public Library and the archives of the Royal Opera House, Covent Garden in London, the State Library of New South Wales in Sydney, and records of Le Théâtre des Champs-Elysées in Paris.

Editor & Production: Loraine Brown

Notes

Frequent abbreviations
GW – Ganna Walska
GWLA – Ganna Walska Lotusland Archive
ART – Ganna Walska's 1943 autobiography "Always Room at the Top"

Prelude

Based on reminiscences of GW's former physician, estate-owning neighbor and close friend, Dr. Warren Austin, recorded at his Montecito estate, Val Verde, by the author on October 23, 1998. Additional material from interviews with Patricia Tarkowska (GW's secretary and confidant) and Hania Tallmadge (GW's niece) in Santa Barbara on 24 and 28 September 1999 respectively.

Chapter 1: *Birth of a Legend* 1887-1910

Litovsk - or Litowsk - meaning "of Lithuania" - refers to when the city belonged to that country: from the eleventh century. It became Polish territory before being annexed by the Russian Empire in 1795. Brest-Litovsk, or Brzesc nad Bugiem in Polish (Brest on the Bug river) became part of Poland again between 1919 and 1939, then the USSR from 1939 to 1951, before incorporation in the independent nation of Belarus.

GW was notoriously evasive - or sometimes just careless - about her age, though a certified copy of her baptismal certificate from Brest-Litovsk was in her possession, originally dated October 23, 1887 and reissued as a copy on November 29, 1934. It was probably obtained for one of her many unsuccessful applications for a United States passport. GWLA.

A clipping from an unidentified and undated Polish newspaper refers to a Polish tradesmen's association meeting in Mlawa (about two hundred kilometers north-west of Brest-Litovsk); among the newly-elected board of directors is a "Mr. Puacz" - GW's father? GW must have thought so by keeping the clipping. Napoleon's given name suggests someone who stood up for his rights and principles, proud that his father had participated in the 1863 Polish revolt against Russian domination. This, and other sketchy information about him, comes from published obituaries in unidentified Polish newspapers in GWLA. Some indicate that, belonging to a minority, it was imperative for GW's father to bend

456

to the Russian Tsar's regime for economic survival, and, whatever his education prepared him for, he took various jobs as a tradesman and shopkeeper. Napoleon Puacz also worked for the railways according to one report, until forced to leave through persecution. His social standing in Brest-Litovsk may not have been as prominent as family members liked to recall. GW herself, however, left no detailed records or information about her parents.

GW tended to ignore her childhood until reviewing it for her autobiography, when she characterized herself as a feisty, rebellious little girl, brought up in an orthodox Roman Catholic family, never remembering playing with dolls. "But I can see, as if it were today" she wrote in "Always Room at the Top," a little girl of six or seven seated on the floor and trying for hours to catch with her tiny fingers the mercury taken from the broken window thermometer in a moment of no supervision. That happened so often that scarcely was a new thermometer put up than it was down again. . . Severely punished for breaking something that was forbidden for a nice girl to touch, she was undaunted and did not hesitate to repeat the experiment, knowing the consequences of disobeying again but sure at heart that the next time she could imprison the rebellious matter. . . The perseverance of that little girl was a symbol of my whole life."

Hania Tallmadge, formerly Hanka Puacz, the daughter of Maria (Marysia) and Leon Puacz, Walska's brother and sister-in-law, received through her late aunt's will several of GW's portraits, a piano from Lotusland, copies of Madame's jewelry, some gowns and hats, and an extensive photo archive.

The article by Robert Murray about GW for Hearst Syndication Service was never published. Madame may have failed to approve the draft manuscript sent to her by Cosmopolitan News Service, Inc., New York on March 24, 1923.

Baron Arcadie d'Eingorn remains a shadowy figure beyond what GW wrote about him in ART, and suggestions in the American press were that he followed his father's profession (one of Tsar Nicholas II's doctors) by becoming a physician or, more-likely, a veterinarian in the Imperial Russian Army.

St. Petersburg-born Mikhail Fokin [the English transliteration - more commonly known by the French version of his name Michel Fokine] after training to become a dancer from the age of nine, made his début at the Mariinsky Theatre on his eighteenth birthday in *Pasquita*. Four years later he became a teacher at the Mariinsky's ballet school, numbering Bronislava Nijinska (of Polish descent) and the Baroness d'Eingorn (likewise) among his students - the former serious, with a brilliant career as a dancer and choreographer ahead of her, the latter headed in a different direction. Fokin's radical ideas about choreography and the future direction of classical dance were not welcomed by the highly conservative Imperial Theatre management and in 1909 he accepted Sergei Diaghilev's invitation to become the choreographer of the Ballets Russes in Paris. His ballets for the impresario included *The Firebird*, *Petrushka*, *Le Spectre de la Rose*, *Carnaval* and *Daphnis et Chloé*. Fokine's works remain in the repertoires of the world's leading companies and some regard him as "the father of modern ballet" because of his reformist vision of dance.

Joachim Tartakov was born in Odessa, southern Russia in 1860, and studied singing at the St. Petersburg Conservatory from where he graduated in 1881, and then joined the Odessa Opera Company. He became the leading baritone and principal stage director at the Mariinsky Theatre, St. Petersburg in 1900, as well as teaching at the Conservatory. A distinguished operatic career took Tartakov to sing leading baritone roles in Berlin, Copenhagen and other European cities, and he recorded a number of songs and arias which are available on CD and MP3. He became an Honored Artist of the USSR in 1923, the year he died in what had then become Petrograd.

Chapter 2: *From Russia with Love* 1911-1914

A Russian émigré writer in Paris, N.N. Breshko-Breshkovskii, recalled that he was approached in the early 1900s to organize a ball at St. Petersburg as a charity fund-raiser. Its high point was the selection of a beauty queen whose prize was to be a portrait painted by the famous Alfred Eberling. This information is included in correspondence from the exiled Grand Duke Alexander, uncle of Tsar Nicholas II, to GW July 28, 1924. GWLA.

GW's version of acquiring her stage name in ART differs from others, suggesting something more elevated than cabaret: "I was not able to use my husband's name at an occasion when I was to sing for charity. At the eleventh hour I had to think up a substitute and, like all Poles, I loved to dance, especially to waltz." The Kiev cabaret connection is quoted by her costume designer, Romain de Tirtoff (Erté) in his autobiography "My Life/My Art."

A press report from1921 (the New York *Evening Telegram*) suggested that GW shared a flat during some of her time in Paris before the First World War, with the Polish-born vaudeville entertainer Anna Held (1872-1918.) She was a former Florenz Ziegfeld star on Broadway who had gone to the French capital to perform after ending her relationship with the famous showman. Held spent the years of the war touring France entertaining the troops. The same article stated that GW initiated divorce proceedings against Arcadie d'Eingorn on the grounds of drunkenness by serving a writ of divorce on him through a Russian Orthodox priest in Paris.

Polish-born (in 1850) Jean de Reszke was famed for his stylish looks and silky quality tenor voice that made him the biggest male star of opera in the late 19th century. He became the darling of the Paris Opéra, and the Royal Opera House, Covent Garden - also of the British royal family for whom he gave private recitals. In the later years of a dazzling career, de Reszke performed in every season at the Metropolitan Opera House in New York from 1891. He married a countess in 1896, gradually reduced his stage appearances, and retired from singing in 1904, handing over his mantle as the world's most famous tenor to Enrico Caruso. He subsequently bred horses in Poland and taught singing in Paris and on the French Riviera. A measure of his celebrity impact was the successful marketing for some thirty years in Britain - between 1920 and 1950 - of an upmarket brand of cigarettes "de Reszke," promoted as "the right cigarette in the right company" and "the aristocrat of cigarettes." They continued to be available long after the singer's death in 1925, together with many series of cigarette cards now prized by collectors.

Ganna Walska was fortunate to have direct contact with some of the giants of European culture during her formative years. Associating with Mikhail Fokin, Joachim Tartakov and Jean de Reszke - however half-heartedly, together with experiencing the best of the St. Petersburg and Paris performing arts scenes during the early years of the new century – fired her passion to be someone in those creative worlds.

Chapter 3: The Promised Land 1915-1918

Syndicated stories about GW appeared in the American press as early as February 27, 1915, a few weeks after her arrival in the United States. They report cancellation of a New York theatrical engagement because of her husband's death on the Prussian battlefield: "While the public was applauding her play - and another singer - Madame Walska was grieving over news of her husband's death, news of which arrived before she was about to make her American stage début." Unidentified and undated newspaper cutting in GWLA.

With military stalemate on the Western Front, the Germans' military strategy was to defeat the Russians in East Prussia and then transfer their forces to fight the Allies in the West. Arcadie d'Eingorn probably died in the Second Battle of the Masurian Lakes between February 7 and 22, 1915.

GW's first New York lodgings may have been at 226 W.59th. St. (telephone Columbus 4221.) This address and telephone number are printed on a flyer issued soon after her arrival in the United States. GWLA.

Levi "Lee" (Schubart) Shubert (1871-1953) was born in Poland and migrated to the United States with his family at the age of seven. He was the eldest of seven siblings of the Shubarts [sic] who became managers and producers of the largest theater empire of the 20th century which included New York's Wintergarden and Shubert theaters. Presumably his Polish background played a part in his attraction for GW.

GW must have arrived in the United States with enough convertible roubles or francs from the d'Eingorn fortune to allow her to live in the style to which she'd become accustomed in Europe. Her meeting with a New York producer on the voyage from Liverpool, noted in ART, and notably the Lee Shubert connection, probably led to being introduced to the influential financier and patron of the arts, Otto H. Kahn, because both men were associated with the Century Theatre. The dapper, German-born Kahn (1867-1934) became a British subject when working for Deutsche Bank in London and then moved to the United States, taking American citizenship. He joined the powerful German-Jewish élite of bankers, using his business and management skills to finance the reorganizing of America's railroad systems. His passionate nature was also deeply rooted in culture and the arts, making him the most influential patron of the arts in the United States during the early years of the twentieth century. Kahn's wealth, influence and personality saw him becoming a friend of the greatest stage and music performers, producers, writers, painters and sculptors of the age, and of creativity in all its forms. He was known as a capitalist with soul. Among many official positions, he was on the board of the Metropolitan Opera and vice-president of the Century Opera Company, formed to bring the best of the lyric art to New Yorkers at affordable prices. Otto H. Kahn delighted in fostering the careers of new talent and must have been enchanted by GW's possibilities. Referring her to his friend, Dr. Joseph Fraenkel for treatment of her throat problem was a major turning point in GW's life.

Lowell M. Palmer Senior was a prominent Brooklyn businessman, philanthropist and art connoisseur. His business interests included the Manhattan Life Insurance Company, the Union Ferry Company, Palmer Lime and Cement Company, the Palmer Dock Company, New Jersey's Colonial Trust Company and the United States Lloyds ship insurance. A veteran of the Civil War, he was one of the founders of the Brooklyn Academy of Music. He died on September 30, 1915, at the age of 70

Richard (Ric(c)ardo) Barthélemy (1869-1937) was born in Smyrna of Italian-French origins, studied music in Naples and became a composer of songs and stage works, winning the first Olympic Music Competition in Stockholm in 1912 with his "Olympic Triumphal March." He was a considerable musician, becoming Enrico Caruso's *répétiteur, professeur,* accompanist and close friend for fourteen years. Barthélemey was probably the best-qualified of the myriad singing teachers hired by GW before she met Walther Straram.

Chapter 4: *Unlucky in Love* **1918-1920**

Havana may seem a strange place for an aspiring prima donna to make her opera début. The balmy Cuban capital, however, was the most popular offshore destination for vacationing Americans after the First World War, welcoming millionaires and mobsters alike to its seductive Caribbean climate during the northern hemisphere winter. This rich man's playground could boast among its no-prohibition casinos, grand hotels, gaudy bars, brothels and night clubs, one of the best-equipped stages in the Americas: the neo-gothic Gran Teatro de la Habana, inaugurated in 1838. By the time of GW's appearance there, its 1500-seat auditorium had established a tradition of presenting opera, zarzuela, dance and drama for the entertainment of its resident Spanish immigrant population and cultured American visitors, attracting the top international names to perform on its stage, such as the dancers Fanny Elssler and Anna Pavlova, actresses Sarah Bernhardt and Eleonora Duse, opera singers Enrico Caruso and Adelina Patti and famous musicians Sergei Rachmaninov and Arthur Rubinstein.

Harold Fowler McCormick (1872-1941) with his brothers, Cyrus Jr. and Stanley, were the sons of Cyrus H. McCormick (1809-1884), the Chicago industrialist and inventor, in 1831, of the first commercially-successful mechanical reaper. This horse-drawn machine for harvesting grain crops changed arable farming from an essentially manual operation. Cyrus formed a company in 1848 to market his invention, which he exhibited successfully at the 1851 Great Exhibition at the Crystal Palace in London. In 1878, he was elected to the prestigious French Academy of Sciences for "having done more for the cause of agriculture than any other living man." In 1902, the McCormick Harvesting Machine Company merged with several other similar firms to become the mighty International Harvester Company. Two of the sons - Harold and Cyrus Jr. - presided over the enlarged business for many years.

When his father died, Alexander Smith Cochran (1874-1929) became head of the family, and, after graduating from Yale in 1896, worked in the hugely profitable Alexander Smith & Sons carpet mills for a few years, becoming president of the company in 1902. He cited ill-health for relinquishing any direct control in 1910, and a rich bachelor's life of extensive travel, ocean racing, hunting, playing polo, collecting antique books, and acquiring Western, Buddhist and Islamic art stretched ahead. In the meantime, the family company became the largest carpet manufacturer in the world, and Cochran's personal fortune at the time he proposed marriage to GW was estimated at fifty million dollars. As a philanthropist, he founded Yale's Elizabethan Club in 1911 with a $100,000 endowment and donated many of his collection of rare Elizabethan and Jacobean books. The same year he gave New York's Metropolitan Museum of Art, antique books, works on paper, European tapestries and furniture. Another gift, in 1913, included Persian manuscripts and single-page paintings collected on his travels in the Middle East, which greatly enhanced the Museum's already important collection of Islamic Art.

Chapter 5. *Femme Fatale* 1920

The American Cathedral of the Holy Trinity where GW and Alexander Cochran were married was known as the American Cathedral in Paris. It was designed by George Edward Street (best known for London's Gothic-style Law Courts: the Royal Courts of Justice) as a place of worship for Episcopalians from the United States.

Opera as part of Chicago's cultural and social life developed slowly, with touring Italian and German companies first serving the burgeoning immigrant population with the lyric art in their blood. It was not until 1910, when the Chicago Grand Opera was established as a permanent resident company, that the city achieved national prominence, largely due to its adventurous musical director, Cleofante Campanini, together with lavish patronage from Harold and Edith McCormick. Mary Garden, the Scottish-born lyric soprano was to rule the company briefly as "directa," although her expensive 1921-1922 season (the year following GW's *Zaza* fiasco) which included the world première of Prokofiev's "The Love for Three Oranges" ended with a huge deficit. This was covered by Harold McCormick for over a million dollars, but the company folded, to be succeeded by a new organization, the Chicago Lyric Opera, bringing the medium to a broader audience.

Chapter 6: *Bonjour Paree!* 1920-1921

Soprano Yvonne Gall (1885-1972), Paris-born and specializing in French lyric roles, made her début at the Paris Opéra in 1908 at the start of a long and successful international career, including appearances with the Chicago Opera from 1918, where she sang many of the roles that Mary Garden chose not to take. Two years older than GW, Gall was probably one of the reasons - as a rival - for Walska's trouble with *Zaza,* because of the high standards demanded by the company and its audiences. The French soprano was also one of opera's beauties and it must have been galling for GW being challenged both vocally and physically. Yvonne Gall participated in the Pathé company's early recording of a complete opera in 1912 - Gounod's *Roméo et Juliette* - and became a prolific recording artist. She can be heard to good effect on YouTube.

In choosing Erté as her costume designer, Ganna Walska embraced the height of Art Déco elegance from the man whose striking designs helped define the style of an era - and long after - in fashion, graphic arts, interior décor, costume, and set design for movies, theatre and opera. Although they had never met previously, there was a peripheral link between client and creator because both knew well the St. Petersburg of pre-revolutionary Russia. Erté was born there (as Romain de Tirtoff) in 1892, the son of an admiral in the Tsar's fleet, and both were to adopt pseudonyms to conceal their backgrounds: GW in order to sing in public without causing a scandal, and he because the admiral wanted his son to follow the family tradition of a naval career. In 1915, Erté signed a substantial contract with *Harper's Bazaar* magazine and would produce more than two hundred striking covers for them and other publications. In 1920, when GW first contacted him, he had recently designed the sets and costumes for a movie, "The Restless Sex," starring Marion Davies and Ralph Kellard and financed by William Randolph Hearst for release through Paramount.

The *New York Times*, December 25, 1920 reported that Cochran booked a suite of two rooms and bath for himself and his wife aboard the White Star liner "Olympic" sailing on Wednesday, December 29 for Cherbourg and Southampton.

Walther Straram (1876-1933) at the age of forty-five enjoyed a successful career in training individual singers (*répetiteur* to Mary Garden at New York's Manhattan Opera House in 1910) and opera choruses (*chef de chant* for the Boston Opera's 1914 Paris season.) Following this he became chorus master and assistant conductor to maestro André Caplet at Boston. Then, in Paris, he had GW's voice to train and her money to realize his *grandioso* musical ambitions.

Diaghilev's *The Rite of Spring* choreographed by Nijinsky to music by Stravinsky premièred in Paris on May 13, 1913 causing a late-Spring rumpus at Le Théâtre des Champs-Elysées, with sections of the volatile audience affronted by its brutal assault on their eyes and ears, upsetting the genteel sensibilities of *La Belle*

Epoque. Subsequent presentations were disrupted and the ballet was removed from the Ballets Russes' season after eight performances. In hindsight, the violent response presaged the end of the era itself - the Third French Republic's contented period of peace, prosperity and flowering of the arts - and *Rite* would prove to be a turning point in the history of dance. On the cusp of society being turned upside down by the H.G. Wells catchphrase "The war to end war," the world, let alone ballet, would never be the same again. GW was probably unaware at the time of the ferment that took place on the Avenue Montaigne in Paris in the theater that one day would be hers.

Chapter 7: *The Reaper Prince* 1921-1923

Town Topics, July 28, 1921: "When Alec Cochran married Ganna Walska, those who think (and there are still some of us left), said, 'There is no fool like an old fool . . . All dreams will end, however, and Alec is a grass widower as I write, or else the French courts have not yet found time during their summer session to confirm the decree of divorce, application for which Alec made some months ago. *Sic erat in fatis*, and I might almost add, *Sic transit gloria mundi*."

News of the Cochrans' divorce was all over the newspapers during 1921, allowing the New York *Evening Telegram* of October 4 to give a contemporary opinion of GW: "Those who stood sponsor for her career in America are frank to confess her only assets were a marvelous string of pearls, a face and figure of remarkable beauty, masked in a baffling cloak of coldness and a voice scarcely calculated to call Metropolitan attention to its timbre."

A sequel to Landau's involvement in the Cochran divorce occurred nine years later when he was dealing in *objets d'art* in Paris. He asked by letter for GW to help him pay government taxes of 30,000 francs ($1,200) which he described as "a sum, actually not so frightening," adding, "I would like to feel that you will be inclined kindly towards my appeal and its effective satisfaction." Landau to GW March 13, 1930. GWLA.

The *New York Times* reported on May 2, 1922, that Cochran had left orders that his wife - who was in Dieppe with Harold McCormick when they officially separated - was not to be admitted to their Paris mansion. Once in her home, Mrs. Cochran had it guarded like a fort, and remained there "as in a besieged castle, resisting all efforts to oust her." Her attorney, Malone, charged that by barring his wife from the conjugal home, Cochran gave her sufficient grounds for a French divorce. GW engaged some well-known, well-connected and colorful lawyers to represent her over the years. Dudley Field Malone (1882-1950) was a leading attorney as well as a politician, liberal activist, and later a screen actor. In 1920 he ran unsuccessfully for Governor of New York and then served in the Woodrow Wilson administration. GW knew him through his wife, Doris Stevens, the writer and women's activist. Malone made his living principally as an international divorce lawyer, but in 1925 he was one of the defending attorneys (with Clarence Darrow) in the famous "Monkey Trial" with its leading questions about creationism and academic freedom. During the 1930s he moved to Beverly Hills to begin a new career as a movie actor, notably playing Winston Churchill in Michael Curtiz' "Mission to Moscow" (1943), made at the behest of F.D.R. to gain extra support from the Soviet Union in WW2. Dudley Field Malone left the world a memorable quote when speaking in support of academic freedom during the "Monkey Trial" – "I have never learned anything from any man who agreed with me."

An extract dated December 22, 1922 from the Divorce Register, Préfecture of the Seine Département, refers to the judgment of the Tribunal de la Seine of May 19, 1922 pronouncing a divorce in favor of GW, who had been married to Cochran with official approval at the same Mairie on September 15, 1920.

In later stories about "monkey gland" operations, The New York *Daily News*, April 3, 1971 refers to "a battery of high-priced foreign surgeons" and *Chicago Tribune* magazine of October 23, 1983, notes McCormick's "secret gland operation" as performed by Dr. Serge Voronoff, "a controversial surgeon."

Feodor Ivanovich Chaliapin (1873-1938) on a concert tour in 1926, discovered that Australians were more interested in sport than culture. Writing to Maxim Gorky, his biographer, from Sydney on September 6, 1926: "They're rich, they know nothing, they're interested in nothing, except sport." "Chaliapin - an autobiography as told to Maxim Gorky." Moscow 1957/58.

When it was known in the United States that GW had acquired a

Paris theater it was often referred to in the press as a wedding gift from Harold McCormick. In denying this, she told the Chicago *Tribune* in December 1922 that her own funds [provided by Cochran] had paid for the building, not those of her wealthy husband. She added: "I will never appear in my own theater until I have gained recognition solely on my merits as an artist."

Because of her status as a celebrity (famous for being famous) GW received mixed notices for her singing, particularly in the American press. They were often by news or social journalists whose reportage was rarely based on musical knowledge. Accepting that she was not equipped vocally or psychologically to join the ranks of the top sopranos, Walska suffered from contradictory criticism that makes it difficult to know how bad - or good - she really was. An exception was the well-regarded music critic of the Chicago *Evening American*, Herman Devries, whose knowledge of opera and the workings of the human voice exceeded that of most of his colleagues. Born 1858 in New York City into a musical family of Dutch descent as Hermann Devriès, he studied with one of the foremost French composers and teacher of his generation, Gabriel Fauré, and became a leading bass in the chorus of the Paris Opéra at the age of twenty. Devries sang key baritone roles at the Opéra-Comique in Paris and appeared at the Metropolitan Opera in New York between 1898 and 1900. Later, as a critic in Chicago, with his wife working a as a vocal coach, he was particularly interested in the development of new musicians and singers. His account of the informal gathering at the McCormick residence provides one of the most reliable assessments of GW's capabilities and deficiencies as a singer.

Chapter 8: *A Musical Mentor* 1923

Dr. Edward J. Kempf's report on Stanley McCormick (Harold's brother) incarcerated at Riven Rock estate, Santa Barbara. Undated - probably 1926: "As to Stanley's medical condition. Most of his behavior and thoughts since I have been working with him are not characteristic of any form of dementia praecox. If we consider the whole picture of his life, all its stresses from childhood until his illness, such as the strict Puritanism of his home making his sexual traumas abnormally severe, the seductions by his nurse Marie when he was a little child, suppression of his love to become an artist, his mother's attachment of herself to him when he was a young man, making him believe she had heart disease, the resistances to his marriage, the deep sexual incompatibilities after marriage, despairing struggle with masturbation, and his unfortunate reticence and self- suppression when in conflict with the wishes of other people, have produced a condition of malignant compulsion neurosis and not dementia praecox." [literally premature dementia - a form of schizophrenia] GWLA.

Edward J. Kempf (1885-1971), a distinguished American pioneer in the field of psychosomatic medicine, was the author of a number of books on psychiatric and psychological subjects. In 1923 he met with Sigmund Freud in Austria and the two men discussed their respective theories of the personality and methods of dealing with schizophrenia Dr. Kempf's textbook "Psychopathology" (1920) describes an acute or reactive psychosis - which became known as "Kempf's disease" - suffered by the target of unwanted homosexual advance. He explained that the condition resulting in "the pressure of uncontrollable sexual cravings" originated in the typical case of a young man becoming convinced through innuendo and insults from those around him that they believed he was a homosexual.

Grey Gardens is a 1975 film documentary by the Maysles brothers (Albert and David) about two reclusive former New York socialites, both named Edith Beale (aunt and first cousin of Jacqueline Bouvier Kennedy Onassis) living their eccentric lives at a decaying mansion in the Hamptons: the then-decrepit Grey Gardens. Their story was adapted into a Tony-winning musical which ran on Broadway from November 2006 for eight months. In 2009 an HBO film with the same title, starring Jessica Lange and Drew Barrymore, won six Prime Time Emmys and two Golden Globes.

GW agreed to at least one silent screen test, in spite of her haughty opposition to what she considered a tiresome formality, not worthy of her attention. A can of disintegrating 35mm nitrate film found in a cupboard at Lotusland after her death shows Walska in close-up, full-face, half-profile and full-profile - all with differing hairstyles: old-fashioned and contemporary. Following off-camera directions, she alternately smiles and looks serious, vampish and gauche, confident and embarrassed, in sequences running for a total of about ten minutes. The unidentified test may

468

have been for Madame's thwarted role of Joséphine in Abel Gance's *Napoleon* in 1925. Whatever its provenance the camera fails in doing justice to GW's legendary beauty.

Chapter 9: *Diva by Default* 1924-1925

The original version of *Madama Butterfly* was in two acts and had its première at La Scala, Milan during February 1904. It was not a success, due mainly to late completion and inadequate rehearsal time. Puccini made an immediate revision, splitting the second act into a third part, and the new version was given at Brescia four months later to great acclaim. *Madama Butterfly* soon became a staple of the standard repertoire, ranking regularly among the top ten operas performed worldwide. Perhaps the most interesting singer to take the title role was the diminutive Japanese soprano, Tamaki Miura (1884-1946), who built a career on performing Cio-Cio San, often praised for her "authentic" portrayal, but criticized for a rather thin voice matching her physical stature. The *New York Times* reviewed Miura's performance at the Manhattan Opera House in October 1915, noting that her personality charmed the audience but the voice in its lower ranges was seldom good. Their critic asked readers in a headline if she was an artist or a curiosity, which is exactly how Ganna Walska tended to be treated by the musical establishment. Miura was three years older than GW and they met during the San Carlo Opera Company's tour of the United States in 1924, during which Walska sought advice for her own performances of *Butterfly* throughout Europe - the only sustained operatic success of an otherwise blemished career. Tamaki Miura, who died in 1946, is commemorated in Nagasaki, where Madama Butterfly is set, with a statue in the city's Glover Park showing her in costume for her role.

An obituary notice from an unidentified and undated Polish newspaper for Napoleon Wladyslaw Puacz, who died November 21, 1924, states that he was the son of a participant in the 1863 uprising against the Russian Empire, worked on the railway, and later operated a store in Warsaw. A second clipping, also Polish, notes that he left the railway after persecution by the Tsar. Buried in Powazki cemetery, Warsaw, he is said to be survived by a wife, daughter (GW), sons, daughters-in-law, sister, brother, grandchildren and other relatives. Translated by Ted Ross. GWLA.

Singing *Madama Butterfly* at the Nice Opéra was a significant career progression for GW. Performing in the elegant, late 19th century building supervised by Charles Garnier, architect of the Paris Opéra, must have felt like the big time. But a rival center of opera and ballet existed only ten kilometers away along the Riviera's *corniche*, where its bijou contemporary, the Salle Garnier, part of the Principality of Monaco's Casino complex overlooking the Mediterranean, attracted the top critical and social attention, as well as the top stars and world première performances to its compact auditorium. From the start, the Monte-Carlo Opéra's artistic standing and wealthy clientèle attracted the celebrity performers of the day: Sarah Bernhardt (inaugurating the theatre in 1889), Adelina Patti, Francesco Tamagno, Feodor Chaliapin, Nellie Melba and Enrico Caruso. This prominence continued throughout the 1920s, including seasons by Diaghilev's Ballets Russes. Nice and Marseille could not compete on the same level, and their opera houses suffered like poor cousins as second-string or provincial.

Chapter 10: *International Celebrity* **1925-1926**

The *New York Times*, October 4, 1925 announced: "A film on a grand scale entitled 'Napoleon' will be developed in palaces and other settings through which Napoleon himself moved and lived and will tell in gorgeous pictures a story of the First Empire."

Gance's *Napoléon* used several cinematic techniques ahead of their time such as hand-held cameras and widescreen sequences. This blockbuster silent movie, running 330 minutes with an accompanying music score by Arthur Honneger, was premièred at the Paris Opéra on April 7, 1927 with Gina Manès in the role of Joséphine, originally offered to Ganna Walska. The film is regarded as one of the triumphs of silent cinema.

Ganna Walska's Fabergé Easter egg - the only large example thought to have been commissioned by an American (Consuelo Marlborough in 1902) was sent for auction to Parke-Bernet in New York, together with other items in 1965. It was acquired by Malcolm Forbes.

GW envied Angelica Catalani (1780-1849) for her legendary abilities as both a bel canto singer with a range of nearly three octaves and a shrewd business sense. Contemporary reports of her vocal brilliance suggest a powerful voice combined with

470

formidable technique. She was noted for the role of Susanna in Mozart's *The Marriage of Figaro*. Catalani's musical taste, however, was questionable, and she was sometimes regarded as an artist only in name. As a businesswoman, she gave bravura displays of charging outrageously, and it was said that she took half the total box office receipts for each production in which she appeared. Word of GW's interest in Catalani memorabilia circulated among the opportunistic Paris dealers, and one of them, R Strakosch on the rue Pigalle, contacted her by letter: "Having heard that you take great interest concerning the great singers of the past, I hereby take the liberty of informing you that I have a very fine oil painting of Madame Adelina Patti, who was my aunt, by Gustave Doré, and should you desire to acquire the same, I should willingly make arrangements with you." Strakosch to GW. March 2, 1924. GWLA.

Chapter 11: *Dollars from Scents* 1927-1928

The Infanta Eulalia, Duchess of Galliera (1864-1958) was the youngest daughter of Queen Isabella II and her husband Francis of Spain, whose brother succeeded to the monarchy as King Alfonso XII. In spite of being at the core of a conservative court and suffering a miserable marriage, disdaining her husband "with the same violence" that her mother showed to her father, the beautiful and intelligent Eulalia held progressive views that pitched her into constant conflict with the royal family. The Infanta (a title given to daughters of the Spanish monarch) shocked everyone by her independent spirit, expressed in a book exploring her thoughts on a wide range of contemporary issues including women's rights, socialism, education equality of the classes, religion, marriage, prejudices and traditions. Her nephew, King Alfonso XIII demanded that its publication be suspended until he read the manuscript and gave his approval - or not. Eulalia refused and "The Thread of Life" appeared under a pseudonym in 1912 in French and was subsequently translated into several languages. During her long and adventurous life, she wrote two other books under her own name and traveled extensively in Europe. Eulalia was hailed in the United States as a direct descendent of Christopher Columbus and became a member of the Daughters of the American Revolution as a descendent of Carlos III, under whose reign Spain began to be recognized as a nation. As GW's

471

friend with radical views on independence for women in modern society, the Infanta Eulalia was a strong influence in shaping her thoughts about feminism - albeit from a privileged perspective.

Vladimir Samoylovich Horowitz (1903 -1989) is widely recognized as one of the greatest pianists of the 20th century whose name became a byword for keyboard virtuosity, helped by a prolific discography. Born in Kiev in the Russian Empire, he gave his first solo recital under a different political regime in Kharkov, aged seventeen. Horowitz became famous across the Soviet Union giving concerts for which, in the economic circumstances caused by the Civil War, he was often paid in food instead of money. He defected to the West, making his first appearance in Berlin in December 1925 where GW's agent heard him and suggested his introduction to the music lovers of Paris at one of her regular recitals at rue de Lubeck. In 1928 the pianist, who claimed he really wanted to be a composer, made his American debut at Carnegie Hall on the way to becoming a huge musical celebrity over the following decades.

$240,000 is quoted in the text as the approximate exchange rate for the time when GW gained complete control of her Théâtre des Champs-Elysées: $1 = 25 French francs.

Martha Wheatley in the Binghamton *Press* (circulation 34,800) commented on GW's concert: "She never imitates, and if her real hope of success is only a fluttering bird of passage that plumed creature is sure to be faultlessly preened and exquisitely feathered. . . ." Quoted in *Time* magazine, December 17, 1928.

Names given to the GW range of perfumes seem to reflect some of Madame's attitudes to life and love. They included Près de Toi (Close to You), Chypre (literally Cyprus - a generic description for a family of fragrances with citrus overtones created by François Coty in 1917), Divorçons (Let's Get Divorced), Blue Ribbon (symbolizing high quality), Gardenia, Pois de Senteur (sweet pea) and Pour le Sport (presumably for the active woman because GW showed little interest in sport, with the possible exception of horse racing as a social ritual.) An indication of the Ganna Walska Perfume Company's standing in the arcane world of collecting antique perfume bottles can be gauged from an online auction in 2010 when a 1927 Divorçons in its original packaging was expected to bring $200, when a 1938 Baccarat bottle for Elizabeth

Arden's Cyclamen was estimated at $4000.

Paul Claudel (1868-1955) was a towering figure in French literature, though his renown as a poet and dramatist was tarnished in certain literary circles by his devout Catholicism and right-wing political views, as well as accusations of being anti-Semitic and a misogynist. Claudel had a parallel career as a diplomat, but he did not always regard the profession over-seriously: "It is fortunate that diplomats have long noses since they usually cannot see beyond them." When he was appointed France's ambassador to the United States his controversial reputation made the cover story for *Time* magazine of March 21, 1927. On the day GW lunched with him in Washington, D.C. during her American concert tour she could never have imagined that later in the afternoon she would be singing in competition with a caged lion. It must have amused her host when he heard about it, being a man of letters with a fine turn of phrase - such as his oft-quoted "Intelligence is nothing without delight."

Chapter 12: *Flirting with Feminism* **1929**

Djamgaroff to GW September 17, 1929 and October 11, 1929 pointed out in memoranda that American sales of Ganna Walska beauty products made during the month of September were greater than those of the Paris factory for three years "notwithstanding the fact that Paris has had 2,740,000 francs and New York only one-tenth of that amount; these figures are enough to show you what possibilities the New York Company has and how far it could go if it had a reasonable amount of working capital." GWLA.

Frederik Herman Gade (1871-1943) was a Norwegian-born, Harvard-educated diplomat and lawyer who became an American citizen and was prominent in Chicago social circles, where he served as the honorary Norwegian consul for several years, while running his own law practice. Gade lived at Lake Forest, where the McCormick family had their out-of-town estate, and was the municipality's mayor on four occasions. He acquired the splendid 16th century château of Le Mesnil-Saint-Denis around the same time as GW's bought her own, more modest, bijou château at nearby Galluis

Although the press and rumormongers gossiped long and loud about GW and her "Svengali," there could be no denying that Walther Straram was a major figure on the Paris concert scene, particularly in the years between 1923 and 1933 when Madame engaged him as her private singing teacher, appointed him as *administrateur délégué* of the Théâtre des Champs-Elysées, and financed a full symphony orchestra for him to conduct, described by several critics as the best in France. In seasons at the Salle Gaveau, the Grande Salle Pleyel and the Champs-Elysées, Straram presented the standard concert repertoire of the day as well as introducing much contemporary music. He conducted a number of première performances of works by Lennox Berkeley, Villa-Lobos, Marcel Dupré, Milhaud, Hindemith, Messiaen, Castelnuovo-Tedesco and Roussel. Well-known composers were sometimes invited to conduct their own compositions with the Orchestre des Concerts Straram, as it was known, including Richard Strauss, Igor Stravinsky, Arthur Honegger and Manuel de Falla. Straram's baton was handed over occasionally to the visiting giants of the era like Toscanini, Furtwangler, Stokowski, Koussevitsky and Ansermet. In addition to symphony concerts, the Straram orchestra was conducted by Stravinsky for his first recording of "The Rite of Spring" in 1929 and again, in 1931, for the world première recording of "Symphony of Psalms." Straram himself won the Prix Candide, the first classical music award for the phonograph, with Debussy's "Prélude à l'après-midi d'un faun." Several compilations have been issued on CD and MP3 from the Straram recorded repertoire and are listed on Amazon, allowing GW and her mentor's musical marriage - the one that *was* made in heaven - to live on. A famous poem by Shelley published posthumously in 1824, and the inspiration for many composers to set the words to their music, might provide an appropriate postlude for their fruitful collaboration:

> **Music, when soft voices die,**
> **Vibrates in the memory;**
> **Odors, when sweet violets sicken,**
> **Live within the senses they quicken.**
> **Rose leaves, when the rose is dead,**
> **Are heap'd for the beloved's bed;**
> **And so thy thoughts when thou art gone,**
> **Love itself shall slumber on.**

Leopold von Hoesch (1881-1936), a career diplomat who served as the German ambassador to France from 1923, was a cultured and gentlemanly figure from the tradition of old-world diplomacy.

In Paris, he devoted his energies to smoothing relations between his defeated country and its Western neighbors following the horrors of the Great War. During 1932 he became the German ambassador to the Court of St. James and was generally welcomed by British government ministers for his anti-war sentiments during the rise of Nazism. He criticized Hitler's invasion of the Rhineland as an act designed to provoke the French only a month before his untimely death in 1936 from a heart complaint. Hoesch's replacement in London was the notorious Joachim von Ribbentrop, the Fuhrer's favorite foreign policy advisor, later to be hanged for war crimes.

Chapter 13: *A Date with Mussolini* 1930-1931

When GW visited Rome with an official invitation to meet Benito Mussolini, the Italian dictator's concordat with the Vatican was already in place protecting the honor and dignity of the Pope, and all school teachers had to swear oaths of allegiance to the fascist regime. Newspaper editors were personally selected by Il Duce and no one without a certificate of approval could work as a journalist. Trade unions had no independence, and the nation was run, in effect, as a police state. Since his March on Rome in 1922 at the head of the notorious black shirts, Mussolini had attained a despotic position with virtually no constitutional restraints on his powers. In foreign policy, Il Duce encouraged a form of aggressive nationalism with the intention of making his country respected - but feared - throughout Europe, portraying himself as a caring, paternal statesman. Against this highly propagandized background, with an ambition to make the Mediterranean *mare nostrum* - "our sea," and in spite of what friends in Paris told her, GW was pleasantly surprised to find the Eternal City operating in a way that she thought perfectly normal, with an impressive program of public works and services. They included the ultimate political cliché of the leader succeeding to make the Italian railways run on time. GW enjoyed her visit and returned home to France with a glow of satisfaction for what she saw and experienced. But the atmosphere had changed dramatically a few years later. In ART she records that in 1935 she tried to pay her respects to Mussolini when passing through Rome and was almost arrested on approaching Palazzo Venezia: "When I did come near it, two husky men jumped on the steps of my car to prevent me from putting my feet on the ground in Il Duce's vicinity."

In 1930, when GW received her surprise birthday gift from Harold McCormick, the International Harvester Company, with headquarters in Chicago, was one of the world's leading multinationals, recognized everywhere by the IH trademark on its range of trucks, tractors and general agricultural machinery made by the largest and most influential manufacturer of farm equipment of the twentieth century. It had originated from the amalgamation in 1902 of the McCormick Harvesting Machine Company and Deering Harvester Company, together with three smaller agricultural equipment firms. The giant corporation was named after the first product it mass-produced: the mechanical reaper invented by Cyrus McCormick in 1831 and later known as a harvester. By 1910, IH was one of the leading corporations in the United States with gross annual sales of around a hundred million dollars, seventeen thousand workers, its own steel mill in the Chicago area and foreign manufacturing plants located in Sweden, Russia and Germany. The first harvester-thresher was marketed in 1915 and became known as a combine harvester. IH had moved quickly into motorized vehicles and equipment, with a sales network across the world, and GW was the recipient of this legacy through generous trust funds set up by Harold McCormick, which seemed to remain inviolable in spite of the grim economic conditions of the 1930's, and their looming divorce.

Excerpts from the Department of State's instructions on Madame's passport applications are contained in a communication of June 12, 1930, attached to a letter from Marc L. Severe, American Vice-Consul, Paris, to Walska. GWLA.

Walter Lowrie Fisher (1862-1935) was Harold McCormick's divorce lawyer in his action against GW. He moved to Chicago from his native Virginia to establish a successful law practice and become a potent force in the city's civic affairs. Fisher was prominent as a reformist, railing against corrupt city aldermen and striving to free Chicago's transport system from rampant corruption during the early years of the 20th century. His longtime friend, President William Howard Taft, appointed him Secretary of the Interior (1911-1913) and as a progressive Republican he helped Taft during the 1912 presidential campaign, which was lost to Woodrow Wilson. Fisher continued his career in law and civic matters, and Phelan Beale had reason to caution GW about his abilities.

Chapter 14: *Curtains* **1932-1935**

Society gossip in Chicago *Daily News*, October 5, 1928, noted that Baroness Violet Beatrice Wenner recently returned from Vienna to open her studio apartment for the winter at 619 North Michigan Avenue was entertained "quite informally at tea at the Saddle and Cycle Club by Mrs. Alister McCormick."

In June, 1933, the ailing Walther Straram managed to conduct a rare GW appearance on the stage of the Champs-Elysées in a private performance of Debussy's *Pelléas et Mélisande*, and then traveled to Ostend in Belgium for a festival of French music: Berlioz, Saint-Saens, Lalo, Debussy and Ravel, ending with Chabrier's *Marche Joyeuse*. It was as joyous a way as any to end the career of a brilliant musician, too ill to conduct any more. The Orchestre Concerts Straram continued to perform during October, 1933 under Toscanini, and Straram died on November 23. The Italian maestro admired the man as well as his musicians, describing the orchestra as "One of the most consistent, the most perfect, the most prestigious that I have ever had the occasion to conduct." Honoring those sentiments, Toscanini returned to Paris for a quartet of concerts during June, 1934 billed as *Hommage à la Mémoire de Walter Straram*. He then took the players to the Palais des Beaux-Arts in Brussels before returning to the French capital for two further appearances at the Champs-Elysées. A year later, the feisty little Italian conductor came back to Paris to conduct the remnants of the Orchestre Concerts Straram, which then disbanded.

The signatories recommending the award of GW's Légion d'honneur were Charles Widor, permanent secretary of the Académie de Beaux-Arts; Phillipe Gaubert, conductor of the Orchestre de la Société des Concerts du Conservatoire de Paris; Albert Wolff, conductor of the Concerts Pasdeloup; composers Darius Milhaud, Jacques Ibert, Louis Aubert, Albert Roussel; together with Professor Philipps of the Conservatoire de Paris and director of the Conservatoire de Versailles.

Chapter 15: *New York, New York* **1936**

Cordell Hull (1871 -1955) is America's longest-serving Secretary of State: for eleven years 1933 - 1944. He received the Nobel

Peace Prize in 1945 for his work in establishing the United Nations, and President Roosevelt called him the "Father of the United Nations."

Thirteen disks recorded privately by GW were found in a cupboard at Lotusland in 1992. The piano accompanist is unknown. No specific date is noted for recordings 1 and 2. Numbers 3 -13 are from February 22, 1936:

1. Giordano, "Caro mio ben."
2. same.
3. Schubert, "Die Forelle," Op.32; D.550.
4. Schumann, "Der Nussbaum," Op.25, No.3.
5. unidentified.
6. Brahms, "Von Ewiger Liebe," Op.43, No.1.
7. Charpentier, *Louise*: "Depuis le jour."
8. Schubert, Wiegenlied: "Schlafe, schlafe holder susses Knaabe," Op. 98, No.2 a.D.498.
9. Schubert, Die Winterreise: ADie Post," D. 911.
10. Wolf, "In dem Schatten meiner Locken."
11. Richard Strauss, ADie Nacht," Op.10, No. 3.
12. Richard Strauss, "Morgen," Op.27, No.4.
13. Bach-Gounod, "Ave Maria."

When GW finally met the woman who had fired the affections of Dr. Fraenkel, the former Alma Mahler claimed to be her soul sister and they became, according to Walska, firm friends. They must have had an interesting tete-a-tete at their meeting in Venice, perhaps reminiscing about strangely similar lives associated with powerful, older men - but never controlled by them - becoming contemporary icons of independent womanhood while being perceived widely as celebrity femmes fatales. Both were beauties who needed to be surrounded by creative genius, with Alma regarded disrespectfully at this time as "The widow of the four arts," referring to music, architecture, painting and literature, through her marriages, or close liaisons, with Gustav Mahler, Walter Gropius, Oskar Kokoscha and Franz Werfel. Ganna Walska had tended to go for the money first with her spouses (Fraenkel, Cochran, McCormick) and then employ her acquired wealth to satisfy her cultural ambitions with close, non-marital relations (Stokowski and Straram to mention but two.) After similar, hair-raising escapes from Europe following the German occupation of

France in WW2, the two women met each other in the United States and had much more to talk about.

Chapter 16: *Doldrums* 1936

The Indian mystic Meher Baba ("compassionate father") took a vow of silence on July 10, 1925 and observed it until his death in 1969. His life was spent alternating between periods of seclusion with his disciples, and traveling in the West where he attracted many followers, particularly women. His tomb-shrine in Meherabad in India remains a place of pilgrimage. Baba's teachings are much-quoted and he even had a worldwide song hit in 1988 with Bobby McFerrin's "Don't Worry Be Happy" - the limited lyrics taken from an expression used by the mystic when cabling his followers.

Undated and unsigned instructions to be observed for Baba's visit to the Château de Galluis are written on notepaper from the Hotel Metropolitain, Paris. GWLA.

Norina Matchabelli (1880-1957) was born Norina Gilli in Florence, Italy and became well-known in Europe and the United States under the name of Maria Carmi, a beautiful stage and silent screen actress and mystic. She studied drama at Max Reinhardt's acting school at the Deutsches Theater, Berlin and joined his company for two years from 1907, performing in Germany and Italy before appearing in London and New York as the Madonna in the pantomime-play *The Miracle* written by her first husband Kurt Vollmoller. It was a role she played more than a thousand times during her stage career. During 1917 in the United States she married for a second time to Prince Georges Matchabelli, a Georgian aristocrat, senior diplomat, amateur chemist and co-founder with his wife of the perfume company Prince Matchabelli. Norina became known as Princess Matchabelli. The couple divorced in 1933, two years after Norina became a devoted follower of the Indian spiritual leader Meher Baba. Matchabelli died in 1935 leaving the company to his wife, who sold it a year later for $250,000.

Sam Waagenaar (1908-1977) was born in Amsterdam's Jewish Quarter, the son of a diamond worker. As a young man he lived and worked in Paris where he studied singing with Cécile Gilly [meeting GW] and performed in operetta, later becoming publicity manager for the French MGM Company. He emigrated to the

United States in 1939 and acted in Hollywood films, then becoming a correspondent for the U.S. Army. Waagenaar reported the D-Day landings in Normandy, arrived in Paris for the Liberation and visited Auschwitz. He became a successful photojournalist after the war and settled in Rome.

Chapter 17: *Cause and Effect* 1937

Rudolf Joseph Lorenz Steiner (1861-1925) the Austrian social reformer, philosopher and architect founded a spiritual movement called Anthroposophy, seeking a fusion of mysticism and science. He immersed himself in a variety of media including drama, eurhythmics and art, culminating in building his Goetheaum with two performance stages and several event spaces as a cultural center to house all the arts, and as a place to cultivate individualism with no limit to human knowledge. On her whistle-stop tour of the Steiner village at Dornach, near Basel, GW was impressed by what she saw and enjoyed meeting with Steiner adherents, though she thought, on reflection, that their lives, rather than expressing uplifting individualism were too rigidly utopian. Steiner's greatest legacy was probably in education, founding the first of his Waldorf Schools in 1922. There are now Steiner Schools, kindergartens and university colleges numbering into the thousands, claimed to be the largest independent educational movement worldwide.

GW's friend and admirer, Dr. Josef Orlowski, an American-based Polish journalist, visited Padarewski in Morges, Switzerland - a small town on Lake Geneva near Lausanne - where he found the former statesman and piano virtuoso living in penurious circumstances. Orlowski to GW. March 20, 1937. GWLA.

Léa Martin-Daszkiewicz. Recollections of the Château de Galluis faxed to the author, February 23, 1999.   .

"The King and Dr. Cannon," BBC Radio 4, December 6, 2008: In 1939, having moved to the Isle of Man to set up a clinic for nervous diseases, Dr. Cannon was investigated by the British internal security organization MI5 on suspicion of being a Nazi sympathizer and a German spy. He was described in their reports as "a queer fish" and "a quack and a compulsive liar." After the war, Cannon continued to present live magic shows with psychological overtones and he died in 1963, aged sixty-seven.

Chapter 18: *The Mad Inventor* 1937

Details of the London performances of GW's private production of *Daphnis et Chloé*, for which she paid the entire cost, come from the archives of the Royal Opera House, Covent Garden. The striking décor and costumes by Boris Blitsky were much-admired. Blitsky (born 1900) was a Russian artist and designer working in Paris, famous for his posters and publicity material for Fritz Lang's expressionist science-fiction movie *Metropolis* in 1927.

Receipt for GW loan to Grindell on 6 September, signed by him at the Ritz Hotel, London. GWLA.

Pre-nuptial documents for GW signature sent to the Ritz Hotel from London solicitors Perowne & Co. September 14, 1937. GWLA.

Chapter 19: *Saving Britain* 1937-1939

Telegrams of seasonal greetings were sent to Joan and Lestock Reid in England; Mrs. Pinchard in Mayfair, London; Miss Morris, Grindell's housekeeper in Wales; with a special one to Mr. Lindsay Rea, Grindell's eye surgeon in London's Harley Street: "Merry Xmas. Happy 1938, Which Is For Me Happiest Of All Thanks To Sight You Gave Me Back. Grindell And Ganna Walska." GWLA.

Invoice for purchase of Terraplane vehicle for Grindell from George Newman & Co., London. March 4, 1938. GWLA.

Coutts & Co., London, notification of remittance from GW June 14, 1938. GWLA.

Chapter 20: *Mecca of Equality* 1940

Pierre Arnold Bernard, born Iowa 1875, assumed several names over the years, including Perry Baker, Peter Coon and Homer Stansbury Leeds, before settling on Pierre Bernard in 1909 after founding his Sanskrit College in New York. He was also dubbed by the press "The Great Oom" and "Omnipotent Oom." Bernard was a larger-than-life character whose skills embraced a quirky combination of sex, mysticism, money and celebrity, ranging over myriad activities from religious scholarship and philosophy to con man and seducer. He was said to own the largest Sanskrit library in the United States and the first to introduce the practices of yoga to Americans. He also made sure to obscure many details of his motley activities, including the facility to attract rich widows and relieve them of their money, to be used for his various business schemes. Bernard died in 1955 at the age of seventy-nine, and his nephew, Theos Bernard, inherited his celebrity uncle's reputation as an engaging hustler, while maintaining a veneer of scholarly respectability.

Letter from Don Brown, professor of religious studies at University of California, Santa Barbara, to Bob Easton, reminiscing about GW and Theos Bernard. Dated July 4, 1982.

Chapter 21: *The White Lama* 1940-1941

Vanity Fair, **January 2000**. Published letter to the editor from Beatrice Welles (Orson Welles' daughter) refers to the origins of *Citizen Kane*.

"Our Family - Stevens, Jacques and Tallant" and "Our Montecito Valley Home" by Kinton B. Stevens, February 1961 and February 1963 respectively, provide full details of GW's Montecito estate's early history.

Chapter 22: *Tibetland* 1942

The air attacks on Darwin and those against other targets in the Northern Territory and Western Australia were part of Japan's strategy to prevent the Allies using Australia's northern ports, airfields and military installations to defend Timor and Java against a Japanese invasion. The first attack on Darwin on February 19, 1942 by 242 aircraft, dropped more bombs than used during the raid on Pearl Harbor two months before, and killed at least 243 persons, injured up to 400 and made hundreds homeless. The lightly defended city in the tropics was abandoned as a major naval base, and Darwin would be attacked from the air on sixty-four subsequent occasions. The federal government in Canberra downplayed the deaths and damage from enemy bombing raids in the north of the continent, believing that the news would be a huge psychological blow to the nation and affect wartime morale. The bombing of Darwin was described after the war as "Australia's Pearl Harbor."

GW's secretary, Miss Finlay, had first written to American Express in Los Angeles about arranging travel for Tibetan Lamas on October 13, 1941. GWLA.

The distinguished landscape architect Lockwood de Forest Jr., son of a key figure in the American Aesthetic Movement as a designer and landscape painter, was born in New York City in 1896, studied landscape design at Harvard and after the First

World War returned to the West, where he had been educated as a youngster, to study at the University of California, Berkeley. He then traveled in Europe looking at Renaissance villas in Italy and Moorish gardens in Spain. Lockwood's return to California coincided with an era of garden ferment, particularly around Santa Barbara, and for the next two decades he was commissioned to design some of the areas great estates, working with Ralph Stevens and George Washington Smith, among other top designers until he went off to war in 1942. He planned his last large-scale garden in 1946 and died in 1949;

GW, in marrying Theos Bernard and making him her sixth spouse, matched Henry VIII's tally of wives. Unlike the calculating monarch, however, no executions were needed to divest Madame of any of the passing parade of husbands, though her published and unpublished memoirs contain character assassinations of most of them.

Chapter 23: *Life with Yogi* 1943

Transcription of GW's radio broadcast in Polish translated by Lucy and Chester Radlo. GWLA

All aspects of American daily life were regulated during the Second World War. A swingeing scheme introduced in 1942 rationed gasoline and automobile tires (because of a shortage of rubber) and a year later the government issued ration coupons for purchasing a wide range of goods, including clothing and fuel oil, shoes, meat, cheese, margarine, dried fruits and canned food. Controls placed on economic activity applied to wealth, wages and prices; increased taxes affected the wealthy, with top marginal rates ranging from 81% to 94%. The income level attracting the top rate was reduced from $5 million to $200,000, which directly affected GW, as did a scarcity of labor for developing Tibetland and Penthouse of the Gods. In 1940, Congress had introduced the first peace-time legislation for the draft, which was renewed the following year. Those classified 4F were not called for military service, and this applied to Theos Bernard, who managed to lead a reasonably "normal" life throughout the entire conflict with the help of GW, but not without constantly complaining of the inconvenience.

In her introduction to "Always Room at the Top," GW stated: "I did not want these memoirs to be written by a literary collaborator who might take the facts of my life and by romanticizing my personality through his interpretation of my character thus obscure the true psychological issues and not conform to reality." She said she could not remember "what gave birth to her memoirs," deciding it was because of extreme loneliness: "I suppose my secretive nature desired a confidant and could think of no other possibility than the friendly white pages of a confessional." In other words, the diaries and notes she kept over the years. The cover blurb of ART described her book as "the story of the life of an internationally known personality - a woman of beauty and wit. . . Through these pages there pass the most famous personages of our time in the fields of music, art, politics, statesmanship, religion and philosophy." ART was published with a recommended price of $3.50 and contains 504 pages (similar to this biography!) A prominent review appeared in the *New York Times* under the byline of Effie Alley, October 10, 1943, drawing heavily on quotes from the book and including the percipient comment that GW rarely engaged in light flirtations: "She was one of those all-or-nothing girls."

Viola Wertheim (1907-1998), who married Theos Bernard in 1934, was the youngest child of Jacob Wertheim, founder of the United Cigar Manufacturers Company, and at one time a director of General Motors Corporation and the Underwood Typewriter Company. He was also a founder of the Federation for the Support of Jewish Philanthropic Societies. Viola lived at Pierre Bernard's ashram at Clarkstown, Rockland County, New York between 1926 and 1930, practicing yoga and studying Eastern philosophy, where she met Pierre's nephew Theos Bernard. They married in 1934 and following her graduation from medical school in 1936 the couple traveled extensively in Japan, China and India. Viola returned to the United States to begin her medical internship at Cornell, while her husband continued on to Tibet. They divorced in 1938. A woman of unwavering social conscience, Viola engaged in a wide range of causes, including a vocal defense of the alleged Cold War spy Alger Hiss, and was herself investigated by the Federal Security Agency of suspected "un-American activities" in 1951-52. A pioneer in the field of social psychoanalysis, Viola Wertheim, made a major contribution over many years to community psychoanalytic research and practice at Columbia, and at her death in 1998 was the university's clinical professor emeritus of psychiatry.

Chapter 24: *Burbank Blues* 1944-1946

Dr. Herbert Koteen, GW's New York physician was interviewed by the author, Santa Barbara, October 14, 1998. He died in 2003 aged ninety, leaving in his will The Herbert Koteen, M.D. Scholarship for students enrolled in the Johns Hopkins Medical School, his alma mater.

Born in Germany in 1902, Mr. John (Hans Piocelle Harberger) was an American milliner whose name, according to obituaries, was as famous in the world of hats as Christian Dior's in haute couture. In 1929 he formed a partnership with Frederic Hirst to establish the millinery label John- Frederics. His clients included stars of stage, screen, opera and high society, including Gloria Vanderbilt, Lauren Bacall, Joan Crawford and Ganna Walska. Mr. John's creations were seen by millions on screen worn by Vivien Leigh in *Gone with the Wind*, Marlene Dietrich in *Shanghai Express*, Greta Garbo in *The Painted Veil* and Marilyn Monroe in *Gentlemen Prefer Blondes*. Mr. John's headwear for *Gone with the Wind* (1939) made bonnets popular again, and his version of the snood added a touch of glamor to women's wartime fashion. He died in 1993.

Chapter 25: *Freedom!* 1946

At the time of GW's divorce action, the hottest name in criminal defense was Jerry Giesler, known as "Attorney to the stars" for defending, and usually obtaining, acquittals for his celebrity clients. According to the "Guinness Book of World Records," he became "the highest-paid attorney." In 1935 Giesler represented movie choreographer and director Busby Berkeley, charged as the responsible driver in a terrible automobile accident in Los Angeles County, in which two people were killed, five seriously injured, with Berkeley himself badly cut and bruised. When the first two trials for second degree murder ended with hung juries, the director was acquitted in the third and went on to make many further hits such as *Gold Diggers of 1935* (1935) and *Gold Diggers of 1937* (1936.) Giesler continued to serve Hollywood's leading names, including Errol Flynn. The star's raunchy lifestyle as a serial womanizer caught up with him in 1942 when two under-age teenage girls accused the actor of statutory rape. Giesler successfully defended Flynn in a trial that made headlines around the world, and his swashbuckling career, rather than becoming irreparably tarnished, went from strength to strength. How Giesler came to be involved in Theos Bernard's divorce case against GW is not known, but as first president of the Criminal Courts Bar Association in Los Angeles he risked his credentials by visiting Tibetland to suggest an out-of-court settlement to GW without discussing it with her own legal team. The superstar lawyer achieved more notoriety by representing Marilyn Monroe in her much publicized divorce from Joe di Maggio in 1954.

GW's letter to Frank P. Dow Co., Los Angeles, Calif., December 10, 1965 refers to her 1946 visit to France and arrangements to send a second consignment of furniture from the Château de Galluis to Lotusland: ". . . the form asks when I was last abroad. It was in 1946, I believe (I am never sure of the year) after World War II was finished. I went to France to attend to my homes there. In those days planes were going only twice a week and so I went with one and returned five or six days later with the other plane. I believe at that time the airport was called La Guardia but I am not quite sure." GWLA.

GW wrote to Wagenaar seeking information about "my family" on October 25, 1945: "Did you see Madame Gilly. Probably not as she is not in Paris. Did you send her my book or did you lose [it] on the way? My brother wrote me that my niece fell in love with you, that you were the first man in her life. She was tiny when I saw her last time; she was very pretty. Is she still? GWLA.

Chapter 26: *Life without Yogi* 1947

Three affidavits sent to Warsaw - for GW, Leon Puacz and Phelan Beale - were drawn up by the Bouvier Beale legal office. GW's and Beale's documents were sworn before Katharine A. Woods, Notary Public, State of New York on April 16, 1947, before being sent together with Leon's to Poland. GWLA.

Oswald da Ros was interviewed by the author, Santa Barbara. October 15, 1998.

Stanley McCormick's long incarceration in Santa Barbara is the central theme of T.C. Boyle's gripping 1998 novel "Riven Rock."

David Kamansky interviewed by the author in London, UK, November 20, 1998.

Theos Bernard's third wife (or partner as she also called herself) was Helen Graham Park, with a career in architecture and a passion for Tibetan Buddhism. She spent a year with Bernard as his research colleague when he returned to the Indian Himalayas in 1947 following his divorce from GW. After his untimely death, Park resumed her work as an architect and organized her small, but important, collection of Bernard's Tibetan acquisitions, as well as his unpublished essays, notebooks, correspondence and historical documents. In 1994 the Helen Graham Park Foundation was established in Florida to honor her life and work.

Chapter 27: *Family Matters* 1948-1951

One of GW's heroines was Alexandra David-Néel, born in Paris in 1868, who showed and early and precocious talent for singing and a curiosity about far-flung places. She acquired a taste for Eastern philosophy during a journey to India in 1891, returning to France to perform in opera and operetta as Mlle. Myrial – perhaps like GW changing her name for the sake of propriety. David-Néel sang works by Delibes, Gounod, Massenet and Puccini in the French provinces, then in 1895 was chosen to tour Indo-China, billed in Hanoi and Haiphong as the Opéra-Comique's *première chanteuse.* She received acclaim as Violetta in *La traviata* and then attempted *Carmen*, which was beyond her abilities and almost ruined the voice. Returning to Paris, Alexandra was unable to build upon her former successes and embraced occultism, while going to perform in Tunis with the municipal opera company where she met Phillip Neel, her English husband-to-be. They were married at the French consulate in 1904 and eventually moved to London, becoming involved with the Buddhist revival movement. Alexandra's passion for occult studies took her to India and, incredibly, toward Tibet. Suffering all kinds of privations, she went to live in Sikkim, where the Buddhist monks ordained her in 1914, and later, in 1916, the Panchen himself bestowed on her the robe of a graduate. David-Néel reached Lhasa on foot in October, 1923 and would describe her extraordinary experiences in "My Journey to Lhasa," published in London, New York and Paris during 1927. She was quoted as saying "Adventure is my only reason for living," and GW, admiring such spirit, determined to emulate her.

Anne Dewey interviewed by the author, Santa Barbara, September 30, 1999.

.U.S. Department of Justice, Immigration and Naturalization Service, Los Angeles, references: D.P. 5638: 5637: 5639 - Maria Puacz, Hanka Puacz, Leon Wladyslaw Puacz. Issued January 3, 1951.

Ralph Stevens was well-qualified to play a prominent role in Lotusland's development for GW. Born in Montecito in 1882, he graduated in landscape architecture at Michigan State College and worked in Chicago before taking up a teaching post at the University of California, Berkeley from 1913. He entered private practice as a landscape architect at Santa Barbara in 1917 and taught at the Santa Barbara School of Arts. Stevens became superintendent of the city's Parks Department and then Parks Commissioner and consultant. His designs amalgamated strands of international and Californian ideals of landscape and planting in which Mediterranean influences merged with the local Spanish Colonial Revival in architecture to produce a less formal, and identifiably local style. A notable property for which Stevens designed the original garden plan is Casa del Herrero, which became a National Historic Landmark in 2009. Ralph Stevens died in 1958, and Santa Barbara's Stevens Park is named after him.

Alien registration numbers issued for the Puacz family: (Leon) A#6942764, (Marysia) A#6965838, (Hanka) #A6965639.

.Chapter 28: *Queen of Lotusland* 1952-1958

Phelan Beale, GW's long-serving attorney was known as a wealthy sportsman in New York City society. He graduated from Columbia Law School in 1905 aged twenty-four and founded the law practice of Bouvier Beale with Jacqueline Kennedy Onassis's grandfather, John Vernou Bouvier Jr. Beale married Bouvier's daughter, Edith Ewing, in 1917, separating from her around 1926 and they were legally divorced in 1931. He is best remembered, not so much for his legal expertise and sporting activities, as the absent father in the *Grey Gardens* saga on stage and screen.

Beale's successor as GW's principal attorney was Alfred Rice, a prominent Manhattan lawyer who numbered several famous authors among his clients, including Ernest Hemingway and E.E. Cummings, the celebrated American poet and essayist. Rice graduated from Fordham University Law School and specialized in copyright law. He began representing Hemingway in 1944, looking after his literary, radio and movie properties, often visiting Cuba to meet with his client living there. Ernest Hemingway died from a self-inflicted gunshot wound in Idaho during July 1960 and the Nobel and Pulitzer prizewinner's will was found shortly after with his publishers, Charles Scribner's Sons, in one of three leather valises, together with what Alfred Rice called some "very personal items." These were transferred to the attorney's office at 640 Fifth Avenue and found to include several original handwritten manuscripts, two of which, "A Farewell to Arms" and "For Whom the Bell Tolls," Rice said at the time "Will probably go to Harvard University, Mr. Hemingway had intended to give them to the university in 1956 but never got around to it." Their value was described as "substantial." As well as his legal and literary activities, Alfred Rice was a trustee of the Hospital for Joint Diseases Orthopedic Institute for many years and served as its president for eight years. He died in 1989 aged eighty-one.

Chapter 29: *Cactus and Codicils* **1959-1965**

An undated letter from Richard Gentry, "Donroven," Delaplane, Virginia to GW Invites her to accompany him to *The Sound of Music* on Friday, January 29, 1960 at Broadway's Lunt-Fontanne Theater, starring Mary Martin and Theodore Bikel. GWLA.

William Paylen interviewed by the author, Santa Barbara. October 20, 1998.

Bruce Van Dyke interviewed by the author, Santa Barbara. October 23, 1998.

GW vacillated about the disposal of the uninhabited - and uninhabitable - Château de Galluis causing it to deteriorate even further, leading to a French surveyor's conclusion that the buildings on her property had no value, as such. Local zoning restrictions were imposed to preserve the park-like character of the estate, and in particular the striking avenue of trees from the main gates. The upgrading of the RN12 meant that a busy highway bordered the estate and further affected its value. GW finally accepted a much reduced price for the land; the main building was torn down, leaving only the gates, the avenue and "Le petit château" or guest house where Grindell Matthews and Walther Straram had lived, as the only tangible reminders of Madame's tenure.

Patricia Tarkowska memoirs recorded by Santa Barbara

489

Historical Society's Oral History Program in January 21, 1987. Also author interview - see details in Notes: *Prelude*.

Chapter 30: *Put the House in Order* 1966-1972

Katharine Dexter McCormick's generous underwriting of the work of Gregory Pincus, the reproductive biologist at Boston's Worcester Foundation for Experimental Biology, led to the development and subsequent marketing of the oral contraceptive pill for women.

A reminder of GW's passion for fine jewelry surfaced forty-two years after the sale of her prized collection at Parke-Bernet in New York. In Geneva, Switzerland international collectors were excited by the auction of the "Walska Briolette Diamond" brooch which had been purchased from the New York sale by the French jewelers Van Cleef & Arpels and transformed into a golden Bird of Paradise brooch with the addition of other precious stones. Originally in the form of pendant, it sold in the low tens of thousands of dollars. In November, 2013 at Sotheby's Madame Walska's 96.62 flawless yellow diamond attracted a winning bid of $10,555,778 - the highest price ever paid for one Van Cleef & Arpels' pieces.

GW's commitment to the performing arts continued throughout the 1960s and into the seventies. Her long friendship with the impresario Sol Hurok led to Dr. Warren Austin's Val Verde Enterprises presenting the Metropolitan National Company's *Madama Butterfly* under Hurok management at Santa Barbara's Granada Theatre in March, 1966. It was more than forty years since GW first sang Cio-Cio San in Puccini's masterpiece.

Chapter 31: *New Direction* 1972-1976

Reminiscences of Charles Glass in this chapter, Chapter 33 and *Postlude* come from his unpublished manuscript "Ganna Walska's Lotusland (experiences of 12 years as Director of 'Lotusland' the Fabulous Estate of Mme. Ganna Walska.)" deposited with GWLA April 28, 1992. Additional information from *Cactus and Succulent Journal (U.S.)* Vol. 65: "Cacti, Shells, and Music - The Charles Glass Story" by Larry W. Mitchell - Cactus *and Succulent Journal (U.S.)* XLIV: 6 (Nov. - Dec. 1972): "Lotusland the Fabulous Garden of Mme. Ganna Walska" by Charles Glass and Bob Foster; *Cactus and Succulent Journal (U.S.)"* Vol. XLVI, "The Succulents of Lotusland" by Charles Glass and Bob Foster.

Michael Monteabaro. Interviewed by the author, Santa Barbara, October 20, 1998.

GW's undated draft correspondence, presumably intended for Guru Rinpoche, suggests that donating her collection was far from a *fait accompli*, as far as she was concerned. In one draft GW states: "From the beginning of my acquaintance with Mike [Monteabaro] there was nothing normal and simple, everything was deceptive, strange and unusual . . . Later I discovered that he begged Elden [the tree man from Griffin's Nursery] to take him as a helper because he desired to see this great Collection. So even the first step was not truthful and sincere but [a] calculated act." GW's initial response to the Colorado foundation was surprise at their interest: "I was happy to get your very kind but puzzled letter proposing help to move my Tibetan collection, which fact never crossed my mind and never, never would I consider to part with my Tibetan collection which is, and will be, a part of my home for more than 40 years." Rinpoche expected to visit Santa Barbara for a few days to see his students and expressed the desire to see a "little Tibet." This was inconvenient for GW because, as she explained, the house was being used "as a storehouse for much garden furniture during winter time. But I was persuaded to make an exception for such [an] illustrious visitor." Apparently, a whole team turned up. "Certainly I was more than surprised when, instead of yourself alone - expecting you alone with Mike - seeing six men walking to my bedroom as the best parts of the collection are on the wall of my bedroom." The collective persuasion of the visitors was enough, however, to convince GW to leave her treasures to the Colorado foundation in her will. GWLA.

Chapter 32: *Nirvana* 1977-1984

The Last Will and Testament of Ganna Walska dated August 7, 1979 replaced an earlier version signed and witnessed in Santa Barbara on April 28, 1959. Codicils to the 1979 document are dated: (1) March 6, 1980, (2) April 9, 1980, (3) April 21, 1980, (4) May 15, 1980, (5) June 13, 1980, (6) June 13, 1980, (7) July 30, 1980, (8) July 30,1980, (9) November 6, 1980, (10) March 11, 1981, (11) March 11, 1981, (12) April 17, 1981, (13) May 22, 1981, (14) December 9, 1981. GWLA.

The remarkable Dr. Pearl Chase (1888-1979) was a tireless community activist in Santa Barbara from the early 1920s when its small-town population was little more than 20,000. Born in Boston, she was a graduate of the University of California, Berkeley, and became a pioneer in conservation, the promotion of public health, social services and civic planning, committing herself to preserving the natural beauty and history of the area, particularly its Spanish colonial past. The Pearl Chase Society, established in 1995, supports and advances her vision for a beautiful city whose population has increased five-fold since she began her invaluable work. The Dr. Pearl Chase Scholarship in Environmental Studies is awarded to a qualified undergraduate majoring in the area of environmental studies at the University of California, Santa Barbara.

Postlude

The Breitweiser-Studio 2 auction in Santa Barbara, January 18 through January 25, 1986, included GW's Venetian painted rococo furniture, Louis XV sofa and chairs, a Louis XVI mahogany dining table, a Biedermeier corner shelf, antique French clocks, a Fabergé silver tea set, Chinese porcelain and lacquer work, oriental rugs, Dutch paintings and French watercolors, a Cartier alligator skin vanity case, Louis Vuitton luggage, antique stringed instruments, the Pleyel harpsichord, and much more. Proceeds were to benefit the Ganna Walska Lotusland Foundation. Other antiques and artifacts were auctioned at Phillips in New York, May 2, 1987.

Kamansky to author: "Most of Madame Walska's Sino-Tibetan material came from Grace Nicholson through the great explorer Sven Hedin. Miss Nicholson purchased them through an agent in Chicago where they were in storage for many years. Some of her Tibetan material and part of her fine jewelry collection came from Nancy Anne Miller, who was at one time the Maharani of Indoor. She sold her collection of jewels through Grace Nicholson after she divorced the Maharaja." Fax November 26, 1999.

Steve Timbrook. Interviewed by the author, Santa Barbara, September 29, 1999.

The question of road access to Lotusland, in the objection from Montecito residents against opening Lotusland to the public, was discussed by the Land Use Committee of the Montecito Association just before review by the County Planning Commission, with the majority supporting a plan for shuttling all visitors to the estate. *Montecito Life* of January 10, 1991, reported local resident, Diane Morgan, saying that the shuttle-only policy would prevent garden visitors from touring the area after visiting Lotusland, indicating Montecitans' determination to keep their neighborhood safe from intrusion. Director Timbrook told the committee that this plan would be too expensive for the foundation to finance, and there were no places for the shuttles to board and park.

After leaving Lotusland under a dark cloud of suspicion, Charles Glass continued writing for the *Cactus and Succulent Journal* and working as a botanist until moving to Mexico in 1991. He became curator of cacti and other succulents at the botanical garden of Churco del Ingenio at San Miguel de Allende, Guanajuato, in a country with the richest variety of cacti in the world, as well as a great diversity of other succulent families. Glass died there in 1998, leaving to his credit new plant descriptions, and publications about his special field of study and joy, including "The Illustrated Encyclopedia of Cacti" (with Clive Innes.)

The Lotusland trustees' battle to maintain their tax-free status as a public garden operating in a private, residential neighborhood continued against a background of rancor between the estate and its surrounding residents long after GW's death. The local Planning Commission in November 1998 approved a maximum of 18,000 people and up to 5,000 students and teachers to visit annually. But an appeal against their decision was filed by sixty-six "aggrieved persons," together with their opposition to special night events and increased vehicle parking. This caused the Board of Supervisors of Santa Barbara County to review Lotusland's conditional use permit after the appellants disagreed with the Commission's original findings in 1998 that their decision "would not be detrimental to the health, safety, comfort, convenience, and general welfare of the neighborhood." In May 1999, the Board, after considering the appeal, issued revised conditions for Lotusland's permit, including a cap of 13,500 visits annually for a period of eighteen months, rising to a maximum of 15,000 afterward, together with the elimination of all activities after dark and before 9 a.m. These strict conditions, and others, were to be observed, to the letter, for the next ten years.

Dr. Warren Austin and his wife Florence wanted their historic 17.4 acre estate to have a future similar to GW's neighboring Lotusland, by establishing the not-for-profit Val Verde Foundation. But both died before the property's legacy was secured: Florence "Bunny" Heath Horton Austin in 1991 and her husband in 1999.

Horace E. Horton founded the Chicago Bridge & Iron Company in 1889 and it would become widely known as CB&I, a multinational conglomerate with a worldwide workforce of more than 16,000. His heiress daughter became one of the richest women in America on his death, marrying Warren Austin in 1955 and they bought Val Verde. The estate became renowned for some of the smartest parties in the area, often attended by Hollywood royalty, and carrying on a tradition that had seen the house welcome many celebrity guests to stay, like Charles Lindbergh, Gloria Swanson, Georgia O'Keeffe and Cole Porter. After Bunny died, Dr. Austin lived alone among his huge collection of antiques, books, paintings and sculptures in the impressive Mediterranean Revival mansion from 1915, surrounded by spectacular landscaped gardens. He was determined to open the estate to the public, following the example of Ganna Walska's Lotusland. In December 1996, a resolution of the Board of Supervisors of the County of Santa Barbara deemed Val Verde worthy of protection because it represented an important era of local history, being one of the few Montecito estate homes by a nationally known architect (Bertram Goodhue) with gardens designed by the noted landscape architect Lockwood de Forest, together with a lower garden representing an important period of early hybridization, with ties to Britain's Royal Botanic Gardens, Kew

Architect Bertram Grosvenor Goodhue (1869-1924) was celebrated for his Neo-Gothic and Spanish Colonial Revival designs. After completing his apprenticeship in New York City, he established his own practice and worked extensively throughout the United States, particularly in California, where he reintegrated the Spanish Colonial style that produced El Fureidis and Val Verde in Montecito, both of which were to become national historical monuments. Goodhue's later creations veered to the Romanesque and a generalized archaic style. He died in 1924 with many commissions still to be constructed and, according to his wishes, was interred in a wall vault of his 1913 Church of the Intercession in New York City, a building the architect considered his finest. Other notable designs, among many, are St. Thomas Church - New York City (1906), Hotel Washington - Panama (1913), San Diego Museum of Art (1913), Los Angeles Central Library (1924), National Academy of Sciences-Washington, D.C., Nebraska State Capitol - Lincoln (1924.)

This writer visited Val Verde in October 1998 for dinner with its owner, during which I recorded our long and entertaining conversation, followed by an exhaustive tour of the extraordinary Val Verde mansion, including a section discreetly given over to celebrating gay marriages. Warren Austin was still waiting to hear if permission would be granted to open his estate to the public in the face of open hostility - as he described it - from local residents, "I'm trying to give it away so that everyone can enjoy it," he told me in an emotional *cri de coeur*. He died a year later without knowing if the Board of Supervisors would grant a permit for public visits. In the event, they did not, effectively leaving the estate without the prospect of income to maintain the property. In addition, I missed out on being his guest on my next visit to Santa Barbara, staying in the estate's Lindbergh Suite, as he'd promised.

The Austins had arranged a $7 million trust fund to preserve the future of their property, but during 2006, the trustees found themselves in financial difficulties and mortgaged Val Verde and its contents for thirteen million dollars to avert a foreclosure auction sale. Three years later and $1.4 million in arrears, the foundation was declared bankrupt. A wealthy Russian banker, Sergey Grishin, bought it out of bankruptcy for $15.3 million in 2009 and then sold it a few months later - with reduced land - to a Montecito neighbor, Peter Muller of Morgan Stanley for a reported $14.8 million. Already the owner of the spectacular El Fureidis ("Little paradise" or "Pleasure gardens"), designed by Bertram Goodue in 1906, Grishin was reported saying that he sold Val Verde because of its poor condition which would mean years of renovation.

As a designated historic landmark Val Verde's future remained shrouded in uncertainty as dense as the occasional sea fogs that drift in from the Pacific Ocean to transform Montecito into a magical fairyland, but the property remained protected by regulations allowing no demolition, removal or destruction, together with a ban on alterations, repairs, additions or changes without approval from the Santa Barbara Historical Landmark Advisory Commission.

In the meantime, the spirit of Ganna Walska Lotusland, probably the last of the great Montecito estates to be open to the public (by reservation because of the strict conditions of its permit) continues to astound, delight and stimulate visitors.

**Full information about
GANNA WALSKA LOTUSLAND
available at www.lotusland.org**

Selected bibliography

Alda, Frances. Men, Women and Tenors. New York: Haughton Mifflin, 1937.

Barwell, Ernest H.G. Death ray Man. London: Hutchinson, 1943.

Penthouse of the Gods. New York: Charles Scribner's Sons, 1939.

Heaven Lies Within Us. New York: Charles Scribner's Sons, 1939.

Land of a Thousand Buddhas (British title for Penthouse.) London: Rider and Company, 1940.

Hatha Yoga. New York: Columbia University Press, 1944.

A Simplified Grammar of the Literary Tibetan Language. Santa Barbara: Tibetan Text Society, 1946.

Philosophical Foundations of India. London: Rider & Co., 1ç'-.

Hindu Philosophy. (same as previous title) New York: Philosophical Library, 1947.

Boyle, T.C. Riven Rock. (novel) New York: Viking Penguin, 1988.

Brady, Frank. Citizen Kane. New York: Macmillan, 1989.

Chernow, Ron. Titan – the life of John D. Rockefeller, Sr. New York: Random House, 1998.

Crawford, Sharon. Ganna Walska Lotusland – The Garden and its Creators. Santa Barbara, Ganna Walska Lotusland Foundation, 1996.

Music Academy of the West – Fifty Years 1947-1997. Santa Barbara, Music Academy of the West, 1997.

Dedmon, Emmett. Fabulous Chicago. New York: Random House, 1953.

Erté. Things I Remember. London: Peter Owen Limited-Sevenarts, 1975.

My Life/ My Art. London; Sevenarts Limited, 1989.

Evans, Sara. Born for Liberty – A History of Women in America. New York, The Free Press, 1989.

Foster, Jonathan. The Death Ray - The Secret Life of Harry Grindell Matthews. U.K. Inventive Publishing, 2009.

Foster, Michael and Barbara. The Life of Alexandra David-Néel. New York: Harper & Row, 1987.

Garden, Mary and Biancollii, L. Mary Garden's Story. New York 1951.

Gardner, Theodore. Lotusland – A Photographic Essay. Santa Barbara; Knoll Publishers, 1995.

Glass, Charles and Foster, Bob. Lotusland and the Fabulous Garden of Mme Walska. Cactus and Succulent Journal (U.S.) November – December 1972.

Hackett, Paul. Theos Bernard, the White Lama. Columbia University Press, 2012.

Matz, Mary Jane. The Many Lives of Otto Kahn. New York/ Pendragon Press, 1963.

Meeker, Arthur. Chicago, With Love. New York: Alfred A. Knopf, 1955.

Padilla, Victoria. Southern California Gardens. Berkeley & Los Angeles, University of California Press. 1986.

Parks, Stephen. The Elizabethan Club of Yale University and its Library. New Haven, Conn: Yale University Press, 1986.

Rebic, Michael. Landmarks Lost and Found. An Introduction to the Architecture and History of Yonkers. Yonkers (N.Y.) Yonkers Planning Bureau, 1986.

Spencer, Charles. Erté. London: Peter Owen Limited-Sevenarts, 1970.

Straram, Enric. Histoire Croisée d'une Institution et d'une Famille. Paris: Société Immobilière du Théatre des Champs-Elysées, 1998.

Streatfield, David. Landscaping the California Garden. New York: Abbeville Press, 1994.

Thomson, David. Rosebud – The story of Orson Welles. New York: Alfred A. Knopf, 1996.

Veenhof, Douglas. The Life of Tantric Yogi Theos Bernard. New York: Harmony Books, 2011.

Vogt, Elizabeth. Montecito – California's Garden Paradise. Santa Barbara: MIP Publishing, 1993.

Walska, Ganna. Always Room at the Top. New York: Richard R. Smith, 1943.

Index

A

Abbey Garden Press, 408
Abrams, Joseph, 365, 369
Alda, Frances, 52, 55, 163, 248
Alexandra, Her Majesty Queen, 237
Alfonso XIII, King of Spain, 150, 471
Amacher, Fritz, 441
Anderson, Judith, 372
Antheil, George, 376
Aphrodite, 88
Aquitania, 65, 67
Arabic, 36, 378
Arden, Elizabeth, 472
Arizona Heritage Center, 355
Astor, John Jacob, 39
Astor, Mrs Vincent, 50
Astruc, Gabriel, 156
Aubert, Louis, 477
Austin, Dr Warren, 7, 9, 10, 347, 351,
   362, 366, 412, 437, 439, 453, 454,
   456, 490, 493, 494, 495

B

Baba, Shri Meher, 222
Bacon, Mark Addison, 383
Baker, Josephine, 135
Balch, Earle, 256
Baldwin, Stanley, 231
Ballets Joos, Les, 191
Ballets Russes de Monte Carlo, Les, 90,
   191, 458, 465, 470
Ballets Suédois, Les, 152
ballo in maschera, Un, 353
Barrymore, Drew, 468
Barry-Orlova, "Gita", 206, 234
Barthélemy, Richard, 49
Barthou, Louis, 173, 200, 204
Bartok, Bela, 124
Baruch, Bernard, 85, 343
Baruch, Rosemarie, 85
Barwell, Ernest, 256, 285, 286, 288,
   289, 497
Bassan, Jonathan, 444

Batory, 346
Beale, Phelan, 65, 110, 164, 167, 182,
   183, 187, 213, 225, 244, 248, 252,
   279, 289, 299, 300, 317, 332, 337,
   341, 344, 350, 354, 360, 363, 365,
   366, 367, 382, 476, 486, 488
Beckman, Frederick H., 71
Beecham Opera Company, 101, 233
Beethoven, Ludwig van, 49, 101, 175,
   196, 221
Belle Hélène, La, 42
Belmonte, Juan, 150
Benvenuto Cellini, 90
Berengaria, 122
Berg, Alban, 174
Berlin Philharmonic Orchestra, 174
Berlioz, Hector, 90, 140, 477
Bernard, Dr Pierre, 260, 261, 481, 484
Bernard, Glen A., 331
Bernard, Theos, 9, 260, 261, 262, 263,
   266, 268, 272, 273, 276, 279, 280,
   282, 288, 289, 290, 291, 293, 295,
   300, 304, 311, 320, 328, 329, 344,
   347, 348, 352, 354, 355, 356, 358,
   359, 379, 442, 481, 482, 483, 484,
   486, 498
Bernhardt, Sarah, 462, 470
Besant, Annie, 144
Bizet, Georges, 49, 50
Bloch, Ernst, 349
Boléro, 254
Bonelli, Richard, 349
Bori, Lucrezia, 211, 249
Boris Godunov, 184, 185
Bormans, 254, 255, 257
Bortolazzo, Rosetta, 433, 434
Boston Symphony Orchestra, 174
Bothin, Henry E., 322
Boucher, Francois, 375
Bourdin, Roger, 235
Bouvier, Edith Ewing, 110
Bouvier, John Vernou, 65, 488
Brahms, Johannes, 189, 196, 478
Branly, Edouard, 240
Bremen, 194
Brown, Don, 263, 276, 289, 301, 354,

502

THE AUTHOR

Brian Adams has had a long and distinguished career in the arts, as a writer, and as a producer/director in television. He was in charge of arts programming for the Australian Broadcasting Corporation for more than twenty years.

In 1990 he was awarded an Order of Australia, in recognition of his outstanding contribution to the arts and entertainment.

His books include the biographies of opera diva Dame Joan Sutherland ("La Stupenda") which sold worldwide and was translated into several languages; the great 18th-century English botanist Sir Joseph Banks ("The Flowering of the Pacific"); and Australian painters Sir Sidney Nolan ("Such is Life") and Sir William Dobell ("Portrait of an Artist"). He is also the co-author of "Australian Cinema: The First Eighty Years."

His media memoir "A Pain in the Arts! Culture without Cringe in Australia" is now available as a paperback and Kindle edition; also an expanded biography "Sidney Nolan's Odyssey" is available as a paperback and Kindle edition through amazon.

Brian Adams lives in the South of France

Made in the USA
Coppell, TX
07 September 2020